Canada and World Order

The Multilateralist Tradition in Canadian Foreign Policy

Second Edition

Tom Keating

OXFORD
UNIVERSITY PRESS

OXFORD

UNIVERSITY PRESS

70 Wynford Drive, Don Mills, Ontario M3C 1J9
www.oup.com/ca

Oxford University Press is a department of the University of Oxford.
It furthers the University's objective of excellence in research, scholarship,
and education by publishing worldwide in

Oxford New York

Auckland Bangkok Buenos Aires Cape Town Chennai
Dar es Salaam Delhi Hong Kong Istanbul Karachi Kolkata
Kuala Lumpur Madrid Melbourne Mexico City Mumbai Nairobi
São Paulo Shanghai Taipei Tokyo Toronto

Oxford is a trade mark of Oxford University Press
in the UK and in certain other countries

Published in Canada
by Oxford University Press

Copyright © Oxford University Press Canada 2002

The moral rights of the author have been asserted

Database right Oxford University Press (maker)

First published 2002

National Library of Canada Cataloguing in Publication Data

Keating, Thomas F.
Canada and world order : the multilateralist tradition in Canadian
foreign policy
2nd ed.
Includes bibliographical references and index.
ISBN 0-19-541529-9

1. Canada—Foreign relations—1945–   2. Canada—Foreign relations—1918–
1945. I. Title.

FC242.K42 2001   327.71   C2001-902288-3
F1034.2.K43 2001

Cover design: Joan Dempsey
Cover image: Canadian Soldiers in Bosnia—Hidajet Delic/CP Picture Archive

2 3 4 - 05 04 03 02
This book is printed on permanent (acid-free) paper ∞.
Printed in Canada

Contents

Abbreviations

ABM	anti-ballistic missile	EADRCC	Euro-Atlantic Disaster Response Coordination Centre
ACCT	Agency for Cultural and Technical Co-operation		
ALCM	air-launched cruise missile	EC	European Community
APEC	Asia-Pacific Economic Cooperation	ECM	European Common Market
		ECOSOC	(UN) Economic and Social Council
ASEAN	Association of South-East Asian Nations		
		EDC	European Defence Community
CAST	Canadian Air-Sea Transportable	EEC	European Economic Community
CCF	Co-operative Commonwealth Federation	EFTA	European Free Trade Association
		EPTA	Expanded Program of Technical Assistance
CCIC	Canadian Council for International Cooperation	EPU	European Payments Union
CCW	(UN Convention on) Certain Conventional Weapons	EU	European Union
		FAO	Food and Agriculture Organization
CHOGM	Commonwealth Heads of Government Meeting	FIRA	Foreign Investment Review Agency
CIDA	Canadian International Development Agency	FTA	(1988 Canada–US) Free Trade Agreement
CIEC	Conference on International Economic Cooperation	FTAA	Free Trade Agreement for the Americas
CMAG	Commonwealth Ministerial Action Group		
CSCE	Conference on Security and Cooperation in Europe	G-7	Group of Seven
		G-8	Group of Eight
		GATT	General Agreement on Tariffs and Trade
DAC	Development Assistance Committee	GDR	East Germany (German Democratic Republic)
DEA	Department of External Affairs	GNP	gross national product
DEW	Distant Early Warning		
DFAIT	Department of Foreign Affairs and International Trade	IBRD	International Bank for Reconstruction and Development
DND	Department of National Defence	ICAO	International Civil Aviation Organization

ICBL	International Campaign to Ban Landmines	MICIVIH	OAS/UN International Civilian Mission in Haiti
ICC	International Criminal Court/International Control Commission	NAC	North Atlantic Council
		NACC	North Atlantic Co-operation Council
ICRC	International Committee of the Red Cross	NAFTA	North American Free Trade Agreement
ICTR	International Criminal Tribunal for Rwanda	NATO	North Atlantic Treaty Organization
ICTY	International Criminal Tribunal for the Prosecution of Persons Responsible for Serious Violations of International Humanitarian Law Committed in the Territory of the Former Yugoslavia since 1991	NGO	non-governmental organization
		NIEO	New International Economic Order
		NORAD	North American Aerospace (previously Air) Defense Command
IDA	International Development Agency	NPT	Non-Proliferation Treaty
IFOR	Implementation Force	OAS	Organization of American States
IGO	inter-governmental organization	ODA	official development assistance
ILC	International Law Commission	OECD	Organisation for Economic Co-operation and Development
ILO	International Labour Organization	OEEC	Organization for European Economic Cooperation
IMF	International Monetary Fund	OPEC	Organization of Petroleum Exporting Countries
INF	Intermediate-Range Nuclear Forces (Treaty)	OSCE	Organization for Security and Cooperation in Europe
ITO	International Trade Organization		
KLA	Kosovo Liberation Army	P-5	permanent five
		PHP	post hostilities problems
MAI	Multilateral Agreement on Investment	PJBD	Permanent Joint Board on Defence
MBFR	Mutual Balanced Force Reduction	PLO	Palestine Liberation Organization
MCC	Military Co-operation Committee	PMO	Prime Minister's Office
		PRC	People's Republic of China
MFA	Multifibre Agreement		
MFN	Most Favoured Nation	RCAF	Royal Canadian Air Force

RCMP	Royal Canadian Mounted Police	UNDOF	UN Disengagement Observer Force
RTA	Reciprocal Trade Agreements Act	UNEF I	UN Emergency Force
		UNESCO	UN Economic, Social and Cultural Organization
SACEUR	Supreme Allied Commander in Europe	UNGA	UN General Assembly
		UNIFCYP	UN Interim Force in Cyprus
SAP	structural adjustment policy	UNIFIL	UN Interim Force in Lebanon
SDI	Strategic Defence Initiative		
SSEA	secretary of state for external affairs	UNPROFOR	UN Protection Force
		UNRRA	UN Relief and Rehabilitation Agency
START	Strategic Arms Reduction Treaty		
		UNSCOM	UN Special Commission
SUNFED	Special Fund for Economic Development	UNTCOK	UN Temporary Commission on Korea
		UPD	Unit for the Promotion of Democracy
UDI	unilateral declaration of independence		
		USAF	US Air Force
UN	United Nations	USSEA	under-secretary of state for external affairs
UNCLOS	UN Convention on the Law of the Sea		
UNCTAD	UN Conference on Trade and Development	WEU	Western European Union
		WTO	World Trade Organization

Introduction

The Sources of Multilateralism in Canadian Foreign Policy

The two inescapable realities of Canadian foreign policy, based on our geographical and historical development, are: the necessity of maintaining unity at home, especially between the two founding nations; and living distinct from but in harmony with the world's most powerful and dynamic nation—the USA. These factors tend to restrict initiatives being undertaken by Canada alone, and favour the pursuit of limited international objectives through international organizations. —George Ignatieff, 1980

We have . . . a lasting and visceral commitment to multilateralism which is ingrained, and endemic to the Canadian character. —Stephen Lewis, 1985

INTRODUCTION

Multilateralism has been an article of faith in the practice of Canadian foreign policy for decades. Since the 1940s, successive Canadian governments have actively supported a wide-ranging network of multilateral institutions and associations. By the 1980s, Canada's then foreign minister Joe Clark could justifiably report that 'no other major power has Canada's institutional reach'.[1] Much of Canada's relations with the international community of states has been conditioned by the country's membership in institutions such as the United Nations (UN), the North Atlantic Treaty Organization (NATO), the Commonwealth, and the General Agreement on Tariffs and Trade (GATT), among many. With the noteworthy exception of the United States, multilateral contacts have generally taken precedence over bilateral ones and multilateral diplomacy has been the preferred instrument for the pursuit of foreign policy objectives. This strong and persistent commitment to multilateralism has survived various attempts to circumscribe or replace it. It has also survived in the face of the opposition of some of Canada's principal allies to the entire spirit of multilateral co-operation and to specific international organizations. Finally, the commitment has cut across party lines and received substantial support from organized groups and the Canadian public.

Canada's active role in multilateral institutions has been widely acknowledged in the literature on Canadian foreign policy. Numerous works have discussed Canadian policies as they have involved international organizations or the activities of these organizations, and countless government statements have identified multilateralism as one of the most prominent and persistent themes in the practice of Canadian foreign policy. While some have celebrated Canada's participatory activity as indicative of the country's commitment to a constructive global order, others have discounted it as a facade for close collaboration with the Americans or for the pursuit of narrow self-interest. As suggested later in this introduction, there is some merit to each of these views. Clearly, one of the benefits of multilateralism from the perspective of Canadian foreign policy makers has been its ability to fuse different policy objectives.

The multilateralist tradition in Canadian foreign policy is the subject of this work. The central objective of this book is to demonstrate the significance of multilateralism as a guiding principle and operational strategy in the conduct of Canadian foreign policy across a spectrum of policy issues in the political, economic, and security arenas. The following chapters provide an overview of the history of Canadian involvement in multilateral associations and institutions since the 1940s. This overview reveals the vast range of Canada's multilateral activities in international institutions with particular reference to the most significant of these: the UN, the Commonwealth, the GATT/World Trade Organization (WTO), and NATO. The book also touches on Canadian involvement in other associations, such as the World Bank, the International Monetary Fund (IMF), the Organization of American States (OAS), the Francophonie, and the Conference on Security and Cooperation in Europe (CSCE).

What follows is not intended to be a comprehensive account of Canada's multilateral activities. There are too many of these to review in a short volume. It is also not intended to be a definitive account of specific Canadian policies. In some instances, such accounts already exist. In others, the work remains to be done. Rather, the primary purpose of this work is to provide the reader with a survey of Canada's involvement in multilateral associations and to argue that over time and across different issues, Canadian policy makers have repeatedly relied on multilateralism in the pursuit of a diverse range of foreign policy objectives. In addition to arguing that multilateralism has been one of the most important defining characteristics of Canadian foreign policy, this review will also illustrate how multilateralism has been used to meet quite distinct policy objectives, ranging from milieu goals, involving a more peaceful and stable international order, to possessive goals, intended to satisfy narrow national interests.[2] Another consideration in writing this book is to examine how Canada's involvement in multilateral associations has changed over time and across different issues. Finally, given the significant transformations that are taking place in the world today and the historic opportunity that exists for a renewal of effective multilateral co-operation in the interests of a more peaceful, stable, and just international order, it is important to assess Canada's contribution to world order in the past and to speculate on its potential to contribute in the future.

The book is organized to examine Canadian policy in three different but related policy spheres and in three historical periods. The first three chapters of the book review Canada's involvement in the formation of post-war multilateral institutions. The first chapter deals with the UN and its affiliated agencies; the second addresses post-war economic institutions, principally the Bretton Woods system; and the third concerns post-war security arrangements and the formation of NATO. These chapters discuss the active role that Canadian officials played in the late 1940s and their efforts to construct a multilateral framework that would offset the dominant and potentially domineering power of the United States and, at the same time, provide a stable structure of peace and prosperity. These chapters also review Canada's early experiences in these institutions.

The second section examines the evolution of Canadian policy in each of these spheres from the 1960s through the 1980s. During this period, there was a transformation in the attitudes of many Canadians toward a multilateralist foreign policy. By the end of the 1960s, many Canadians, including members of the Trudeau cabinet, had become more skeptical and more critical of the benefits of multilateralist connections for Canada, and there were attempts to steer clear of multilateral commitments. In most instances, these attempts did not persist. Chapter 4 looks at the effects of the Cold War on Canadian activities at the UN in such areas as membership, peacekeeping, and arms control. The fifth chapter, in examining international economic institutions during this period, reviews the North–South debates that dominated the global political economy at the time, the evolution of the multilateral trade regime, and the demise of the Bretton Woods financial order. The sixth chapter assesses Canadian policy at NATO during the 1960s as the North Atlantic Treaty, despite Canadian reservations, was transformed into an unequivocal military alliance with a prominent nuclear strategy. It also examines Canada's NATO policy in a period of détente and describes the government's effective diplomacy in securing participation in the CSCE. During this period, Canada's multilateralist arrangements often did little to prevent more intensive bilateral arrangements with the Americans. On the other hand, Canadian officials did seek wider objectives as well. Throughout this period, Canadian policy makers attempted on occasion to use the UN and NATO to bridge the East–West divisions of the Cold War. Within the commercial sphere, however, the primary concern was to protect the Canadian economy from the demands of developed and developing economies alike.

The final section looks at Canada's multilateralist policies during the 1990s in the aftermath of the Cold War and during the process of globalization. Chapter 7 examines the UN's role in the 'new world order' and Canada's contribution to the UN's more interventionist and normative agendas. The eighth chapter reviews Canada's response to the demise of the Bretton Woods system, the globalization of the international political economy, and the gradual multilateralization of a continental trade relationship that became too large to ignore. It also discusses Canada's attraction to and involvement in the more selective plurilateral club (having a limited number of members): the Group of Seven (G-7) leading industrialized countries that began meeting in annual summits in the mid-1970s. Chapter 9 reviews Canada's participation in two wars during the 1990s and its relationship with NATO as the alliance adjusted to the loss of an enemy. Each of these chapters addresses in a preliminary manner the profound developments of recent years that have resulted in a dramatic transformation of the associations and institutions that have served as the foundation for Canada's multilateralist foreign policy for the past 40 years. This section examines Canada's response to these revolutionary changes and attempts to indicate the direction in which Canada's multilateralist tradition might carry on in the future.

Before undertaking this review, the remainder of this introduction briefly discusses the phenomenon of multilateralism, considers the sources of multilateralism in Canadian foreign policy, and previews the interests that this policy has served.

MULTILATERALISM

Multilateralism has not received much attention in the literature on international politics and foreign policy. International institutions, on the other hand, have been widely discussed and analyzed. The volumes written on international institutions have focused both on the characteristics and operations of the organizations and on the factors that have supported their establishment and maintenance. Multilateralism, on the other hand, calls attention to the foreign policy activity of states. States, in designing their foreign policy, can select from a variety of orientations, ranging from isolationism and economic self-sufficiency to active interaction with other states. As compared with unilateral or bilateral strategies, *multilateralism*, as used here, refers both to the practice of multilateral diplomacy and to policies supporting the establishment and maintenance of institutions and associations that facilitate and support the practice of multilateral diplomacy. Robert Keohane has defined *multilateralism* as 'the practice of co-ordinating national policies in groups of three or more states, through ad hoc arrangements or by means of institutions'.[3] Multilateral diplomacy involves working with coalitions of states, primarily but not exclusively within formal associations or institutions, to achieve foreign policy objectives. It also implies a willingness to maintain solidarity with these coalitions and to maintain support for these institutions. In practice, it often involves greater attention to the process by which decisions are made than to the more substantive elements of those decisions. Support for multilateral diplomacy also necessitates encouraging others to follow the same procedures.[4]

John Ruggie has written that multilateralism should be viewed as having some substantial content as well as the procedural ones already noted: 'What is distinctive about multilateralism is not merely that it coordinates national policies in groups of three or more states, . . . but that it does so on the basis of certain principles of ordering relations among those states'.[5] These principles, in Ruggie's view, 'specify appropriate conduct for a class of actions, without regard to the particularistic interests of the parties or the strategic exigencies that may exist in any specific occurrence'.[6] When viewed from this vantage point, a commitment to multilateralism involves more than a procedural strategy for conducting one's foreign policy. It suggests a subjective approach and a conscious commitment to the process and substance of the associations—more specifically, a conscious interest in the substantive content of the international order that is supported by multilateral activity. Multilateralism, in this sense, shares certain characteristics with how international regimes have been described in the literature. Support for regimes, analysts note, derives from their ability to reduce the costs and risks to governments from co-operation. International regimes also provide a greater degree of predictability for governments because they make it easier to anticipate the response of other governments involved in the same regime. Each of these views of multilateralism emphasizes the role of states in the process of co-operation and tends to look upon international co-operation primarily as a top-down process, one organized and implemented by states in service to interests that have been defined by the states involved.

In contrast to this, some analysts have argued that for both empirical and norma-tive reasons, multilateralism needs to be examined from the bottom up. This argu-ment stems from the increased prevalence and participation of non-governmental organizations (NGOs) in global politics. This 'new multilateralism', as it has been described, takes a different view from that of realist, liberal, or constructivist views of multilateralism. In these more traditional approaches, as Michael Dolan and Chris Hunt describe them, 'the actions of elements of civil society serve to legitimate or delegitimate decisions made in state-centric multilateral institutions, rather than in any way transforming the terrain of political sovereignty'.[7] In contrast 'the bottom-up element embodies the reconstitution of civil society, and is most glaringly manifest in the rise of new social movements, which are "no longer willing to allow governments to act as exclusive agents on [their] behalf"'.[8] In considering this new multilateralism, Robert Cox has noted that multilateralism becomes 'highly "schizophrenic" in that one part is situated in the present predicaments of the state system, and another prob-ing the social and political foundations of a future order'.[9]

Cox has also argued that world order and the multilateral activity that supports it can support different interests and ideas. He describes world order as 'neutral as regards the nature of the entities that constitute power; it designates an historically specific configuration of power of whatever kind'.[10] As a result, world order may exhibit different tendencies under different configurations of power. Multilateralism, in turn, may support more or less progressive or conservative ordering principles for global political relations. Furthermore,

Cox's critical IR [international relations] perspective also points to the way in which discursive meanings of multilateralism become important in shaping concrete mate-rial practices. This brings in an inherently normative aspect to the new multilateral-ism, in that it seeks to uncover whose voices are represented (or not) in international politics as well as revealing the nature of particular sites of struggle and contestation.[11]

These distinctions are worth considering as we review Canada's multilateralist activities. One should not assume that support for multilateral processes and institu-tions is inherently enlightened and reflects an abnegation of national interests, nor that there is an inconsistency between the pursuit of milieu goals and serving national objectives. On the contrary, as will become clear in examining Canada's policies and practices, multilateralism has frequently been viewed as the most effective strategy for pursuing national policy objectives. For example, Denis Stairs has written that 'Canadians contributed to the construction of the postwar international order—to the creation, that is, of institutions of global governance—with clearly defined inter-ests in view and on the basis of a "realist" calculus of power from which they derived relatively clear notions of what they could get away with and what they could not'.[12] Mark Neufeld argues that Canada's interest in multilateralism or middle power diplomacy acts to serve the interests of a hegemonic and unequal world order, one that reinforces and legitimates the interests of dominant capitalist powers such as the United States.[13] David Black and Claire Sjolander concur: 'The norms and principles associated with [multilateralism] have been central to the construction and preservation of hegemony, at the levels of both world order and the Canadian social formation'.[14] A more critical or reflective reading of multilateralism and Canada's contribution to it in the post-1945 world would reveal that the rhetoric or assumptions of multilateralism as a benign, pacifying, equalizing force have seldom been matched by the actual practice or results. On the other hand, results are not always the best indicators of either intentions or alternative possibilities. As Ruggie's essays on international co-operation and Craig Murphy's analysis of international institutions indicate, the underlying ideas, norms, and motivations of those contributing to the multilateral process provide a critically important, but by no means coherent or consensual, foundation for shaping the substantive content and practices of multilateralism.[15] We will revisit this issue in the conclusion, but it is worth considering, in reviewing the nature and sources of Canadian participation in multilateral institutions, the ideas and interests that have been supported. It is also important to consider the frequency with which and the manner in which these ideas and interests have been rejected or modified through the process of multilateral diplomacy. Finally, it is noteworthy that much of Canadian activity in this area has been more concerned with procedural notions of order than with substantive notions.

The persistent Canadian interest in multilateralism is based on a number of factors, ranging from Canada's relative power status in the international system to the personalities of particular officials. The convergence of these factors in the 1940s was instrumental in setting Canadian foreign policy on a multilateralist course that has been followed with few deviations since that time. After more than 50 years, many of these factors have undergone a significant transformation such that the future viability and direction of multilateralism and Canadian support for it may be poised for change. Before reviewing and assessing the link between Canadian foreign policy and multilateralism during the post-1945 period, it is worth considering the various factors that have encouraged this orientation.

HISTORICAL SOURCES OF MULTILATERALISM

The substance of Canadian foreign policy underwent a transformation during the 1940s. Until the Second World War, foreign policy had been devoted to securing autonomy from Britain, settling bilateral disputes with the Americans, and avoiding any further participation in the affairs of the world, especially the European world. The coming of the war was not unforeseen in Canada. Many of Canada's foremost diplomats of the day recognized it as a possibility and later, after Britain's efforts to appease Hitler's designs failed, accepted it as an inevitability. Still, some officials were reluctant to view the war as being in Canada's interest or as Canada's responsibility.

These sentiments reflected the prevailing isolationist mood of the Department of External Affairs (DEA) and the government during the inter-war years. When the League of Nations made a half-hearted attempt at implementing collective security measures in 1935 in response to the Italian invasion of Ethiopia, Canadian delegates, under explicit authority from newly elected prime minister Mackenzie King, turned away knowing full well that a commitment to collective security was a commitment to war and that the government wanted none of it.[16] For many officials in Ottawa, the coming war was an illustration of the folly of European power politics. A desire to avoid entanglements in British foreign policy had guided Canadian foreign policy during the inter-war years. This policy was also in accord with popular opinion. As suggested by the lament of Frank Underhill, a prominent liberal academic and commentator, that 'all these European troubles are not worth the bones of a Toronto grenadier',[17] many Canadians favoured a policy of isolationism, secure in what they thought was a 'fireproof house'.

The prevalence of these isolationist sentiments did not convince the government to reject membership in the League of Nations as such views had in the United States. Indeed, membership was actively sought as an avenue for furthering Canadian auton- omy in foreign affairs. Autonomy was necessary to preserve the policy of non-involve- ment. The First World War had acquainted Canadians with the human and political costs of international politics and had made many in Canada aware of both the need for and the ability of the government to assume more control over foreign policy. Faced with the memory of the conscription crisis of 1917 at home and with still strong colonial links abroad, the governments first of Borden and later of Mackenzie King attempted to steer the delicate course between a foreign policy that would retain some colonial ties and the protection of national unity at home. Multilateral arrangements such as the Imperial Conferences of prime ministers and the League of Nations were an important part of the government's strategy to gain recognition for Canadian autonomy while limiting the country's commitments to the international commu- nity. It was a matter of acquiring rights without the concern for duties. At the end of the First World War, Borden argued that Canada's contribution to the war had quali- fied the country as an 'international personality' and entitled it to an independent status in the international system. As a result of Borden's diplomatic efforts, Canada signed the Versailles Treaty and took its own seat at the League of Nations. Membership in the League had been secured to enhance Canada's independence and status and to keep the country away from European conflicts; 'indeed', noted R.A. MacKay and E.B. Rogers, 'Canadians generally, in so far as they thought about the matter, seem to have supported membership primarily because it indicated recogni- tion by other nations of Canada's new status'.[18]

Canada's initial involvement in international organizations was significantly differ- ent from the pattern that emerged in the post-war period. Membership in the League was sought not to involve Canada in international affairs, but to keep the country free from such involvements. Canadian delegates at the League struggled for over four years to have Article X deleted, especially the commitment on the part of all League members to protect the territorial and political integrity of other members, and failing that, were satisfied to have it rendered ineffectual. 'Canada's influence' in the League, according to its official historian, 'had regularly been on the side of cutting down the obligations of the Covenant'.[19] Nor, should it be mentioned, was Canada unique in this regard; its views on Article X were widely shared by other League members. For the Canadian government, then, the League was important only insofar as it secured Canadian independence from Britain and thereby reinforced Canadian sovereignty. Nonetheless, the utility of multilateralism had been established. The League was 'the first international political peacekeeping agency that provided a supplementary multilateral mode of conducting foreign policy in addition to the traditional bilateral diplomatic contacts'.[20] For Canada, R.A. Preston noted, 'having known no other kind of world, . . . External Affairs has probably found it easier than older chancelleries to think in terms of UN diplomacy'.[21] Even before the more active period of Canadian internationalism, the government had turned to multilateral diplomacy in a remodelled Empire and to an emaciated League to protect its isolationist objectives.

The isolationist view was not shared by all Canadians. For those who sought a more active foreign policy, the League of Nations became a rallying point. It was also an important focal point for those Canadians who sought to avoid the horrors of another war. Many of these sentiments were expressed through participation in the League of Nations Society, whose membership peaked in the late 1920s. As the principal historian of the Society, Donald Page, has written, 'There has probably been no other time when so many scholars from across the country were so active in the espousal of a single means of promoting peaceful international relations'.[22] There was, however, a basic inconsistency, if not contradiction, in these 'peace movements' at home. As with similar efforts in the UK, while they supported the League's collective security provisions, they remained strongly opposed to the use of force to implement them. When political leaders in Europe turned to war to redress grievances, supporters of the League opposed the implementation of collective security measures. For some—such as Escott Reid, who would soon join the Department of External Affairs—opposition to League sanctions against Italy in 1935 was justified because a League that was 'ineffective in dealing with causes of international tension was not a League which was worth supporting because peace had to be founded on justice between nations'.[23] For others, sanctions and other collective security measures increased the risks of war and were to be avoided at any cost. Even the internationalists turned isolationist when confronted with the political realities of the 1930s.

Isolationism did not save Canada from the war. War did come—for Ethiopia in 1935, and for Canada in 1939. The crisis of 1935 and the ensuing war had a profound effect on some members of External Affairs. For future foreign minister and prime minister Lester Pearson, the Ethiopian crisis 'confirmed my own conviction . . . that only by collective international action and by a consequent limitation of national sovereignty through the acceptance of international commitments, can peace and security be established and maintained, and human survival ensured'.[24] For others, the outbreak of war in 1939 and the rapid fall of France one year later led to a reappraisal. Some of those who had pressed for isolationism in the 1930s lamented their misguided vision. For Reid, these developments had an equally profound effect on his own views and on the course of Canadian foreign policy: 'Perhaps a persistent uneasy feeling that I might have been remiss in pressing for a policy of neutrality in the second half of the thirties', he wrote in his memoirs, 'contributed to making me a fervent advocate in the second half of the forties of a strong United Nations and a powerful North Atlantic alliance'.[25]

The government approached the United Nations in a decidedly different frame of mind. The country emerged from the Second World War as a significant global power. Its economy had expanded substantially. The political system had survived the conscription crisis, as had the Liberal government of Mackenzie King. Policy makers also enjoyed considerable access to the major power centres in London and Washington. Canada's enhanced status, when combined with the country's historical experiences, encouraged a more enthusiastic response on the part of policy makers to proposals for post-war organizations. A more activist strategy of international involvement emerged as the favoured policy option in Ottawa. Policy makers' historical experience encouraged them to look at multilateralism as the preferred mode to pursue this activism.

External Sources

The defining characteristic of Canada's approach to international institutions, when viewed from a systemic perspective, is the country's position in the international hierarchy of power. Canada has most commonly been described as a middle power.[26] This is a description that was, at least initially, self-imposed. In attempting to distinguish Canada's position in the international system from that of small powers and in recognizing that Canada had neither the desire nor the capability to press for great power status, Canadian officials, on repeated occasions, sought special recognition for middle powers. They hoped, by proclaiming middle power status and encouraging the great powers to recognize it, to obtain some influence over post-war deliberations. For a power with limited military capabilities in a global power balance that was largely based on such capabilities, middle power status was a way of avoiding domination by the great military powers.

The idea of middle powers is not a new one in discussions of international politics.[27] Many writers have noted that middle powers display a greater interest in and commitment to international institutions and a more stable international political and economic order than do other powers. Middle powers have also often been identified as displaying a tendency to support community-wide objectives; 'the powers who by definition were without "general interests"', wrote Martin Wight, 'were more capable than the great powers of pursuing consistently what might be regarded as the universal interest of upholding international law and order'.[28] The interest that middle powers have shown in international organizations is a reflection both of their interests and of their capabilities. They have more of the former than of the latter and therefore are more vulnerable to the actions of greater powers. As Cox writes, 'the primary national interest of the middle power lay in an orderly and predictable world environment that embodied some limits to the ambition and the reach of dominant powers'.[29] Institutions become a device both for regulating and constraining great power activities and for enhancing the capabilities of these middle powers. Middle powers have also been viewed as having the necessary combination of characteristics to make a significant contribution to international organizations:

> They are in a unique position to contribute personnel because of their reputation for neutrality. They have not been tainted with imperialism, nor with the exception of the North Atlantic Treaty Organization, with association with movements that jeopardize their reputation for impartiality. They have sufficient economic resources to meet the costs involved without undue citizen sacrifice. Their position in world affairs is such that they have a heavy stake in the avoidance of military conflict. Leaders such as Lester Pearson of Canada have emerged as enlightened advocates for the strengthening of techniques, including peacekeeping, that may ensure world peace. The humanitarian concerns of a discerning citizenry furnish a base for generous support for causes that promote world peace as well as for a wide range of United Nations economic and social activities. These countries perceive a close affinity between their national interests and United Nations goals and principles.[30]

John Holmes, among others, has pointed to the significance of Canada's middle power status in accounting for the interest and support shown toward multilateralism: 'Lesser powers always feel the need of international institutions and international law and regulation more acutely than stronger powers. . . . It is through international institutions, furthermore, that lesser powers can, by consolidating their interests with those of other countries, hope to have some impact on the great powers'.[31]

Canadian foreign policy has been shaped by the structure of the international system and by the foreign policies of other states. Systemic wars involving the great powers have and will continue to have grave repercussions for Canada. Mechanisms that would constrain these powers have therefore been of vital importance. For a country that relies extensively on international trade to support domestic economic prosperity, a system of international rules was essential to provide the stability and security in which trade would be conducted. The government in the post-war period had neither the will nor the capability to impose order on others in either the security or the economic realm. The only viable option was to establish institutions and procedures that would bring about such an order. The experience of the League of Nations convinced most policy makers (some more belatedly than others) that mere token support for international organizations would not prevent Canada from becoming embroiled in international conflict. Not only was an effective international organization necessary, but so was an effective Canadian presence. Additionally, Holmes notes, Canada had little hope for exercising influence independently outside of an international organization: 'As a middle power, our role is more constructive if it is played not in isolation but in association with many other countries—with friends and allies and fellow members of the world community. For us, international associations, and above all the United Nations, are of supreme importance. Without them we are impotent'.[32]

The apparent tendency of middle powers to show a greater interest in community-wide objectives does not mean that many of these objectives are not also serving the particular interests of these same powers. Canadian support for multilateralism has not been an altruistic commitment to international order, but a means of meeting vitally important national objectives. This is not to say that such policies have not contributed to order at the international level or that policy makers have not been aware of the systemic implications of their actions. For example, Cox has argued that in addition to considerations of the national interest, 'Canada had an overriding interest in the development of institutions and practices conducive to peace, tranquility and orderly adjustment in world politics'.[33] However, multilateral contacts, especially through institutionalized arrangements, were seen by policy makers as a method for furthering Canadian interests without the necessity of possessing large military and economic capabilities; as Holmes writes, 'There is nothing particularly high-minded or unselfish about a strongly internationalist policy on the part of a country that so obviously cannot protect its people and its interest except in collaboration with others'.[34] It would be misleading to assume that in the pursuit of multilateralist goals, policy makers were sacrificing the country's national interests. It was, instead, a strong concern with these national interests that tended to favour active support for and involvement in international organizations. Multilateral organizations would best protect Canadian interests in matters of security, trade, currency stability, political contacts, and many functional areas. Multilateralism was also the most effective strategy for advancing such interests in an anarchical international system:

> As Canada's historic sense of vulnerability to the military activities of great powers was heightened after 1945, the neo-isolationist idealism of the inter-war years was replaced by internationalist idealism. Canada's statesmen of that era saw in internationalism a means to fuse Canada's own particular security interests with idealist notions of a better world order. Internationalism came to be an expression of a close relationship between ideals and self-interest in Canadian foreign policy.[35]

In short, multilateralism became a device for protecting the wide-ranging interests of a middle power, especially one sharing a continent with a superpower.

Some observers suggest that Canada has emerged as a principal power in the international system and, as a result, no longer relies on strategies more suitable to middle powers.[36] David Dewitt and John Kirton, in defining the concept of principal power, argue that Canada has maintained its activity in multilateral associations but has worked with new partners and assumed more leadership roles. They go on to argue that as a principal power, Canada has been more likely to undertake unilateral initiatives, to develop more selective and autonomous bilateral relations, to pursue 'a more full and equal association with a larger number of nonuniversal organizations', and to have 'relatively less involvement . . . with international organizations having universal membership'.[37]

There is room for debate on Canada's position in the international hierarchy of power; but even if that position has changed, it has not necessarily affected the strategies employed by Canadian policy makers. There is some evidence, discussed in the final four chapters of this book, for the types of activity described by Dewitt and Kirton. Much of this activity, however, continues to rely on multilateral strategies in the pursuit of foreign policy objectives. On a series of recent issues—from Canadian policies toward Southern Africa, to Canada's role in North–South debt negotiations, to its policies in response to crises in the Persian Gulf, Yugoslavia, and Haiti, to name a few—policy makers have displayed a preference for working through multilateral coalitions and under the auspices of international organizations. The members of these coalitions may have changed and the organizations may have more selective memberships, but the techniques have remained quite constant over time. Even deliberate attempts to restructure this multilateralist orientation, as evident in the Trudeau foreign policy review of 1969 and in the proposed shift to bilateralism in the early 1980s, eventually yielded to the dominant multilateralist tradition.

Canada's approach to international politics has also been greatly influenced by its location next to and its relationship with the United States. The extensive contacts that currently link the two countries in defence and commerce have been shaped by both external and domestic developments. Two world wars, the decline of Britain, and the bitter Soviet–American rivalry of the Cold War have all acted as pressures that encouraged both Canadians and Americans, albeit for different reasons, to design an extensive array of bilateral defence schemes. In the economic realm, the collapse of the British economy and its global influence and the collapse of the continental European economies led Canada and other world traders to rely on the American market. The subsequent recovery of Europe, matched as it was by economic integration, mitigated Canadian efforts to redirect trade in an effort to offset its reliance on the United States. Much of Canada's foreign policy since the Second World War has been designed to adjust to the conditions resulting from the country's geographic proximity to the United States, the asymmetrical distribution of power that exists between these two countries, the extensive transnational contacts, and especially the emergence of the United States as a global superpower.

Canada's geographical proximity to the United States, when combined with the extensive transnational connections that link the two countries in everything from sports to defence, has encouraged Canadian policy makers not only to devise means for regulating these bilateral links, but also to view international organizations as a forum in which a distinctively Canadian presence can be manifested. Multilateralism becomes important as a counterweight to an exclusively continentalist foreign policy. The shift to a more active internationalist foreign policy has been one way of coping with Canada's bilateral links with its southern neighbour. Pearson, who as foreign minister was instrumental in advancing a multilateralist agenda, thought that Canada's involvement in international organizations 'helped us to escape the dangers of a too exclusively continental relationship with our neighbour without forfeiting the political and economic advantages of that inevitable and vitally important associa- tion'.[38] Extra-continental multilateral connections have also acted as a corrective to continentalist preoccupations. Reid, who in a variety of diplomatic roles supported active participation in multilateral institutions, viewed the Commonwealth in this light:

> In the 1950s membership in the Commonwealth helped Canada to break out of the confines of Canadian isolationism, North American isolationism, North Atlantic isolationism. It helped to inoculate Canada from some of the misleading simplicities of much of the cold war propaganda of the time. It helped us realize sooner than we otherwise would have that most of the crucial problems before the world are not in their pith and substance aspects of a struggle against communism. It helped us to face these crucial problems: colonialism and its aftermath, racial discrimination, cultural imperialism, the misery of half of the people of the world.[39]

In addition to balancing American pressure and correcting a potentially myopic view of the world, some also saw multilateralism as an effective method for influenc- ing American foreign policy, because of

> the importance to us of influencing United States policy in directions which we conceive to be right, either through direct diplomatic action, or through the various bilateral and multilateral associations in which we share common membership. Our capacity to do this by direct diplomatic action is limited, however, and can only be strengthened by active participation in such multilateral associations, and when necessary, accepting the responsibilities of leadership in certain matters ourselves. We should therefore oppose any policy which would have the effect of isolating Canada as a comparatively weak northern neighbour of the United States.[40]

Multilateralism became more important for Canada as American power and involvement in the international system grew. The country was severely limited in the capabilities it could exercise to control American activities. By bringing the Americans within formal institutions, it was hoped that some constraints could be placed on them.

A more critical perspective on this has argued that the government's interest in institutionalizing the post-1945 international order reflected an interest in securing and legitimating American hegemony. Reg Whitaker's analysis of Canada's post-war activism of the late 1940s argued that Canadian policies worked to support American capitalist hegemonical aspirations in the emerging Cold War environment.[41] Neufeld has also argued that much of Canadian diplomacy can be understood as an effort to legitimate support for the existing international order.[42] This raises the question of whether Canada's commitment to multilateralism is better viewed as a reflection of its location in the global capitalist order or of domestic sources. Either way, it is difficult to disagree with Stairs when he writes that Canada's 'interest in the development of rule-governed international processes has thus had something in common with the affection of wealthy classes everywhere for the values of law and order'.[43]

Domestic Sources

In considering the influence of domestic politics on Canada's commitment to multi-lateral institutions, it is important to recognize that the level of commitment will vary depending on domestic political coalitions; Keohane writes that 'theories relying on changes in domestic politics should expect to observe shifting political coalitions in major countries, with policy change instituted by new political leadership or prompted by pressure from below'.[44] John Ravenhill's review of middle power diplomacy notes that 'the personal interests, beliefs, personality, ambitions, energy and skills of prime ministers and foreign ministers affect the extent to which, and the issues on which, their governments play activist roles in foreign policy'.[45] The political history of Canadian foreign policy suggests the relevance of these considerations. In the post-war context, there occurred a fundamental change in the politics surrounding the Department of External Affairs and its role in foreign policy making. The departure of William Lyon Mackenzie King from his positions first as secretary of state for external affairs (SSEA) and later as prime minister opened the way for a number of officials to exert their influence on foreign policy. A new wave of political actors shared a common view that a more activist and internationalist foreign policy would be in the country's best interests.

Active participation in international organizations provided an opportunity for Canadian policy makers to become more directly involved in international politics. If policy makers were to have any influence on international issues, they would need a forum in which to articulate their concerns and a coalition of supporters. Policy makers in Ottawa, especially officials in the Department of External Affairs, were unwilling to be left on the sidelines in post-war decision making or to abandon to the great powers complete control over the international order. They reacted quickly to the first hints of superpower collaboration in the early 1940s. Pearson, in claiming for Canada a position of leadership among lesser powers, devised a middle power response to the Moscow Declaration in which, among other issues, he noted: 'The government and people of any nation, however small, must desire to participate in the great task of ensuring its own security'.[46] For Pearson, and indeed for many other policy makers, it was imperative that Canada have some control over its own foreign policy. Moreover, there was widespread recognition that multilateral associations were the most effective means for maintaining this control because they were seen as the most effective way of dealing with Canada's 'American problem'. For these reasons, policy makers were suspicious of many of the post-war proposals that did not provide an opportunity for Canadian involvement and that threatened to revert to regional organizations. When domestic issues became more intertwined with international developments, the need and opportunities for strategies that could effectively influence international developments took on greater significance. This was evident, for example, throughout the law of the sea negotiations. The pursuit of national interests often required effective diplomacy, and this in turn benefited from multilateral connections.

It has been argued that the Canadian state enjoyed relative autonomy from domestic groups in the making of foreign policy. But it is also evident that until more recent years and with some notable exceptions, the country's multilateralist foreign policy orientation has enjoyed strong popular support. Kim Nossal has identified 'internationalism' as one of the dominant ideas that have structured debates on Canadian foreign policy since the 1940s. He identifies four features of internationalism: (1) responsible involvement, (2) multilateralism, (3) commitment to international institutions, and (4) willingness to make prior commitments to these institutions.[47] As Nossal points out, these ideas did not spring forth from the body politic; they were cultivated by policy makers anxious to win approval for the various commitments the government was undertaking. Their efforts were successful, and Canadian participation in post-war institutions occurred with barely a whimper of dissent.

For many years after the Second World War, there was a rather stable consensus in support of Canada's multilateralist orientations. This consensus began to break down in the early 1960s, in part in response to the nuclear weapons debate, but also in response to international developments such as the American war in Vietnam. Despite the fragmentation of public views on some issues, critics and supporters alike found common ground in the need for and desirability of supporting active involvement in international institutions. Even during the 1960s, when critics of Canadian foreign policy became more vocal and numerous, there remained an underlying commitment to international institutions and to the spirit of multilateralism. Indeed, critics often argued that the Canadian government had abandoned its multilateralist orientation in deference to a closer association with the United States. A similar tendency is evident in recent years; opponents of such policies as the Free Trade Agreement with the United States and Canadian participation in the Gulf War have argued that both policies indicated a rejection of long-standing multilateral commitments to the GATT and to the United Nations.

Domestic economic interests have also been important in shaping the government's involvement in multilateral activities. The Canadian economy has been very dependent on international trade. Moreover, the changing shape of the international economy has placed new demands on Canadian policy. The waning influence of Britain's role in the international economy and the declining utility of benefits for Canada in Britain's sterling system made policy makers acutely aware of Canada's growing dependence on the American market. Nor were they secure in the belief that this market would remain open to Canadian products. In the international community at large, there was also an emerging consensus that some system of globalized international trade would be desirable to prevent a recurrence of the economic turmoil that had spread throughout the system in the 1930s. This support for multilateralism has always been qualified in the economic sphere by some who favour a closer and special relationship with the Americans and by others who support a more nationalistic and protectionist orientation. Shifts among these interests have been instrumental in determining the strength of the government's commitment to multilateralism over time.

The historical, external, and domestic factors that supported a shift to a multilateralist foreign policy in the 1940s remain relevant today. As the international political, economic, and social environment undergoes a profound transformation, many of the conditions that have influenced Canadian foreign policy—its relative power position, its trade dependency, its asymmetrical relationship with the United States, its internationalist-oriented bureaucracy—continue to shape foreign policy options. As will be discussed in the chapters that follow, these conditions have often encouraged policy makers to rely on multilateral diplomacy, conducted primarily through international institutions, as Canada's best option. Support for multilateralism has not, however, been unconditional. Nor has it been the only option pursued by foreign policy makers. Canadian foreign policy has been influenced by many factors, including the predispositions of policy makers, prevailing public attitudes, the nature of the issue involved, and the policies and interests of other states in the system. At different times throughout the post-war period, in response to one or more of these factors, the government has set aside multilateral considerations and turned to unilateral action or to selected bilateral arrangements. What has become apparent over time, however, is that these alternatives are deviations from the norm, are short-lived, and are frequently combined with complementary multilateral activities.

Chapter One

Designing the International Order:
Canadian Interests in Post-War International Organizations

If there is one conclusion that our common experience has led us to accept, it is that security for this country lies in the development of a firm structure of international organization. —Louis St Laurent, 1947

INTRODUCTION

Canadian planning for the post-war world began in earnest in 1943. For the next two years, amidst a flurry of activity and numerous multilateral meetings, idealists and realists alike in the Department of External Affairs (DEA) worked to construct organizations that would secure the peace and win a place for Canada in the council of nations. In the end—but not for lack of effort—they would be disillusioned and disappointed. The United Nations (UN), launched amidst the chaos of the Second World War, was buffeted by balance-of-power politics and came adrift on the shoals of the Cold War. The experience was not without some success for Canada. Perhaps most important among these was that a relatively new corps of Canadian diplomats achieved a 'reputation for discreet statecraft [that] was to carry Canadian diplomacy far in the post-war world'.[1] Despite the setbacks experienced in the mid-1940s, Canadian officials continued to pursue active involvement in world affairs through international institutions and willingly responded to new challenges by accepting additional responsibilities in the decades to follow. There were historical precedents to Canada's multilateralist foreign policy. The most intensive period of multilateral diplomacy, however, surrounded the establishment of post-war international organizations in the 1940s.

This chapter focuses on Canadian policy during the formation and early years of the United Nations. The UN and its affiliated agencies absorbed most of the attention of government officials, especially those in the DEA. (The Commonwealth was a secondary, but not incidental, consideration.) The initial optimism and idealism of some officials quickly yielded to a more sober assessment of the limitations of the new organization. By the end of the 1940s, and especially following the UN's experience in Korea in the early 1950s, the government's approach to the UN had been thoroughly reassessed. Despite this shift in attitudes, this chapter reveals that support both for the principle of multilateral co-operation and for the institutional role of the UN in facilitating such co-operation remained strong. Whereas the primary Canadian objective throughout this period was to secure effective representation in the newly created organizations, Canadian practices reveal that these objectives were frequently set aside in an attempt to secure the UN's place as a source of negotiation, compromise, and peace in the emerging post-war world order. The viability of the institution was the fundamental policy objective.

BACKGROUND

The United States and Great Britain, later to be joined by the Soviet Union and China, initiated discussions during World War II on post-war international organizations. British prime minister Winston Churchill and American president Franklin Roosevelt were originally attracted to the idea of three regional organizations overseen by the great powers or, in Roosevelt's words, 'the four policemen'. Roosevelt's favoured approach to post-war organization was to combine the forces of the United States, Britain, Russia, and China, disarm all others, and rely on regional organizations to implement security provisions. When confronted by members of his own State Department on the need for an international secretariat to handle conferences, Roosevelt laughed and responded, 'I'll give you the Pentagon or the Empire State Building. You can put the world secretariat there'.[2] Within months, however, officials in the State Department convinced Roosevelt of the limitations of regional groupings and the necessity for an international organization. By October 1943, these officials had drafted the statement that was subsequently accepted by the other great powers and included in the Moscow Declaration. It argued in part for 'the establishment of "a general international organization, based on the principle of the sovereign equality of all peace-loving states, and open to membership by all such states, large and small, for the maintenance of international peace and security"'.[3] Churchill remained unconvinced, but he too encountered the opposition of his Foreign Office and of the Commonwealth prime ministers at a meeting in the spring of 1944. The objective of an international organization had been accepted; the structure remained to be worked out.

Having decided to create an organization that would be open to all states, the great powers were determined that effective control would remain in their hands. These four powers, led by the Americans, negotiated the initial draft of what would become the UN Charter. During a series of meetings in the late summer of 1944 at Dumbarton Oaks, a Georgetown estate in Washington, DC, the four powers agreed that 'there should be established an international organization under the title of the United Nations, the Charter of which should contain provisions necessary to give effect to the proposals which follow'.[4] The Dumbarton Oaks Proposals became the basis on which other states, including Canada, formally joined the negotiations. Six months later, following the meeting between Stalin, Churchill, and Roosevelt at Yalta in February 1945, the United Nations Conference on International Organization convened in San Francisco. On 26 June 1945, representatives from the 46 participating states signed the Charter of the United Nations, and on 10 January 1946, the newly formed United Nations met for the first time.

The UN was not the lone pillar of post-war plans. It was, however, the most widely discussed and publicized. It also exercised most of the energies, if not the talents, of Canada's beleaguered foreign service officers. By the time the Canadian delegation reached San Francisco, they were already well schooled in the intricacies of multilateral diplomacy.

The ABCs of Post-War Organizations

Telegrams from London in June 1943 requesting Canadian views on the post-war settlement prompted the government, preoccupied with fighting the war, to explore Canada's interests and options in the emerging international order. To facilitate this process, the government established the 'post hostilities problems' (PHP) committee under the direction of Hume Wrong, then assistant under-secretary of state for external affairs. Unlike Lester Pearson (at the time the minister-counsellor at the embassy in Washington) and Escott Reid (a second secretary in the department, who, among others, would also play a prominent role in the government's planning for the post-war period), Wrong was more of a realist than an idealist. He once numbered among the qualifications of a diplomat the need for 'cynicism about governments and pessimism about human nature, with both of which I am amply provided'.[5] These attributes would serve him well as he oversaw Canada's contributions to the negotiations on the post-war international order.

The objectives of the PHP committee were modest. Its primary task was to respond to initiatives taken in London and Washington. Canada, like other lesser powers, was not involved directly in any of the great power talks that led to the final preparatory meeting at Dumbarton Oaks. More than those in any other state, however, Canadians were kept well informed of the deliberations, principally by officials in London. As a result, there was a great deal on which to comment. Wrong, on behalf of the committee, and no doubt the government, eschewed more grandiose assignments: 'It would be wasted effort for Canada to attempt to plan from the foundation upward. As a secondary country we have not a great enough influence to make our views prevail. We should, however, be in a position at least to know what is not acceptable and to advocate changes or additions to fit our particular interests'.[6] This view was not a unanimous one. For Reid, such a position was both disappointing and ineffectual. Based on the Canadian experience at Bretton Woods and on his personal experience at the Chicago aviation conference, Reid maintained that a completed draft charter could serve as the basis for negotiations and thus be more influential than mere reactions to the drafts of others. But Wrong's more practical views prevailed and Reid's 'personal charter for sanity' was published anonymously as the San Francisco meeting opened.[7]

There was surprisingly little debate over whether Canada should participate in post-war international organizations. Prior to the formation of the PHP committee, Canadian officials had expressed an interest in organizing a more orderly international system along multilateral lines. The country's inability to avoid involvement in the war, a more activist and internationalist-oriented group of officials, and the American government's commitment to be involved all weighed heavily in favour of participation. There was also the historical precedent of Canada's membership in the League of Nations and in such associations as the International Labour Organization.

There was wide recognition that Canadian interests would best be served through multilateral associations. 'Under a collective system', wrote Reid in 1942,

> a small state like Canada would have an opportunity to exert a reasonable amount of influence in international politics at the cost of putting various aspects of its sovereignty into an international pool. But under the conditions of international anarchy which exist today the number of big states is likely to decrease and the few that are left are likely to run the small states which come within their respective spheres of influence.[8]

Finding room for the expression of Canadian interests in the emerging international order would become somewhat of a fixation for foreign policy makers.

Specific Canadian interests were not the only consideration. Within the DEA, the prevailing view was that the war had been a result of the failure of the League of Nations to secure the peace that had been gained at such terrible costs in 1918. James Eayrs has noted that Prime Minister Mackenzie King did not share this position, was skeptical of the benefits of international organizations, and worried over the commitments the country was undertaking.[9] For both the PM and his advisors, however, preventing another war was the overriding concern, and this concern provided the strongest impetus for the government's decision to become actively involved. The strength of this motivation is perhaps best attested to by the government's willingness to maintain support for the UN and other institutions despite repeated failures to secure effective Canadian representation on the decision-making councils of the new organizations.

Once Canada had decided to participate, attention in Ottawa shifted to the nature of Canadian involvement. Long before Canadian delegates reached San Francisco, a variety of international conferences were convened at which the framework of post-war organizations were devised. At these meetings, Canadian officials were preoccupied with securing recognition for what they saw as Canada's special status. There was little debate on involvement itself, or indeed—with some notable exceptions, such as the International Civil Aviation Organization (ICAO)—on most of the substantive matters that would preoccupy the institutions.[10] This was in part a result of the very preliminary nature of many of these negotiations. It was also a clear reflection of the fact that the overriding Canadian objective at most of these meetings was to further the process and to gain a place for Canada at the decision-making table. At a meeting of the Commonwealth prime ministers in 1944, Mackenzie King put forward the position that would direct the Canadian negotiating approach to post-war organizations: 'Although the special responsibility of the four great powers for maintaining political security must be recognized, nevertheless an effort should be made to give the smaller powers a larger share in the direction of the many functional organizations which will be set up'.[11]

Not surprisingly, in view of Canada's special interests and capabilities in various non-security areas such as raw materials and food, policy makers in Ottawa displayed a particular concern for the many specialized agencies that were established during the course of the war. The members of External Affairs displayed no common ground on the motives for this concern; John English writes that 'Pearson and Escott Reid fought against great power domination because they were, in Reid's own words, utopians; Wrong, King, and, to a lesser extent, [Norman] Robertson [under-secretary of state for external affairs (USSEA)], did so because they wanted Canada's national interests recognized and represented'.[12] The utopians, including Pearson, saw the great powers as the problem, not the solution: 'The history of the League proves that not small powers but big powers cause most of the trouble and prevent most of the solutions. It also shows that smaller powers—when not the pawns of larger—can do good and constructive international work'.[13] Despite these differences in motives, the government was united in its commitment to direct Canadian representation in international councils, a commitment that was expressed in the pursuit of functional representation.

Functionalism was the organizing principle behind the government's approach to representation in international organizations.[14] The fundamental idea was that decision-making responsibility had to be shared and that it should be shared with those who were most capable of making a contribution. The Canadian government had indicated its willingness to take on greater responsibilities. In return it wanted recognition and influence. The government's concern with adequate representation emerged before concrete plans for post-war organizations materialized. As the war progressed, and especially after the Americans became involved in 1941, the government had less and less say over the course of the war; the Americans and the British held a duopoly of power and were unwilling to share it with the other combatants.

The initial battlegrounds for Canada's fight for functional representation were the Combined Boards that directed the Allies' campaign against the Axis powers. The Boards were American and British efforts to co-ordinate their own and other allies' wartime efforts. They encompassed not only strategic planning, but also raw materials, shipping, food, production and resources, and munitions. Canadian representatives in Washington expressed concerns over Canada's role on the Boards from the outset in the early months of 1942. Canadian participation on the Boards became an important test of American and British recognition of Canada's extensive contributions to the war effort. As Jack Granatstein has noted, participation also became a symbol of Canadian nationalism: 'In the course of fighting to secure a place commensurate with Canada's new power, the Department of External Affairs made nationalism equal involvement. . . . Nationalism now marched hand in hand with internationalism'.[15]

Initial representations for Canadian participation on the Boards met with little success. The British were unwilling to lend their support for a Canadian seat at the table out of concern for the possibility of demands from other states. Yet it was this very distinction from other states who were contributing substantially less that was the crux of the Canadian position. The tendency of the Americans and the British to ignore Canadian demands for more effective participation created a dilemma for

Ottawa. It was necessary to press Canadian claims in such a way that other governments in support of the allied cause would not all press for similar access. Wrong, as
early as January 1942, wrote to Robertson from the embassy in Washington that the
principle, which might be more difficult to implement than to articulate, was that
'each member of the grand alliance should have a voice in the conduct of the war
proportionate to its contribution to the general war effort. A subsidiary principle is
that the influence of the various countries should be greatest in connection with those
matters with which they are most directly concerned'.[16]

Part of the difficulty the country's diplomats confronted in arguing for greater
access to decision-making circles was the government's past unwillingness to take on
greater responsibilities. Another problem was whether to seek representation alone or
on behalf of other secondary powers (as they were referred to at this time). Some, such
as Pearson, suggested working with these other states to acquire representation on the
Combined Boards. Another view supported the notion of Canadian distinctiveness.
This would be a problem that would recur in various circumstances throughout the
post-war period: Should Canada attempt to lead the middle powers or seek privileged
access to great power corridors? Pearson believed that the country would derive additional benefit if it led a coalition of lesser powers: 'This might be not only desirable in
itself, but also would supply a useful corrective to those who think that we should
exercise no influence except within the confines of the British Commonwealth'.[17] In
spite of these arguments, the government decided to pursue membership on the
Combined Boards on the basis of Canadian distinctiveness. In making this decision,
the government set a precedent that it would follow throughout subsequent negotiations on the UN. Australia would become the 'spokesman of the chorus' and would, in
Reid's view, win the respect of other lesser powers.

Pursuing functional representation was both a necessity and an opportunity for
Canadian policy makers. It was necessary because Canada was one of the few states in
the early 1940s that had the capabilities to make a substantial contribution to the war
effort. Canadians were the second-largest suppliers of food and raw materials, after
the Americans, and the country was also making a disproportionately large contribution of personnel. Relinquishing control over the size and deployment of these contributions raised potential political difficulties at home. The opportunity was to increase
significantly Canada's potential influence in shaping the war and its aftermath. Never
before, or since, had Canada reached so near the pinnacles of international power.
European and Pacific powers were threatened with their very survival. Governments
and economies in these regions were in tatters. In Canada, however, the economy was
flourishing and the government enjoyed solid public support. Only the looming
threat of conscription created a sense of uncertainty. Even this problem, however,
could be used to justify greater access to allied decision making. In this context, there
was an opportunity to make a mark, and many Canadian diplomats were anxious to
try their hand.

However logical the argument for functional representation appeared to its
Canadian (and other middle power) proponents, it was a tough sell in Washington

and London. Despite being rebuffed, Ottawa repeated its demands ad nauseam. In doing so, it refrained from aligning with other secondary powers. The objective was to distinguish Canada's capabilities from those of other states, not to argue for some principle of middle power representation—that would come later. For now, the primary motive was to secure some degree of control over the disposition of Canadian resources, and the Combined Food Board was to be the test case.

In July 1942, Canada requested membership on the Food Board, on the grounds that 'she considers herself the largest holder of surplus exportable food'.[18] In the face of strong British resistance, the Cabinet conceded defeat in the autumn. External Affairs was unwilling to let the matter drop, however, and when an opportunity came to put forward another request for representation, it did so. This time, opposition in London and Washington wavered, and in October 1943, Canada accepted an offer for a seat on the Board. Functionalism and its External supporters had achieved their first victory, but the war had not been won. A more important struggle was already underway.

From the early stages of the war, the allies recognized the need for a major relief effort at the end of hostilities. Plans for this effort were released in June 1942. The United Nations Relief and Rehabilitation Agency (UNRRA) was to be the prototype of post-war international organizations. For Ottawa, it was imperative that this organization accept the principle of functional representation. This was not only a matter of symbolic importance; policy makers recognized that Canada's advantageous position would compel the country to make substantial contributions to the relief effort. Principled concerns opposed to great power domination were joined with the practical realities of acquiring some say in how Canadian resources would be used. Unlike the Combined Boards, UNRRA involved all of the United Nations. It was not enough to convince the British and the Americans; the Russians and Chinese would also have to agree to Canadian participation and others would have to be left out.

The Canadians defended their claim in stark terms in the spring of 1943: 'It will be very difficult or even impossible to persuade the Parliament and people of Canada to accept the financial burdens and other sacrifices . . . unless they are satisfied that their representatives exercised their due part in its direction'.[19] The Americans bent in response and suggested that Canada, 'as chairman of the supplies committee of UNRRA, [sit] on the executive committee whenever supplies were being discussed'.[20] This proposal received the support of officials in External, but this time Cabinet would not bend and held out for full membership. Their resistance did not last long. Opposition from the Soviets to more Anglo-Saxon members of the committee and a meeting between British foreign minister Anthony Eden and Mackenzie King led the Cabinet to accept the compromise position. In its statement, the War Committee of the Cabinet informed the Americans that the acceptance had 'been determined by the desire that international organization in this field should get under way as soon as possible'.[21] External officials made the argument that this would not be a precedent for future organizations to which the four powers acceded, but Mackenzie King was perhaps more to the point when he referred to it as 'one of the cases where it is clearly impossible for a lesser power to really do other than be largely governed by the views of the greater powers'.[22]

As the British and Americans shifted their attention from the course of the war to the shape of the post-war order, Robertson pressed Mackenzie King to speak out in support of the functionalist principle:

> While experience between the wars has shown the great practical difficulties of apply-ing to membership in international bodies the legal concept of the equality of states, we are confident that no workable international system can be based on the concen-tration of influence and authority wholly in bodies composed of a few great powers to the exclusion of all the rest. It is not always the largest powers that have the greatest contribution to make to the work of these bodies or the greatest stake in their success. In international economic organizations such as the Relief Administration represen-tation on such bodies can often be determined on a functional basis and in our view this principle should be applied wherever it is feasible.[23]

As Wrong predicted, the functionalist principle presented many practical difficul-ties. The UN was to be based on the principle of the sovereign equality of nation states, yet Canadian diplomats sought to compromise this principle in practice. English has written that 'in a sense "functionalism" was a Canadian attempt to exaggerate the significance of a small nation in a fashion that contradicted the liberal, democratic, and universalist notions on which a true world government would have to be based'.[24] The contradiction, however, was not Canada's alone. The big two powers were already controlling the war effort, and the big four were in the process of drafting the UN Charter, which would offer special protection for the interests of the great powers. These powers had little hesitation in pressing ahead to consider post-war matters, declining requests for wider consultation and accepting only minimal input from lesser states. It is not surprising, in this context, that the four readily accepted a veto over all important UN matters. Canadians were willing to recognize the necessity of great power co-operation and the need for a limited veto. They accepted the nature of power and the practical benefits of reflecting the distribution of power in the new organization. Indeed, the Canadian position was consistent with such a position in arguing that there should be a further differentiation between secondary and lesser powers. The distinction that concerned Canadians was not between the United States and Canada, but between Canada and El Salvador—between secondary powers that had contributed substantially to the war effort and would continue to contribute in peacetime and smaller states that had neither the interest nor the capability to make a substantial contribution. Functionalism may have contradicted 'liberal, democratic' notions of world government, but it was more in tune with the institutionalization of the balance of power that was to become the UN.

Despite its limited success, functionalism remained the foundation of Canada's approach to post-war organizations. Perhaps this is not surprising in view of Nicholas Mansergh's assessment that functionalism was 'a principle that commended itself to

Canadian altruism, good sense and self-interest alike'.[25] What is noteworthy, however, is that even when functionalist arguments failed to secure for Canada a voice in decision making, the Canadian commitment to active involvement in the organization remained. This was a remarkable shift for a government led by a prime minister who had been extremely reluctant to accept foreign commitments. Functionalism was designed to secure some Canadian control over the commitments it would make to these new institutions, but Canadians were clearly willing to make a commitment regardless. Three-quarters of the public surveyed in 1943 supported participation in the maintenance of post-war peace, even if it required sending Canadian forces to other parts of the globe[26]—such was the strength and degree of the change that had taken place in the country. Further testimony to this new thinking can be found in the Canadian reaction to the Dumbarton Oaks Proposals and in its negotiating tactics at the San Francisco meetings where the UN charter was finalized.

FRAMING THE CHARTER

More so than most of the other 46 delegations that came to San Francisco in the spring of 1945, the Canadians had had ample opportunity to plan. The government, although lacking direct access to the discussions at Dumbarton Oaks, had been fully apprised of their content by the British government. Canadian diplomats were also already well versed in the political struggle for recognition of the rights and responsibilities of secondary powers. Most important, the political commitment to participate had been taken. One month prior to the conference, the House of Commons approved, by a vote of 202 to 5, Canadian participation in the new organization. Government planning for the organization had been underway for more than a year through the PHP committee. By the time the Canadian delegation reached San Francisco, the Canadian positions had been widely debated within the DEA. Canadian concerns about the new organization were both procedural and substantial. The dominant procedural issue was, of course, recognition of the important role of secondary powers; the substantial concerns ranged widely.

Surprisingly, for a government that had turned its back so quickly on the League of Nations, the delegation supported a strong collective security system. Perhaps this was a result of the changed personnel in External Affairs. The three officials leading Canada into the UN were Wrong, Robertson, and Pearson. Each had viewed Canada's ambivalence as the world drifted toward war in the late 1930s as seriously mistaken. Pearson had already registered his deep displeasure with the failed collective security effort of 1935. He wrote to Robertson in 1944 that 'we now know—or should know—that there is no safety in a League of Nations which does not make adequate provision for peaceful change and police action against the aggressor. We shall, I think, have to revise our attitude toward any future Article X or Article XVI of an international covenant'.[27] An international organization that could wield effective power to prevent aggression was a high priority for these officials. There had also been an important shift in the public mood. Perhaps this was the result of the ongoing war, which reinforced among the public the belief that future wars must be avoided and that Canada could and should make a contribution to this effort. Even the prime minister was willing to accept a collective security system. In Mackenzie King's case, it was the lesser of two evils, the greater being the regional security arrangements originally proposed by Roosevelt and Churchill.

Early in the planning, External Affairs officials favoured the establishment of international—or perhaps more precisely, multilateral—forces, drawn from the experience of allied forces in wartime. This proposal, although it was unlikely to receive the support of the PM, was indicative of Canadian officials' attitudes toward sovereignty. The country had willingly yielded control of its armed forces during the early stages of the war, and only as the war progressed had it demanded a greater say in allied operations. The ease with which Canada had sacrificed sovereignty to shirk responsibility had perhaps made it easier for the diplomats to think that it could now be done in assuming greater responsibilities. Some in the East Block wanted to go further. Pearson lamented the lack of commitment on the part of the great powers to strengthen the collective security provisions. Reid questioned the value of an organization that would stay out of domestic conflicts, which in his view were 'very often, if not most often, the occasions for the really serious disputes between nations'.[28] These proposals were ultimately forced to give way to the real necessity of maintaining the tenuous co-operation of the great powers as the war drew to a close and post-war planning intensified. In the words of Robertson, the department had come to the decision that the government should 'take the Organization that we can get and . . . refrain from further efforts to pry apart the difficult unity which the Great Powers have attained'.[29] Not for the last time, Canadians decided to abandon particular objectives in order to support the more important institutional objectives.

The Canadian approach to the San Francisco conference was decidedly low-key. The idealistic visions of Reid and Pearson had been overruled by Robertson and Wrong as impractical in light of great power agreements. These visions were also unlikely to win much political support from Mackenzie King. The 'realists' turned their attention to maintaining what remained of great power unanimity and to the more practical concerns of gaining representation for Canada in the new organization. The focus was on obtaining a seat on the proposed Security Council and on ensuring that Canadian forces would not be called into service without some say in when and how they would be used. The main threat was that the UN would develop into a concert system in which the big four powers (at this time France had not yet been admitted to the great power club) would dictate to the smaller states. In their approach to the negotiations, the Canadian delegation recognized the importance of keeping all of the large powers within the new organization and, unlike the more outspoken Australians, did not want to antagonize these powers and thereby threaten the very existence of the organization in their drive for recognition. Nonetheless, they wanted some say in how the new organization would use the contributions of smaller powers. One can find in the Canadian approach to the San Francisco negotiations evidence of a view that the organization itself was of primary importance and Canadian representation a secondary concern. Australia, in comparison, took a more aggressive stance against great power domination of the UN. Reid, in a prophetic memo to Robertson, questioned the government's tactics: 'If Canada swings too much to the support of the Great Powers position it may lose more small power votes [in elections to the Security Council] than it will gain from the votes of Great Power satellites'.[30] At the first meeting of the General Assembly in January 1946, Australia won a seat on the Security Council; Canada did not.

The middle powers were successful at San Francisco in winning support for some of their demands. On representation on the Security Council, they secured in Article 23 an amendment originally proposed by the British (under pressure from Canada) that in electing non-permanent members to the Council, 'due regard' would be paid 'in the first instance to the contribution of Members of the United Nations to the maintenance of international peace and security and to the other purposes of the Organization'. Article 61 of the UN's Economic and Social Council (ECOSOC) also included provision for the re-election of members of the Council. Canadian representatives hoped that this would allow for near-permanent representation for those members who made substantial contributions to the work of the Council. With respect to enforcement measures, Article 44 was included in the Charter to enable non-members of the Security Council to participate in its deliberations when such members of the UN were called upon to contribute forces. In this way, the Canadians intended to gain some say in the disposition of forces that it might contribute to UN enforcement measures. The success of these efforts to amend the Charter in accordance with functionalist principles had little effect on the actual operations of the organization. Canada was not immediately elected to the Security Council and in practice, the representation of non-permanent members on the Council has been based primarily on equitable geographical representation. Article 44 would not become relevant for 50 years, until the Security Council invoked Article 43 on enforcement measures.

Perhaps the main advantages that Canadian officials gained at San Francisco were a good dose of realism about the future prospects for the new organization and the experience of working in a multilateral setting. Some of this had, of course, already occurred, especially in negotiations on UNRRA, the Food and Agriculture Organization (FAO), and the ICAO. Canadians were moving into ever wider international settings, taking on new responsibilities, and attempting to inject a Canadian voice into the formation of the evolving international order. In doing so, however, they were still preoccupied with the North Atlantic triangle. Greater freedom of action would now come not by balancing the power between Britain and the United States or by using one against the other, but in joining both in a wider network of states that would open opportunities for independent Canadian initiatives while minimizing the risk of injury to important bilateral relations.

BEYOND THE NATIONAL INTEREST

It would be misleading to conclude that the sole motivation for Canada's approach to post-war organizations was to gain recognition for the country's contribution to the war effort. Holmes has argued that 'the Canadian theory of functionalism was more than an argument for a larger Canadian role. It was a philosophy for world self-government'.[31] There has been some skepticism expressed about this view, but it is evident that some officials—such as Pearson, Reid, and Dana Wilgress, the Canadian ambassador to the Soviet Union—did seek a more effective and authoritative system of international management than the UN eventually provided. Underlying the persistent references to functional representation in many Canadian statements was a commitment to a system of rules that would govern international behaviour. International organizations were favoured not simply because they would enhance Canadian influence or offer a wider range of tasks for an expanding corps of diplomats; they were viewed as a way of entrenching a more stable and secure international order that would both support Canadian interests and provide an ongoing site in which Canadian representatives could operate. The willingness of policy makers to set aside narrow concerns over representation in the interest of building such firm structures was evident in Canadian diplomacy throughout this active period of institution building.

Beyond the issue of representation, much of Canadian diplomacy reflected an ambivalence to sovereignty and to national interests narrowly conceived. Many officials in Ottawa favoured authoritative institutions, ones that would have some control over state sovereignty. This was evident in the government's position on the ICAO. It was also apparent in its views on the UN Secretariat, which it thought should be made up of international civil servants and not national representatives. There was also a persistent interest in facilitating the ongoing operations of these organizations despite the failure to receive special recognition for Canadian representation and the obvious disappointment that many officials experienced after the San Francisco meetings. Reid was among the most disappointed, both with the results of the various UN negotiations in which he was involved and with aspects of Canadian policy. Nonetheless, in a letter of instructions to Canada's first delegation on the Security Council in January 1947, he wrote, 'One way in which Canada can help to remedy the weaknesses in the Security Council is by acting in the Security Council not in defence of the special national interests of Canada but in defence of the interests of the United Nations as a whole'.[32] It is perhaps for these reasons that Holmes writes that Canada's approach to international organizations in the early post-war period was marked by a commitment to the institution and that 'any immediate interest would often be sacrificed for the conservation of the structure'.[33]

The structure of international institutions that was established in the mid-1940s encompassed a wide variety of objectives. The system of collective security embodied in the UN was the core, but few, and especially few in Canada, saw it as sufficient. It would have been futile to deal with war without addressing some of its underlying causes. This was evident in Canada's interest in the Economic and Social Commission of the UN and in the various Specialized Agencies that were created during the war. Indeed, Holmes notes, 'the part played by Canadians in the conferences at Hot Springs, Bretton Woods, Chicago, where the great agencies to deal with food and money and aviation were set up, was closer to the international centres of power than was their activity at San Francisco'.[34] The country had both a greater interest in and a greater capability to wield influence in these areas; these were the functional areas in which Canada could claim special status. They were also areas in which multilateral co-operation would provide the experience on which a wider and more developed system of international co-operation and multilateral management would be based. This was not a completely new position. In the waning days of the League before the outbreak of war, Wrong had argued that 'more frequent initiative by the Canadian representatives on questions of economic, social and humanitarian importance would contribute towards preserving the practice and technique of international collaboration'.[35]

Effective international co-operation was a central objective, and one can see that even at this early stage, Canadian policy makers were keenly interested in fostering this co-operation. Substantive issues, regardless of their significance to the country's interests, were commonly set aside in an effort to maintain co-operation. The reconciliation of divergent British and American interests was always an immediate concern, and in meetings at Bretton Woods (see Chapter 2) and at the Chicago air convention, the Canadian delegation tried valiantly to do this. Throughout this period, Canadian policies frequently rested between British and American proposals. Often, Canadian policy shifted closer to that of the Americans. This was not so much out of deference to the emerging power of the United States as it was out of recognition that Canadian interests were frequently more in tune with those in Washington. It was also, in part, a result of an interest in resisting pressures for a common Commonwealth position on the new institutions. The Canadian government had struggled to identify Canada as an independent northern neighbour and hence had avoided adopting policies that might suggest that Canada was merely the Commonwealth's representative on the North American continent.

Canadian concerns also went beyond the North Atlantic triangle, however, and extended to efforts to avoid alienating the Soviets and to mollify the demands of lesser powers. Even at this early stage, conciliation in the interest of institutional maintenance had become a principal policy objective.

COMMONWEALTH RELATIONS

Much of Canada's pre-war foreign policy had been devoted to securing Canadian autonomy within a looser association of the Commonwealth. As the war progressed and attention turned to other matters, the idea of a unified Commonwealth had still not been put to rest. There remained pressures in Britain and elsewhere for a common foreign and defence policy. For the British, such pressures resulted in part from concern over Britain's declining power relative to that of the United States and the Soviet Union. For governments in Australia and New Zealand, the concern was to retain Britain's commitment to an active defence role in the Pacific. These countries had not yet worked out security arrangements with the new Pacific power, the Americans. Canada had already settled its immediate security concerns with the

United States through the Ogdensburg Agreement of 1940, which had established the Permanent Joint Board on Defence for ongoing bilateral military co-operation, and it looked to the UN and not the Commonwealth as holding the greater promise for international security. For these reasons, along with the predilections of Prime Minister Mackenzie King, Canada often stood alone in resisting pressures for a unified Commonwealth voice. Officials in Ottawa were also wary of the American reaction to closer Commonwealth co-operation and feared losing, in the words of Pearson, 'the national and international position we have gained'.[36] The country was at long last exercising its independent voice on the world stage and, despite the occasional contrary view in the House of Commons, had little interest in returning to the confines of Dominion status.

The prevailing political view in Ottawa remained firmly opposed to any suggestion of a Commonwealth foreign policy. When various proposals were raised during the war that Britain represent Canada on the Combined Boards or that Canada have a seat and represent the Commonwealth, these were flatly rejected by the Canadian government. Fear of a common foreign policy voiced from London was also among the reasons for a rejection of regional approaches to security. Unlike in the pre-war period, however, the main objective now was to internationalize policy, not to remain cloistered in a nationalist, isolationist shell. Despite rejecting a unified voice, Canada was quick to defend a new and vital role for the Commonwealth. As Mackenzie King told the meeting of Commonwealth prime ministers in May 1944, where he dismissed calls for a more unified stand, 'the Commonwealth is not a Power bloc exploiting its own selfish interests but a group of like-minded nations whose close association has in the past and may in the future form the most reliable element within the framework of the world order'.[37] The new Commonwealth must allow for the independence of its members and depend on consultation and not collaboration. As Lord Garner said, this meeting 'marked the apotheosis of Mackenzie King and all that he stood for. . . . This was for him virtually the last round—and he won completely'.[38]

Commonwealth relations, and especially links with Britain, were extremely valuable to Canada throughout the events leading to the formation of the UN. Despite fears of co-optation, to which were now added concerns about upsetting the Americans, Canada's Commonwealth connections provided an indispensable source of information and, on occasion, support for Canadian policy makers:

> External Affairs was increasingly realizing that, whether they liked it or not, the big decisions were being made among the great powers and the best channel of information as to what was going on at those levels, and also of providing some outlet for Canadian views, was the British bureaucracy, which shared its confidences with the Canadians and Australians in a much more familial way than was conceivable at that time from Washington. If the bogey of a single voice could be laid, then the advantages of the Commonwealth association could be exploited.[39]

Indicative of the value of such consultations was a meeting of the Commonwealth prime ministers in May 1944 to discuss what would become the Dumbarton Oaks proposals. This meeting and numerous bilateral contacts also kept Canada and other Commonwealth members well informed on great power deliberations while other governments had to wait for the public release of the proposals in October 1944. Perhaps as much as anything else, this provided the government with an indication of the value the Commonwealth could have in the emerging post-war system.

There were other reasons to keep Canadian support for the Commonwealth alive. One was the continued affinity of many Canadians for the association. While there was little opposition to the repeated attempts to disassociate Ottawa's policy from that of London, the public remained supportive of Commonwealth membership. For the government, retaining Commonwealth connections would not only appeal to these Canadians, but might also mitigate a tendency, in Canada and elsewhere, to view Canada as a North American power with limited interests, dwarfed by a hegemon. There was also a certain affinity, despite different tactics, between the Canadians and other Commonwealth members. A shared experience in winning greater autonomy from London had perhaps encouraged their mutual aspirations for functional representation in the new institutions being created. For example, although Canada and Australia soon became rivals for a seat on the Security Council and adopted different strategies in San Francisco, they shared many common objectives.

Thus, despite periodic uneasiness over too close an association with the Commonwealth, support for continued involvement remained strong. With the end of the war and with the struggle for autonomous foreign policies secured, other considerations took on greater significance. Declining British capabilities and the emergence of American power and assertiveness raised new fears in Ottawa. Commonwealth membership could now be seen as a means of balancing an ever-increasing number of North American contacts without any threat of subservience to London. In addition, the growth of anti-colonial pressures and the independence of states on the Indian subcontinent raised questions about the very future of the Commonwealth itself. The Commonwealth, if successful in integrating these and other new states, could become not only a counterweight to the Americans, but also a window on a wider world, one that would complement and support rather than constrain Canadian policy in the UN. These concerns led to a re-evaluation of the importance of the Commonwealth for the conduct of Canadian foreign policy. They also influenced the manner in which the government reacted to developments in India. The government was hesitant in its response to Indian independence in 1947 and to its membership in the Commonwealth; it did not wish to get involved in the former, but it did not want Britain to have the sole voice in the latter. Indian independence was for Britain to work out. Canada concentrated on reforming the club to make it more appealing for the next wave of ex-colonies.[40] This was done by resisting pressures for a single voice, dropping the Dominion status, allowing for the membership of republics, and, much later, removing the stain of racial discrimination. In helping to set the Commonwealth on this new course, there was little sense of future direction. It seemed more a matter of keeping a trustworthy association available in case of future needs.

PUTTING THE CHARTER INTO PRACTICE: KOREA

The first real test of the UN's collective security provisions came in June 1950 as the result of the outbreak of hostilities in the Korean peninsula. Prior to the outbreak of war in Korea, the Canadian delegation had already reconsidered the utility of an enforcement role for the UN. Effective collective security may have been the original goal, but it was clearly unobtainable under the circumstances. In response, the Canadian delegation argued that the organization must limit its aspirations. Pearson, who in 1948 became the secretary of state for external affairs (SSEA) in the Cabinet of Prime Minister Louis St Laurent, outlined three principles that he believed should govern the Security Council's approach to problems of peace and security. The first was that the Council 'should not initiate action that it cannot complete with its present resources'; the second was that 'to the greatest extent possible the responsibility for solving a political problem should be left with the people who are immediately affected by it'; the third was that the Council 'should in all cases immediately concentrate its influence on putting an end to hostilities or disorders whenever they occur'.[41] In articulating these principles, Pearson acknowledged both the constraints that now limited UN action and the changes that had occurred in his government's approach to the UN's peace and security role. With the establishment of NATO, Canada's security would rest with a military alliance and the goal of universal collective security would be set aside, to be replaced with more modest objectives. In place of its collective security role, the Canadian delegation took the view that 'the United Nations should act more as a mediator than a policeman, not only because its effective police powers are so very restricted, but also because their use is apt to lead to heightened controversy within the Organization'; for these reasons the delegation sought to emphasize 'the maximum use of conciliation with a minimum use of intervention' and a 'reliance on persuasion rather than coercion'.[42]

By moderating their expectations of the UN's role in international conflicts, Canadian officials could also minimize the need for Canadian contributions to international peace and security. The failure of the great powers to reach agreement in the Military Staff Committee over the establishment of a common UN military force meant that there would be no need for national contributions to such a force. This, in turn, would make it possible to keep defence expenditures limited. The government was accepting new commitments for the defence of Europe through NATO, and although this had not as yet brought about the deployment of forces to Europe, it did make the government wary of additional commitments to the UN. The Cold War provided the main threat to peace and security, and the UN was ill prepared to take a definitive position in that conflict without alienating the Soviet bloc and many neutral states. Ottawa saw little value in turning the UN into an anti-communist organization. In the interest of maintaining the organization's diverse membership, Canadian officials wished to avoid driving the Soviets out of the UN and sought instead to take advantage of opportunities within the organization to bridge the East–West divide. This became even more difficult as the Cold War intensified and the UN was dragged into it.

The war in Korea was a watershed in the Cold War. It had an immediate and long-lasting effect on the West's response to the Soviet challenge. Containment came to be viewed as primarily a military policy, and defence budgets escalated accordingly. Western arsenals, especially those of the United States, underwent an expansion that has yet to subside. Co-operation across the ideological divide became even more difficult as militant anti-communism emerged as the orthodox view in American political circles. For Canadians, the long-term effects would be felt more distinctly in NATO and in bilateral defence relations with the Americans, but the immediate repercussions were in the UN and in Canada's commitment to that organization.

Canada's initial contact with the Korean dispute occurred innocently when the Canadian delegation accepted an American nomination to sit on the United Nations Temporary Commission on Korea (UNTCOK) in 1947. UNTCOK was mandated to assess the viability of holding supervised elections throughout the Korean peninsula, which had been divided by Soviet and American occupying forces at the end of the Second World War. As with the divisions in Germany and Berlin, the Cold War made early unification unlikely. Nonetheless, the Americans were anxious to force the Soviets to reject American *qua* UN proposals for elections and to proceed with their own American-run elections in South Korea. The Canadian delegation viewed the commission as another of many UN committees that would try to make a report on an intractable political problem. Their willingness to participate despite surprise at the invitation was also, in part, 'to save the United States from embarrassment'.[43] Reflecting the delegation's view of the pedestrian nature of the commission, the acceptance was made without informing the Cabinet. The decision, however, was anything but routine. There was great surprise and consternation when the prime minister registered his strong opposition to the decision during a subsequent Cabinet meeting. Mackenzie King's opposition and his concern over the participatory inter-nationalism displayed by officials in External Affairs stemmed from his isolationist sentiments, his antipathy toward the UN, and his fears about American intentions in the region (and, perhaps, the warnings of a London spiritualist).[44] The issue led Mackenzie King, on one side of the issue, and Minister of Justice J.L. Ilsley and Minister of External Affairs Louis St Laurent, on the other, to threaten resignation if their respective positions were not accepted. In the end, Mackenzie King yielded, with the proviso that the Canadian representative, Dr George Patterson, support the position that the commission could only supervise elections if both the Soviets and the Americans agreed. This Patterson did, to no avail, and in the end, King's view that the Americans 'were seeking to make the United Nations a political arm of the State Department' proved accurate.[45] Canadian opposition to the holding of elections in the South did not prevent the commission from deciding to proceed, and elections were held on 10 May 1948, after which the government of the Republic of Korea was established.

UNTCOK was an early indication of American intransigence in the Cold War politics of the early 1950s. Events during the ensuing war in Korea confirmed this pattern and created serious problems for Canadian diplomats anxious to bridge the East–West divide. In the end, desires for a mediating role would yield to the interests of bloc solidarity. Equally important, the UN's short-lived attempt at collective security gave way to a more sober assessment of its potential contribution to international peace and security.

War in Korea, and especially the American reaction to it, caught Canadian officials by surprise. Pearson, in his earliest public reaction to the crisis, did not think that the United States would intervene because the peninsula lay outside the American security zone in the Pacific. When the Americans did respond, and when their response was sanctioned by the United Nations, Canadian policy was devoted to attempts to enhance the role of the organization even when this brought the government into conflict with the Americans. For Canadians, the foremost consideration in assessing the Korean situation was the integrity of the UN. As the Opposition leader, George Drew, informed the House of Commons, 'On the outcome of this issue in Korea depends the future effectiveness of the United Nations. For that reason it is not only the fate of South Korea that hangs in the balance; it is the fate of the United Nations, the fate of that organization upon which the hope of peace in the years ahead now rests'.[46] The war did have a notable effect on the UN and on Canadian assessments of the organization's peace and security function, but it was not the one intended. It also had a significant influence on Canadian appraisals of American Cold War policies. As Pearson succinctly stated in 1951, 'Our preoccupation is no longer whether the United States will discharge her responsibilities, but how she will do it and how the rest of us will be involved'.[47]

The war exposed the UN's role in the conflict as little more than an instrument of American policy:

> Rightly or wrongly, the fact remains that the decision to repel the North Korean invasion by force was an American decision, just as the decision to refer the crisis to the Security Council was at American behest. The United Nations did not decide collectively to condemn the aggression and then to obligate its members, including the United States, to take action to stop it; rather, the United States decided to oppose the aggression and then to ask the members of the United Nations for moral and material support.[48]

The Canadian government attempted to put the best light on this situation by working with other UN members to increase the organization's control over American actions, to bring the operations in the field under UN control, and to ensure that the Security Council's mandate not be exceeded in the field. In his history of Canadian involvement in the war, Stairs takes note of the problems this created for Canadian policy makers:

Every attempt by the American authorities . . . to extend the objectives or the conduct of hostilities beyond the limits which defined the United Nations role in the crisis produced a conflict between Ottawa and Washington. For the Canadians most directly involved, the politics of the Korean War consisted largely in the attempt to make the collective, or United Nations, aspect of the crisis the dominant one, and since to succeed in this was to constrain the United States, friction in their official relations with their American counterparts was the result.[49]

For Canadians, the results of these efforts were very disappointing and indicated the difficulty they would encounter in controlling the Americans through the collective voice of the UN.

There were many aspects of the Korean War that troubled Canadian officials. Although not a member of the Security Council at the time, the Canadian government was in agreement with the initial Security Council resolutions that called for a cessation of hostilities and for the withdrawal of North Korean forces from the South and that requested UN members to give support to the South Koreans. Following the commitment of American forces to the war zone and the Council's resolution of June 27 calling on members 'to furnish such assistance to the Republic of Korea as may be necessary to repel the armed attack and to restore international peace and security in the area',[50] the government was under pressure both from the Americans and from many segments of the Canadian public to make a tangible contribution. As Stairs notes, 'it was a small caprice of Canadian history that on the day [Mackenzie King] died, leaders of opinion among the populace whose isolationist views he had nurtured for so long were clamouring to send troops to an obscure and ugly war in the Far East'.[51] This the government did, but not before making a concerted effort to bring the military operation under strict UN control and guidelines. Officials in Ottawa were concerned that the war would become an exclusive American operation, thus undermining the 'collective' dimension and, further, that hostilities might be broadened to encompass Formosa.

Canada's contribution to the war, while insignificant and insufficient in the view of many Americans and some Canadians, was substantial when considered in light of the capabilities of the Canadian armed forces at the time. In July 1950, the government committed three destroyers to support the UN effort in Korea. The Americans, who constituted the overwhelming majority of forces, considered this completely inadequate and called for additional armed forces. Using UN secretary-general Trygve Lie as the demandeur, the Americans continued to press for additional commitments. The Cabinet eventually agreed to recruit a force for Korea but, on the advice of the military, delayed its deployment until 1951 to ensure that they were prepared for conflict. By the end of the conflict, about 20,000 Canadians had gone to Korea, and more than 300 lost their lives there.

Ottawa wanted the operation limited in scope and as closely governed by the UN as possible to lend credibility to the UN, to gain the support of the non-aligned countries, and to win political support at home. In this as in so many other aspects of the conflict, Canadian efforts failed. Canadian frustration over the course of the conflict in Korea was heightened by two developments. First, in August 1950, the Soviet Union returned to the Security Council, which it had been boycotting to protest the lack of representation from the People's Republic of China (PRC), an absence that had allowed the Council to authorize the military operation. The second involved uncertainty about American objectives in the region. As the Soviets returned to the Council chambers, US general Douglas MacArthur, commander of UN forces in Korea, began making statements that linked the defence of Formosa with the UN operations in Korea. Although such statements had little support in Washington—and none whatsoever in allied capitals such as Ottawa—they did generate confusion over American intentions. The confusion did not disappear once UN forces reversed the initial invasion through their spectacular landing at Inchon. By the end of September, North Korean forces had been pushed back over the original boundary line, the 38th parallel. Earlier in the month, and in the absence of specific guidelines from previous UN resolutions, MacArthur was given orders by the American government to pursue North Korean troops north of the 38th parallel provided he did not encounter resistance from Soviet or Chinese troops. The Americans once again turned to the UN to approve action that had already been undertaken in its name. To gain UN approval, the Americans had to turn to the General Assembly, because the Soviet Union blocked action in the Security Council; this the Americans did on 7 October 1950. The Canadian delegation reluctantly supported the resolution based, in part, on verbal understandings with Washington that MacArthur would not proceed too far into North Korea so as not to antagonize the Chinese. Canadian fears were confirmed when, contrary to such assurances, UN forces were led to the Yalu River on the Chinese border and bridges spanning the river were bombed. The Chinese had by this time entered the fray and, after a momentary pause in November, launched a counteroffensive that by the middle of December returned the UN forces south of the 38th parallel. From Ottawa's vantage point, the situation in Korea had gotten out of control and Washington bore much of the responsibility. Efforts to contain the conflict had clearly failed. The priority now was to prevent the outbreak of a general war.

Chinese intervention in the conflict made crystal clear what had already been perceptible to some. For the United States, the war in Korea was not primarily an implementation of the UN's collective security provisions: it was first and foremost an example of Cold War diplomacy. As such, it gave rise to concerns in Ottawa and other Western capitals over the nature and extent of American military plans. Such concerns were encouraged by loose statements by President Truman over the possible use of atomic weapons. In Ottawa, the deteriorating military situation generated renewed demands for limiting UN objectives in Korea and encouraged officials to seek a negotiated solution to hostilities. To achieve this objective, Pearson participated, along with Iran and India, in formulating a set of five principles that would form the basis for a settlement of the Korean conflict. These five principles were subsequently endorsed by the First Committee of the UN General Assembly (UNGA) and presented to authorities in China. By virtue of their earlier decision to seek the legitimacy of the UN, American policy makers were forced to allow some time and space for such negotiations to proceed before they branded the Chinese as aggressors. Dean Acheson described the situation: 'The choice whether to support or oppose [attempts to reach a settlement with the Chinese] was a murderous one' for the Americans, 'threatening, on one side the loss of the Koreans and the fury of Congress and press and, on the other, the loss of our majority support in the United Nations'.[52] There was little doubt that in the end the UN would lose out. The Americans left enough time for the Chinese to respond to the five principles, dismissed the response as a 'contemptuous disregard of a world-wide demand for peace',[53] and pressed ahead with their resolution to label the Chinese as aggressors. This resolution, with the affirmative vote of the Canadian delegation, was approved in the UNGA on 1 February 1951. The war itself dragged on until 1953, when an armistice was finally signed.

The Korean War sparked a full-scale reappraisal of the United Nations within the Department of External Affairs. The concerns expressed ranged widely, from a consideration of the general principle of collective security to the specific policy priorities of the Canadian government. Generally, the views expressed concluded that the UN's operations in Korea had been a failure but that there were important lessons in this failure.

Collective security, at least in the existing international circumstances and perhaps in general, carried with it the possibility of another world war. For that reason, it must be avoided, or at least not used until conditions warranted such a possibility. More narrowly, UN military actions during the Cold War of the 1950s carried the risk of turning the organization into an anti-communist coalition. Canadians had categorically rejected this idea when the government decided to enter into NATO. If this change in the nature of the UN happened, it would not only drive out the communist states, but would also alienate those states attempting to maintain non-alignment in the East–West conflict. An added concern was the possibility that the UN would become nothing more than an instrument of American foreign policy. Canadian officials had a strong interest in avoiding this and subsequently worked to bridge the Cold War divide in the UN. These officials tended 'to be profoundly suspicious of any attempt to use that organization for the defense or advance of any particular set of ideas'.[54]

At the same time, the war left many American policy makers wary of turning to the UN in the future. From their perspective, the UN's failure in Korea was a failure of adequate material and political support for the American cause. They tended to look upon other UN members as chronic complainers who contributed little to the fighting. Thus the war created the possibility not only of Soviet rejection of the UN as an anti-communist forum, but also of American rejection of the institution for failing to support its foreign policy goals. It was unlikely that member states, including Canada, could have done or would have been willing to do anything to satisfy them both. The only option was to keep them both involved but not to allow them to dominate the organization, even if this ran the risk that their policies increasingly turned away from the organization.

This is not to say that all of the fallout from the war was negative. In keeping the conflict under UN auspices, Canada and other governments were able to have some say, albeit limited, over American actions. This was one of the original objectives in establishing the institution. It was also one of the reasons Canada was willing to contribute forces to the war; as Stairs notes, 'the price of this multilateral involvement was that it gave those, like the Canadians, who were obliged to contribute to the military campaign a license to intervene in the decision-making process'.[55] The interventions were far from successful, but they may have gone some way to discouraging Washington from pursuing other options, such as those favoured by MacArthur. The events also demonstrated that there was room for flexibility in the UN Charter, especially in allowing the UNGA to take up issues the Security Council was unable to deal with. The Uniting for Peace Resolution, which sanctioned such activity, was subsequently used to overcome the British and French vetoes over UN action in Suez in 1956. Most important, the legacy of Korea was the immense cost involved in launching collective security; says Holmes, 'In spite of the advantages in principle of organizing military action and economic sanctions through UN institutions, sober second thought suggested that this was not a very practical proposition'.[56] It became a good deal less practical as the organization's membership expanded.

FROM COLLECTIVE SECURITY TO PEACEKEEPING

Collective security was, for many Canadian policy makers, the initial raison d'être of the United Nations. Despite this, the belief that the UN should possess the clout that the League of Nations had lacked and should have the authority to order a multilateral military force into the field to repel aggression eventually yielded to a more modest alternative: peacekeeping. A number of factors contributed to this change. First, the veto had made it clear that collective security could never be used against one of the great powers. Second, the Cold War and, subsequently, its global scope made it unlikely that the United States and the Soviet Union would ever agree to launch a collective security operation. Finally, the Korean War, even as a modified collective security effort, suggested that the human costs of collective security were greater than had been imagined and were perhaps greater than the results. In a world divided into hostile blocs, each in possession of nuclear weapons, collective security measures ran a real risk of global war. 'As soon as the bomb fell', Reid wrote, 'the security articles in the Charter became archaic'.[57] The primary objective under these new conditions was to contain war and not to universalize it.

It had become clear that if the UN was to have any role in responding to international conflicts, it must act within the circumscribed conditions of the Cold War. Canadian officials were instrumental in moving the UN toward such a response. Holmes has argued that 'by 1948–49 Canada had begun creating for itself "foundations for its reputation as a moderate mediatory middle power"'.[58] These efforts continued after the Korean War as Canadian officials looked for alternatives to collective security.

Preventative diplomacy, or 'peacekeeping' as it is more commonly known, was the alternative, and it became the primary mechanism by which the UN maintained a profile in the international community during the height of the Cold War. It also became a primary area of activity for Canadian foreign and defence policy, one that for many would continue to define Canadian internationalism into the 1990s. Peacekeeping has been an area of activity that fit well with Canadian interests, insofar as Canada is both as a committed member of the Western alliance and a strong supporter of the United Nations. Paradoxically, peacekeeping has been an illustration both of the UN's failure and of its ability to adapt. It reflects the inability of the UN to mount collective security operations and suggests the inappropriateness of such measures in a world in which states possess large arsenals. It is also indicative of the difficulty that the institution has had in reaching and imposing settlements for inter-national conflicts. At the same time, peacekeeping is an indication of the willingness and ability of the member states to accept the institution's limitations and to work in spite of them to support peaceful methods of conflict resolution.

Peacekeeping is 'the use of military personnel to monitor and supervise a cease-fire between belligerents'.[59] Unlike collective security, peacekeeping does not take sides in a conflict. No attempt is made to determine an aggressor and no prejudgments are made about a solution to the conflict. Peacekeeping was intended for conflicts among lesser powers; as David Cox says, it 'was not designed to be used at all in uncompro-mising conflicts between the rival power blocs, but instead for conflicts amongst smaller powers, in non-bloc areas, and in situations where the great powers might find their hardcore interests so little threatened that international intervention might be preferable to unilateral interventions which could lead to unwanted great-power confrontations'.[60] The main objective has been to keep the fighting parties separated and secure and thus to provide them with the time and opportunity to reach a settle-ment. Peacekeeping, unlike collective security, is far more suitable to the ambiguities that proliferate in relations between states. It was especially so in the ideologically charged atmosphere of the Cold War.

Canadian policy makers had long taken an interest in more peaceful methods of conflict resolution. They had played an active mediatory role in the UN in the late 1940s and were involved in UN truce observer missions in the Middle East and Kashmir in the early 1950s. It was not until the Suez crisis of 1956, however, that a peacekeeping force was established by the United Nations. It was also in response to the Suez crisis that the Canadian delegation in New York, under the able direction of then external affairs minister Lester Pearson, took the lead in securing the support of the UN General Assembly for this force. In discussions with Secretary-General Dag Hammarskjöld and others, Pearson played a significant role in defining the makeup and mandate of this innovative multilateral operation. It was, in many respects, natural and thus inevitable that the Canadian government responded to the Suez crisis as it did. The crisis raised many serious problems for Canada, none of which were directly related to the issues under dispute in the region. Indeed, Canada's acknowledged disinterest in the region was one of the factors that gave Pearson's proposals credibility. It was one of those instances in which a concern for international order blended well with specific national interests; in contributing to the former, the government could protect the latter.

The Israeli invasion of Egypt in November 1956, aided and abetted by the British and the French, caught Canada and the rest of the world by surprise.[61] The invasion had been precipitated by Egypt's decision to nationalize the Suez Canal in order to finance the construction of the Aswan Dam, which had previously lost the financial support of Washington after Egyptian president Nasser approached the Soviet Union for assistance. The British and French did not want to see Nasser in control of the canal, which was a vital passage for their foreign trade. Anxious to re-establish their control over the passage, they decided to use the pretext of an Israeli invasion to secure their objectives. In collusion with these two governments, Israel launched an attack on Egypt. In response, the British and French moved their forces into the canal in an attempt to 'settle the conflict', enforce a ceasefire, and most important, wrest control of the canal from Egyptian hands. The reaction of the international community was swift and punishing. Despite the Cold War overtones of their own dispute with Nasser, the Americans condemned the invasion and were highly critical of the British. For many newly independent states, including the Commonwealth members, Nasser was a symbol of their own aspirations for greater autonomy, self-determination, and non-alignment. Not surprisingly, they too were quick to condemn the attack. The Soviet Union, no doubt pleased by the tensions emerging within the Western bloc, likewise offered a condemnation and a threat. In Ottawa, policy makers were both upset by what they saw as a foolhardy act and anxious to prevent it from damaging a number of important relationships.

In addition to the wider risk of war, the Suez crisis presented a number of specific problems for Canadian foreign policy. First, as a clear violation of the UN Charter by two of the permanent members of the Security Council, the invasion further undermined the credibility of the organization. This also rendered the Security Council incapable of responding to the crisis, because the British and French vetoed action by that body. British actions also threatened to disrupt Anglo-American relations and thereby tear apart the North Atlantic triangle that had been an important cornerstone of Canadian foreign policy. In addition, Anglo-American conflict threatened to weaken the NATO alliance. Equally important for Canadian policy makers, the crisis posed a threat to the transformation of the Commonwealth. The imperialist actions of the British government were a direct affront to those members of the Commonwealth who were freeing their countries from colonial rule. It is perhaps true that no other crisis of the period posed such a direct threat to so many important foreign policy connections. As such, a resolution of this conflict required all the skill that a moderate mediatory middle power could muster.

If the Suez crisis demanded a Canadian response, it was also apparent that Canada possessed the capabilities necessary to respond effectively. Its connections in London and Washington gave it credibility in both capitals and made it possible to moderate the growing animosity between them. Canadian representatives could also use past connections and common multilateral affiliations to convince the French and British to accept a UN peacekeeping operation. Furthermore, Canadian credibility in the Middle East, and especially with the Egyptians, was aided by its past peacekeeping experiences in the region, especially in the person of General Burns; by its disinterested position on Mideast disputes; and by its lack of an imperial past. Good connections with India were also helpful in encouraging their support and that of other non-aligned countries for the peacekeeping efforts. All of these factors, when combined with an effective record of multilateral diplomacy at the UN, were helpful in winning international support for the establishment of the UN Emergency Force (UNEF I).

Domestic support proved to be a more difficult challenge. The St Laurent government fell victim to the criticisms of the opposition Conservative party for its failure to support the 'mother country'. It was one of the rare instances in which bipartisanship broke down on Canada's internationalist foreign policy and it may have had some influence on the Liberals' fall from power in the 1957 federal election. Domestic critics could not blunt the international reaction, however; Pearson received widespread recognition from the international community and a Nobel Peace prize. Whether or not the government anticipated the hostile domestic response, it is evident that it was more interested in responding to foreign policy interests, both national and multilateral, in pushing for the establishment of UNEF I. The Suez crisis contained both risks and opportunities for Canada. In response, the government demonstrated that there was not only room for middle power interventions in the midst of the Cold War, but a role for the United Nations as well.

CONCLUSION

The United Nations was seen by foreign policy makers as the cornerstone of Canada's post-war multilateralist foreign policy. It was also intended to be the basis for a more peaceful and stable international order—an order that while accepting the prominence of great powers, recognized the significant contribution that middle powers could make. Canadian officials, through their active participation in the negotiations that established the UN and its affiliated agencies and, in the early years of the organization's existence, demonstrated a firm commitment to making the UN work. Their unqualified support for the organization was a reflection of a strong consensus within the government that the UN could best serve Canada's long-term security and political interests. Canadian support remained strong despite a number of setbacks, the most important of which was the breakdown of superpower consensus and the fallout from the Korean War. When the Cold War entered the UN, Canadian delegates worked that much harder to find room for dialogue and compromise. No longer would the UN be seen as a guarantor of security, but it would remain a vitally important forum for discussing political conflicts, particularly those that were susceptible to superpower intervention.

Chapter Two

Reviving the Global Economy: Canada and the Bretton Woods System

One of the results of the establishment of the Fund that has not received enough empha-sis is the great increase in international consultation and collaboration. This seems so obvious that it may seem jejune even to mention it, but to those of us who saw what international co-operation in these matters was before the war the difference is drama-tic. . . . If one contrasts that with the frequency and intimacy of the discussions which now take place on the board of the Fund and in other forums one becomes aware of a very major achievement. —Louis Rasminsky, 1972

INTRODUCTION

Canadian contribution to the formation of the United Nations (UN) suggested a strong interest in supporting and strengthening the institution, even to the neglect of some specific national objectives. A similar commitment to the process of multilater-alism is evident in Canadian policies toward the financial and commercial institutions reviewed in this chapter. The examination of the formation of the International Monetary Fund (IMF), the World Bank, and the General Agreement on Tariffs and Trade (GATT) does indicate, however, that national economic objectives, as opposed to more internationalist objectives, were a major influence on Canadian officials. The pursuit of multilateralist objectives in this area was intended to serve Canadian inter-ests first. This is evident in the willingness on the part of policy makers to shed multi-lateral commitments to protect specific interests such as the value of the Canadian dollar in the late 1940s. What is clear from the period discussed in this chapter is the strong preference for a multilateral alternative to the creeping continentalism that was beginning to overwhelm Canada's commercial options. The multilateral management of trade and currency exchanges was seen as a way of stabilizing the international economy while protecting Canadian interests on both sides of the Atlantic. This chap-ter also points to what would become a persistent problem in Canada's foreign economic policies: a tension between multilateral interests and commitments and bilateral ones.

When Roosevelt and Churchill met at sea in Placentia Bay off the coast of Argentia, Newfoundland, in August 1941, they set the course not only for the UN, but for Bretton Woods as well. At American insistence, the Atlantic Charter included commit-ments for post-war economic collaboration. The two leaders agreed to 'endeav-our, with due respect for their existing obligations, to further the enjoyment by all States, great or small, victor or vanquished, of access, on equal terms, to the trade and to the raw materials of the world which are needed for their economic prosperity' and 'to bring about the fullest collaboration between all nations in the economic field with

the object of securing, for all, improved labour standards, economic advancement, and social security'.[1] The supporters of post-war collaboration in the United States pressed for firmer guarantees in support of these objectives during the subsequent negotiations on mutual aid with Britain and other states. Less than one year later, in Article VII of the Mutual Aid Agreement reached in February 1942, the Americans and British repeated their commitment to post-war co-operation in the economic field while making it more explicit and opening the way for others to participate:

> In the final determination of the benefits to be provided to the United States . . . in return for aid . . . the terms and conditions shall be such as not to burden commerce between the two countries, but to promote mutually advantageous economic relations between them and betterment of world-wide economic relations. To that end they shall include provision by agreed action . . . directed to expansion by appropriate international and domestic measures of production, employment and exchange and consumption of goods which are the material foundation of the liberty and welfare of all peoples; to the elimination of all forms of discriminatory treatment in international commerce and to reduce tariffs and other trade barriers.[2]

This article became a standard part of each agreement the United States made to extend wartime assistance to other governments. Although Canada was not a recipient of American aid during the war, the two governments concluded an exchange of notes in November 1942 that included the terms of Article VII. In this manner, the United States established the foundation for a series of negotiations the objectives of which were to liberalize post-war economic relations.

Guided in large measure by the free trade convictions of Secretary of State Cordell Hull and other members of the US State Department, the Roosevelt administration presented the rest of the industrialized world with a challenge to move toward a multilateral system of international finance and trade. The British, who until the early 1930s had been unequivocal supporters of free trade while the Americans were supporting protectionism, were skeptical and reluctant participants to these early agreements; the need for American support in the war effort made it necessary to go along. Watching from the sidelines in the early 1940s, the Canadians were more enthusiastic and cheered on the American cause.

Although many in Britain were skeptical of the American conversion to freer trade, support for multilateral institutions to oversee the governing of the international economy was widespread throughout the governments in Washington, London, and Ottawa. This trio—the United States, Great Britain, and Canada—orchestrated the formation of what has become known as the Bretton Woods system, itself a threefold scheme encompassing the International Monetary Fund (IMF), the International Bank for Reconstruction and Development (IBRD, or World Bank as it is more commonly known), and the stillborn International Trade Organization (ITO), later superseded by the General Agreement on Tariffs and Trade (GATT). Established in the midst of the fighting, Bretton Woods was very much an ABC affair. The European powers were

fighting for their survival and the Soviet Union had little interest in aiding the long-term prosperity of the capitalist powers. Each member of the trio had its respective part to play, with the Americans as the conductor. In spite of Canada's secondary role, the formation of the Bretton Woods system was an important part of the Canadian effort to establish an international order that would be based on multilateral co-operation and, most important, co-operation between the British and the Americans.

THE COMMITMENT TO MULTILATERALISM

John Maynard Keynes, then an adviser in the British Treasury Department, and Harry Dexter White, an assistant to the US secretary of the Treasury—one in London, the other in Washington—independently developed their governments' positions on post-war financial co-operation. Keynes and White shared a common philosophy but had distinctly different views on post-war co-operation, reflecting substantially different national conditions and interests. They also shared a commitment to a multilateral system of liberalized trade based on an equilibrium in the balance of payments between states and full employment within them. Both Keynes and White accepted the view that stable international monetary relations were a necessary prerequisite for an international economic order; they also accepted the need for an international institution that would play an integral role in managing these relations. The objective was to regulate international financial transactions to facilitate freer trade.

Formal negotiations to this end commenced in 1943 when the two plans, White's Stabilization Fund and Keynes's Clearing Union, were released. These negotiations culminated at a conference of the United Nations at Bretton Woods, New Hampshire, in July 1944, where agreement was reached on the IMF and the World Bank. The third pillar of the Bretton Woods system, a proposal for an international trade organization, was delayed until the war's end and never received final approval from the US Congress. By the early 1950s, only the GATT remained in the wake of the arduous negotiations on a mechanism for governing post-war trade relations.

It was both inevitable and natural that the United States and Britain would take the lead in organizing the post-war economic system. As the world's two largest capitalist powers, they had the most to gain or lose in any arrangements that would be made. It is perhaps more surprising that they decided to act so quickly and before arrangements for post-war political and security co-operation had been reached. The fact that the first moves were made in this area suggests both the overriding importance American secretary of state Hull gave to economic co-operation and the precarious economic position of Britain during the early years of the war. In an often-quoted phrase, Hull wrote that

> unhampered trade dovetailed with peace; high tariffs, trade barriers, and unfair competition with war. . . . If we get a freer flow of trade—freer in the sense of fewer discriminations and obstructions—so that one country would not be deadly jealous of another and the living standards of all countries might rise, thereby eliminating the

economic dissatisfaction that breeds war, we might have a reasonable chance of lasting peace.[3]

It was Hull who pushed to have economic co-operation included in the Atlantic Charter, and Hull who continued to press for formal commitments to post-war economic co-operation.

The Americans were, of course, very well placed to benefit from freer trade. The war had devastated the continental economies in Europe and was draining Britain of capital (to pay for the war and for the defence of the far reaches of the Empire), in addition to destroying industrial capacity at home and severely curtailing Britain's previously pre-eminent position in such areas as foreign investment and shipping. The growth of American financial and industrial power enabled the United States to dictate the terms of various financial arrangements, such as the Mutual Aid Agreements and the subsequent post-war loan with Britain in 1945. While the administration's terms usually favoured multilateral endeavours, there remained strong sentiments of isolationism and protectionism in various sectors of American society and within the government itself. There was some support for multilateralism in Washington, especially in Hull's State Department, but once one moved beyond Foggy Bottom into other departments, such as Agriculture, protectionism was the principal article of faith and multilateralism a heresy. In Congress as well there was vocal and influential opposition to any proposal that would relinquish aspects of American sovereignty to international institutions. Many Americans were concerned about any form of economic co-operation with Britain, which was still seen as a leading rival to American pre-eminence in the capitalist world. Thus, although some of the strongest pressure for multilateral economic co-operation came from Washington in the 1940s, this was more a reflection of the temporary influence of Roosevelt New Dealers and the Department of State than of a strong consensus among the American body politic.

As Richard Gardner has argued, Britain too had interests in post-war economic co-operation, although these interests did not completely match those of the United States.[4] While the Americans saw Britain as one part, albeit an important part, of a universal system of liberalized trade, London looked upon Washington as an essential partner in the economic, political, and military revival of British power. The war had destroyed Britain's capacity to act as a great power, and if it were to return to this favoured status, it would require American support. In addition, Britain had long experience in the area of multilateral co-operation. The British, despite occasional lapses, had been ardent advocates of the League of Nations and did not share the suspicions and skepticism—so evident in American discussions of post-war plans— of the value and potential reach of international institutions. Finally, in the commercial arena, the British commitment to imperial preferences was both recent and half hearted. Imperial preferences allowed members of the Empire or Commonwealth to trade at lower tariff rates than non-members, but such preferences went against generations of support for free trade. Imperial preferences were as much a result of the unique combination of the Depression and of initial misgivings over the decentralizing implications of the Statute of Westminster as they were a complete and final rejection of the free trade philosophy that had previously governed British trade policy. There remained many committed free traders in the British government throughout these wartime negotiations, but their voices were often stifled by outspoken opponents, such as Lord Beaverbrook of publishing fame. Their principles were also severely shaken by American demands and practices.

The Canadian government showed little hesitation in giving its full support to plans for post-war economic co-operation on a multilateral basis. As long as the Americans and the British were partners to the plan, Canadians believed that their immediate interests would be served. Indeed, the prospects of a multilateral system in which both its principal trading partners were fully committed members was the best option for Canadians.

Trade had long been an integral part of Canadian foreign policy. Many of Canada's earliest ventures abroad were in search of foreign markets for Canadian raw materials and of investments and immigrants to fuel economic prosperity at home. The Second World War had a dramatic effect on Canada's position in the global economy, but in retrospect, the winds of change were already blowing before the war broke out. After the First World War, there had been an expansion of Canadian trade and a shift in Canada's trade balance. During the 1930s, the structure of Canadian trade had developed to the point where American imports (which made up nearly two-thirds of the total) were paid for by exports to Britain, Europe, and other members of the British Empire. Only about one-third of Canadian exports were sent to the United States. Thus, a diversified export market compensated for an unfavourable balance of trade with the United States. The Depression of the 1930s had been accompanied and reinforced by policies of economic nationalism and protectionism, especially in the United States, that had catastrophic consequences for the Canadian economy. The Depression was only finally crushed by the outbreak of war in 1939, but it had made abundantly clear the vulnerable state of the Canadian economy; Canada's dependence on foreign trade would require close and constant attention. Future economic prospects, for many officials, would rest on securing American support for freer trade in a multilateral trading system.

Wartime experiences with capital flows also provoked a strong interest in convertible currencies. The war dramatically reinforced Canada's close economic ties with the United States; what was true for most countries in the world was even more pronounced for Canada. The devastation of the war took its toll on Canada's traditional export markets in Britain and Europe and made even more profound the consequences of its import dependence. The demise of Britain as an economic counterweight to the United States confirmed the latter's position as Canada's pre-eminent economic partner. While most other countries would have gladly accepted Canada's position, it was the source of considerable concern in Ottawa. In response, policy makers looked to the creation of an effective multilateral system to offset the bilateralism that had come to govern Canada's economic orientation. There was also an interest in regulating the more politicized American trade policy under a multilateral rules-based order.

For Canadian officials involved in post-war planning, questions of economic co-operation assumed a high priority. Not only was it necessary to work for a financial and trading system that would serve Canadian interests, but many also saw the economic conflict that accompanied the Depression as one of the primary causes of the war. Many Canadian policy makers believed, along with Hull, that a freer system of international commerce would support a more peaceful international order: co-operation in the economic field would facilitate collective action in other important areas of policy, such as collective security. Canadian policy makers saw support for the emerging Bretton Woods system as a necessary and desirable complement to its participation in post-war political organizations. For them, and for many others at the time, a stable and open global economy was indeed as much a prerequisite for a peaceful international order as it was a means of securing domestic prosperity.

Support for the negotiations was also a reaction to the significant changes that had taken place in the Canadian economy. Prior to the war, there had been not only a shift in Canadian trade patterns whereby imports from the United States were supported by exports to Britain and the rest of the Empire, but also a sizable expansion in the volume of Canadian trade. This expansion continued during the war, as did the appetite of Canadian consumers. More than ever before, Canada's economy—and significant interests within Canada—were linked to the international economy. In response, the government did what it could to shape the emerging economic order. Even if Canada failed to redesign the new order to meet the country's specific interests, the effects of whatever arrangements the Americans and British arrived at would be profound for Canada.

Unlike negotiations on the UN, the discussions on financial and commercial relations did not attract much attention within External Affairs. There were in Ottawa only a limited number of officials with the time and intellect to devote to the technical details of the various proposals under discussions, and they resided in the Bank of Canada and the Department of Finance. Bank of Canada governor Graham Towers, his executive assistant Louis Rasminsky, John Deutsch from the Bank of Canada, financial attaché A.F.W. Plumptre at the embassy in Washington, and assistant to the deputy minister of the Department of Finance W.A. Makintosh led the Canadian delegation at Bretton Woods and—especially Rasminsky—played a major role in the negotiations that preceded the conference. One of Keynes's biographers and an observer of these negotiations, Sir Roy Harrod, has remarked that 'almost alone outside the ranks of the British and Americans, the Canadians seemed capable of understanding the international monetary problem as a whole'.[5]

In addition to their intellectual acumen, the Canadian negotiators worked with a strong supportive consensus in Ottawa. Even the limited role played by External Affairs was indicative of that department's overwhelming support for the policies being pursued in both Finance and the Bank. There was also strong support for Canadian involvement among parliamentarians, with the only opposition being heard from the Social Crediters, who believed they knew better than international bankers how Canada's economy should be managed. As Holmes has noted, 'because of the widely recognized dependence of Canada on international commerce, Canadian officials had less difficulty with the prejudices of their legislatures than had those in Washington and London'.[6] In December 1945, Canadian participation in the IMF and the World Bank was approved by the House of Commons with only nine dissenting votes.

Thus it was with a mixture of very immediate national interests and a longer-term view of international order that Canadian policy makers entered into discussions to establish the post-war international economy. In the end, as with the political organizations, the mechanisms established fell short of Canadian expectations. In part, this was a result of a certain reluctance on the part of all the participants, including Canada, to embrace the regulatory regime adopted at Bretton Woods. But it was also a reflection of the asymmetrical positions of the principal negotiating partners. Even more than in other areas, negotiations on post-war economic relations were shaped by the tone and substance of Anglo-American talks, and in these deliberations, the hegemonic position of the United States in the global economy dominated.

THE ROAD TO BRETTON WOODS

The long-term objective of freer multilateral trade required prior arrangements for a regulated financial order defined by convertible currencies, stable exchange rates, and a sufficient supply of capital.[7] Trade could best expand when the respective trading partners were certain of both the value and the convertibility of the currency that was being exchanged. The dramatic and rapid fluctuations that had taken place in currency markets in the inter-war period placed monetary stability at the top of the agenda for post-war economic planning. A second fundamental requirement was the reversal of the economic isolation of the United States, the removal of the US administration from the protectionist constraints of Congress, and the integration of American economic planning into a multilateral system. Canadian officials were thus faced with a delicate operation as they approached the preliminary discussions on what would become the IMF and the IBRD after the initial invitation for consultations came from London in the summer of 1942. Canadians were anxious that some form of multilateral co-operation involving the British and the Americans be obtained. In entering the negotiations, Canadian officials were concerned both about the British, who were viewed as reluctant converts to the idea of multilateral co-operation with the Americans, and about the US Congress, renowned for its protectionist sentiments when it came to international commercial relations.

During initial negotiations with the British in autumn 1942—discussions that Rasminsky referred to as 'the high spot intellectually in the discussions that preceded Bretton Woods'[8]—the Canadian delegation expressed qualified support for Keynes's proposal for the establishment of an International Clearing Union. The Clearing Union would provide financial reserves that would support economies experiencing balance of payments difficulties in order to allow them to continue trading without relying on exchange controls or currency devaluations that would otherwise interfere with international commercial relations. As described in its initial presentation to the Canadian government, it would 'provide in the international sphere an organisation which would perform for participating States the functions performed for individuals by the ordinary banking system i.e., the clearing of accounts debit and credit between different customers and the provision of overdrafts for those who need them'.[9] An international unit of account, referred to as *bancor*, would be created and would serve as the basis for international transactions. The plan would allow for a very large borrowing capacity and would have considerable flexibility in its operations. The original plan, as presented by Keynes, viewed the institution as 'a centre around which other international agencies could gather'.[10]

Keynes's proposal was soon joined by a plan produced independently in Washington by Dexter White. The two plans shared the fundamental premise that an international agency would be required to oversee and manage financial transactions and that such an agency should have the ability to support countries that experienced balance of payments difficulties in order to make it unnecessary for these countries to revert to drastic exchange rate adjustments; 'broadly, the object [was] to remove much of the incentive to the adoption of measures of a discriminatory, trade-throttling, or "beggar-my-neighbour", character by countries'.[11] The White plan proposed a Stabilization Fund that would be used for a similar purpose to the Clearing Union but that would rely on contributions from participating states and thus draw from a smaller pool of capital. Drawing rights, which would be unlimited under Keynes's plan, would in the American proposal be restricted and dependent on the size of a country's contribution. White proposed a fund of US$5 billion, considerably less than the approximately US$25 billion envisioned by Keynes.

Ottawa reacted very favourably to these proposals. Most important, London and Washington displayed a willingness to support an international agency to oversee a vital area of economic policy. There were concerns, however, that the principles shared by the two plans might fall victim to the different approaches taken. There was also concern that the American Congress might reject the proposals, Keynes's simply because it was British and White's because it came out of the Treasury Department, which had little political support in the United States. Finally, officials in Ottawa thought other governments would find it difficult to make a decision if they were forced to choose between the two plans.

In response to the Keynes and White plans, and as a result of these concerns, officials in Ottawa developed a set of Canadian proposals. The recommendation had come from Plumptre and was readily adopted by Rasminsky, who had already been working on a plan that would attempt to bridge the differences between the British and American proposals. With a third plan under discussion, it was hoped that 'attention might shift from the details to the broad principles'.[12] In the spring of 1943, the prime minister was advised that 'the diplomatic and technical difficulties in the way of reaching general agreement on either the British or the American scheme are great' and that 'the only country which might conceivably put forward a third scheme with some hopes of the others accepting it is Canada'.[13] News of the Canadian plan caught officials in London by surprise despite the fact that there had been some encouragement from Keynes for a synthesis of the British and American proposals. 'I am convinced that such a synthesis is possible', Keynes wrote to Wrong, 'and very possibly you in Canada might use your good offices to put something forward on these lines at the right time'.[14] The right time for the British was after the Americans had given full consideration to Keynes's proposals. Despite British reservations, the government decided to release its compromise plan to the Americans, who were quick to include it on the agenda of a meeting of the UN held in Washington in June 1943.

The Canadian proposals accepted the American form of a fund, but proposed a larger pool of capital (US$8 billion) based on members' contributions and lines of credit. The plan also eliminated the American veto and attempted to limit the rigidity of the American plan without accepting the degree of flexibility proposed by Keynes. The Canadians did not want the fund to take on other tasks and instead favoured the creation of other institutions to handle such matters as trade and capital needs for reconstruction. This was consistent with the functionalist approach that the government was taking toward other international institutions.[15] The support for the American plan reflected, in part, tactical considerations:

> Intellectually the Canadians seemed closer to Keynes than to White, but they understood, as the British did not fully, the changes that the war had forced on the world economy. In particular they were sensitive to the American desire for a fund with a limited liability. They had to be, for increasingly there was every likelihood that Canada too would emerge from the war as a creditor in current account. The civil servants in Ottawa were also worried by the unpredictability—even the bloody-mindedness—of the United States Congress.[16]

Indeed, one of the arguments in support of an independent Canadian initiative was a belief that 'a Canadian plan would probably attract more support in the United States than a [US] Treasury plan'.[17] Canadian officials thought they had a better image in the American Congress than did some branches of the American executive.

This Canadian initiative, which stands in marked contrast to the usually more low-key approach to high-level negotiations between its two most important allies, was a reflection not only of the intellectual quality both of the Canadian draft and of its author, Rasminsky, but also of the profound interest at stake. It was considered essential in Ottawa that the British and the Americans reach an agreement. Of the two, the Americans were the more important, both because they would have to supply most of the necessary capital and because they were considered the more unpredictable. If there was any doubt that the devastating effects of the war on the British economy had left London with a weak hand in the negotiations, subsequent negotiations on the post-war loan confirmed it. The Canadian draft may have appeared 'off-White' to the British, but it suggested a more accurate reading of the mood in Washington and of the limited influence that Britain could exercise in that capital.

The meetings in Washington effectively finalized the terms of the fund, which were subsequently confirmed one year later during a relatively brief three-week sojourn at Bretton Woods. The plan of the International Monetary Fund more closely resembled that proposed by the Americans. The IMF would supply short-term credit to member countries experiencing balance of payments difficulties, working with a limited supply of capital (US$8.8 billion, of which only about $3 billion would be available for loans, the remainder taking the form of unpaid subscriptions). Exchange rates were to be fixed and to be allowed to float within only a very narrow margin. Currencies were to be fixed in terms of the price of gold and, by implication, in terms of the US dollar, the value of which was fixed at $35/ounce in gold. Provisions were made for a transitional period during which members could retain restrictions on payments and transfers in order to adjust to post-war circumstances. The IMF was also excused from providing interim financing for post-war reconstruction. This task was given to the World Bank, which—despite its objective of restoring the economies that had been destroyed by the war—would prove to be too conservative and undercapitalized to be of any value in this regard.

The Canadian government had little difficulty in accepting these terms in 1944. Although officials had pushed for a larger pool of capital and had yet to face the problems of administration that would appear at the Fund's first meeting, the IMF essentially met the government's interest in securing both Britain's and, more important, the United States's commitment to developing post-war economic policies through multilateral institutions. Canada would soon enough encounter problems in adhering to its own commitment to the Fund, but in the mid-1940s, the main objective had been secured.

There have been a few comments made regarding Canada's influence in the events that led to the agreement on the IMF. Gardner, for example, refers to Bretton Woods as 'very much an Anglo-American affair, with Canada playing a useful mediating role'.[18] Another observer has noted that 'the International Monetary Fund and the International Bank were the product of English and American brains, with valuable assistance from the Canadians'.[19] Jack Granatstein refers to Canadian actions at this time as not only unprecedented, but quite out of the ordinary diplomatic style.[20] The Canadian initiative may have had some influence in altering aspects of the American plans and may have helped to convince the British that their own plan had to be abandoned in deference to American objections. What is certain is that the quality (as one British document described it)[21] of the Canadian proposal, as well as the country's privileged position during the closing stages of the war, earned Canada an important voice in the deliberations and—in the short term, at least—perhaps helped to gain the necessary credit for future deviances from the Fund.

The Illegitimate Offspring: The GATT

The IMF and IBRD were never expected to stand alone. They were always viewed as part of a larger set of proposals in which the expansion of liberalized international trade on a multilateral basis was the overriding goal. There was a strong consensus in Ottawa on the significance of this objective:

> It is especially in Canada's interest, first, because our trade extends over many countries and it would be difficult, if not actually impracticable, to achieve any pattern of bilateral agreements which would serve our interests so effectively, and second, because the United States will undoubtedly press for the removal of preferences, even though under the Trade Agreements Act, should it be renewed, there is comparatively little that she can offer as a quid pro quo to Canada.[22]

The Canadian government had, since the early 1930s, attempted to balance the country's position in the system of imperial preferences with rapidly expanding trade links with the United States. As negotiations between the British and Americans turned toward the post-war trade regime, it quickly became evident that the Americans' prime objective was to dismantle the system of imperial preferences. In return, the Americans were willing to offer a reduction in tariffs. Once again, the Canadians found it desirable to lend support to the American cause. For Canadians, a multilateral system of trade liberalization would provide the benefits of better access to American markets without the political liabilities inherent in an exclusive bilateral arrangement. It would also open alternative markets and thereby render acceptable the dismantling of imperial preferences that threatened to disrupt the all-important bilateral trade. But while the objective was clear, getting there would prove to be most difficult.

The system of imperial preferences—which the American Hull once referred to as 'the greatest injury, in a commercial way, that has been inflicted on this country since I have been in public life'[23]—were agreed on at the Imperial Economic Conference held in Ottawa in 1932. Pressed by the economic disaster that was confronting Britain, Canada, and the other Dominions, the Conference was viewed by its chairman, Canadian prime minister R.B. Bennett, as a lifeline amidst the Depression. But as Nicholas Mansergh has written, 'the exhilaration which undoubtedly prevailed in Ottawa appeared to some as having an air not of natural spontaneity but of the enforced gaiety of a septuagenarian wedding'.[24] The idea of imperial preferences ran counter to the free trade ideology that had motivated British commercial policy for decades, but it found favour among the protectionist left and among those Tories who were concerned about the decentralization of the Empire. It was seen as a mixed blessing by many in Canada and Australia, which had already begun to diversify their trade relations with the United States and Japan respectively. Mackenzie King, then leader of the opposition Liberals, was opposed to a system that would increase protectionist measures against other states and, most important, might harm Canada's trade links with the United States. Imperial preferences were, in his view, no match for the attractions of the American market. Nonetheless, the Bennett government signed on. Subsequently, during the 1930s, Canada concluded reciprocal commercial treaties with the United States and Britain. As Canada's two leading trade partners began devising plans for the post-war order, the government sought to secure this North Atlantic triangle not by a continuation of these bilateral deals, but by embedding them in a wider network of multilateralism.

The system of imperial preferences had only a marginal impact on trade flows, but it aroused considerable opposition among the free traders in Washington. As a result, it became one of the prime targets in subsequent negotiations on the proposed International Trade Organization. Negotiations on post-war commercial relations were more arduous and raised even more national hostilities than had those on monetary relations. In some respects, this was not surprising given the domestic dimensions of trade policy and especially the overriding importance of policies of full employment in all of the major industrialized countries as they converted to peacetime economies. It was also a particularly troublesome situation for Britain, which had seen its leading position in international commerce devastated by the war. One estimate noted that Britain would require a 75 per cent increase in exports just to match pre-war levels of import purchases. While only a handful of experts saw the linkages between monetary policy and domestic conditions, the public and their elected representatives saw only too clearly the domestic effects of trade.

The Americans, for their part, had begun to move toward a more liberal approach to trade in the 1930s. In the Reciprocal Trade Agreements Act (RTA) of 1934, Congress delegated some powers over trade policy to the executive. As a result, the administration was now able to adjust tariff rates by as much as 50 per cent from the high levels that had been set in the Smoot-Hawley Act of 1930. As Gilbert Winham says, 'From the standpoint of international politics, the RTA was revolutionary in that it implicitly accepted that setting tariff rates could no longer be unilateral policy by a nation-state, but was rather a bilateral matter to be settled through negotiations'.[25] With this mandate, the Roosevelt administration negotiated a series of bilateral agreements, including two with Canada in 1935 and 1938. The Americans had recognized their advantageous trading position, and they worked quickly to exploit it until the war stalled their progress. Non-discrimination on the basis of Most Favoured Nation (MFN) status was an essential part of these agreements. The commitment to non-discrimination, in Gardner's view, was an important influence on the American hostility to imperial preferences.

Negotiations on post-war trade policy did not begin until 1945. Discussions had taken place between the Americans and the British as early as 1943, but more formal talks were delayed for a number of reasons, not the least of which was Britain's serious imbalance of payments problems. As the war drew to a close, and with it the end of Lend Lease (or Mutual Aid as it was referred to in Britain), London looked to Washington for more financial support. The final compromise on trade would be delayed until Britain and the United States agreed on loan arrangements for facilitating Britain's transition to the envisioned post-war order. The negotiations concentrated on three themes: employment, quantitative restrictions, and tariffs and preferences. Full employment was a primary concern in Britain and had also generated some interest in the United States, although the US Congress had rejected full-employment measures. Yet the two sides were only able to reach vague statements that full employment was desirable and that domestic programs to achieve full employment should not adversely influence employment in other countries. In the final analysis, Gardner writes, 'neither government had any well-developed views on how the employment problem could usefully be handled in any international agreement'.[26]

Quantitative restrictions on trade were not a major source of contention, although in this area the agreements had a more substantial effect on future trade relations. Both the Americans and the British agreed that quantitative restrictions on trade should be prohibited except where such restrictions were necessary to protect the balance of payments. They thus agreed on safeguard measures to deal with this contingency. More important for the longer-term prospects of liberalized trade were restrictions on trade in agricultural products. Both countries had an interest in such restrictions; however, the strongest pressure came from the US Department of Agriculture, which had only recently secured the administration's support for price-support programs. These restrictions were not seen as a major concern in 1945, but they would become a significant point of contention in trade negotiations over the ensuing decades.

The principal area of disagreement at these early meetings was the linkage between the reduction of American tariffs and the elimination of imperial preferences. Whatever support there was in both countries for multilateralism was severely tested by these negotiations as well as by subsequent negotiations on the American loan to Britain, which were concluded in December 1945. The basic British position was that imperial preferences could only be curtailed in exchange for large and automatic reductions in the American tariff. But American officials, who had boldly embraced freer trade, now found their policies modified by other members of the Administration and, perhaps most important, by the US Congress, whose members were reluctant to see tariffs pushed too low. Gardner writes that 'when it came to the decisive test the Administration's promises of a bold foreign economic programme were quickly dissipated by the hard domestic political realities'.[27] American negotiators wanted imperial preferences eliminated, but in return they could offer only negotiated and partial reductions in tariff levels.

A resolution of these differences was not quick in coming. The Americans proposed bilateral negotiations for selective tariff reductions in a multilateral setting where bilateral agreements would be extended to the other participants through the Most Favoured Nation principle. This was to be the method that would be used during the first 15 years of GATT negotiations. As Gardner notes, 'this "multilateral-bilateral" method of negotiation would enable participating countries to make reductions not just on the basis of concessions offered to them directly but on the basis of concessions gained indirectly through the operation of the unconditional most-favoured nation clause'.[28] In response, the British became even more skeptical of the American commitment to substantial tariff reductions and, in turn, concluded that the British would not be committed to the elimination of imperial preferences. The two sides walked away from meetings in 1945 with quite different perceptions of the agreement that they had reached.

The Anglo-American negotiations took place in a very uncertain climate. There was a great asymmetry in the bilateral relationship. But officials in both countries seem to have misperceived the situation. The Americans overestimated Britain's capacity to adjust smoothly to the post-war situation, and the British appeared reluctant to accept their diminished status. It was not until December 1945, when Keynes came to Washington to negotiate the terms of a post-war loan, that the serious state of the British economy became somewhat clearer. Nonetheless, the negotiations were at times bitter and the subsequent domestic debates in both Britain and the United States highly acrimonious. The British eventually accepted the terms of the loan before the end of 1945 in order to proceed with final ratification of the Bretton Woods agreement. The American debate dragged on into 1946, by which time attention had shifted from concerns about post-war economic relations to growing apprehension about future relations with the Soviet Union. These emerging security considerations were enough to shift the debate in favour of the loan, but a sour taste remained. *The Economist* concluded with considerable foresight that Congress could not 'be relied upon to pursue with any consistency the policy of moderation and liberality without which the whole structure of the loan, of Bretton Woods and of non-discriminatory trade is built on sand'.[29] The proposed International Trade Organization would be the first victim.

Difficulties in the Anglo-American negotiations created concerns among Canadian policy makers. In citing the rift that was widening between the Americans and the British in 1944, Robertson took the view that 'if effective multilateral action is to be indefinitely deferred and, when achieved, prove modest, then I think we may have to look at the question again from the continental viewpoint'.[30] Bilateral free trade was clearly not the preferred option, but it remained among the formal options until 1948. In the meantime, there was widespread support for freer global trade; public opinion polls taken during the war indicated that a clear majority of Canadians supported freer trade.[31] As in other areas of post-war economic relations, however, progress on the trade front would have to wait for a resolution of Anglo-American differences.

Negotiations on the International Trade Organization emerged out of wartime discussions between the Americans, British, and Canadians. In 1946, the United States released a document entitled 'Proposals for Expansion of World Trade and Employment' that summarized the American position on these wartime discussions and recommended a UN conference on trade and employment. At the first session of the UN Economic and Social Council (ECOSOC), a preparatory commission (of which Canada was a member) was established to set the agenda and to make other arrangements for the conference. By the time the preparatory commission met for the first time in October 1946, it had accepted a US draft charter as the basis for discussing the establishment of an ITO. The American proposals also recommended a preliminary round of tariff discussions that would serve as a set of interim rules and arrangements until the ITO was finalized. This the preparatory commission agreed to, and at its second session in Geneva in 1947, concurrent talks were held between 23 states dealing with tariff reductions and with the drafting of a General Agreement on Tariffs and Trade. Immediately prior to the start of the UN Conference on Trade and Employment, which opened in Havana in November 1947, the 23 states that had participated at the Geneva meetings signed the GATT. It entered into effect on 1 January 1948 while discussions continued in Havana.

In March 1948, the nearly 60 UN members who were in attendance at the conference gave approval to the Havana Charter and to an ITO. The scope of the proposed ITO was very broad. As Jack Finlayson describes it, 'the ITO was intended to have a very expansive regulatory scope, encompassing not only trade barrier issues but also such matters as international investment rules, the operation of commodity agreements, and restrictive business practices'.[32] Almost immediately, the Charter aroused opposition in Washington, where the approval of both houses of Congress was required. Protectionists viewed the Charter as too liberal, liberals saw too many safeguards and restrictions, and most Americans saw too much room for the intervention of international institutions and for multilateral control over the national economy. In the face of such opposition, the Havana Charter never had a chance; it was withdrawn in 1950 without a vote. Canada and most other countries had waited expectantly but not optimistically while Congress deliberated; ratification on their part would be a wasted effort if Washington did not join in. As a result, the ITO was stillborn and its premature predecessor, the GATT, was left to oversee post-war trade relations.

Unlike the IMF and the World Bank, the GATT was not established as a formal institution. It was an agreement among contracting parties to abide by certain principles and practices in conducting trade with one another. Three principles are of particular significance in understanding how the GATT was designed to operate. The first article of the agreement stipulates that 'any advantage, favour, privilege of immunity granted by any contracting party to any product originating in or destined for any other country shall be accorded immediately and unconditionally to the like product originating in or destined for the territories of all other contracting parties'. All the contracting parties were to be treated as the Most Favoured Nation of any one of the parties. This would, it was intended, prevent the emergence of discriminatory trade policies. A second principle was that of national treatment, which meant that once foreign products had cleared whatever border measures were in place, such as tariffs, they would be treated as if they were a domestic product. As Article III states, 'internal taxes and other internal charges and laws . . . should not be applied to imported or domestic products so as to afford protection to domestic production'.[33] GATT procedures, especially in the area of tariff reductions, emphasized a third principle, that of reciprocity. This meant that any concessions should be reciprocated so as to provide a balance of concessions or benefits. Additionally, any punitive trade practices could be reciprocated to yield a similar effect on a country that initiated punitive practices. The overriding objective of the GATT was to liberalize international trade from national policy constraints by making trade restrictions transparent and then by reducing these restrictions.

The Canadian government had strongly supported the ITO. In responding to the American draft charter, the Department of External Affairs (DEA) concluded that 'with all its weaknesses, the ITO project is an inspiring internationalist approach to world-trade problems, and the Charter represents perhaps the most ambitious and far-reaching project of international legislation yet attempted'.[34] The subsequent abandonment of the ITO, although disappointing, did not lead to a full-scale retreat from multilateralism. Instead it encouraged Canadian officials to work for the strengthening of the GATT.

As in so many other areas, a system of multilateral trade was dependent on the full support of the United States. Unfortunately, in this area, the US administration was far more susceptible to domestic pressures. The Americans were not, however, the only significant player. If international trade was to be liberalized, other markets outside of North America would also have to be available and the GATT could help to secure these. Nowhere was this more evident than in Canada.

The GATT, despite its initial interim status, received the unqualified support of the prime minister, who believed that in the GATT 'there are incorporated the results of the most comprehensive, significant and far-reaching negotiations ever undertaken in the history of world trade. . . . The Agreement clearly charts our long-run course'.[35] The GATT had not only provided for a number of tariff reductions, nego- tiated bilaterally by participating states, but had extended these reductions to all signatories as a result of the Most Favoured Nation principle. It also included a number of the key provisions of the Havana Charter that applied to trade relations. As Gardner writes, 'It provided a forum for the discussion of trade problems and a mechanism by which the Contracting Parties could modify their tariff conces- sions in the light of changing economic and political conditions. It also provided a set of commercial policy principles to assure that the tariff concessions were not offset by other instruments of trade relations'.[36] Thus, although it lacked the institutional support that the ITO was designed to provide and failed to account for the difficult position of developing economies, the GATT included most of the substantial commitments that would in practice facilitate a liberalization of inter- national trade.

PUTTING BRETTON WOODS TO WORK

The negotiations leading to the establishment of the IMF, the IBRD, and the GATT were difficult and at times acrimonious. The instability of wartime conditions belied a more stable and prosperous peace once hostilities ceased. It was not that policy makers were unaware of the dangers: the weakness of the British economy, the immense costs of reconstruction on the continent, and the American public's limited commitment to multilateralism. It was more a matter of underestimating these while overestimating the capacity of the institutions that had been created to deal with post- war problems. Just as the UN was abandoned by the great powers in the wake of the Soviet–American conflict, so too did the IMF, the World Bank, and the GATT fail to thrive in the harsh economic realities that confronted Europe and Britain after the war ended. In every area, the institutions were incapable of meeting the onerous demands that were placed upon them.

Gardner refers to 1947 as the end of the Bretton Woods system.[37] From a longer-term perspective, most observers see it not as the end but as the start of a long hiatus during which the United States, as the hegemonic power, assumed primary responsibility for managing the global economy. What was supposed to have been multilateral institutional management of the global economy was replaced by the unilateral intervention of American policy in what Robert Keohane refers to as the 'long decade'.[38] From the late 1940s to the early 1960s, the United States assumed primary responsibility for implementing the provisions of the Bretton Woods agreements. The result was not as anyone (even the Americans) intended, but the success of multilateralism now rested more than anyone had planned on American shoulders and the institutions that had been created to lead were relegated to supporting roles.

Canada also experienced difficulties that were, in part, a result of the transitional problems being experienced by other states. The difficulties, which were related, included finding an acceptable par value for the Canadian dollar and restoring a balanced pattern of trade. In addressing these problems, the government attempted to maintain its support for the principle of multilateralism while compromising it in practice. The imbalance that developed in Canadian trade placed the government in an embarrassing and contradictory position when on 17 November 1947, the prime minister's announcement of the signing of the GATT in Geneva was followed by Finance Minister Douglas Abbott's introduction of quantitative restrictions on imports from the United States. A multilateral trading system had been pursued to provide the answer for the imbalances in Canada's trade relations. But multilateralism could not provide the short-term cure; at best it was a longer-term solution. In the short term, the government was confronted with sizeable imports from the United States and limited markets for Canadian exports. The government had made an effort to generate export opportunities in Britain and the rest of Europe, but this effort was insufficient.

In a memorandum circulated in Ottawa by Graham Towers, then governor of the Bank of Canada, entitled 'Post-War Commercial Policy Prospect: A Proposal for Averting a Breakdown in International Trade Relationships', a case was made for post-war financial support for Britain. Not only would the loan provide much-needed capital, it was also proposed that Canada and the United States assume some responsibility for Britain's heavy indebtedness to countries in the sterling area. In return, the Canadians asked for non-discrimination of their products on currency grounds. Canada's commitment to the multilateral organization of the post-war economy was clearly evident in these proposals. The loan would allow Britain to avoid implementing restrictive trade policies and would ease the transition to a more open trading system. In the words of one of the participants at this meeting, Douglas LePan, who was at the time second-secretary at the High Commission in London, the Canadian proposal would serve Canadian interests by fostering 'a world in which trade would be multilateral and currencies would be convertible'; the proponents of the plan were, however, 'also thinking of the havoc that had been wrought throughout the world during the inter-war period by currency mismanagement and rivalries and by proliferating trade restrictions and were hoping to avoid a repetition of that melancholy chapter'.[39] These wider concerns led LePan to conclude that Canadian interests 'were set out with such largeness and daring and magnanimity as to become almost identified not only with the interests of Britain and the sterling area but also with the interests of international prosperity and, yes, of international peace and security'.[40] Hyperbole aside, the Canadian contribution was certainly magnanimous. It was also to have unforeseen repercussions.

Canada and Britain eventually agreed on a loan of CAN$1.25 billion, which represented more than 10 per cent of Canada's GNP in 1946 and was one-third the size of the American loan of CAN$3.75 billion agreed to in the previous year. The effect of the loan on Canada's balance of payments was that exports to Britain did not yield the return of dollars needed to purchase imports from the United States. Imports were increasing dramatically in response to pent-up consumer demand for products denied during wartime and an expansion in the Canadian economy. In addition to these abnormal conditions, there was also the chronic problem related to the practice of foreign-owned firms operating in Canada.[41] The government had anticipated some of these problems when it set its par value equal to the American dollar in 1946; but as was typical during this period, the extent of the problem was not anticipated. Despite the 'high' dollar value, imports continued to increase until restrictions were put in place. The final blow came when Britain, in conforming to the terms of the American loan of 1945, attempted in July 1947 to make sterling convertible. The result was a disaster, and by the time sterling was blocked one month later, Britain had drawn almost CAN$1.3 billion in dollar and gold holdings. The Canadian and American loans were seriously depleted, and Canada looked to emergency measures. Trade restrictions were taken under the emergency provisions of the GATT as the government attempted to adhere to the recently concluded agreement. These measures, combined with Marshall Plan purchases in Canada, provided a temporary respite. In defending its actions, the government argued that it was essential to give continued support to international commitments. At the same time, however, it began to look for alternatives.

In the midst of these difficulties, the government began to negotiate a free trade agreement with the United States. Kenneth Wilson recounted the difficulties that confronted the government:

> During 1947, it became clear that our long-range programme was not 'paying off'. Our gold and United States dollar reserves were dropping dangerously; our loans rapidly exhausted. The proposed or established international agencies were not satisfactory, and prospects for sterling convertibility and free multilateral trading, far from being realized, seemed to be receding rapidly. Finally, in November 1947, we ourselves were forced to back-track on our own long-term programme and impose severe short-term trade restrictions designed to save United States dollars.[42]

Robertson had foreseen the possibility of these developments in 1944 and proposed, at that time, a bilateral deal with the Americans.[43] The proposal was received favourably by some Canadian officials, most notably by John Deutsch, who was posted to the Canadian embassy in Washington. Initially, it also received the approval of the prime minister. Negotiations began in earnest in 1948, and within a matter of months a tentative agreement had been reached. But by this time, Mackenzie King was having second thoughts and the immediate problem of the dollar shortage had been alleviated. In March 1948, the initiative was withdrawn as quickly and quietly as it had been initiated.[44] For the time being, Canada would rely on the fledgling multilateral system. The success of this system would depend, in part, on the revival of strong and open economies in Britain and Europe. European governments, however, had different plans.

European Integration and Canada's Options

The expansion of Canada's offshore markets required a revitalization of the European economies, and the revitalization of these economies required an infusion of capital beyond the capacities of the World Bank or the IMF. The United States, the only viable source of capital, launched the Marshall Plan in 1947. To acquire Marshall Plan aid, the European states would have to co-operate in longer-term economic planning, and they formed the Organization for European Economic Cooperation (OEEC) and the European Payments Union (EPU). American support for such initiatives meant that 'the emphasis in American policy changed from the pursuit of multilateralism on a universal scale to pursuit of multilateralism within a specific region'.[45]

The change in emphasis was not motivated by economic considerations alone. By 1947, the American administration had gained more sympathy for the economic difficulties confronting Britain and other European states. More important, however, they became aware of the necessity of maintaining the support of these states in stemming the growth of Soviet power on the continent. Potential economic rivals had become security allies, and as Gardner notes, 'when it came to a choice, American opinion subordinated the immediate enforcement of multilateralism to the political and economic interests of the Western World'.[46]

Although Canadian officials were sympathetic to the American objectives, the means employed created serious difficulties for them. The slow recovery of the British and continental European economies was a continual source of frustration for Canadian policy makers during the late 1940s and early 1950s; as a result, there was a strong interest in facilitating the recovery of these countries and in encouraging the opening of their markets. Most important for Canada was to secure a much-needed supply of American dollars to offset the chronic and substantial trade deficit that existed with the United States. The emergence of integrationist pressures on the European continent raised concerns not only because these pressures might provide an additional barrier to Canadian exports, but also because they might push Canada into ever closer alignment with the United States. The integration process in Europe also created real problems for Canadian exporters, problems that grew in significance with Britain's application to join the European Common Market (ECM) in 1961. Discussions of Canada's response began in the early 1950s. While politicians such as C.D. Howe expressed little concern over growing dependence on American markets, others disagreed. Pearson, for example, 'believed that a good portion of Canadian trade should be directed toward third countries, such as the United Kingdom, as a counter-balance to a powerful American presence'.[47] Pearson's views may have been influenced by LePan, who sent a memo to Pearson in 1951 expressing great concern over the repercussions for Canada of closer European integration:

> This development, unless it is accompanied by progress more or less *pari passu* towards co-operation in the North Atlantic area, will prove unfortunate for Canada, I am convinced. European economic integration could very easily mean the creation of new trade barriers against Canadian imports; and military co-operation among the countries of Western Europe could mean a great growth in neutralist sentiment. Both these possibilities would imperil the success of the North Atlantic Treaty. They would be particularly dangerous for Canada, since we would be left to deal with the United States on our own and almost inevitably would sink into a policy of simple continentalism.[48]

These differing views (which were also evident in the debate on free trade in 1947–8) indicated a growing divergence of opinion within the government over the future direction of Canadian trade and its political ramifications. They also cast doubt on the viability of the multilateral system that had been established for protecting Canadian interests.

By the mid-1950s, the hope that Europe would recover quickly and once again become an outlet for Canadian exports had been dashed as Europeans resisted pressures from both Canada and the United States to adopt convertible currencies and reduce tariff levels. These problems were exacerbated when the Europeans refused to grant tariff concessions to Japan when that country entered the GATT in 1955. As a result, the United States and Canada absorbed relatively larger volumes of Japanese exports. Repeated pressures were put on the Europeans to ease their tariff restrictions on the Japanese; 'these efforts were well and consistently supported by Canada and other countries that already applied the General Agreement to Japan, in part because restrictions in other countries caused Japanese exports to concentrate on their more open markets'.[49] The establishment of the ECM in 1957 added further complications, as progressive reductions in intra-European tariff levels were replaced with a common external tariff that yielded no substantial benefits to Canadian exporters. Those Canadians who had been worried about the implications of European integration were beginning to see their worst fears confirmed. If Europe would not return as a major export market for Canadian producers, the United States would be left as Canada's pre-eminent trading partner.

For security reasons, the United States adopted a rather benign view of European trade and monetary practices. As Stone has noted, Canadians did not share this view and were more concerned about the trade implications of what was taking place in Europe:

> Canada was less willing than the United States to allow its broad support for Western European recovery to override its objections to discrimination against Canadian exports. Through the 1950s, in OEEC, GATT and the International Monetary Fund, as well as through other channels, Canadian protests grew louder as the OEEC-member countries progressively dismantled quantitative restrictions against one another's exports without giving equal treatment to Canada.[50]

Canadian officials repeatedly emphasized the importance of abiding by the rules of the GATT during negotiations with the Europeans, but this did little more than build up resentment in Europe. And such objections lost some credibility in the 1960s when Canada too sought relief from its multilateral obligations.

DIEFENBAKER AND TRADE DIVERSIFICATION

The Diefenbaker government paid particular attention to the evolution of European economic integration. In part, this suggested a concern about the violation of the rules of international trade that had been laid down in the GATT. Yet given the government's later violation of these rules, there was more involved here than concern for the viability of multilateral trading rules. A more important consideration was an interest in diversifying Canadian trade away from its growing dependence on the United States. Diefenbaker had pledged to redirect 15 per cent of Canadian exports to Great Britain, but he never developed a precise plan for how this was to be done. Without an effective strategy to bring about such a shift in trade, the only possible encouragement was a dramatic shift in European tariff rates.

The objective of trade diversification was made even more difficult when Britain applied for entry into the ECM in 1960. The fears aroused in some Ottawa circles by Britain's application were based in part on commercial considerations. Canada and other Commonwealth members had been able to maintain their British preferential tariff arrangements when they signed the GATT in 1947, and these remained of some significance. With the prospect of Britain's entry into the Common Market, such preferences, already of declining value, were clearly at risk of being abandoned. With trade diversification a major policy theme and with Britain having been identified as the key market for this diversification of Canadian exports, preventing British entry into the ECM became a major policy objective of the Diefenbaker government, and somewhat of a *cause célèbre*.

Diefenbaker's decision to oppose British entry did not win the support of either his advisers or the Canadian press. Officials in External Affairs were concerned that Diefenbaker's opposition to a British foreign policy priority would seriously damage Anglo-Canadian relations in other important areas. The opposition from the Canadian prime minister was certainly not appreciated by the Macmillan government, which had domestic difficulties of its own to face along with the ever-obstinate

French president Charles de Gaulle. This had little effect on Diefenbaker. The issue was brought to a climax at the 1962 meeting of the Commonwealth Heads of Government in London. In his initial statement at the meeting, Diefenbaker raised concerns about the effects of British entry into the ECM and about the failure of negotiations to protect Canadian and Commonwealth interests. He closed his statement with an 'impassioned declaration of faith in the Commonwealth'.[51] As Robinson describes it, 'the British ministers were not among those applauding', as the speech 'had amounted to exactly the kind of performance they had hoped to head off'. Diefenbaker, despite reassurances that the French would veto Britain's application for membership in the ECM, had identified himself and Canada 'as the principal obstacle to UK objectives'.[52] De Gaulle did eventually veto the British application, and Britain's entry into the ECM was postponed until 1973.

However laudable his defence of the Commonwealth and his concerns with protecting Canadian trade interests, Diefenbaker's actions caused serious problems in Anglo-Canadian relations. It also had little effect on the structure of Canadian trade, which did not change despite Britain's exclusion from the ECM; diversifying Canadian trade required a great deal more than keeping Britain out of Europe. Moreover, Britain's European overture was not the only trade problem that confronted the Diefenbaker government. A more serious problem emerged as a result of balance of payments difficulties and the exchange rate crisis of 1961–2.

FINDING A VALUE FOR THE CANADIAN DOLLAR

Much of Canada's frustrations with the GATT and the international monetary regime resulted from the unwillingness of other states to adopt the new principles that were intended to liberalize trade. In the area of international monetary relations, however, Canada's troubles with the IMF were largely self-created. The root of Canada's balance of payments problems may have been found in the failure of other states to accept convertibility, but they were also complicated by Canada's own trade, investment, and monetary policies.

In its various attempts to cope with post-war adjustments, the government at times violated IMF regulations. This could be viewed as a less than wholehearted commitment to the multilateral system that Canada had helped to design. There were, however, a number of mitigating factors that put in question this assessment. First and foremost, the transitional problems that confronted these newly created institutions were far more severe than anyone had anticipated. Many states were slow to respond to the new directives for international consultation and co-operation. The weakness of the institutions provided little relief; they could not support the pressing needs of many member states. In this situation of rather tenuous multilateralism, it was understandable that even committed participants such as Canada would find more solace in unilateral measures or bilateral deals. With so many states in violation of the terms of agreement, what was perhaps more noteworthy than the deviations was the degree of Canadian compliance. Second, the Canadian decision to adopt a floating exchange rate in 1950, perhaps Canada's most serious violation of the IMF regulations, was a clear signal to the institution of the need for greater flexibility in the application of its rules. It also was an indication that flexible exchange rates were not always a sign of instability and need not always lead to beggar-thy-neighbour policies. By the 1970s, this had become the majority view. Finally, the Canadian violations can also be seen as a reflection of Canada's unique place in the global economy. It was (and is) a wealthy state with a serious trade imbalance and a prime market for foreign investment. All of these factors encouraged the government to take initiatives that were at times unilateral and at times in violation of the specific rules, if not the general principles, of the Bretton Woods organizations.

Canada's initial difficulties with the IMF over currency evaluation occurred in July 1946 when the government, without informing the IMF, upwardly adjusted the Canadian dollar from approximately US$.90 to parity with the American dollar. As Plumptre writes, 'the legal department of the Fund expressed the opinion that consultation with the IMF should have taken place, but the point was not pressed'.[53] In establishing this par value, the government underestimated the problems that would follow. As a result of Canada's loan commitments to Britain and of a rapidly expanding economy at home that was being fed by a growing supply of American imports, Canada's dollar reserves fell rapidly. Initially, the government met the crisis with a policy of import restrictions. Once the government imposed import restrictions in 1947 and began receiving purchases under Marshall Plan aid, Canada's dollar shortage problems were alleviated. They were also helped by a 10 per cent devaluation in the fall of 1949 that was part of a worldwide readjustment in the wake of the devaluation of sterling taken in consultation with the Fund. There remained, however, considerable concern over the future state of Canada's balance of payments. The Canadian economy continued to experience a sizeable trade deficit with the United States and was offsetting that by capital inflows in the form of foreign investments. By 1950, it had become clear to the government that it would be impossible to maintain a fixed rate of exchange.

When the Canadian director, Louis Rasminsky, informed the Fund in September 1950 that the Canadian government had decided to let its foreign exchange value fluctuate in response to market forces, the staff of the IMF recommended alternative measures in order to ensure that exchange rates not be used to serve domestic monetary policy. The government, however, was opposed to any form of exchange controls and was unwilling to absorb the inflow of capital by accumulating additional debt. Unlike most other currencies, Canada's was heavily dependent on international capital flows and these flows exerted continuous pressure on the country's exchange rate. In response, the executive directors of the Fund agreed that although they could not approve a floating rate, they would permit the Canadian government to attempt it. This was initially seen as a temporary measure, but Canada did not return to a fixed rate until 1960. The directors of the Fund made several attempts during the 1950s to encourage Canada to return to a fixed rate, but the government consistently refused. Rasminsky argued that 'the Canadian experience had been that a fixed rate of exchange produced wide swings in capital movements [and that] where foreign capital movements were large, a fluctuating rate controlled them better than a fixed rate'.[54] Furthermore, the Canadians argued that by adopting the fluctuating rates, the government had been able to meet two other IMF objectives: a fully convertible currency and the elimination of all exchange restrictions.

Part of the Fund directors' concerns with the fluctuating rate was that it would establish a precedent for other governments. This did not happen. Indeed it was not until the 1970s that many other countries adopted a floating rate. Viewed from a longer-term perspective, Canada's actions pointed to the difficulty that national governments would have in maintaining fixed rates as currency markets became more interdependent. Although the decision to adopt a fluctuating exchange rate placed Canada at odds with the IMF, the country's overall record with both the IMF and the GATT was better than that of most other states at the time. In this vital area of economic policy, the country had clearly linked its future prosperity to an open and orderly multilateral system.

The government adopted what has been described as a 'clean float', in which the Canadian dollar floated freely on international markets and the government refrained from intervening to set or keep the exchange rate at any particular level. By the late 1950s, representatives of the IMF had come to accept Canada's unique position as a country with a trade deficit and a sizeable capital inflow and, further, they had accepted that in light of the country's special circumstances, 'the Canadian policy did not threaten the maintenance of the Fund's par value system. As a result Canada remained a member of the Fund in good standing'.[55]

This monetary stability was threatened in the early 1960s when the Diefenbaker government encountered a serious shortfall in capital reserves. Diefenbaker's dollar dilemmas were part and parcel of an economic downturn that hit the Canadian economy in the late 1950s and continued into the 1960s. The post-war boom was coming to an end and competition from Europe and Japan was on the rise. The US economy moved into a downturn, and Canada's close links with it meant that Ottawa could not avoid some of the spillover effects. As unemployment rose, attention turned to the value of the Canadian dollar as one possible source of the problem. The crisis developed when the Diefenbaker government attempted to fix the rate of the Canadian dollar after more than a decade of floating exchange rates. The decision to fix the currency at 92.5¢ in US dollars was taken after a move was made in the 1961 federal budget to devalue the Canadian dollar to deal with a chronic balance of payments deficit. Once the government had let slip its intentions to devalue the dollar, the situation began to deteriorate: as Plumtre describes the scenario, 'not until 1961, when the government expressed a view as to the level of the exchange rate, did market operators begin to speculate on the wishes and intentions of the government'.[56] In advocating a lower dollar, the government opened the door to extensive speculation and instability.

The problem was further exacerbated in May 1962 when the government established the new fixed rate. Despite the problems this created for trade policy, the IMF approved of the government's attempt to establish a fixed rate for the Canadian dollar for the first time since 1950. The decision did not, however, resolve the country's economic problems; attempts to maintain the fixed rate created a rapid and serious depletion of the country's capital reserves. In response, the government borrowed from the IMF and imposed a surcharge on $3 billion worth of imports. As Peyton Lyon writes, 'the Canadian tariff surcharges were instituted without prior consultations within the GATT (as required) and little effort was made to demonstrate that they were consistent with the letter of Canada's commitments'.[57] Despite this, Canada escaped with relatively little censure from the GATT, although there were complaints from some of the contracting parties. As Kenneth Dam recounts, 'the CONTRACTING PARTIES recognized that surcharges were "inconsistent" with Article II and recommended that they be "eliminated expeditiously"'.[58] 'More significant', Lyon argues, 'was the damage done to Canada's ability to promote the multilateral trading environment' and to Canada's reputation as 'the most consistent and emphatic advocates of multilateral trade'.[59] Canadians could no longer adopt a 'holier than thou' attitude toward the Europeans. Nonetheless, they were successful in gaining further exceptions when the contracting parties of the GATT embarked on an ambitious round of trade negotiations in 1963.

Three rounds of negotiations were held under the GATT through the late 1950s and early 1960s. Prior to 1958, the GATT had achieved little liberalization beyond what had been achieved during the first meeting in 1947. Tariff negotiations under the GATT were held in Annency in 1949 and in Torquay in 1951, but the results were less than satisfactory for Canada. The Torquay meetings confirmed the pattern that was emerging: 'While the delegation was merely half-way through a six month negotiating session at Torquay under the aegis of the multilateral GATT, it was ready to turn its collective back on Canadian trade philosophy of the past decade to try to work out a bilateral deal with its southern neighbour'.[60] Under the GATT arrangements, negotiations took place bilaterally and then were extended to other members through the Most Favoured Nations principle. At this time, in effect, the Americans were the only member with something to negotiate. Progress had been slowed by the process of European recovery and integration, but 'from 1958 onward, GATT ceased to deal with postwar problems and began to occupy itself with the questions raised by peace, prosperity, and economic development'.[61] Negotiations in Geneva in 1956 dealt with the entry of Japan into the 'traders club'. The Dillon Round of negotiations held in 1960 and 1961 resulted from the formation of the ECM and the European Free Trade Association, and the main issue was the ECM's common external tariff. Few substantial reductions in tariff levels emerged from these negotiations, and neither organization had a substantial effect on Canada's trade policy. The country retained relatively high tariff rates when compared with other industrialized states and was still disproportionately favoured in exporting to the American market.

Progress in the GATT appeared stalled until changes in American trade legislation initiated the Kennedy Round of negotiations, which lasted from 1963 to 1967. For the first time since 1947, the contracting parties to the GATT participated in a comprehensive set of negotiations that would make substantial reductions in tariff levels. And once again, Canadian officials looked to maximize their trade benefits through these multilateral talks.

The net result for Canada was the liberalization of ever greater amounts of bilateral trade. But 'ironically, what the GATT negotiations did do for Canada was to draw it closer to the American orbit. For Canada, the multilateral General Agreement had turned into a bilateral institution and American tariff reductions did play a major role in reorienting trade' along North–South lines.[62] Increased access to the American market also had an effect on Canadian producers. Exporters confronted with the diffi-culties of penetrating and holding offshore markets were now willing, as they had not been in the past, to rely on the American market. In the past, the American market had been considered unstable because of Congressional control over tariff rates. Now, with these rates removed from direct Congressional intervention as a result of the RTA of 1934 and the GATT, the American market was seen as more predictable. The British market in turn was now viewed as the unstable market. Once decisions had been taken to shift export markets, it was difficult to change them. As a result, these developments tended to reinforce a longer-term dependence on the American market. What emerged then was exactly the situation that many policy makers had wanted to avoid.

The changing character of Canadian trade and the frustrations experienced in attempting to push the British and others to respect the multilateral provisions for convertible currencies and freer trade did not lead the government to abandon its longer-term objectives of a multilateral trading order. The DEA concluded:

> On balance, the disadvantages of bilateralism would outweigh the advantages at the present time. As long as there is a hope of restoring a non-discriminatory trading system with convertible currencies, or as long as there is no serious threat of world depression or of a recurrence of indiscriminate protection in the United States, we should continue our present arrangements and endeavour to induce other countries to move along the path to multilateralism in accordance with their undertakings in GATT and the Fund.[63]

Years of frustration in prodding the Europeans and British along this path in the 1950s did not alter these views. Said Plumptre, 'The only basis on which Canada should consider an enhanced relationship with the United States would be one that was developed through multilateral negotiations'.[64]

Throughout this early period, commercial and financial relations were intimately linked with security considerations. These were perhaps more important for the Americans and the Europeans, but they had ramifications for Canadian policy as well, tending to reinforce the commitment to multilateralism. There were also continuing concerns about maintaining a good standing within the Commonwealth. Some in External Affairs expressed fears about the repercussions resulting from the elimina-tion of Commonwealth preferences. Here too the concern was with losing a counter-weight to the economic power of the United States:

The result has been a great increase in our trade with the United States, a historically unstable market. Our bargaining power in political and economic matters has been reduced because of our closer economic relations with the United States. Our policy should now be to maintain economic connections with Commonwealth countries as a support for a cohesive political association which can be used to offset United States pressure. This political consideration should be given more weight when negotiating future reductions in preferences.[65]

On balance, while such considerations left many policy makers reluctant to develop too close a relationship with the Americans, pressing economic considerations at times led them to abandon such concerns in the pursuit of immediate economic benefits.

CONCLUSION

The Canadian approach to post-war international economic relations closely resembled that which had been adopted for the political institutions. Despite the emergence of divergent views and considerable pressures for a purely bilateral arrangement with the United States, the government gave its full support to a multilateral system. The policy was in certain respects a natural solution to Canada's position in the international economy at that time. Although dependence on the United States was growing, it had not yet reached the degree that would be experienced in later decades. Moreover, there was still considerable hope for the early revival of strong export markets in Britain and Europe. Canada's active participation in the negotiations that led to the formation of the IMF, the World Bank, and the GATT was also facilitated by Canada's privileged position in the global economy. When the Cold War intensified and security interests assumed greater prominence, and as the European economies recovered in the 1950s, Canadian influence lost ground. The discussions on Canada's floating exchange rate, however, demonstrated that Canada retained a position of considerable importance. Throughout this period, the Canadian commitment to multilateralism and its ability to play a leading role in these negotiations indicated not only Canada's stake in the global political economy, but also the intelligence and skill of its civil servants and a generally supportive domestic constituency. In this area, Canadians were very much present at the creation.

Chapter Three

Confronting the Security Dilemma:
Canada and the Formation of NATO

We are making an alliance not a federation. —Hume Wrong, 1948

I believed that we were making an alliance which would be the foundation of a federation. —Escott Reid, 1977

INTRODUCTION

The ending of World War II brought little satisfaction to Canadian diplomats involved in negotiations to establish the United Nations. The hope and optimism that had surrounded planning for the organization gave way to disillusion and pessimism as discussions among the great powers during the spring and summer of 1945 revealed the deep rifts that would keep them apart during the post-war period. At the end of the San Francisco conference, Norman Robertson cautioned his colleagues against revealing the extent of their disappointment lest they 'destroy the public's faith in the new organization'.[1] Yet less than four years later, Louis St Laurent, then secretary of state for foreign affairs, launched a 'crusade' to convert the public's faith to a new organization founded on the North Atlantic Treaty. The transition from a universal political organization based on collective security to a regional alliance for purposes of collective defence was accepted with relative ease in Ottawa and the rest of the country. Attitudes had changed dramatically between 1944 and 1949. One thing did not change, however, and that was the government's commitment to a multilateralist foreign policy.

This chapter reviews the origins of Canada's Cold War policies and the government's active support for the establishment of the North Atlantic Treaty Organization (NATO). For Canadian policy makers, NATO was the obvious alternative to the UN. Once the UN failed to provide effective security in a multilateral framework, a more limited multilateral alternative was favoured. This chapter makes clear that NATO responded to real concerns in Ottawa over American pressure for bilateral arrangements to defend the continent. As with the trade policy considerations discussed in Chapter 2, a multilateral alliance was a way of being onside in the Cold War without having to stand alone with the Americans. The creation of NATO marked the end of this intense phase of post-war institution building. It was also Canada's last major effort to shape the character of these institutions. The successful struggle for Article 2 discussed in this chapter indicates that Canadian officials were still looking for institutions that did more than meet immediate and self-serving objectives.

In reviewing the government's active role in the formation of NATO, it is evident that the strength of the Canadian commitment to the UN and to the principles of multilateralism had a significant influence on the government's pursuit of the North Atlantic Treaty. Collective action was by this time widely accepted as a guiding principle of Canadian foreign and defence policy. Amidst extensive discussion within the government of the options the country should pursue in response to the deteriorating international situation, there was no sentiment in favour of isolationism or nonalignment and there was considerable resistance to an exclusively bilateral defence pact. Instead, debate focused on what sort of multilateral alignment would be acceptable and with which states such an arrangement would be made.

The North Atlantic Treaty was the last creation of the ABC powers. During the late 1940s, Canada continued to play a prominent, if diminishing, role in discussions on post-war organizations. A small group of diplomats and ministers took a leading role in initiating discussions on the North Atlantic Treaty and had some influence on the final product. By the time the treaty was completed and the period of post-war creativity had passed, Canada's privileged access to the corridors of international power had been circumscribed by the onrush of events and circumstances. The renewed prominence of European powers, the now-established hegemonic status of the United States, and the emerging Cold War limited both options and opportunities for independent Canadian initiatives and influence. During the negotiations on the North Atlantic Treaty, however, Canadian officials made a final effort to establish the foundation of an international order that would meet their aspirations and interests. Comparable to their experience at the UN and with the financial institutions, their efforts met with only partial success and the final product was once again soon overtaken by events.

THE TREATY CONCEIVED

By 1947, Canadian policy makers had accepted the inevitability of Soviet–American conflict and had indicated their strong support, however qualified in some quarters, for the American side. They had also come to accept the necessity of developing a collective defence policy to meet what was seen as a Soviet threat to Western interests in Europe. Canada's interest in collective approaches to security had by this time been widely acknowledged. The government accepted that it would be unable to avoid participation in any future war in Europe or in any conflict between the United States and the Soviet Union. In addition, there was a concern that the American government adopt an internationalist foreign policy rather than retreat to its inter-war isolationism, even if this internationalism was going to be based on anti-communism. While some in Ottawa were also concerned about controlling American reactions to Soviet policies, as Denis Smith points out, there was no strategy for doing so.[2] Instead, policy makers favoured a multilateral alliance that would commit the Americans to participate while bringing them within the framework of collective decision making. Finally, support for an alliance of Western states was seen by some, including Escott Reid and Lester Pearson, as a possible foundation for a North Atlantic community.

The proposal for a Western alliance was launched by Reid in a speech he delivered at a conference of the Canadian Institute of Public Affairs in August 1947:

> If the peoples of the western world want an international organization with teeth . . .
> they do not need to amend the United Nations Charter. . . . They can create a regional
> security organization [in which] each member state could accept a binding obligation
> to pool the whole of its economic and military resources with those of the other
> members.[3]

Reid's statement had the support of both Pearson and St Laurent. The latter followed up with a statement of his own in an address to the UN General Assembly in September of the same year. If the UN would not provide security, St Laurent said that states 'may seek greater safety in an association of democratic and peace-loving states willing to accept more specific international obligations in return for a greater measure of national security'.[4]

Both of these statements were premised on an agreement among all non-communist states. A more narrow version limited to the North Atlantic was favoured by the British. Following the breakdown of talks on Germany among the four occupying powers in London in December 1948, the British concluded that 'there is no chance that the Soviet Union will deal with the west on any reasonable terms in the future'.[5] Within a matter of months, following the communist coup in Czechoslovakia in March 1948, the British, along with France, Belgium, Luxembourg, and the Netherlands, reached agreement on the Brussels Pact. This would set the stage for the North Atlantic Treaty.

The Canadian government's response to the Brussels Pact stands in marked contrast to historical attitudes toward foreign commitments. Prime Minister Mackenzie King—who in 1922, in response to a request from Britain to send troops to support them at Chanak, had stated that 'Parliament must decide' if Canadians are to be committed to foreign wars[6]—now committed his country unequivocally:

> This pact is far more than an alliance of the old kind. It is a partial realization of the
> idea of collective security by an arrangement made under the Charter of the United
> Nations. . . . The peoples of all free countries may be assured that Canada will play her
> full part in every movement to give substance to the conception of an effective system
> of collective security by the development of regional pacts under the Charter of the
> United Nations.[7]

This marked a very significant change in attitude for a prime minister who had been skeptical of the UN's collective security provisions and who only months earlier had driven his foreign minister to the brink of resignation by initially refusing to allow Canada to participate in a UN commission to oversee elections in Korea. Perhaps the change was a result of King's view that the UN was impotent, along with a good dose of fear over the prospect of war in Europe that had been instilled in him during his trip to London in December 1947. Whatever the reason, the government was now committed to participating actively in the formation of a regional alliance. The invitation from the British to participate in tripartite talks with the Americans had been received in Ottawa and accepted without hesitation.

Canadian support for participating in a regional security scheme was not unanimous. Opposition came from academics such as Harold Innis and Frank Underhill, from within the ranks of the CCF (although not from the party leadership), and from certain quarters in Quebec, notably *Le Devoir*.[8] Support was, however, generally strong and reflected the success of St Laurent's crusade during the summer of 1948. Among policy makers, a North Atlantic alliance served a variety of foreign policy interests, which were neatly summarized by Robertson:

> Ever since we have been in a position to shape our policy abroad we have had to wrestle with the antimonies created by our position as a North American country and as a member of the Commonwealth, by our special relationship with the United Kingdom and at the same time, although in less degree, with other countries of Western Europe as well. A situation in which our special relationship with the United Kingdom can be identified with other countries in Western Europe and in which the United States will be providing a firm basis, both economically and probably militarily, for this link across the North Atlantic, seems to me such a providential solution for so many of our problems that I feel we should go to great lengths and even incur considerable risks in order to consolidate our good fortune and ensure our proper place in this new partnership.[9]

The alliance would secure the North Atlantic triangle and embed it in a wider collection of states with firm commitments of mutual support.

There was, however, more to the Canadian interest than this. A North Atlantic pact might also enhance the country's ability to deal with the United States. Especially pertinent in this regard were American demands on Canada for continental defence. With an alliance that included members from across the Atlantic, Pearson, for one, hoped that strictly bilateral defence arrangements could be minimized: 'Under such a treaty the joint planning of the defence of North America would fall into place as part of a larger whole and the difficulties arising in Canada from fear of invasion of Canadian sovereignty by the United States would be diminished'.[10] The same message was repeated during the negotiations in an effort to convince the influential American George Kennan to throw his support behind the alliance. This would remain an important consideration for Canadian diplomats throughout the 1950s.

The North Atlantic Treaty, the document that was so revolutionary in Canadian (and American) foreign policy, comprises 14 brief articles and a short preamble. The treaty was signed by twelve governments in Washington on 4 April 1949.[11]

Changing Course

Canadian officials had displayed an interest in an effective system of collective security from the start of their planning for the post-war world order. The experience of the 1930s had left a deep impression on many of them, including the most committed neutralists, such as Reid. The desire for a working system of collective security was in large measure responsible for the frustration experienced during negotiations on the UN Charter. As a result, the decision taken during 1947 to look at alternatives to the UN did not reflect a radical shift in policy; it was more of an effort to find a better means of reaching the same end. Collective security under the auspices of the UN had already been impaired by the veto, which would render action against any great power impossible. Collective security suffered an additional blow when the developing conflict between the Soviet Union and the Western powers spread into UN corridors.

The first session of the United Nations met in London in January and February 1946. The reaction of one of the Canadian delegates, Hume Wrong, left little room for optimism: 'It would be unwise in present circumstances', he reported,

> to attach serious importance to the Security Council as a guardian of world peace. . . . Without a great alteration . . . in the attitude towards each other of the great powers— and it should be emphasized that this alteration is required not only on the part of the Soviet Government—the first meetings of the Security Council and the Assembly leave open the question whether the establishment of the United Nations has in fact furthered its primary purpose—the maintenance of international peace and security.[12]

The failure of the UN to overcome great power animosities did not come as a complete surprise to Canadian officials. There had been some hope that the great powers might have been able to co-operate on matters in which their interests were not directly involved, but such matters were few and far between. Differences between the Soviets and the Americans soon led to deadlock in a number of major areas, such as disarmament, control of atomic energy, and the work of the Military Staff Committee, which had been charged with establishing military forces under international control. But the ever-diminishing prospects for an effective UN did not dampen Canadian officials interest in and enthusiasm for an effective multilateral security arrangement. It also did not result in any desire to abandon the UN. In response, and in an effort to reconcile these conflicting objectives, officials looked for alternative arrangements.

The principal question to be addressed was whether to rescue the UN from the 'obstreperous' Soviets or to seek security through another avenue. To abandon the UN at such an early stage would have been a difficult decision. The organization was centred on its collective security provisions, but there was a good deal more to it than that. Moreover, there was a strong feeling in Ottawa that an institution in which the principal antagonists shared membership was of some value despite the inevitable propaganda campaigns that would ensue. In a memorandum to Canada's first delegation to the Security Council in 1947, Reid outlined the Canadian position:

> It is important to maintain the UN as a meeting ground between the Soviet world and the Western world. The United Nations is the only constitutional structure which now

exists which includes both worlds. As long as that structure remains in existence—faulty and weak as it is—there is some hope that the two worlds can learn to live together. If that structure goes, the chances of the two worlds learning to live together will become more remote.[13]

The objective of keeping the UN afloat with the Soviets aboard called for a policy that would acknowledge legitimate Soviet interests within the organization and refrain from deliberate attempts to antagonize or ostracize the Soviet delegation. This stood in marked contrast to the position being developed in Washington, which proposed that the United States take a different line toward the Soviet Union and the UN. As described in a memo from Wrong in Washington after Truman's March 1947 speech to Congress, the Americans intended to use the UN to criticize the Soviets:

> The way in which issues are being faced by the Administration involves giving up much support of the public pretense which has surrounded the conduct of relations with the USSR and support of the United Nations. The United States Government will speak more bluntly and briefly than hitherto. They are likely deliberately to make use of United Nations meetings as a forum for putting the Russians on the spot by the methods of psychological warfare. They will be more unready to continue to take part in protracted and unproductive discussions such as those in the Atomic Energy Commission. The effect would be to employ the United Nations as a means for building up an anti-Soviet bloc.[14]

Canada's interest in keeping the UN as a forum in which the Soviet Union and Western powers could interact was made easier by the recognition that collective defence measures could be established without violating the Charter. In the same memo quoted earlier, Reid made this point explicitly:

> A United Nations without the Soviet Union and its satellites and without the veto would be a western alliance directed against the Soviet Union. Such an alliance can be created at any time under Article 51 of the Charter. It is not necessary to drive the Soviet Union out of the United Nations in order to create it. We can have the alliance and at the same time have a United Nations which includes the USSR.[15]

In this way, the UN could be preserved until such time that East–West differences were resolved and the organization could begin to work as it was intended. In the interim, security objectives could be achieved without ruining whatever chances there were for the long-term viability of the UN. The UN served both immediate and long-term needs. In the longer term it was, from Canada's viewpoint, a more desirable basis for a system of world order. In the immediate circumstances of the late 1940s, however, as Pearson recognized, it was incapable of meeting the emerging threats to security with collective action:

We in Canada hoped that our own economic well-being and the national security of our country would be assured through the extension into peacetime of the international co-operation of the war. We have had to admit, however, that in present circumstances the organization which we created for this purpose in the United Nations, is not equal to this task.[16]

IDENTIFYING THE THREAT

The ineffectuality of the UN did not warrant on its own the hasty moves to organize an alliance of like-minded states for purposes of security. It was the combination of the UN's incapacity and the growing fear among Western governments that the Soviet Union presented a clear and immediate threat to their interests that precipitated the secret discussions between Canada, Britain, and the United States in the spring of 1948. The fear of revolution and war was perhaps most pronounced in the capitals of Western Europe, where governments were still trying to cope with reconstruction, but its reverberations were felt in North America as well. Uncertainty over the aspirations of the Soviet government and the looming fear of another war led to an emerging consensus among Western governments that the Soviet Union was the primary threat to international security. This was perhaps the only point of agreement at the start of negotiations on the North Atlantic Treaty.

While Canadian officials shared this pessimistic assessment of the Russians, they were also motivated by other concerns. Canada had followed the lead of the Americans in refusing to recognize the Soviet state that was created in November 1917. It was not until Hitler abandoned his pact with Stalin and the Russians joined the nations united in the war effort that the Canadian government sent its first ambassador to Moscow. During the next five years, Canada's ambassador in Moscow, Dana Wilgress, attempted to present his superiors in the East Block with an independent assessment of the Soviet Union, one not filtered through the lenses of other Western diplomats in Moscow. Superiors in Ottawa were, as a result, provided with reasoned assessments of Soviet behaviour and objectives. The need to secure great power co-operation was one of the principal concerns influencing the government's wartime attitudes toward the Soviet Union. This need was in part responsible for the government's acceptance of secondary status in the UN Relief and Rehabilitation Agency (UNRRA) and for the Canadian delegation's willingness to yield to Soviet demands during negotiations on the UN Charter. But as the war ended, attitudes began to change.

In his book *Diplomacy of Fear*, Smith provides an account of the evolution of Canadian attitudes toward the Soviet Union and its emerging conflict with the Western powers during this critical period. He emphasizes the opportunity for independent decision making in Ottawa:

The Canadian government possessed its own diplomatic sources of information on Soviet foreign policy, shared its documents and judgments widely with the American

Department of State and the Foreign Office, took part forthrightly in the creation of a common appreciation of Soviet intentions and capabilities. In addition, the Canadians possessed a distinct perspective on the United States, initially more sceptical than that of the United Kingdom because Canada was less desperately dependent on American support; yet in the end more complacent before American power— perhaps because Canada lacked Britain's traditions and presumptions as a fading imperial power. Canada entered the Cold War alliance against the Soviet Union not just as a pawn of the United States, but with its own calculations of interest in mind.[17]

Nonetheless, Canadian attitudes toward the Soviet Union began to mirror many of those that were emerging in the United States. Canadian views of Soviet intentions changed in response to changing assessments from both its own diplomats and from those in Washington and London. They also changed in response to Soviet activities in Canada and Europe. By 1948, the prime minister and Pearson were both expressing fears of imminent war.

The Canadian government was confronted with its first reappraisal of the Soviet Union when Wilgress left to join colleagues at the UN conference in San Francisco in the spring of 1945 and Arnold Smith began sending reports to Ottawa. The mood among Western diplomats in Moscow was changing and Smith's reports reflected these changes: 'The signs of change can be traced over months, in 1944 and 1945, through shifts of tone and emphasis in their dispatches, as the views of the "realists" like George Kennan gradually gained ground and those of the liberal optimists lost it'.[18] Soviet intentions were now viewed more darkly, and a policy of firmness rather than accommodation was encouraged upon the Canadian government, for example by Leon Mayrand: 'A long run policy of increasing the strength of Western civilization, coupled with a flexible diplomatic technique which would use firmness against firmness, yield advantage usually only against advantage, and that would always be ready to encourage cooperation but would offer no temptation through softness for the undue seeking of expansionist advantage, would seem a necessary educational technique'.[19] In line with London and Washington, Ottawa was being advised to accept the inevitably of post-war conflict with the Soviet Union and to adopt new tactics in response.

Additional fodder for a change in policy came with the revelation in September 1946 of a spy ring operating out of the Soviet embassy in Ottawa; as Smith writes, 'from this point on—although policy remained far from clear—the anti-Communist faith dominated the North American public consciousness, providing a touchstone of "loyalty", narrowing the range of speculation and enquiry about Russian intentions, and progressively limiting the margins for diplomatic manoeuvre in relations with the USSR'.[20] Churchill's 'Iron Curtain' speech in the United States in March 1946 and the proclamation one year later of the Truman Doctrine, in which the American government pledged its support for anti-communist regimes, played upon and reinforced these attitudes. By the end of 1947, and following the breakdown of meetings between the foreign ministers of the great powers in London, there was concurrence throughout Western governments that co-operation with the Soviet government was no longer possible and new strategies would have to be devised.

Soviet actions during 1948, especially the coup in Czechoslovakia in March and the blockade of Berlin that was imposed in June, encouraged Western governments to establish collective arrangements for common defence purposes. Some, like Pearson, spoke of the possibility of war: 'Here we go again', he wrote at the time of the Berlin blockade, 'it's the third time we'll be over in Europe fighting and, by God we've got to do something about it'.[21] Others were not so pessimistic but did see the need to establish a collective display of force that would both temper Soviet aspirations and reassure wavering allies. To these were added an additional concern, as some also worried about how to deal with the other superpower: the United States.

COPING WITH AMERICAN INSECURITY

Smith has written that 'American power, American assertiveness, American insensitivity were the preoccupations of Canada's diplomats as they reflected on the world that would emerge from war'.[22] Beginning during wartime and continuing throughout the post-war period, Canadians had been forced to cope with a United States that was an assertive military power of the first order and at the same time more vulnerable to a military attack than at any other time in its history. This situation imposed considerable strains on the bilateral relationship and on Canadian sovereignty. Officials in External Affairs repeatedly expressed concerns during the 1940s about the future course of bilateral relations and the implications for Canada of the United States's emerging position as a global superpower. The most frequently advised solution was to get the Americans committed to multilateral institutions in which their power might be contained through the requirements for collective decision making. The area of defence policy presented special problems in this regard as Ottawa faced persistent demands from Washington for joint planning for the purposes of continental defence.

Following the fall of France and faced with the real possibility of British collapse, Canadians and Americans alike expressed the need for the establishment of bilateral defence arrangements. These demands met with a quick response when Prime Minister Mackenzie King accepted President Roosevelt's invitation for a meeting at Ogdensburg, New York, in August 1940. The two leaders reached an agreement to establish the Permanent Joint Board on Defence (PJBD), a binational advisory board on common defence concerns that includes both civilians and representatives of the armed services. The PJBD, designed initially to meet the needs of wartime, has served ever since as a forum for bilateral consultation on defence matters. Once the Americans entered the war, the PJBD yielded to the Combined Boards and Canada became the third wheel on the vehicle of Anglo-American co-operation. The war's end returned the PJBD to prominence, and the Americans were quick to use it and other forums to press for the co-ordination of continental defence plans.

American interest in Canadian territory for purposes of continental defence was the source of much anxiety in Ottawa. The government had little difficulty in accepting the principle that joint planning would be beneficial; joint planning that provided an opportunity for Canadian input and some Canadian control over the scope and pace of defence plans would be helpful in protecting Canadian sovereignty. What concerned officials in Ottawa, however, was that this opportunity would not be available. In particular, many Canadian officials had a different assessment of future threats to the security of the continent and of the necessary measures required to meet these threats. Lacking the intelligence capability to confirm these assessments and challenge those coming from Washington, and interested in maintaining good relations with the Americans, the government instead adopted a policy of appeasing American insecurities.

American military planning for the post-war period began before the smoke had cleared from the war, and within a matter of months the plans adopted the tenor of a pre-war rather than a peacetime situation. While initial plans from the Pentagon were primarily limited to the need for bases in foreign countries, the demands on Canada were of a different order. According to Joseph Jockel, although the Joint Chiefs of Staff 'wanted to preserve American access to two specific Canadian sites, they also had something broader in mind. They were clearly interested in "signing Canada on" as a faithful postwar ally and as a secure geographical element in that strategy'.[23] Long before political leaders on both sides of the border had even identified potential sources of threat, let alone the extent of co-operation they would accept, the American military moved to gain the support of their Canadian counterparts for their grandiose schemes. The first step was to move discussions out of the political circle, and hence out of the PJBD, and into a newly constituted Military Co-operation Committee (MCC) that comprised exclusively military personnel.

At the first meeting of the MCC in May 1946, agreement was reached on documents that outlined the requirements for continental security and a basic plan to meet these requirements. The requirements were extensive and included comprehensive air-warning and air-defence systems, with radar installations and bases to cover all potential areas of approach and interceptor aircraft to defend against incoming aircraft. The MCC concluded that the threat would be sufficiently credible by 1950, thus warranting immediate action by the two governments to develop adequate defences. These planning documents went far beyond anything higher military authorities in Washington or political authorities in either capital considered necessary. More important, the conclusions had been supported by Canadian members of the committee, who then turned them over to political officials in Ottawa. When presented to officials in Ottawa, however, the recommendations were met with a great deal of skepticism and with some fear that their implementation would merely antagonize Moscow and make a war more likely. In External Affairs, Wrong dismissed the MCC's analysis:

> My feeling is that the appreciation while sound in its general analysis is defective in its estimate of the possible time factors involved and also overemphasizes some of the

potential dangers. It seems to me to assume a greater capacity in the USSR for waging an offensive war than seems likely to exist now or even within the next decade.

He went on to say that 'we need not . . . begin in 1946 to approve plans and incur expenditures based on the conception of a malevolent Russia building up her strength so as to be able to engage successfully in a deliberately chosen contest with the United States'.[24] Canadian assessments of the likelihood of war saw it as remote and as more likely to start from localized conflicts than from a direct attack on the North American continent. They also believed that the mere publication of such a plan 'would be treated as the announcement of a defensive alliance against the Soviet Union'.[25] Canadian authorities were not ready for this—not yet. This seed would, however, bear much fruit in the 1950s.

The Canadian government had foreseen the possibility of strong American pressure for post-war military co-operation and seemed to have won this initial battle. The war, however, had just begun. In accepting the principle of joint planning and the American assessment of the Soviet threat, the Canadians had signed on as a committed ally in the Cold War to follow.

THE SEARCH FOR A COLLECTIVE RESPONSE

The Canadian government was reluctant to limit its defence planning to the North American continent. If there was to be a Cold War and if the Americans were to dominate the Western faction, Canadians did not wish to be isolated with them on the North American continent. Pressures for bilateral co-operation had the effect of further encouraging officials to seek out multilateral associations in which this pressure could be deflected. In attempting to secure American involvement in a multilateral defence pact, Canadians hoped not only to commit the Americans to the next war before it started, but also to extend the American defence perimeter to Europe so that North America would not become the first line of defence. It was for these reasons that Canadian negotiators were opposed to an American proposal of unilateral or bilateral security guarantees to European governments in place of the North Atlantic Treaty.

Among the reasons Pearson gave for supporting a multilateral treaty over a unilateral guarantee were that it would more strongly commit the United States to involvement, the support of the Senate having been secured; that it would be less likely to offend the Europeans; that it would recognize the mutuality of the assistance being provided; that it would lend support to the consistency between such arrangements and Article 51 of the UN Charter; and that it would allow for non-military forms of co-operation.[26] Wrong later added an equally compelling consideration in a conversation with Kennan:

It would be far more difficult for Canada to collaborate in planning against Soviet aggression on the basis of a unilateral US assurance than it would be if both countries were parties to an Atlantic agreement. Furthermore, under such an agreement the joint planning of the defence of North America fell into place as part of a larger whole and would diminish difficulties arising from fears of invasion of Canadian sovereignty by the US. It would be easier to advocate a policy of Canadian aloofness if the present state of affairs was maintained. An Atlantic pact would go a long way towards curing our split personality in defence matters by bringing the US, the UK and Canada into regular partnership.[27]

Canadian opposition to unilateral guarantees was indicative of a wider view that post-war defence planning would be made easier if it was part of a larger framework. Multilateralism was to be used to balance the strong continentalist pressures to which the Canadian government had already been exposed. In the face of the opposition of Canada and Britain, the proposal for a unilateral American guarantee was finally put to rest in July 1948.

Their apprehensions also led Canadian negotiators to oppose a tendency in some quarters in Washington and Europe to adopt a two-pillar conception of North Atlantic defence, in which one pillar would be North America and the other an integrated Western Europe. As conceived, this would have involved an agreement between the Brussels Pact group and the North American group (Canada and the United States). This proposal was as unacceptable as the idea of a unilateral guarantee, and for the same reasons. If North America was to be one of two pillars, this would in effect mean that the United States would act as that pillar: given the asymmetrical distribution of power between Canada and the United States, Canadian views would likely be overwhelmed by American interests. The entire purpose of the alliance was to attempt to redress this imbalance by giving Canada an opportunity to work collectively with other states to counterbalance American power. A two-pillar alliance would limit these opportunities. A multilateral alliance would, it was hoped, enhance Ottawa's ability to influence decisions on Western security taken in that framework, but only to the extent that Canada was able to work with other, European, members.

Finally, it should be added that Canadian concerns about post-war American defence policy were not based on selfish considerations alone. There was in defence policy, as there was in commercial policy, apprehension about the stability of American behaviour. Such fears resulted from the somewhat contradictory notions of American isolationism and American unilateralism. As was evident in the debate on the unilateral guarantee, governments in London and Ottawa wanted to see a firm American commitment to overcome their suspicions of a latent isolationism in the American body politic. The North Atlantic Treaty would, for the first time, place the United States in an entangling alliance, and there were many voices in that country that argued against such a dramatic shift in policy. For most other members of the alliance, nothing less than a formal commitment would be sufficient either to deter the Soviets or to reassure the Europeans. On the other hand, there was a perceived need for the alliance to be used to contain the excesses of American unilateralism. These were perhaps most unsettling at the time of the Berlin blockade.

As early as 1945, in a report from Moscow, Wilgress—after acknowledging the obstructionist tendencies in Soviet policy—added his own caution to Western states:

> But we on our side have much to learn from the recent happenings in London [Foreign Ministers meeting of December 1945]. It is not so much a question of teaching the Soviet Union that there is a limit beyond which the United States will not go. Rather it is a question of the United States learning the difficult art of adjusting its policy to the new fact that accommodation must be found in the family of nations for a newcomer with different manners and different modes of thought.[28]

Others were concerned with more than American sensitivities to Soviet diplomatic culture. There were some fears that war might come as a result of American reactions to Soviet policy. John Holmes, for one, expressed these fears in a memo from his post in Moscow. Holmes did not agree with Westerners in Moscow 'that the real danger of war in the near future comes from the trigger-happy U.S. military who argue that the best way to prevent the next war is to drop a bomb on the Kremlin'. He did, however, think that the government should 'use our considerable influence in the coming months to prevent the United States from taking heady action without calculating the consequences'.[29] The French were also concerned about precipitous US action and expressed these concerns to the Americans. Such fears were fuelled by American military proposals for dealing with the blockade on Berlin initiated by the Soviets in June 1948. When combined with the deployment of supposedly atomic-capable American B-29 bombers to Britain and Germany in July 1948, US military recommendations for armed intervention took on grave overtones. Despite President Truman's argument that 'this is no time to be juggling an atom bomb around', it is clear that the apparent threat of an atomic attack was a part of the American response to the Berlin blockade.[30] Based on these signs, and without the knowledge that the Americans at this time lacked the capability to launch an attack with atomic weapons against the Soviet Union (knowledge that was also unavailable to many in the US administration), the Canadians, British, and French were rightly concerned with the possibility of a preventative war initiated by Washington. There was some hope that an alliance might help to constrain such rash behaviour.

More than a Military Alliance

All of the above factors played some part in the government's decision to proceed with the North Atlantic Treaty. In addition—and probably one of the most important factors for some, such as Reid and Pearson—was the hope that the alliance would provide the basis for a viable North Atlantic community. Reid has noted that this view was shared by others in the United States and Britain: '[John D.] Hickerson, Kennan, [Theodore] Achilles, [Gladwyn] Jebb, St Laurent and Pearson all hoped that a supranational institution . . . would emerge in the 1950s and 1960s. They believed that the formation of a North Atlantic alliance would make more likely the emergence of the supranational institution on which their hopes were fixed'.[31] The UN having failed to provide the foundation for an effective world order, the North Atlantic coalition would be used instead to develop such an order.

Perhaps more than any other, Escott Reid professed this belief. It is reflected in his initial proposal that the treaty be open for any state willing to abide by its provisions; in his strong commitment to emphasizing the economic, social, and cultural basis of the North Atlantic community; in his opposition to the inclusion of non-democratic states in the alliance; and in his relentless advocacy of Article 2. Reid did not win many friends in his hard-fought battle for the inclusion of Article 2 in the treaty; his proposals were met with caustic comments both from Robertson, then posted in London, and, most important, from Wrong, on the front line of negotiations in Washington. Nonetheless, for Reid and others who shared his position, commitment to these values would ensure that support for a North Atlantic Treaty was in no way inconsistent with their support for the UN. The alliance would instead become a way station until other members of the UN were willing to support collective security and Western values.

Article 2 of the North Atlantic Treaty has been referred to accurately as 'the Canadian article', for it would not have appeared in the treaty without the persistent demands of its Canadian proponents. While the principle of the article received support from many quarters, it was inspired by Reid and Pearson and forced through by them over the opposition of Dean Acheson and Jebb and with less than whole-hearted assistance from Wrong at the negotiating table in Washington. As finally approved, the Article stated:

> The Parties will contribute toward the further development of peaceful and friendly international relations by strengthening their free institutions, by bringing about a better understanding of the principles upon which these institutions are founded, and by promoting conditions of stability and well-being. They will seek to eliminate conflict in their international economic policies and will encourage economic collaboration between any or all of them.[32]

The government's commitment to what Acheson regarded 'as the least essential article'[33] was so strong that Canada threatened not to sign the treaty unless the article appeared. On only one other issue (the pledge of military assistance in Article 5) was the Canadian government as strongly committed. In its effort to win support for the article over the opposition of the Americans, the Canadian government went directly to the other governments involved in the negotiations and brought them onside. R.D. Cuff and J.L. Granatstein have written that to have succeeded 'in the face of such opposition and apathy is a commentary on Pearson's influence at the time; to have persisted in the face of such disinterest is a demonstration both of his commitment to the idea and of his worries about Canadian public opinion'.[34] The staunch advocacy for Article 2, however, reflected more than a means for winning political support; it was important in making clear Canada's interest in an international order that did not rely on military force alone. This order was that of the UN modified to take into account the ideological divisions that had scarred the international landscape. The commitment to Article 2 thus serves as an important indication of the continuing Canadian commitment to multilateralism for world order objectives and of its efforts to link national security and other national interests to more internationalist objectives.

It would, however, be remiss to dismiss entirely the political implications of Article 2. The government encountered little opposition to its proposals to enter into the North Atlantic alliance. Throughout the 'crusade', however, St Laurent and others had repeatedly emphasized that this was not to be an alliance like all the others. These statements had created an impression that the alliance would do more than merely commit the members to mutual military assistance. As a result, political considerations were not incidental. As Pearson later noted,

> One reason for our stand on this was, admittedly, political. We did not think that the Canadian people, especially in Quebec, would whole-heartedly take on far-reaching external commitments if they were exclusively military in character; nor should they be asked to do so. These domestic considerations . . . were reinforced by our dedication . . . to the grand design of a developing Atlantic community.[35]

Given the absence of concerted opposition, the treaty was approved by the House of Commons with only two dissenting votes. Thus it would seem likely that political considerations were only a secondary motive behind the government's threat to abandon the treaty if Article 2 was not included.[36] With this victory, Pearson and Reid may have thought they had laid the foundation for a North Atlantic federation. Within two short years, however, little more than a military alliance remained.

The Canadian government's tenacity in pushing through Article 2 was not matched by any substantive mechanism for implementing its provisions. Instead, having secured its inclusion in the treaty, Canadian officials, with the exception of Reid, seemed content to look upon the article as a symbolic representation of Western unity. Part of the difficulty in implementing the economic provisions of the article was that other institutions had already been put in place to foster Western co-operation. A more significant problem was the considerable lack of harmony that existed among Western governments in these other areas. As a result, those who were concerned primarily with security considerations were reluctant to bring non-security issues into NATO discussions for fear that conflict in these other areas would sow seeds of disunity within the alliance. Others, who were primarily interested in economic co-operation, feared that the alliance was not capable of addressing the technically difficult matters of trade and monetary relations. A.E. Ritchie, then head of External Affairs Economic Division, addressed the first concern:

> It is difficult to see how any survey of economic policies and problems prepared for such discussions could avoid dealing with the fundamental difference of approach between Canada and to a lesser extent the United States, on the one hand, and the

European member countries on the other, with respect to the economic and commercial policy that should govern relations between Western Europe and North America. Further discussion of this matter in NATO would be likely to give rise to the same recrimination, ill-feeling and embarrassment that it has already in OEEC and GATT, and to harden further the positions already adopted.[37]

The second concern was raised by the director of the International Economic Relations Division in the Department of Finance, A.F.W. Plumptre:

Neither the Secretariat nor the delegations are properly staffed or organized for this kind of activity. Other international organizations organized for the purpose have developed well-defined responsibilities in the field of economic co-operation, and NATO could not and should not attempt to duplicate their activities. Moreover, the economic interests of NATO members are not always the same, and there is a real danger that an attempt to make NATO into an active force on the economic front would merely emphasize the divergency of interests which exists thereby weakening the common ties which have bound NATO members together. These ties seem hardly strong enough at the moment to run the risk of further strain.[38]

These were compelling arguments, and in light of Pearson's failure to put any substance on the high principles articulated in Article 2—let alone to get the support of other governments for doing so—the Canadian article remained an uncompleted project. By 1956, after the third attempt within NATO councils to come up with a plan for implementing the article, Pearson concluded that he 'was losing hope that NATO would evolve beyond an alliance for defence'.[39]

The failure of Article 2 was in part a reflection of the previous success in establishing institutions that were designed to manage co-operation in economic areas. It was also a victim of the plans and policies that were to lead to the economic integration of Western Europe. As Europeans looked across the Atlantic for military support to ensure their security against the external threat from the Soviet Union, they began working on plans to integrate their economies and to pursue a more functionalist path to internal peace and prosperity. These plans received strong support from the United States, which had made co-operation a necessary prerequisite for receiving Marshall Plan assistance. Canadians were more skeptical, and attitudes toward integration on the European continent received mixed reviews.

The difficulty was that integration limited to continental schemes would leave Canada isolated on the North American continent, hence the strong interest in finding some mechanism that would cross the Atlantic and Canada's resistance to any plan that might interfere with trans-Atlantic links. Others recognized the Canadian dilemma. One British opponent of Article 2, Sir Gladwyn Jebb, recognized Canada's important interest in promoting it:

Escott Reid was not only concerned on ideological grounds to introduce into the treaty some provision tending in the direction of Atlantic unity: he was anxious to do so in order to protect the special position of Canada. He saw very well that if Western Europe ever one day really 'jelled' and the famous dumb-bell became a reality, it was not clear what the role of Canada would be, or how it would be expected to protect its special interests.[40]

But despite Canadian concerns about the European project, it was difficult to oppose the process, especially when it was so heartily endorsed by the Americans.

THE TREATY TRANSFORMED

One of the most important developments in the Cold War and in the history of the North Atlantic alliance was the outbreak of war in Korea in June 1950. Until this time, there had been little interest among the member governments to increase military spending or to consider the forward deployment of forces in Western Europe. The Korean War led Western governments to conclude that the threat from the Soviet Union was no longer limited to domestic subversion but also included the possibility of a direct military attack. It also convinced policy makers that the alliance must adopt more concerted military action in response. Reconstruction in Europe, which had previously been a priority, now gave way to rearmament, and the integrated military command of NATO was born. As Reid wrote,

> The North Atlantic treaty of 1949 was not the result of American cold war policies; it is not an example of the United States persuading other countries to support its cold war policies; but after the outbreak of the Korean War in the summer of 1950, the alliance became the principal instrument of the cold war policies of the United States.[41]

For Canadian policy makers, the transformation of the North Atlantic Treaty into a military alliance that would lead the Cold War struggle diminished the prospects that the treaty would serve as the basis for a viable North Atlantic community. When combined with other developments in trans-Atlantic economic and political relations, it became clear that such a community was a long way off but that, in the interim, NATO would become the strongest link in the trans-Atlantic chain.

The North Atlantic Treaty yielded to the North Atlantic Treaty Organization at a meeting of the North Atlantic Council in September 1950. Foreign ministers of the member states decided at this meeting that paper commitments were no longer sufficient in the face of the military forces that confronted them in Europe. Until this time, member governments had thought that the treaty commitments would be a sufficient deterrent and that additional expenditures and forces would be unnecessary. A report from the Canadian Department of Defence in 1949 had noted that the treaty's 'final result will not be to increase the expenditures which every nation on our side must take. By pooling reserves, the effect of the pact should be to reduce the total expenditures which each of the 12 countries would have found necessary for their security had there been no pact'.[42] The Korean War laid to rest this optimistic view.

MATERIAL CONTRIBUTIONS TO COLLECTIVE DEFENCE

Sparked by the Korean War, the United States doubled its defence expenditures in the summer of 1950. Canada and most other Western states soon followed. Canadian defence expenditures more than doubled, from about $380 million in 1949–50 to about $780 million in 1950–1. They would nearly double again in 1951–2. The high levels of military spending still evident throughout the West were established in the midst of the Korean War.

The war in Korea was also used to emphasize the need for the forward deployment of Canadian forces in Europe. Then minister of national defence, Brooke Claxton, would later write that 'in Canada we did everything possible to bring it home to the people that Korea and NATO were just two aspects of the same operation; two places where we met the communist challenge in precisely the same way, namely by build-ing up our strength'.[43] For Canadian policy makers, the deteriorating situation in Asia tended to reaffirm the priority that would be given to Europe in defence planning. Once it was determined that NATO would respond militarily to the Soviet threat in Europe, it was necessary to determine how much was enough. This became a perma-nent feature of debates on the alliance.

The war in Korea led to a fundamental reappraisal of the resources that would be required to meet the Soviet threat. In Canada, at least, it did not lead policy makers to revise their views on the central significance of Europe as the front line of defence. Throughout the early 1950s, the government continued to stress the importance of Europe; despite the fact that Canadian forces were engaged in battle in the Pacific, the government's gaze was fixed firmly across the Atlantic. Political and economic inter-ests guided and reinforced a military interest in preventing the outbreak of another war in Europe. The commitment to Europe would, however, now have to be supported with more resources. In addition to establishing NATO and designating the need for a Supreme Allied Commander in Europe (SACEUR), the ministers attending the 1950 North Atlantic Council meeting agreed that 'in order to bring the integrated force into effective being all available manpower and productive resources should be fully utilized for the defence of Western Europe'.[44] In response, Canadian forces returned to Europe one year later.

The first peacetime deployment of Canadian forces abroad was made with very little political difficulty. The principle of making a contribution was accepted by the Cabinet in late December 1950. But despite the ready willingness to support the deployment, there were many remaining problems, from finding the available person-nel, equipment, and dollars, to questions of command and control, to meeting the force levels demanded by NATO. The size of the Canadian contribution was consider-ably less than NATO or its leading members had requested. Despite calls for more than 20,000 forces and 600 aircraft, the Canadian government dispatched the newly consti-tuted 27th Infantry Brigade with 6,670 personnel; it became operational in Europe before the end of 1951. The air squadrons would be both more difficult and more expensive, but the government responded in this area as well, deploying 12 squadrons of 16 fighter aircraft each to France by 1954.

The commitment of aircraft reflected an important shift in Canadian military planning that would have a considerable influence on defence policy in the 1950s. This shift was toward a greater emphasis on deterrence than on combat. Along with this went a realignment in the priority given to the various services. These changes were summarized by Jack Pickersgill:

> If as is probable the combined pressure of public opinion at home and in the United States is going to make it necessary for us in 1951 to increase substantially our forces in being, as an effective component of an integrated force designed to deter aggression, it is hard to escape the conclusion that the intelligent course would be to concentrate on enlargement and acceleration as far as possible of the Air Force, and to revise our defence planning as rapidly as possible with a view to giving priority to deterrent planning for actual combat once a war has started.[45]

The RCAF emerged as the pre-eminent service within the Canadian armed forces in terms both of its share of the budget and of capital investment in new equipment. In the age of air warfare, and to keep in step with the even more aggressive USAF, the RCAF pressed for more and better equipment, such as the Arrow fighter aircraft. They also pressed for a larger and more active role in Western defences in Europe, and, more important, in North America.

An interesting aspect of the deployment of forces to Europe was a debate over who would command and control the Canadian forces; the RCAF was anxious to be integrated with American forces, whereas the Army favoured working with the British. The result was a compromise that satisfied both, but the growing influence of the former and the diminution of the latter had a significant effect on the evolution of Canadian defence policy in the 1950s and 1960s.

The deployment of forces to Europe was to become a permanent feature of Canada's contribution to Europe and would subsequently assume a political and symbolic significance out of proportion with its military significance. For a number of years, this commitment of forces went largely unchallenged. There were, at various times, arguments about whether the type of forces deployed were the most cost-effective or whether Canada was contributing enough or too much, but not over the principle of making such a contribution. Harald von Riekhoff suggested that this was because of the multilateral character of the alliance: 'Politically and psychologically this commitment has been rendered more tolerable to Canadian opinion by the fact that it constituted an identifiable role under multilateral assignment which was neither wholly defined nor directed by the United States'.[46] By 1954, it appears that Wrong's comments to Kennan on the greater likelihood that Canada would contribute more readily to a multilateral alliance than to a bilateral one had been confirmed.

On the other hand, it was also becoming clear that the alliance was increasingly being shaped by American policies and American military strategy. During the 1950s, NATO became ever more clearly a military alliance dominated by American military planners with a strategy that rested primarily on the American nuclear arsenal. The alliance adopted a nuclear strategy that removed whatever vestiges remained of Canada's nuclear-free status, much to the annoyance of many Canadians both in and out of the government

Canada's NATO policy became more explicitly a matter of defence policy in narrow terms, and these considerations would dominate alliance discussions throughout the 1950s and 1960s. For Canadian policy makers, three concerns were paramount. First was the size and character of Canada's material contribution. Second was the direction of the alliance's military strategy and its political orientation toward the Soviet bloc. Third was the link between Canada's membership in NATO and its obligations to continental defence. Each of these areas would became a matter of conflicting views within Canada and between Canada and its allies. The outcomes did much to sour many Canadians on the utility of this multilateral connection for serving Canadian security interests.

Building up the military strength of the alliance preoccupied NATO member governments during the 1950s. Early proposals advocated a rapid and dramatic expansion of the alliance's forces. At a meeting of the NATO Council in Lisbon in 1952, force objectives were initially set to rise from 25 divisions (10 of which were to be combat-ready) and 2,400 planes in 1951 to 96 divisions (one-half of which would be combat-ready) and 9,000 planes by 1954. However, as B.S. Kierstead wrote just two years later, 'these original estimates were based on wishful thinking on the part of the Americans who pressed their European allies hard . . . that their economies, with American help, could sustain the effort'.[47] Although never implemented, these force objectives were to become a measure of the needed capability of the alliance to withstand a Soviet attack and thus they played a major role in the transformation of the alliance. By redefining the threat in more explicitly military terms and then arguing that more forces and weapons were required to meet this threat, additional pressure was placed on political leaders to increase defence spending to meet these requirements. Moreover, the failure to meet these self-imposed targets led military planners to conclude that there was a significant 'gap' between Soviet and NATO capabilities that needed to be narrowed with nuclear weapons. Some, including Canada's minister of defence at the time, Brooke Claxton, suggested that the military was in large measure responsible for these developments, because it was the military who 'continued to set military requirements at figures beyond any reasonable hope of realization'.[48]

In addition to reinforcing a perception of Western weakness that would eventually encourage the allies to rely on nuclear weapons, the perceived need for ever-increasing military forces also touched off debates over burden-sharing. Member governments used force-level targets as one means of assessing the contributions that other member governments were making to the collective defence effort. But all members, including Canada, were often chided by the Americans, most often for shirking their responsibilities and not contributing more to the alliance. All members, including Canada, tended to resist such demands, and for the most part, contributions were determined as much by economic priorities at home as they were by the views of military planners in Paris. This was not merely a case of serving the national interest first (although there was a good deal of this involved). It was also based on a widely shared view in Canada, identified by Kierstead, 'that NATO defence needs in the short run must be measured against the long-run needs of the European powers to re-establish viable economies'.[49] Such sentiments reflected an emphasis on the non-military dimension of the alliance, which had always been prominent in Canadian policy toward NATO—a view that the political, economic, and social character of Western states would play a large role in determining the success of the West in its confrontation with the Soviet Union. Pearson repeatedly called attention to the need for a balance between military objectives and economic needs: 'We should give the necessary weight to social and economic considerations in deciding the level of defence programmes which should also be continually reviewed in the light of such considerations'.[50] As the alliance continued to emphasize the need for ever-larger force levels, however, many began to fear that the balance of military with social and economic objectives had been upset.

In Canada, NATO's preoccupation with force levels weakened the consensus that had been forged to support Canadian membership in the alliance. The CCF argued that the plans adopted at the 1952 Lisbon meetings threatened the alliance, at least the one they had supported in 1949. In arguing that NATO had come under the control of the military, the party's leader, M.J. Coldwell, told the House of Commons that 'the policy outlined at Lisbon jeopardizes the peaceful and defensive objectives which brought the Organization into being'.[51] In response to these arguments, Pearson expressed the view that if NATO 'had fallen completely under the control of the military I doubt very much whether Canada would be very anxious to participate in its activities'.[52] The preeminence of military considerations within alliance debates was equally worrisome to Pearson, but the Canadian government remained, in its public face, solidly committed to the alliance.

The 'gap' between Soviet and NATO capabilities was a constant refrain, and for many it became the accepted wisdom. In reaction to continuing concern, the Americans went to work on three fronts in an attempt to close the supposed gap. The first move was to seek the rearmament of West Germany and its inclusion in the collective defence effort. The Americans also supported an extension of the alliance into Southern Europe through the admission of Greece and Turkey, a decision that Canada reluctantly supported at the 1951 meetings in Ottawa. Later the Americans recommended that the alliance turn to nuclear weapons in the face of the persistent conventional imbalance. Each of these actions raised concerns in Canada and had some effect on diminishing support for the alliance. The decisions concerning the alliance's nuclear strategy, however, would become the most divisive and would contribute to the fall of the Diefenbaker government in 1963.

One plan to enhance NATO's capabilities as member governments failed to increase their contributions to the alliance was to allow for the early rearmament of the West German military and its full integration into the alliance. This proposal, which was pushed by the Americans primarily as a quick solution to the sizeable imbalance of conventional forces in Central Europe, generated considerable debate among alliance members. Much of the debate centred on French opposition to the plan. The French were not alone in being sensitive to German rearmament, but in light of their historical experiences with the German military, they were the most vocal. In an effort to deal with the problem, the French proposed a number of alternatives, most notably a plan for a European Defence Community. The EDC received strong support from the United States, which was anxious to see any plan that would allow for the rearmament of Germany.

Having been first proposed by France, it was perhaps inevitable that the EDC was finally rejected by the French National Assembly. In response to its rejection, Pearson expressed a concern that its defeat not put 'an end to the healing and hopeful process of European integration'. One solution, in Pearson's view, was 'the association with NATO of a Germany, with her sovereignty restored and the occupation ended, brought about in such a way that will remove the anxieties of Germany's neighbours, and which will strengthen the whole Atlantic system of collective defence and, therefore, strengthen the peace'.[53] This solution was not an easy one for many, not only the French, to accept. It was, however, in the wake of the failed EDC, the preferred solution and was approved by the foreign ministers of Canada, France, the United States, and Britain at a meeting in London in September 1954. This agreement had a number of stipulations, including a limit on the number of West German troops, set at 500,000; the placement of all of these troops under NATO command; a prohibition on the manufacture of atomic, chemical, and biological weapons; and a pledge from the Germans never to use force to unite their divided country. With these guarantees accepted by the four governments, the agreement was taken before the full NATO membership in Paris in October 1954. On 5 May 1955, West Germany became the 15th member of NATO.

Canada's role in this debate was largely one of working toward a solution that would maintain alliance solidarity; as Kierstead put it, 'the official Canadian position was that the rearmament of West Germany was a calculated risk, and that the degree of risk could be reduced by bringing Germany into the European Defence Community and having her armies integrated with the European Army of EDC'.[54] Although Canadian officials seemed to favour West Germany's integration through the NATO alliance, they were willing to support the EDC because of its apparent acceptability to the Americans and to some European states. Pearson and others also suggested that Canada intervene to encourage the Americans to be more sympathetic to French concerns, a suggestion that was turned aside by the Canadian ambassador in Washington. When the NATO council met in London in an effort to resolve the impasse brought about by the collapse of the EDC, the Canadians attempted to find a solution acceptable to all:

> The Canadian role at the [London Conference] appears to have been that of the good neighbour, who wants to see every body else getting along well together. We made it clear to our allies that the collapse of the EDC did not shake Canadian faith in

NATO . . . when every body else was undergoing an agonizing reappraisal of practically everything, Canada did not.[55]

In the end, Pearson's immediate reaction to the demise of the EDC was designed to ensure that the opportunity to integrate West Germany not be lost and that it be done in a way that would reinforce NATO and, by implication, the 'Atlantic' (as opposed to European) connections. For Pearson, the ultimate objective was to avoid policies and plans that would foster isolationism of either the American or the European model.

CANADA IN A NUCLEAR ALLIANCE

One of the most important issues confronting Canadian policy makers as they examined Canada's participation in NATO during the 1950s and 1960s was the role that nuclear weapons would play in alliance strategy and in Canada's military activities. The alliance's nuclear strategy was an outgrowth of the high force-level targets and of the resulting gap between these targets and actual deployments. It was also a reflection of revisions in American military planning. The increased attention given to nuclear strategy would have profound implications for Canada. As James Eayrs describes it,

> Canada had now become the ally of a nuclear weapons state, whose stockpile of such weapons had been made possible by and would in future depend upon Canadian resources. A major atomic exchange between the United States and the Soviet Union would in all likelihood contaminate her airspace and her lakes and turn her lands into a killing-ground. Her industry would become a prime supplier of military equipment for the armed forces of Western Europe. Her troops and airmen would serve in the West European integrated force—the 'shield' for which the US Strategic Air Command would provided the 'Sword'.[56]

Canada was always part of the American nuclear strategy. The debate that would paralyze the Diefenbaker government in the early 1960s was in effect a debate over what part this country would play and how much. Although much of the history of Canada's struggle with American nuclear strategy and nuclear weapons has been viewed in bilateral terms, the country's multilateral security connections have been most influential in shaping the direction of Canadian policy in this area. The government's nuclear activities should be viewed as much as part of its involvement in NATO as of its bilateral defence relations with the Americans. It was also within NATO that Canada fought its initial battles over American nuclear strategy, and NATO commitment was the rationale used by Pearson in changing the Liberal Party's position on nuclear weapons acquisition. Finally, Canadian officials repeatedly stressed the need for control of nuclear weapons through multilateral channels.

Pearson provided an early indication of Canadian views of American nuclear strategy in his reaction to a speech delivered by American secretary of state John Foster Dulles to the Council on Foreign Relations in January 1954. In his speech, Dulles outlined the 'new look' in American military planning. This 'new look' would combine economic efficiency with military extravagance. Nuclear weapons were to be its centrepiece, and threats to the peace, of whatever character in whatever part of the globe, would be met with 'massive retaliation' on American terms and at a time and place of Washington's choosing. To Pearson, this was unilateralism clear and simple, and his first objective was to reassert the need for consultation with allies. As he once said, 'We want to be let in at the take-off so that we can do our part to help avoid a crash landing'.[57] Consultation would not necessarily guarantee better policy, but Pearson and others believed that it would forestall reactionary ones. A more critical problem with the 'new look' was that it marked a significant turning point in post-war American military strategy: a shift to a more explicit nuclear strategy as the basis for American defence policy. Its initial impact was on American defence policy, but the 'new look' quickly spread throughout the Atlantic community.

The problem of consultation already mentioned was only one of the concerns raised by allied governments. A more substantive concern was the effect of the new American strategy on force levels and conventional defence spending. An alliance strategy based primarily on nuclear weapons raised the prospect of reduced defence expenditures, or at least of slower growth in these expenditures. Conventional force levels would be 'compensated for' by the deployment of nuclear weapons. Such benefits had a price, and for some the price was too high.

Another problem raised by the new strategy was the increased dependence of all the allies on the Americans—on American weapons, on American strategy, and, ultimately, on American decisions about the use of these weapons. The implementation of the 'new look' led to the deployment of American nuclear weapons in Europe, initially of so-called tactical weapons; later, in 1957, intermediate-range ballistic missiles were placed at the disposal of the SACEUR. The virtual monopoly of the United States in the area of nuclear weaponry raised new questions about the command and control of these weapons systems.

The deployment of these weapons also became a source of considerable debate, and perhaps nowhere more than in Canada. Canada's great debate on nuclear weapons was not focused primarily on the deployment of nuclear weapons to Canadian forces operating in Europe. Instead it concentrated on the issue of the deployment of nuclear weapons on Canadian soil. Yet it was Canada's commitment to NATO that was used by the Pearson Liberals and readily accepted by many others that proved to be the determining factor in the debate.

The Canadian government's commitment to accept nuclear weapons for the Canadian forces operating in Europe was made at a meeting of NATO heads of government in Paris in December 1957. The commitment was somewhat less than a whole-hearted one, reflecting much reticence within the Canadian ranks. Robinson writes that even Minister of Defence George R. Pearkes 'was privately discouraging of too open endorsement by Canada of the US proposals', in spite of his general support for placing nuclear stockpiles in Europe.[58] A more sustained critique was offered from within the Department of External Affairs by John Holmes:

We must try to remember, even with all the emotions of December in Paris, that NATO is only one of several associations which is important to us. . . . We must maintain enough flexibility in our diplomacy to associate when necessary with non-NATO countries in the United Nations and elsewhere, to pursue policies with which other NATO countries do not agree, and even to support non-NATO countries in disputes with NATO countries. The NATO association implies an obligation to seek agreement with other members and to oppose them with special reluctance, but it does not involve any more than that.[59]

In his speech at the Paris summit, Diefenbaker accepted nuclear stockpiles as a necessary part of a defence strategy that had already been adopted by the alliance in 1954. But he favoured postponing further action on the ballistic missile deployments to allow time for further reflection and debate. Diefenbaker went on to emphasize the need for the alliance to consider ways of improving contacts with Soviet authorities as well as other détente-oriented strategies. As Robinson writes, 'on the whole, with its emphasis on disarmament, on limiting NATO commitments, on balancing the political with the military purposes of the alliance, and on contacts and readiness to negotiate with the USSR, it placed Canada close to two of its traditional partners in NATO—Norway and Denmark—without antagonizing the major NATO governments'.[60] No doubt one reason for the favourable reception of Diefenbaker's speech in London and Washington was Diefenbaker's willingness to go along with NATO's emerging nuclear strategy. Unlike Norway, which rejected a nuclear role and the deployment of nuclear weapons on its soil, the Canadians had accepted a role for the Canadian forces in NATO's nuclear-armed 'Shield' forces. The decision to accept their deployment on Canadian soil would come later. Robinson argues that the decision at Paris to acquiesce despite misgivings reflected a tendency within External Affairs to accept the military's rationale: 'Within the department there was little, if any, disposition to question openly the judgment of the military authorities in both the United States and Canada that the deployment of nuclear weapons in Europe was necessary as a counter to possible Soviet military probes'.[61] Howard Green had not yet arrived on the scene as foreign minister to become the major voice of opposition to the proliferation of nuclear weapons within and beyond the alliance.

In agreeing to equip NATO forces with nuclear weapons, the government was implicitly accepting that its own forces in Europe would be carrying nuclear weapons. This commitment proved to be a major point of consideration in the ensuing debate on nuclear weapons. The main point of contention was not, however, commitment to NATO; it was how closely Canadian territory and the Canadian military were to be drawn into the nuclear weapons–based strategy of the United States for continental defence. Concern over the political implications of exclusively bilateral projects for continental defence was one of the motivations behind the government's decision to join NATO in 1949. That continental defence would emerge as a significant point of conflict in Canadian–American relations was yet another indication of the alliance's inability to satisfy all of the objectives for which it had been envisioned. Debates over continental defence also served as a rallying point for many critics of the government's defence policy and reinforced demands for a withdrawal from all defence commitments. NATO and NORAD were viewed as two sides of the same alliance coin and both were to be rejected by the increasingly vocal critics of the 1960s in favour of a declared policy of neutrality.[62]

CONCLUSION

Canadian officials had instigated debate on the North Atlantic Treaty in order to preserve the UN while developing more effective means of ensuring collective defence. A multilateral alliance among Western states would, it was intended, support Canadian security objectives at a reduced cost, but would also do so in a way that would not isolate Canada in a bilateral defence pact with the Americans and would in turn preserve trans-Atlantic linkages that were important for political and economic interests as well as security ones. It was also hoped that the North Atlantic Treaty would enhance Canadian influence in debates over how best to preserve Western security and in attempts to reach a settlement of differences with the Soviet Union. These aspirations never materialized. While the treaty did ensure that the Americans participated in a multilateral process, it could not prevent the rapid growth and virtual dominance of American influence within the alliance. As the East–West conflict took on more explicit military overtones, NATO emerged as an armed camp and American military power dominated the scene. Beyond pushing for more consultations in other areas, Canadian officials also urged caution as the alliance moved into the uncharted waters of nuclear strategy. Additionally, while making contributions to the collective defence effort, the government resisted inflated military American and NATO demands that threatened to drain the budget.

Despite these problems, NATO emerged as the foundation for Canada's post-war security policy. For most officials and members of the public, the multilateral setting of NATO was more conducive for the pursuit of Canadian interests than the alternative of an exclusively continental arrangement. Equally significant, the alliance served as the primary institutional link between Canada and the states of Western Europe. In performing this role, NATO would remain an important multilateral connection long after its military rationale had been questioned. The changes in NATO precipitated by the Korean War, when combined with developments in American military and especially nuclear strategy, led to an early reappraisal of this assessment. It was not, however, until later in the 1960s that the government adopted a more critical attitude toward the alliance.

Chapter Four

Coping with the Cold War:
Canada's Response to the Superpower Impasse

It is not very comfortable to be in the middle these days. —Lester Pearson, 1951

INTRODUCTION

The heady days of constructing post-war institutions during the 1940s gave way to the cold realities of making these institutions work during the 1960s and 1970s. These were not favourable decades for international co-operation. International institutions were being racked by two significant developments in the international community. The first was the Cold War between the competing military strategies and ideological views of the Soviet Union and the United States. This conflict was the source of constant tension throughout this period and brought the world to the brink of war during the Cuban Missile Crisis of 1962. The Cold War reinforced polarity in the international system, a polarity that too frequently was extended to the United Nations and its specialized agencies. Attempts to bridge the ideological divide were as difficult as they were necessary in order to maintain the institution.

If this was not enough, a second momentous development was transforming the organization. A wave of decolonization swept across the southern hemisphere between 1957 and 1968 and flooded the international system with dozens of new independent states. The membership of the United Nations more than doubled from 1955 to the end of the 1960s. The influx of new members put an end to what had been for Canada and others a mostly comforting Western majority in the United Nations General Assembly (UNGA) and transformed the white-dominated Commonwealth. In both organizations, these new members brought with them new priorities. In response, the agendas of these bodies were taken over by issues of colonialism, economic development, and racism. East–West and North–South were the axes on which political agendas were formed as member states positioned themselves into ever more cohesive blocs. Co-operation and compromise became exceedingly difficult as international institutions attempted to weather this stormy period.

In this environment, Canadian policy makers attempted to steer a moderate course. Canada was clearly and closely aligned with the Western and Northern blocs. It was not, however, viewed as being at the centre of either one. It lacked the military power and global presence to be a major force in East–West relations, and it lacked the imperial past and economic clout to be a primary target in the anti-colonial debates that came to dominate discussions in the UN. It was therefore somewhat well placed to seek the sort of compromises that would be necessary to assist the UN and the Commonwealth through this difficult period.

In the UN, Canadian policy facilitated adjustments that would maintain the organization by opening doors to new members and finding new political roles for the organization, such as peacekeeping. Despite the Cold War, Canadian policy toward the UN was still directed primarily to the maintenance and enhancement of the organization. Governments in Ottawa were also strongly inclined to support the UN and the Commonwealth, for they represented important investments for foreign policy makers in Ottawa. Officials in the Department of External Affairs (DEA) believed that these organizations were vitally important for the conduct of Canadian foreign policy. They were a significant, and arguably essential, alternative to the dominant and potentially dominating bilateral relationships with the Americans and the British. In addition, these multilateral associations greatly facilitated other important national interests in the areas of economic prosperity and national security. Finally, these institutions were viewed as a fundamental foundation to a more stable and peaceful international order. Despite these converging interests and policy makers' generally strong commitment to supporting institutional goals, Canada's ability to wield influence in pursuit of these objectives was not as great as it had been during the mid- to late 1940s.

The far-reaching changes in the international system during this period had repercussions for the exercise of Canadian influence. No longer was Canada one of the ABC powers that had been most instrumental in developing these post-war institutions. Instead there had been a relative decline in Canada's capabilities. This decline owed more to developments elsewhere, but the effect was to push Canada more firmly into the middle power status that it had claimed during the wartime negotiations. The growth of American hegemony, the revival of European powers, and the increased significance of military capabilities in a period of heightened international tension all tended to diminish somewhat the country's relative capabilities. In addition, prime ministers Diefenbaker and, later, Trudeau were not strongly infused with the spirit of internationalism that had guided the St Laurent government's foreign policy. What was said of Diefenbaker was equally applicable to much of Trudeau's time in power:

> The forces that would be influential in keeping his government in office, as he saw it, were basically domestic rather than international. . . . The support he gave to the various traditional cornerstones—the Commonwealth, NATO, the United Nations, and disarmament—sometimes seemed to be of lesser weight because it had its roots so conspicuously grounded in domestic imperatives and because he often seemed unconcerned with the way in which his preoccupations affected other governments.[1]

Despite these limitations, Ottawa retained considerable diplomatic skills and a favourable image abroad that were still of considerable value. In addition, and more than in the mid-1940s, Canadian diplomats solicited the support of other middle powers and of lesser powers to check the influence of the great powers in the UN and to facilitate innovative responses that would allow the organization to operate despite the Cold War chill that froze superpower co-operation on the Security Council.

Canadian activities in the UN and the Commonwealth during this period were not without problems, however. For one, they were not always successful. They also often created conflicts in relations with the country's principal allies or with domestic publics at home. Finally, such efforts did not free Canadian foreign policy from the economic and military pressures that were pushing for even closer continental links with the United States. By the end of the 1960s, these problems led to a foreign policy review that questioned the utility of Canada's multilateralist policies and argued for a new approach.

Peacekeeping in Retreat

The next major UN peacekeeping operation took place in Africa and had few Canadian interests involved. In July 1960, on one of the rare occasions in UN history where the secretary-general initiated action, Dag Hammarskjöld called an emergency meeting of the Security Council to send UN assistance to the fledging independent state of the Congo. Torn between secessionist movements in the province of Katanga and a return of Belgian troops to restore order, the recently installed government of Patrice Lumumba turned to both the Americans and the Soviets for assistance. Fearing that the conflict would erupt into a Cold War struggle, Hammarskjöld acted quickly to secure the Council's approval for sending assistance to the country to avoid encountering a veto from any of the permanent members. The Congo operation was larger and more involved than any previous UN operation. It also became the focal point for many of the problems that were plaguing the UN during this period.

In anticipation of the operation, Hammarskjöld issued a request to Canada and other member states for assistance. The response of the Diefenbaker government was not enthusiastic. Ottawa was reluctant to rush in with Canadian support, in part because the prime minister was, in Basil Robinson's words, 'worried about the difficulty of having white troops fighting or potentially fighting in an equivocal role in a black country, especially in view of the Belgian involvement'.[2] Events deteriorated quickly in the Congo and the Cold War moved to centre stage as the Americans and the Soviets backed rival leaders and Hammarskjöld searched for a middle ground that eventually pleased no one. Hammarskjöld's initiatives led to trenchant criticism from the Soviet Union, which proposed in response that the secretary-general's position be replaced by a troika representing the East, West, and non-aligned blocs. The Soviets were not the only critics:

> The hostility . . . of France, Belgium, and some of the African states, the refusal of many countries to pay their share of the cost of the Congo operation, and the failure to solve the problem of Katanga's succession or to find a stable political base upon which to build in the Congo as a whole, soon made it evident that this operation might lead to the collapse of the United Nations itself.[3]

In response to these growing pressures on the secretary-general and the UN, the Diefenbaker government shifted its policy toward more overt support for the organization. Robinson writes that 'the prime minister recognized the danger and, in government decisions and speeches over the following few months, he did what he could to bring support to the secretary-general'.[4] The support was important while the crisis dragged on and the UN remained the only effective authority in a divided country.

Ultimately, the Canadian government became one of the more active members of the UN's Congo operation. Canadian participation, however, reflected as much a concern over the fate of the organization as over that of the Congo itself. With the UN at risk and under attack from all sides, the Diefenbaker government made clear its support for the organization and for the office of the Secretary-General. This support would continue under the Liberals when UN peacekeeping encountered a financial and administrative crisis in the midst of yet another intransigent situation.

The UN force in Cyprus (UNIFCYP) did not resolve the outstanding problems that confronted the UN and peacekeeping. Instead it soon contributed to a new set of problems, for in addition to the continuing lack of financial support—once again, France and the Soviet Union, who had abstained on the resolution, refused to pay—there was concern about the inability of the force to contribute to a resolution of the conflict. UNIFCYP became a permanent feature of the Cypriot political scene, an annual drain on the UN's resources, and a permanent symbol of the limitations inherent in peacekeeping operations. What Paul Martin, Sr, describes as 'one of Canada's most successful ventures in diplomacy'[5] also became an illustration of the financial and institutional constraints of the UN and the practical limitations of peacekeeping.

No permanent solution was reached in response to the financing crisis. The Committee of Thirty Three, of which Canada was a member, was established in the UN to propose a resolution of the problem but was unable to reach an agreement that was acceptable to all member states. Instead the organization put in place provisions for the UNIFCYP, which requested that governments contributing contingents absorb more of the costs and also that voluntary contributions make up most of the remainder. The Cypriot government was also required to make a contribution.

In response to these financing problems and to other, administrative, problems experienced in the early 1960s, there has since been a tendency within the UN to have the Security Council provide the necessary authority for peacekeeping missions. This prevents the General Assembly from taking initiatives that the organization cannot support financially or that do not receive the political support of the permanent members of the Security Council. However, these measures have not provided an effective solution to the financing of UN peacekeeping activities, which have also had an adverse effect on the overall financial viability of the UN. In part because of these financial and administrative problems, no new peacekeeping operations were established between 1964 and 1973. What had looked for a time to be an effective method for interposing the UN in regional conflicts had lost a good deal of its credibility. It had also lost the support of the superpowers. For Canada, that credibility would be further tarnished by the collapse of UNEF I in 1967 and by the country's experiences as a non-UN peacekeeper in Southeast Asia.

The problems of financing, of the lack of effective peacemaking mechanisms, and of the profound indifference of many of the newer members of the UN all played some part in tarnishing peacekeeping's image in the 1960s. These problems tempered but did not eliminate Canadian enthusiasm for peacekeeping; having staked a good deal of its multilateral reputation on this activity, the government was reluctant to give it up. The almost unqualified Canadian support for peacekeeping could not, however, survive Canada's bitter experiences in Suez in 1967 and in Vietnam. The former led many to question the utility of peacekeeping in controlling international conflict. The latter left many Canadians with the view that the government had become compatriots of the Americans in the increasingly ugly and unpopular war in Southeast Asia. These developments undermined the government's support for peacekeeping as a worthwhile contribution to international peace and security and cast doubt on Canada's credibility as an impartial peacekeeper. Combined with growing opposition to Canada's close political and economic ties with the United States, they help account for the Trudeau government's reluctance to embrace the Pearsonian tradition of peacekeeping as a central part of Canada's UN policy.

When Egyptian president Nasser requested that UN forces leave the Sinai peninsula in 1967, UN secretary-general U Thant complied with the request. Pearson accepted that this was within Nasser's sovereign rights and that it had been part of the initial agreement to deploy UNEF in 1956. He did not, however agree with the principle: 'I objected to that arrangement at the time because I thought it might cause a lot of trouble in the future'.[6] It created a great deal of trouble. Even before UNEF withdrew, war broke out between Israel and its Arab neighbours. The war ended six days later and UNEF was still not dismantled. Its impotence was, however, clear for all to see. The Egyptian request to have UNEF withdrawn from its territory touched off a substantial debate between the Canadian delegation and the secretary-general on the question of who had authority over the operation. The Canadian view, as described by Martin, was that Egypt had the 'right to request the force's removal, but the request ought to have been submitted to the General Assembly'.[7] U Thant's position was that the force should be withdrawn if and when the Egyptians requested. U Thant was subjected to widespread criticism, but it was clear that UN forces were not equipped to withstand a concerted effort to displace them.

The Canadian contingent had never received the unequivocal support of the Egyptians; Nasser was skeptical of Canada's connections to the British and Americans. In addition, as Brian Urquhart points out, 'the Egyptian government was deeply provoked by bellicose Canadian statements insisting on UNEF's right to stay in Egypt, as if it was an occupation force'.[8] The Canadian position was further complicated by the government's involvement in and tacit support for a British and American proposal to establish a maritime force to protect Israeli shipping through the Strait of Tiran and the Gulf of Aqaba. With Canadian vessels already in place (albeit for the purpose of removing Canadian peacekeeping forces), Nasser no longer viewed Canada as a disinterested party. Urquhart recalls, 'When Egypt riposted by declaring that, because of these actions and statements, it could no longer assure the security of

Canadian soldiers in UNEF and demanded their withdrawal, the Canadian contingent was withdrawn in forty-eight hours, leaving UNEF with no logistic units or aircraft'.[9] The rapid Canadian withdrawal impaired the dismantlement of UNEF. It also tarnished Canada's impartiality toward the conflict. Martin acknowledges this when he writes that after the war, 'Nasser's hostility towards Canada made it very difficult for us to give a lead in any moves to seek a lasting settlement'.[10] Vietnam would prove to be even more problematic.

It is perhaps ironic that Canadian involvement in Vietnam, which occurred largely as a result of the Chinese view that Canada was the most impartial of the Western states, would—for some Canadians, at least—be viewed as an act of covert complicity in American imperialist activities in Southeast Asia. What began as a reluctant agreement to sit as the Western representative on a Cold War troika overseeing a set of peace accords to which no one fully ascribed ended in a bitter debate that not only affected bilateral relations, but also tarnished Canada's peacekeeping tradition.

Looking back over the 1960s, it is clear that Canadian policy makers viewed peace-keeping as an opportunity for the country to play an active role both in the UN and in the wider sphere of international politics. Peacekeeping was also favoured because it did not compromise Canada's alliance commitments; indeed, it could even be seen as part of the country's contribution to the alliance. The 1964 white paper on defence predicted—incorrectly, as things turned out—that peacekeeping in the Third World would be one way that Canada could support Western interests. Peacekeeping opera-tions had wide support among Canada's allies, especially the United States. The Americans often provided the necessary transportation facilities to get Canada's and other countries' peacekeeping forces in the field. At the same time, peacekeeping had become symbolic of an independent foreign policy, an activity that distinguished Canada from its Cold War allies. Not surprisingly, policy makers were anxious to call attention to this. Pearson suggested that in contributing to peacekeeping, Canada and other middle powers were able to play an independent and constructive role in the Cold War. The middle powers, Pearson said, 'are and will remain the backbone of the collective effort to keep the peace as long as there is fear and suspicion between the great power blocs. They have special responsibilities in this regard which they should be proud to exercise'.[11] The implication was that peacekeeping was a more progressive role for the Canadian military than holding down the front in Central Europe or searching the skies of North America for Soviet aircraft. Such a view has been influ-ential in that observers who were critical of other aspects of Canadian defence policy often registered strong support for Canadian participation in UN peacekeeping oper-ations. It does, however, tend to overlook the numerous occasions on which peace-keeping directly contributed to alliance interests. It was also a view that did not sit so easily after Vietnam.

Canada's experience as a member of the International Control Commission (ICC) has been the subject of considerable debate, with opinions ranging from this being another illustration of well-intentioned liberal internationalism to it being a case study of Canadian complicity with its capitalist mentor in perpetuating oppression and injustice in Southeast Asia.[12] That Vietnam even became as significant an issue as it did in Canadian foreign policy attests to the government's effectiveness in its past efforts to offer compromises in areas of Cold War politics, such as Korea, which had impressed Chou En Lai and led him to support Canada's involvement.[13] Participation was, however, complicated by the uncertain status of the Geneva Accords that ended French control over Vietnam. The Americans, for example, never agreed to them. There was as well no clearly designated authority to which the ICC was to be responsible. As a result of the problems this created, subsequent governments have always insisted that such an authority be established before Canadians would participate. Finally, the very nature of the group, representing as it did Western, Eastern, and non-aligned blocs (Canada, Poland, and India respectively) was a recipe for internal conflict and for difficult relations with allies.

As suggested earlier, UN multilateral peacekeeping operations had been favoured because they allowed opportunities for independent action without compromising alliance commitments. Such operations had also been deployed in areas where the superpowers did not want to get directly involved. Vietnam was of a different character entirely. The scope for independent action while adhering to alliance commitments was severely constrained. Canada was effectively isolated as the sole spokesperson for the Western bloc, or at least this is how the position was viewed in Ottawa. In addition, as in other areas, Canada was forced to weigh the costs of opposing American policies against the likely effectiveness of such opposition. Pearson made it clear that in his view, the costs were simply too great.[14] Moreover, the government's commitment to multilateralism and the need to keep the major powers involved meant that substantive principles would be sacrificed in order to maintain the process. Vietnam was the most blatant illustration of this, but it was not the only time the government had encountered such a dilemma. In the end, the absence of a viable multilateral presence in the ICC left Canada more directly exposed to the direct pressures and manipulations of American foreign policy. The end result was to jeopardize Canadian support for future peacekeeping initiatives.

Decolonization, the UN, and the Commonwealth

Among the problems confronting the UN during the early 1950s were the growing number of states anxious to become members and the Cold War conflict that prevented them from doing so. The root of the problem was China, about which more will be said later, but the ideological visors of the superpowers imposed a barrier to many other states as well. By 1955, there were more than a dozen states awaiting admission to the organization. The Security Council had not approved the admission of a new member since 1950. Applicants in close affiliation with the Soviets were defeated by the Western majority on the Council, while the Soviet veto denied entry to those states sponsored by the West. Despite repeated discussions during the early 1950s and the appointment of special committees to examine the problem, both sides remained implacable. The impasse threatened to render the UN's membership roll as poor a reflection of international realities as that of its predecessor, the League of

Nations, had been. In response, the Canadian delegation, with an able assist from its Soviet counterpart, broke the deadlock during the 10th session of the UN General Assembly in 1955.

The Canadian initiative was launched by Paul Martin, Sr. Martin, who was then serving as the minister of national health and welfare in the St Laurent government, had long held an interest in international organizations, and in the absence of Pearson, he headed the Canadian delegation to the 10th session. The Canadian government had never taken a firm position on the membership impasse. The government had considered universal membership desirable and had consistently resisted suggestions that the UN become an exclusive Western club. At the same time, there was a concern that the obligations of membership, as outlined in Article 4 of the UN Charter, be taken seriously. As John Holmes writes, 'While not accepting the view that any state, simply by reason of its existence, had a right to membership, Canada supported proposals "that tended towards the principal of universality"'.[15] At San Francisco, the Canadian delegation had also opposed, unsuccessfully, the use of the veto on membership applications. The concern that each applicant be considered on its respective merits had also made the government skeptical of package deals. An External Affairs document noted that 'in the past, certain states have attempted to trade in this matter of membership. . . . I need hardly say with what concern the Canadian delegation looks upon this type of dealing in the all-important matter of membership. It is not only deplorable, it should not be associated with the name of any present member of the United Nations in good standing'.[16] Such views became more difficult to hold when deserving states were excluded because of the Cold War. Beginning in the early 1950s, there were hints of support within External Affairs for package deal. By 1955, Martin concluded that a package deal was the only way to overcome the impasse. In launching the initiative, Martin was not only acting out of character with the practice of previous Canadian delegations, he was also presenting a direct challenge to Canada's principal allies.

Canadian support for the package deal provoked one of the more intense exchanges between American and Canadian representatives at the UN during a time when such exchanges were rather frequent. But the United States was not the only government affronted by the Canadian action. Both Britain and France were equally opposed to the Canadian proposal. These governments tended to view the membership issue less in East–West terms than in North–South ones. The real danger for France and Britain was that an influx of new members would intensify pressure for rapid decolonization. Britain eventually yielded and gave its support to the Canadian proposal largely as the result of Canada's successful lobbying of other Commonwealth members. If Canadians saw further decolonization as a potential outcome of their 'package deal', it was obviously a matter of little concern to Canada. In response to French complaints, Pearson said, 'Surely the UN was not formed to protect the Colonial powers'.[17] It was the Americans, however, who were most upset about the Canadian actions. In Washington, Dulles registered his opposition with the Canadian ambassador and complained that he had not been not informed. He had been. In New York, the United States's UN ambassador, Henry Cabot Lodge, scolded Martin for dealing with the Soviets and threatened retaliatory action against Canadian exports to the United States market. By this time, support for the Canadian proposal in the General Assembly was overwhelming and the American bluff was called.

The admission of 16 new members to the UN in 1955 stands as a prominent illustration of effective multilateral diplomacy on Canada's part during the height of Cold War animosities. The Canadian proposal encountered strong opposition from the United States. In response, the Canadian delegation was able to marshal the support of a wide collection of middle powers in the General Assembly, securing the co-sponsorship of 27 members. In securing the support of other Western middle powers and eventually winning British support through Commonwealth connections, Canada was able to isolate the Americans and force them to accept the package when it came before the Security Council. Unblocking the membership impasse led to the rapid expansion of the UNGA and to a fundamental change in the organization, its practices, and its priorities. For better or worse, the UN was at least a better reflection of global realities and no longer a sanctuary of Western privilege.

The issue of China's representation at the UN presents a radically different picture. On the Chinese membership issue during this period, American Cold War attitudes prevailed and successive Canadian governments reluctantly followed along. The admission of the PRC to the UN did not take place until 1971, more than 20 years after Mao Zedong came to power in October 1949. The primary reason for the delay was the opposition of the United States and the Americans' successful use of diplomatic pressure in the UN. Canada experienced that pressure on numerous occasions when successive governments broached the idea of admission only to retreat in the face of American opposition. It was not until 1970, when American concern over the issue of Chinese admission began to wane, that the Liberal government, led by Pierre Trudeau, proceeded to recognize the PRC.

In helping to break the UN membership impasse in 1955, Canada had fostered a dramatic change in the agenda of the UN. As the founding members lost interest, the newly independent states looked upon the UN as an important platform for conducting their international relations. One of the issues that most animated these states in the late 1950s and early 1960s was decolonization. A second issue was the racist policies of the South African government. On both issues, Canada found itself in uncomfortable and somewhat unfamiliar territory, as it was reluctant to push the UN into a more activist role in addressing these issues. Part of the explanation for this reluctance was a genuine concern for the capacity of the organization to handle the tasks. Part of it was also the government's unwillingness to abandon friendly allies or to upset other important multilateral connections, such as NATO. A further problem was the government's own discriminatory policies in such areas as immigration. In response to these policies, Canadian policy makers often kept their head low and their hands down. Abstentions became the order of the day when these issues appeared on the UN's agenda.

There were, however, some quarters where the issue could not be ignored and where the government, however reluctant, was forced to take a position. Such was the case on the matter of South Africa's membership in the Commonwealth. Having helped to free the Commonwealth from the remnants of British imperial policy and having encouraged its members to accept ethnic and political diversity by granting India continued membership after 1947, Canada and the other white dominions were forced to confront the racist policies of the South African government that were such an affront to the increasingly non-white majority. If the Commonwealth was to survive the dismantling of the British Empire in Africa, it would have to take a position on the apartheid issue.

South Africa raised many problems for Canadian policy makers at the UN, but it was within the context of the Commonwealth that the Canadian government under Diefenbaker made clear its opposition to South Africa's apartheid policy. In the UN, the Canadian delegation had been able to avoid taking a clear stand on South Africa by supporting further study of the organization's capacity to deal with the issue. For the most part, the delegation held firm to the position that as a domestic affair, apartheid was beyond the bounds of UN action, protected by Article 2 (7) of the UN Charter, which restricted the UN from intervening in the domestic affairs of member states. Pearson explained the Canadian position in the House of Commons:

> We drew a distinction between consideration in the form of discussion and consideration in the form of intervention. We felt . . . that the Assembly is now competent to discuss anything as the town meeting of the world, but that does not mean that the assembly is competent to interfere in the domestic affairs of member states by certain types of resolutions or by setting up committees or commissions to visit those countries and report and possibly take action at succeeding assemblies.[18]

This position allowed the government to avoid troubling questions not only about its foreign relations with South Africa and with such colonial powers as Portugal, but also about its own policies in such areas as immigration.

Canada's approach to the apartheid issue throughout the 1950s was in line with what would later be called 'constructive engagement'. Pressure should not be so great as to isolate the South African government; instead encouragements should be offered for a change in policy. This position became less and less tenable, however, when the South African government scoffed at proposals for change and political pressure mounted in the UNGA for some action on the issue.

The Diefenbaker government seemed inclined to continue with Liberal policies, but there were signs of change. On the domestic front, the Conservatives moved to eliminate the more overt racist elements of Canada's immigration policy. This change was encouraged by the growth of non-white members in the UN and, in turn, made it easier for the government to criticize the racist policies of other states. It was within the Commonwealth, however, that the government was forced to act. The Commonwealth had special significance for Diefenbaker, who, in addition to seeing it as a way of maintaining a link to Britain, viewed it as a means of offsetting American economic and political pressure. Initially, Diefenbaker was opposed to excluding South Africa from the Commonwealth. This policy remained unchanged after a massacre in Sharpeville in March 1961 brought waves of international condemnation down on the government in Pretoria. The Canadian government's sensitivities to its own domestic problems were, in part, responsible for Diefenbaker's view that 'Canada would not become involved in the direct criticism of the internal affairs of a fellow member state, particularly in multilateral consultations'.[19] Other developments were moving more quickly, however, as African members demanded action against South Africa.

The issue came to a head when South Africa decided to become a republic and reapplied for admission to the Commonwealth at the 1961 Heads of Government meeting. The first ministers required a new application instead of an automatic re-admission 'to prevent any misunderstanding by South Africa or the international community as a whole that the association condoned the Union's racial policy'.[20] This is somewhat surprising in that many of the ministers, Diefenbaker included, were reluctant to take the lead in keeping South Africa out. Nonetheless, it was Diefenbaker who proposed that racial equality be accepted as one of the guiding principles of the Commonwealth. In accepting this Canadian proposal, the Commonwealth was effec-tively erecting the barrier to continued South African participation for, as Verwoerd stated to his colleagues on his return to Pretoria, 'no country could honourably remain as a member unless it submitted itself to those principles. It would mean that South Africa would have to change its policy, and that we would not be prepared to do so'.[21] Perhaps unintentionally, Diefenbaker had moved the Commonwealth temporarily past the South Africa barrier. The issue would, however, continue to haunt the Commonwealth as it would the UN, and Canadian policy makers would return to play effective mediatory roles in the 1970s and 1980s.

Having successfully negotiated the transition to a racially mixed organization free from the taint of South Africa, the Commonwealth embarked on a process of insti-tutionalization during the mid-1960s that would give it a greater degree of perma-nence in the face of Britain's decline. In addition to its useful role as a forum for consultation at the UN, the Commonwealth became an important place in which to bridge the North–South gap. The African members of the Commonwealth, led by Kwame Nkrumah of Ghana, proposed the establishment of a permanent Secretariat for the association. The Secretariat was viewed as a way of both facilitating consulta-tion and providing ongoing support for Commonwealth activities in the areas of technical assistance and economic development. The Canadian government, while encouraged by the interest that new members displayed, was reluctant to endorse a proposal that, said Pearson, would create 'an organization of general scope or exten-sive activity'.[22] But the government eventually decided to support the proposal, and a Canadian, Arnold Smith, was appointed as the Commonwealth's first secretary general. The Secretariat confirmed the change that had taken place in the Commonwealth. It was no longer centred in Britain and British foreign policy;

instead it moved without a centre, but its agenda was determined largely by the concerns of the newest members.

As membership shifted, Britain found itself in a minority within the group. It was, for example, virtually isolated in its reaction to Commonwealth initiatives following the unilateral declaration of independence (UDI) by Ian Smith in Rhodesia in 1965. Effective interventions by Pearson in 1965 and again one year later prevented black African states from turning their back on the organization. The interventions did little to change British policy, nor did they have any influence on the Rhodesian question itself. They were successful in their prime objective, however, which was to save the Commonwealth for another day. It would not be the last time that Canadian prime ministers would play such a role.

Nineteen seventy marked the 25th anniversary of the United Nations. The Canadian government was invited to send its prime minister, Pierre Elliott Trudeau, to the General Assembly to lead off the debate on this historic occasion. Trudeau declined the invitation. Unlike every other post-war prime minister, Trudeau did not rush off to New York to make an appearance at the General Assembly. Instead he would wait nearly a decade after assuming the post of prime minister to make his first speech at the UNGA, on the occasion of the UN's Special Session on Disarmament in 1978. The absence of the Canadian prime minister at the UN's anniversary celebration reflected the new thinking that was guiding Canadian foreign policy with its greater emphasis on the national interest and its denigration of the country's mediatory middle power roles. As J.L. Granatstein and Robert Bothwell note, 'though the United Nations had its partisans in External Affairs and in the Canadian foreign-policy community, its reputation by the late 1960s was in something of an eclipse'.[23] Foreign policy was no longer to be directed primarily at supporting a stable international order at the expense of domestic concerns (as it had allegedly done in the past). Instead it would be devoted to serving the national interest. As the white paper stated, 'External activities should be directly related to national policies pursued within Canada, and serve the same objectives. . . . In essence, foreign policy is the product of the Government's progressive definition and pursuit of national aims and interests in the international environment. It is the extension abroad of national interests'.[24]

The Trudeau government's rejection of multilateralism as it had been pursued by previous governments was based on a view that multilateralism did not serve Canadian interests. The desire to be an active participant in post-war international politics, in Trudeau's view, had had the unfortunate effect of leading to a reactive foreign policy that rested more on aspirations of influence than on any actual benefits to Canada or others. In a favourable commentary on the new policy, Alan Gotlieb and Charles Dalfen wrote that 'the stress would be on national self-interest and the development of national goals which would reflect this self interest'. Foreign policy would now be better suited to giving primacy to those domestic interests that required action at the international level. The government could turn away from its previous commitment to multilateral discussions and to international acceptance of policy proposals and instead pursue unilateral methods for achieving or realizing foreign policy objectives. 'There has been a continuation of the earlier emphasis on international solutions', Gotlieb and Dalfen maintained, 'but with less reliance on the need to fall back on compromise solutions' and more reliance on 'the route of taking matters into its own hands and asserting national jurisdiction'.[25]

The changes recommended in the review did not result in a revolution in Canadian foreign policy. There were some policy areas in which the government displayed the interest, will, and capability to proceed unilaterally. Yet Trudeau's personal intervention in disputes in a number of venues, including the Commonwealth, the UN, and NATO, at various times throughout his tenure suggests that even his critical views of these associations could not obviate the need for or negate the utility of multilateral diplomacy. Multilateral diplomacy was Canada's principal means for influencing international politics, and it was used as frequently by Canadian officials during the 1970s and early 1980s as it had been in the past. In practice, even a skeptic like Trudeau could not resist the pressures that were often placed on Canada to play intermediary roles in international disputes. Canadian diplomats and politicians had acquired a reputation that was not easily abandoned. Subsequently, Trudeau's government came to rely on the extensive multilateral contacts that previous governments had established not only to foster a more stable global order, but to protect and enhance national interests. The apparent shift toward unilateralism and the need to protect national interest that many saw in the early Trudeau government had overstated the past neglect of these interests in pursuit of multilateralist objectives. Throughout the post-war period, policy makers identified a close correspondence between Canadian interests and contributions to world order.

Part of the explanation for the apparent change of heart lies in the problems that confronted international organizations during the 1970s and 1980s. For years, institutions such as the Commonwealth and the UN had relied on the support of Britain and the United States. Policy makers in these countries were not always in agreement with the substantive actions undertaken by these institutions, but they were nonetheless willing to pay the bills and to lend political and technical support when necessary. This began to change as these governments were subjected to repeated rhetorical attacks at international gatherings. Britain was frequently criticized by non-white African states over issues such as Zimbabwe and South Africa. As the Commonwealth grew in significance for these states, it declined in significance for Britain. A similar experience influenced American attitudes toward the UN, to the point where Daniel Moynihan, a one-time American ambassador to the organization, referred to it as 'a dangerous place'.[26] Americans, and especially the American Congress, took a more critical stand toward UN policies and budgetary practices during the 1970s and 1980s. This was particularly evident in some of the specialized agencies such as the United Nations Educational, Scientific and Cultural Organization (UNESCO), the Food and Agriculture Organization (FAO), and the International Labour Organization (ILO), where attacks on Western principles, policies, and allies (especially Israel) led to withdrawals of both financial support and formal participation by the United States.

The future viability of these institutions, which were critically important for the conduct of Canadian foreign policy, was being threatened, and Canadian officials took considerable pains to ensure that the institutions would survive and, it was hoped, prosper. In these circumstances, it was not possible for the government to abandon the international organizations that had served Canadian interests so well in the past. In areas such as the development of a Commonwealth policy on Zimbabwe and South Africa; UN peacekeeping operations in the Sinai, the Golan Heights, and Lebanon; arms control initiatives; and negotiations on the law of the sea, Canadian delegations made effective use of multilateral diplomacy to secure important foreign policy objectives. They also supported the institutions and, in this way, countered claims that the institutions were becoming irrelevant.

UNCLOS III

Canadian diplomacy during UNCLOS III (United Nations Convention on the Law of the Sea) is a good example of Canada's ability to serve the national interest through effective multilateral diplomacy while making a contribution to international order. The law of the sea treaty has been criticized for not establishing the basis for the redistribution of the wealth of the oceans and thereby violating the spirit of the principle first articulated by Malta's representative, Arvid Pardo, at the start of the negotiations that the oceans were to be the 'common heritage of mankind'.[27] Canada has been subjected to similar criticism for its pursuit of expanded territorial seas, greater control over the continental shelf, and protection of land-based mining interests. What is also noteworthy about Canada's participation in this UN conference, however, was Canada's effective use of multilateral diplomacy and its extensive use of new coalitions in doing so. Departing for the most part from its traditional post-war partnerships with fellow NATO allies, the Canadian delegation was instrumental in forming a number of coalitions around special interests, coalitions such as coastal states, states with wide continental shelves, land-based producers, and states with environmental concerns. As Clyde Sanger writes,

> Canada gained a reputation for helping launch a number of these groups, often at working lunches for delegates invited to the Canadian mission offices in New York or Geneva, and later handing on the leadership to other delegations. The main reason why Canada did this was because only a handful of developed countries—Norway and Iceland, in particular, Australia and New Zealand to a lesser extent—shared many of the Canadian objectives; and so new alliances were needed.[28]

The effectiveness of this coalition diplomacy allowed Canada to achieve most of its objectives at UNCLOS III and at the same time to help the entire process along to a successful conclusion.[29]

PEACEKEEPING RECONSIDERED

The limitations and failures of peacekeeping were largely responsible for the denigration of what was once viewed as one of the distinguishing features of Canadian defence policy and of Canada's participation in the UN. The shattering demise of UNEF I and the increasingly virulent anti-Americanism that had branded as complicitous Canada's participation on the ICC had the effect of tarnishing the country's peace-keeping tradition. UNEF I was slighted in the foreign policy review's pamphlet on the UN: 'The foreseeable prospects are not great that the UN will be asked to undertake major operations involving peacekeeping forces on a scale comparable to the UN Emergency Force in the Middle East or the UN operations in the Congo, and most certainly not without great power agreement in the Security Council'.[30] The government's more critical approach to peacekeeping was repeated and made more specific in the defence policy review paper that appeared in 1971, where peacekeeping was demoted to fourth in the listing of defence policy priorities.

As part of the defence policy review, the government also identified a number of criteria that would be used to assess the viability of peacekeeping operations; by implication, this set prerequisites for Canadian participation. The criteria, designed to deal with the likelihood of new peacekeeping operations in Vietnam, were met subsequently by the UN's first operation in nearly a decade. After the war in the Middle East in October 1973, a second peacekeeping force for the Sinai (UNEF II) was approved by the Security Council. Once again, the UN was returning to the Middle East to keep the combatants separated. On this occasion, peace came before another war, thanks largely to the initiative of Egyptian president Anwar Sadat and the summit diplomacy between Sadat, Israeli prime minister Menachem Begin, and American president Jimmy Carter at Camp David, where Israel and Egypt reached agreement on a comprehensive settlement of their differences. UNEF II marked the first successful peacekeeping venture, in that an effective peacemaking process complemented the work of the force.

The Canadian criteria for participation were designed to ensure a greater degree of political, technical, and financial support, and in many areas, UNEF II met the requirements. First, the force would have to have the full confidence and support of the Security Council and would be provided with precise terms of reference. This would not only ensure superpower agreement; it would also eliminate any subsequent concerns about the legitimacy of the force and would potentially ease financial problems. UNEF II was approved by the Security Council with only China abstaining. Authority for UNEF II was delegated to the under-secretary-general responsible for special political affairs, who worked in close co-operation with the Security Council. This provision had some effect on the financing issues, as the costs of the UNEF II operation were borne by all members out of the regular operating budget. There were some problems with China and the Soviets and the arrangement did not establish a firm precedent for future operations, but it was a step in the direction that the Canadian government clearly favoured.

Second, the force must have the full co-operation of all of the parties to the conflict. Given the memory of UNEF I, it is not surprising that an emphasis would be placed on this criterion. A third concern was that membership on the force be based on equitable geographical representation. In practice, and in the Cold War politics of the time, this also raised questions of equal bloc representation, which had direct implications for Canadian participation in UNEF II. The Canadian contribution had to be matched by one from Poland. A fourth consideration was that the force operate as an integrated and co-ordinated military unit.

UNEF II was one of three UN peacekeeping operations that were established in the Middle East after the 1973 war. A second force was deployed to the Golan Heights between Syria and Israel in 1974 (UNDOF) and a third was sent to southern Lebanon in 1978 (UNIFIL). The Golan Heights has remained a point of conflict between Israel and Syria, and despite some harassment from the Israelis, a Canadian commander once described the operation as 'the most successful UN operation ever'.[31] Most important, another war between the two disputants has been avoided thus far. The force in Lebanon has not been so fortunate; it was overrun by an Israeli invasion in 1982. It was powerless in the face of the Israeli action, underscoring once again the fragility of these operations.

Despite the Trudeau government's misgivings about these forces, however, Canadian support continued unabated during the 1970s, and Canadian troops participated in each of these operations. By the mid-1970s, there were more Canadians deployed on peacekeeping operations than there had been a decade earlier. For some observers, this was indication enough that little had changed in this area of Canadian foreign policy. Citing Sharp's active diplomacy in pursuit of a place on UNEF II, one correspondent argued that 'the Government wanted to be involved and I suspect public opinion would agree [it did], because it does give us a world role other than tagging along as a junior partner in the North Atlantic Treaty Organization. Despite the scepticism about being "helpful fixers" in the foreign policy review, the legacy of Lester Pearson is still felt'.[32] For others, the setting of conditions did indeed mark a new assertiveness in Canada's approach to peacekeeping. These conditions did not, however, suggest a radical change in the level of commitment.

The evidence from the 1970s indicates that the Canadian commitment to UN peacekeeping remained strong despite the setbacks of the 1960s and the recurring deadlock on the island of Cyprus. Even some of the problems remained the same. Within the UN, the Canadian delegation continued to press to have peacekeeping operations placed on a more stable base of political and financial support. On this subject there was little change from the mid-1960s. The Canadian position at a UN review of peacekeeping operations in 1978, as described by Robert Mitchell, 'stressed that peacekeeping was an essential function of the United Nations but was not in itself a substitute for the peaceful settlement of disputes; that peacekeeping costs should be borne by all United Nations members; and that practical measures as well as general guidelines were required to ensure the effectiveness of peacekeeping resolutions'.[33] Even a change in government in 1984 had little effect on Canadian policy in this area. Prior to presenting his green paper on foreign policy, the newly appointed external affairs minister, Joe Clark, made it clear that Canada had 'a proven track record of success in peacekeeping and I would think that if the conditions were right, that's a natural role for us'.[34] Clark and his successor, Barbara McDougall, would have more than ample opportunity to demonstrate the sincerity of this commitment.

MULTILATERALISM UNDER ATTACK

The effectiveness of multilateralism for the pursuit of Canadian foreign policy objectives has, in the past, been conditional upon an ability to get other states, principally the United States, involved in these multilateral regimes. If the Americans were at any time to reject this multilateral approach, as they did after the First World War, then Canada would still be confronted with unilateral American pressure for purely continental schemes and many of the issues that had been transformed to a multilateral forum would need to be dealt with on a bilateral basis. Moreover, multilateral regimes would not likely be as effective without American participation. In the early post-war period, the United States was a strong supporter of multilateralism. But beginning in the 1970s, it became one of the UN's principal antagonists in what developed into a sustained attack on the whole practice of multilateral co-operation and international law. As Sir Shridath Ramphal, the former secretary-general of the Commonwealth, wrote,

> The paradox—and the tragedy—of recent times [is] that even as the need for better management of relations between nations and for a multilateral approach to global problems has become more manifest, support for internationalism has weakened—eroded by some of the strongest nations whose position behooves them to be at its vanguard and who have in the past acknowledged that obligation of leadership. This is most true, of course, of the United States, whose recent behaviour has served actually to weaken the structures of multilateralism, including the United Nations itself.[35]

As a result, Canadian policy makers were caught between their long-standing commitment to the UN and multilateralism and their permanent interest in maintaining good relations with the United States.

The effects of American unilateralism reverberated throughout the UN and its Specialized Agencies in the 1970s and 1980s. The crisis was not the result of a single cause but was closely tied to shifting currents in American foreign policy and to developments at the UN. Although the United States was not solely responsible for the crisis, it was obvious that much of the problem flowed from the increasingly critical, and at times hostile, approach that the US government adopted toward international organizations in this period. American criticism resulted in part from the more antagonistic approach that many delegations took toward the United States in the mid-1970s at the UN on such issues as the new international economic order and the Middle East. Resolutions recognizing the PLO, granting it observer status at the UN, and branding Zionism as a form of racism increased American hostility toward the organization. In addition, there were concerns over the budgetary process, in which the majority decided and the minority paid. Finally, Americans took exception to the practices of the Specialized Agencies. The antipathy toward international co-operation that American policy displayed was far greater than had been evident in the past; as Pierre Hassner writes, 'Never has global multilateralism or functionalism, whether in relation to non-proliferation, the international monetary system, or the law of the sea been held in such low esteem'.[36] Many Americans were disconcerted by the perception that these institutions, which had long served American foreign policy objectives, no longer did so with as great as regularity as they had in the past. In response, the Americans eschewed multilateral co-operation, with its inevitable compromise, and increased their reliance on unilateral initiatives.[37]

The shift in American attitudes toward a greater reliance on unilateral actions in violation of international standards was evident in a number of areas, including the invasion of Grenada without consultation; the unilateral adoption of sanctions against the Soviet Union, first in response to the Soviet invasion of Afghanistan and subsequently as a result of the declaration of martial law in Poland; the covert mining of Nicaraguan harbours (without advising allies, whose ships were plying those waters); the forced landing of the Egyptian airliner carrying the kidnappers of the *Achille Lauro*; the bombing raid on Libya; the rejection of the Law of the Sea Treaty; the proclamation of the Strategic Defense Initiative (SDI) and subsequent declaration of its non-negotiability in arms control talks with the Soviets; the rejection of the jurisdiction of the International Court of Justice in the Nicaraguan harbour mining dispute; and the invocation of economic sanctions against Nicaragua. What made these actions significant was not only that the Americans acted unilaterally, but that they indicated a blatant disregard for the opinions of principal allies and for the network of international norms and institutions that the United States had helped to create in order to foster a more stable, secure, and predictable international environment.

The American antipathy to multilateralism created problems not only for strong supporters such as Canada, but also for the international community at large. These actions occurred at a time when the ever-expanding conditions of interdependence demanded the revitalization of co-operation between states rather than a withdrawal to the insularity of unilateral action. John Holmes writes:

> The danger is that American denigration of the United Nations has gone too far to be easily reversed. It has induced amongst the public not only hostility but, even worse, an inclination not to take the United Nations seriously, to disregard it as a factor in world politics. The United Nations could be scorned to death. United States withdrawal from UNESCO, its rejection of the authority of the International Court of Justice over Nicaragua's complaint, withholding of funds for programmes Congress dislikes, the rough assertion of the right to take offensive action in Grenada, Libya, and Nicaragua without seeking the agreement of any of the international organizations involved have undoubtedly undermined the faith in international action built up over centuries. Each action may have its own justification, but defiant unilateralism is cause for concern.[38]

The secretary-general, in his 1982 annual report, expressed concern that the world was 'perilously near to a new international anarchy'.[39] Three years later, he lamented that 'it is ironic that, as we enter a phase in history in which the practical necessity of co-operative internationalism is so patent, there should, in some quarters at least, be a retreat from it'.[40] The American action was symptomatic, in Urquhart's view, of a more prevalent development: 'There is an obvious trend in the opposite, back-to-the-hills direction . . . an anti-internationalism that finds expression in a strangely outmoded chauvinism, in sweeping contempt for international organizations'.[41]

The Canadian government's response to this crisis indicated a profoundly different approach to international organizations from that of the United States or Britain. From a Canadian vantage point, the crisis of multilateralism was in effect a crisis in Canadian foreign policy because of the country's investment in international institutions and because of the significance of multilateral negotiations in achieving foreign policy objectives. In response to the American government's denigration of the UN, international law, and multilateral co-operation, the Canadian government reasserted its own commitment and demonstrated leadership in the face of allied opposition. The problem, which became acute in the early 1980s, was addressed by the newly elected Conservative government of Brian Mulroney.

By the time the Conservatives came to power in 1984, the UN faced a number of internal problems, ranging from serious financial difficulties to ongoing concerns about its ability to respond to international crises through the Security Council and to move beyond the interminable rhetorical exchanges on impotent resolutions in the General Assembly. East–West relations were deteriorating and regional conflicts were intensifying, and the UN seemed incapable of meeting these challenges. While many began to condemn the organization, others, such as former under-secretary-general for political affairs Brian Urquhart, maintained that the UN provided the necessary machinery for dealing with these global problems but that member states lacked 'the will, the mutual confidence, or the vision to use it'.[42]

The decline in support for multilateralism posed a serious threat to Canada and to Canadian foreign policy makers. In the initial Speech from the Throne of the Mulroney government in 1984, the revitalization of multilateral institutions was identified as a major foreign policy priority. Years of neglect by the Trudeau government and the opposition of many of Canada's principal allies had undermined not only the institutions, but the whole process of multilateral co-operation. Most important, the United States—Canada's most important ally—had, under the Reagan administration, nearly abandoned multilateralism and had held up both the institutions and the practice of multilateral diplomacy to persistent ridicule. This created a particularly serious problem for the Mulroney government, which simultaneously sought to revitalize bilateral relations with the United States through high-level political contacts with the Reagan administration. For much of the post-war period, good Canadian–American relations could be pursued in conjunction with strong support for multilateral institutions. In the 1980s, that no longer seemed possible. Yet in its UN policy during the mid-1980s, the Mulroney government demonstrated that strong support for multilateralism could be combined with good bilateral relations.

The Mulroney government's initial review of foreign policy noted that recent developments have 'created a serious challenge to a principal vehicle of Canadian foreign policy, the world's multilateral agencies'.[43] Although the policy statement did not offer specific recommendations for the government to follow to deal with these challenges, there was an indication both in the throne speech of 1984 and in subsequent decisions taken by the government that it was prepared to undertake concerted actions to support these institutions. This approach also received a strong show of support from the parliamentary joint committee that had been established to conduct public hearings on the green paper.[44] The appointment of Stephen Lewis, a member of the New Democratic Party, as Canada's ambassador to the UN may have been a bipartisan coup for the Conservative prime minister. It also, however, provided Canada with an energetic, vocal, and articulate supporter of the UN. Mulroney's objective, and that of the Canadian government, was to bring the UN out of the crisis that confronted the organization in the early 1980s. The appointment of Lewis raised the profile of the organization at home and abroad, and with the government's support, Lewis launched a campaign to reform the UN from within and to generate support from the outside. He criticized American opponents of the UN, such as the Heritage Foundation, and worked with a group known as 'Friends of the UN' in an effort to reform the procedures and budget of the organization. Among the most significant accomplishments of this renewed involvement was Lewis's leadership during the UN's Special Session on Africa in 1985. Operating from the chair, Lewis was able to direct a consensual compromise agreement on the economic revival of Africa that met the demands of African states and of the market economies of the North. As Lewis remarked, the events at the Special Session 'simply confirm[ed] the importance of Canada's place in major international initiatives like this'.[45]

The problems confronting the UN and lending support to the lobbying efforts of American groups such as the Heritage Foundation were a result, in part, of the fragmentation of interests within the organization. Increasingly, the agenda of the UN, as well as its budget priorities, was being set by the majority of members, who were neither major powers nor the principal financial supporters of the organization. The United Nations does not have a large budget; its operating expenses are less than US$1 billion. Nevertheless, many of its expenditures result more from members' desire to support each others' pet projects than from a careful and considered assessment of the globe's, or even the organization's, priorities. When the voting majority pays only 20 per cent of the assessed budget and the largest contributors consistently oppose the majority's fiscal irresponsibility, there are bound to be differences of opinion about how the scarce funds should be spent. The financial crisis was further exacerbated by the unwillingness of some member states, such as the United States, to meet their full financial obligations to the UN. The Canadian government did not ignore these financial and administrative problems but argued that reform must take place by working within the organization and not by carping at it from the sidelines.

CONFRONTING SOUTH AFRICA

Southern Africa brought the Trudeau government firmly within the mediatory middle power traditions of Canadian foreign policy. The Commonwealth was the primary setting for such activities, but the issue of racial conflict in the region was also raised in the United Nations. Rhodesia and South Africa were perennial issues in both of these associations, and the Canadian government was forced to respond. This was especially true in the Commonwealth, where the racial policies of these governments threatened the very existence of the organization. Trudeau did not display much interest in the Commonwealth, but he came to view the biennial meetings of Heads of Government as a valuable opportunity for developing contacts with Third World leaders. Preserving this important forum required Trudeau to mediate the differences between Britain and other Commonwealth governments that were anxious to move rapidly and forcefully in ridding the African continent of white-minority rule. Trudeau's mediatory activities included both South Africa and Rhodesia/Zimbabwe during the 1970s. His successful diplomacy at the 1971 meeting in Singapore prevented the dispute between London and other Commonwealth governments over arms supplies to South Africa from destroying the association. In convening a meeting in Ottawa two years later, he not only closely identified his own political career with the organization, but also helped the organization overcome a possible British withdrawal by inviting Queen Elizabeth II to attend. As Granatstein and Bothwell note, Trudeau would remain an active Commonwealth supporter: 'Canada's compromising, facilitating role became familiar, ironically enough for someone who had been inclined to doubt the usefulness of being a helpful fixer'.[46]

The Trudeau government was not supportive of radical reform in Southern Africa. Canada's presence on the Security Council in 1977, however, landed it with the task of trying to find a Western solution to South Africa's colonialist policy toward Namibia. To this end, Canada joined a number of major powers (the United States, France, Britain, and West Germany) in the Western Contact group. This group had little success in bringing about rapid change, but in this area the Trudeau government showed little inclination to adopt unilateral measures. A change in policy would have to wait for a change in government.

The Mulroney government's commitment to a revitalized multilateralism was clearly evident in the Commonwealth, where Canada emerged as a potential rival to Britain for the leadership by assuming a forceful position against apartheid. Once again, the initiative in this area was made by Lewis at the UN, but it took on a much higher profile and had more significance within the Commonwealth. Many of the non-white members of the Commonwealth were becoming increasingly antagonized by the organization's failure to adopt a tougher policy in opposition to apartheid. Pressure from these states, as well as successive Canadian governments' constructive interventions on Commonwealth matters, particularly those involving South Africa, encouraged the government to respond to the growing racial violence in South Africa. The government's policy was based on a series of sanctions that would, in the words of the external affairs minister, Joe Clark, lead to 'full disruption of economic and diplomatic relations' if change was not forthcoming in South Africa.[47] The government initiated its sanctions policy unilaterally, but beginning in the latter part of 1985, it began to co-ordinate this policy with Commonwealth actions.

The Mulroney government's policy toward South Africa marked a dramatic departure from that of its predecessor. As part of the foreign policy review of 1970, the Trudeau government had acknowledged the contradiction between the pursuit of domestic economic growth through the maintenance of economic contacts with South Africa and the objective of social justice, which demanded the elimination of that government's apartheid policies. The foreign policy review sided clearly with the objective of economic growth and limited its opposition to apartheid to rhetorical condemnations. Even in 1977, when violence in South Africa increased, the government adopted only token sanctions that seemed designed more to appease domestic groups than to effect any real harm on the South African economy or government. As a member of the Security Council, the Canadian delegation went along with other Western states in favouring a negotiated settlement of South Africa's illegal control over Namibia, opposing demands for more forceful actions. Canadian policy during the Trudeau years was closely patterned on that of Canada's principal allies.

Not surprisingly, considerations of the most effective response to South Africa's policy of apartheid touched off very significant debates within the Commonwealth. During the early 1970s, Trudeau, despite his reticence about his own or his country's mediatory skills, nonetheless played the role of mediator in smoothing over differences between Britain and other Commonwealth members on the issue of arms sales to South Africa. Mulroney sought at first to play a similar role but quickly sacrificed this for a more assertive stand in favour of economic sanctions. For the most part, the Thatcher government in Britain found itself isolated on the issue. Many of the front-line states expressed their frustration with the British position by threatening to withdraw from the association. The Canadian government, eager both to avoid a Commonwealth breakdown and to bring effective diplomatic pressure to bear on the South African government, worked, along with the Australians, for a compromise that would essentially allow the British and front-line states to remain within the same association even as they differed profoundly on the best method for handling South Africa. In October 1985, the Heads of Government recommended that a Commonwealth Eminent Persons Group attempt to persuade the South African government to begin the reform process. If they were to fail, a first set of collective sanctions would be implemented. The compromise, according to Ian Cameron, 'was a typical Commonwealth compromise, an attempt to achieve unanimity at the cost of taking substantial action'.[48]

The failure of the Eminent Persons Group to influence the South African government led to a mini-summit of Commonwealth leaders in London in August 1986, at which time Mulroney and Margaret Thatcher argued vigorously about what action would be most effective. At the meeting, 'it was clear [Mulroney] would not serve as the conference's mediator' because the government had abandoned its neutral position and come down strongly in favour of sanctions; as Cameron says, 'Canada's strategy at the meeting would be to press for sanctions and use its influence with non-white members to keep the Commonwealth together'.[49] In this respect, the policy was successful despite the absence of unity; 'as in the case of Rhodesia in 1965 and 1966, the Commonwealth minus Britain had chosen Commonwealth credibility over Commonwealth unity'.[50] In an analysis of the Mulroney government's sanctions policy, Cameron identifies four ways in which the Commonwealth effected Canadian policy: 'First, the Commonwealth added leverage to Canadian policy; second, it helped distinguish Canada's position on South Africa from that of the United States; third, it invested Mulroney's policy with moral and political credibility; and fourth, the Commonwealth served as a veil for the government to hide from domestic opposition to its position'.[51] In linking its South Africa policy to the Commonwealth, the Mulroney government could resist some of the counterpressures that were coming from domestic groups and from competing multilateral associations, such as the Group of Seven. Maintaining the balance between these diverse multilateral connections would be a problem in this and other policy areas.

Conclusion

By the end of the 1960s, many Canadians had lost their enthusiasm for the UN and had become critical of the country's alleged 'middle power' role. Throughout the 1950s and 1960s, as we will see in the next two chapters, continental connections between Canada and the United States had been strengthened in both the military and economic spheres. By the early 1960s, many observers were expressing concerns about the waning influence of Canada in the world and the loss of an independent foreign policy in the face of American power and of the country's economic dependence. Critical commentaries on Canadian foreign policy had become commonplace by the late 1960s. Many of these critics complained of the government's slavish attitude toward American foreign policy interests and about the lack of distinctively Canadian approaches to the pressing issues of the day, most notably the Vietnam War. This critical climate supported the equally skeptical predilections of newly elected prime minister Trudeau in 1968, and the result was a major review of Canadian foreign policy. Rather than challenging the bilateral connections, however, the review appeared to mark a turning point in Canada's commitment to an internationalist foreign policy, as it cast aspersions on the legacy of Pearsonian internationalism and espoused a new direction in Canadian foreign policy, one that would more directly serve the country's national interest.

As presented here, Canadian policy at the UN and in the Commonwealth in the 1970s and 1980s illustrated the continuing significance of multilateralism for Canadian policy makers in the pursuit of foreign policy objectives. Its importance had not receded despite the harsh criticisms that were made as part of the Trudeau foreign policy review of 1968–70 and the more recent attacks on these organizations by some of Canada's principal allies. Instead of accepting the views of allies and going along with this retreat, the Mulroney government undertook policies to renew the pattern of multilateral co-operation in the international system. Trudeau had, in a somewhat more selective fashion and with less fanfare, followed a similar course. Prime Minister

Mulroney was voicing a common Canadian refrain in his 1985 address before the UN General Assembly: 'History shows the solitary pursuit of self-interest outside the framework of broader international cooperation is never enough to increase our freedom, safeguard our security, or improve our standard of living'.[52]

Chapter Five

The Limits of Multilateralism:
Canada's Responses to a Changing Global Economy

I believe that the Colombo Plan has lastingly changed Canadian life, has added to it a new and enduring colouring, a tincture, a dye that will not easily disappear, so that year after year external aid will continue to appear on the agenda of Parliament and volunteers will be setting out from Canada to teach—and to learn—in the countries of the developing world. —Douglas LePan, 1979

INTRODUCTION

The Bretton Woods system was designed to manage the post-war international economic order; it involved a series of compromises in demand, development, trade, and institutions.[1] But when the post-war debris settled, it became clear that the compromises reached in New Hampshire in 1944 could not meet the challenges that emerged in the post-war period. The first challenge, discussed in Chapter 2, was the profound capital shortage experienced by the economies of Western Europe. This rendered ineffective the International Monetary Fund's (IMF) objective of supporting stable and convertible currencies. It also demonstrated the weakness of the capital-starved World Bank and severely slowed progress toward a greater liberalization of international trade. Finally, it left the United States as the principal bulwark of what was supposed to have been a system of multilateral management. The Bretton Woods system became heavily dependent on American policy. In this chapter, we examine the evolution of Canada's multilateralist commitments in the emerging global political economy; Canadian policy makers, while maintaining consistent rhetorical support for multilateral institutions and practices, have at times resorted to unilateral and bilateral measures in an effort to meet specific national objectives.

The challenge arising from the impoverished and newly independent states of the Third World presented a more persistent challenge to Canada and the rest of the developed world than did Europe. The problem of economic development was not only exceedingly complex, it was also quite foreign to many Canadian policy makers. 'Most ministers and at least one very influential civil servant in the Finance Department', wrote A.F.W. Plumptre in a memoir, 'felt on familiar grounds when dealing with the Europeans, but hundreds of millions of Asians, diseased or starving or both, raised questions of a different type and seemed to involve amounts of a different magnitude that stretched interminably in to the future'.[2] Few officials had any direct contact with conditions in the Third World until Commonwealth meetings and other responsibilities brought Canadian officials into closer and more regular contact with conditions in these countries. These contacts had a profound influence on some policy makers. Before the end of the 1960s, two of the principal architects of Canada's post-war multilateralist foreign policy, Escott Reid and Lester Pearson, turned their attention and talents to the World Bank and its efforts to alleviate the sufferings of the world's poor.[3] In this chapter, we see that Canada's response to the needs of the newly independent countries was, in the first instance, influenced by its commitment to a multilateralist foreign policy. The government's involvement in institutions such as the United Nations, NATO, the Commonwealth, and the Organisation for Economic Co-operation and Development (OECD) provided both the initial incentive and the institutional base for the government's response. The particulars of Canada's response, however, reflected a mix of enlightened and more selfish interests.

In areas such as trade relations with developing countries and institutional reforms, Canada often appeared more sympathetic to Third World demands in speeches and statements than in practice. Canadian officials tended to be reluctant at best and resistant at worst when confronted with the demands for global economic reform. The emergence of a North–South debate on global economic reform and the salience of this debate in various international organizations tested not only Canada's commitment to alleviating global poverty, but also its support for multilateralism. Associations that had been designed to deal with matters of peace and security took on different priorities. Those that had been designed to handle economic and commercial relations were subjected to a sustained challenge from the forces of reform.

For the most part, multilateral considerations continued to dominate Canada's foreign economic policies during this period. From attempts to gain a say in development debates at the UN to successive rounds of tariff negotiations under the General Agreement on Tariffs and Trade (GATT), Canadians were active on a number of multilateral fronts. Generally, government policy continued to support the work and objectives of these multilateral associations. In spite of this, bilateral commercial relations continued to grow as more and more of Canadian trade that had formerly been with Europe was redirected to the United States. These continental connections were reinforced by sectoral trade agreements in defence products and automobiles, with the latter being most significant in strengthening Canada's dependence on the American economy. This steady growth in bilateral economic activity eventually raised concerns among some Canadians about the extent of American influence over the Canadian economy. These concerns emerged into a significant political movement by the end of the 1960s, a movement that shaped policy debates in the 1970s and led to a reassessment not only of bilateral economic relations, but also of the value of Canada's multilateral connections. Eventually, these concerns would lead to the decision to conclude the bilateral free trade agreement that had been set aside in 1948.

NEW STATES, NEW PRIORITIES

Many of the economically developing countries of the South were still colonies when the IMF, the World Bank, and the GATT were established. For these countries, the solutions reached at Bretton Woods reflected the interests of the leading capitalist powers. Issues related to the economic development of the world's impoverished majority were largely ignored at Bretton Woods. J.J. Deutsch, one of the Canadians at Bretton Woods, reflected in the late 1960s, 'there was one very important aspect which . . . we did not understand very well at the time of Bretton Woods. That was the position of the under-developed countries'.[4] Little time and effort was spent addressing what would, by the 1970s, become one of the main points of dispute in the global political economy.

There were some indications that the economic development of low-income countries would emerge as a matter of debate in the area of trade. The Havana Charter of the aborted International Trade Organization (ITO) devoted a full chapter to the concerns of developing economies in the global system. It included such items as a system of tariff preferences for Third World exports, provisions for commodity agreements, and exemptions from some of the liberal trade rules being considered. When the Havana Charter was replaced by the GATT, this chapter, of primary concern to the developing world, was dropped. The concerns remained, however, and as states throughout the Third World acquired independence, their demands for substantial reforms to the international trading order grew and over time became more difficult to ignore. As a result, the issue was forced back onto the GATT's agenda in the early 1960s and took centre stage at the inaugural meeting of the UN Conference on Trade and Development (UNCTAD) in 1964.

Trade was not the only concern of these new states. There were also persistent demands for greater capital transfers from the developed world to the developing economies of the South. Most of these were articulated in the United Nations, but their effects were felt in the Commonwealth, the OECD, and the World Bank. Third World demands also encompassed institutional reform. As early as 1950, Third World governments asked for changes in the Bretton Woods institutions and called for an expanded role for the UN in the development field. Working through the UN General Assembly (UNGA), where Third World members had acquired a majority by the early 1960s, these states rearranged the priorities of the UN. By the early 1970s, the organization had become the principal forum for debates on the establishment of a new international economic order.

It was the inability of the Bretton Woods institutions to meet the pressing needs of the developing economies that led Third World governments to turn to the UN. This inability resulted from both procedural and substantive problems. The Bretton Woods institutions were designed so that the wealthiest states held firm control over decision making. Both the World Bank and the IMF awarded voting shares on the basis of a country's contribution to the organizations' respective funds. Negotiations under the GATT are also strongly biased in favour of the largest traders, in part as a result of the principal suppliers rule.[5] These organizations thus provided little real opportunity for Third World influence. In addition, some analysts—such as Raul Prebisch, who would become the first secretary of UNCTAD—maintained that Bretton Woods, with its strong bias in favour of the interests of the leading capitalist powers, was part of the Third World's problems rather than a potential solution. An alternative solution favoured a structural reform of these institutions to increase the decision-making power of Third World governments and, in turn, to make the institutions more effective in reducing the inequalities that existed between the North and the South. Other proposals advocated replacing these institutions with new ones. As one author has noted, 'the primary concern [of Third World governments] has not been organizational neatness or financial responsibility, but immediate results. If traditional UN bodies were inadequate to meet their needs, new ones had to be created in which they would have greater control'.[6] Unlike the IMF, the World Bank, or even the GATT, the UN General Assembly operated on the principle of one state, one vote. The UN provided a semblance of equality that did not exist in these other organizations or in the global economy; it became the focus of Third World diplomacy because it was the only institution that provided economically weaker states with an opportunity to assert some influence over the economic policy agenda of the advanced capitalist economies.

The origins of what would develop into a sustained, often acrimonious, and ultimately futile debate on a new international economic order are to be found in the UNGA in the early 1950s. Edward Mason and Robert Asher, in their history of the World Bank, write:

> From 1950 until at least 1960, 'financing economic development' was the most passionately debated economic issue in the United Nations. The less developed countries, led primarily by Chile, India, and Yugoslavia, showed extraordinary ingenuity in keeping the issue alive and inching forward toward their goal. Their campaign splashed over from United Nations channels into other channels and back again, creating waves and ripples in Washington; in European, Asian and Latin American capitals; in World Bank circles; and among special commissions and committees, national and international. The developed countries, led by an increasingly isolated United States, at first opposed, then postponed, and eventually deflected the campaign.[7]

The campaign from the South generated substantial debate and some action, but it provided little relief from the abject poverty that affected the people in the region.

Two general sets of demands were presented by the developing countries: one was to increase the flow of capital from the developed North to the poorer South; the other was to reform the international trading system to take greater account of the structural inequalities that were seen in the South as a major barrier to their future economic development. On the matter of capital transfers, Third World governments noted the substantially higher levels of assistance flowing into Western Europe for reconstruction and military security and the limited funds available to the World Bank, which was the primary source of financial assistance available for development financing. Alternative proposals favoured expanded government assistance programs and a more active role for the UNGA in the development field. These proposals included a series of specific initiatives, starting with an Economic Development Administration, proceeding to an International Development Authority, and ending in 1957 with a Special Fund for Economic Development (SUNFED). Each of these proposals was designed to provide either grants or soft loans (loans at low rates of interest with long-term repayment schedules) to low-income countries. The proposals were viewed as necessary because of the inadequacy of the World Bank both in terms of its available capital and because of its market-driven lending practices. As a commercial bank, the World Bank could not stray far from standard commercial practices. From its establishment in 1944 until 1955, the Bank provided only US$1.8 billion to the low-income countries. This was grossly inadequate for development purposes and in sharp contrast to the more than US$17 billion that had been sent to Europe under the Marshall Plan between 1948 and 1952. A chronic shortage of capital was widely seen as one of the principal causes of Third World underdevelopment, and arrangements for capital financing under the auspices of these proposed UN programs were designed to rectify this problem.

These proposals for extending the authority of the UNGA and establishing new Specialized Agencies to distribute economic and technical assistance met with the firm opposition of Canada and other industrialized countries, including the United States. 'The Canadian government', reported F.H. Soward and Edgar McInnis, 'has . . . been distinctly cautious to date in its attitude toward the various schemes for accelerating capital development in the underdeveloped countries by grants and long-term low interest loans that have been advocated by delegates from those countries at United Nations meetings'.[8] The American government, for its part, strongly favoured more private investment, supported by the limited funds and conservative practices of the World Bank, and rejected an expanded UN role. The general character, if not the specifics, of the responses of some Western governments, including Canada, tended to be set by the United States. Soward and McInnis note that unlike that of other Western European middle powers such as Denmark, the Netherlands, and Norway, the 'Canadian attitude has paralleled that of the United States and the other advanced industrial countries'.[9] In the opinion of Canadian delegates, little new money could be made available until other concerns were addressed. Most important among these was Western security. In the view of Canadian officials and their American counterparts, increased defence spending, ignited by the Korean War, was the major competitor for development funds and drew first priority. The prevailing view was that 'nations which want to assist in the development of the less fortunate countries often find that for their own security they must limit that assistance in accordance with the burden of national defence which they must also bear'.[10] The persistent pressure from the low-income countries, however, made it clear that the issue would not go away.

Despite the opposition of Western governments to many of their proposals, Third World governments were able to use their majority in the UN to force through some development programs. In 1951, the UN began an operational program of technical assistance for development objectives through the Expanded Program of Technical Assistance (EPTA). A significant objective for the developing countries was to put in place a special UN fund for economic development (SUNFED). In 1957, the Economic and Social Council (ECOSOC) recommended that the General Assembly establish a SUNFED. The recommendation was opposed by Canada, Britain, and the United

States. In response to the recommendation, and to avoid being isolated in an antici-pated UNGA debate on the proposal, the Americans recommended an alternative. In place of and 'to offset the urge for SUNFED',[11] a Special Fund was established in 1958 that would facilitate private capital investment in development projects. The Special Fund and the EPTA would later be merged into the UN Development Program in 1966. These arrangements gave the UN a direct operational role in funding development programs and it emerged as a potential rival to the World Bank in this area. The finan-cial support of the developed market economies for these UN programs during the 1950s was modest at best, though, and was closely tied to the contributions of the United States. The small scale of contributions is reflected in the fact that in 1954, Canada ranked third among the donors to UN development programs despite a contribution of only CAN$1.5 million.

Largely in response to proposals in the UNGA to establish a special development fund, the World Bank, on the instigation of the United States, established the International Financial Corporation in 1956 and the International Development Agency (IDA) in 1960. In a history of the Bank, the authors identify the IDA 'as living proof that the "international power structure" is responsive to persistent peaceful pressure'. They add that 'the IDA confirms one's faith in the ability of bureaucracies to remain afloat, to unfurl fresh sails, and to benefit from prevailing winds'.[12] The self-congratulatory tone cannot hide the fact that the IDA was clearly designed to prevent similar agencies from developing in the UN, where they would lie beyond the control of the voting power of the wealthy states that prevailed at the Bank in Washington. Nonetheless, the IDA did reflect a change in the Bank's approach to lending. The mandate of the IDA was 'to finance the same type of projects as does the Bank, selected according to the same standards, but on terms that place a lighter burden on the balance of payments of the borrowing country. Unlike the Bank itself, the IDA could not rely on the sale of commercial bonds to maintain its capital base. Instead it would require periodic replenishments from contributing governments if it was going to be able to respond to the needs of developing countries'.[13] The initial capitalization of the Agency was US$1 billion, an amount that many observers saw as too small. Since then, 'demand has always exceeded supply, and IDA has been unable to escape the rationing problem'.[14]

Moreover, like the IDA, its parent provided funds on loan. As Mason and Asher note, 'spokesmen from high-income countries such as the United Kingdom, France, Canada and the Netherlands argued as eloquently as did spokesmen from the low-income countries that the IDA should have the authority to make grants. But the United States, intensely aware of the congressional preference for loans no matter how soft, disagreed'.[15] The IDA was, as a result, at best a partial response to the demands of the developing countries for concessional financing of development projects.

TRADE AND DEVELOPMENT

An even more contentious area of debate emerged when Third World states, acting through a coalition known as the Group of 77, pressed for negotiations to reform the international trading order. These demands emerged in response to a widespread view in the South that the GATT had failed to address the principal concerns of Third World traders and was in fact allowing, if not encouraging, widespread discrimination against Third World exporters. The Group of 77, which could trace its origins to the Non-Aligned Movement launched in Bandung in 1955, became the voice of the Third World in these global economic negotiations. They also gained support from the Soviet bloc. Despite the initial resistance of the developed market economies, including Canada, on the grounds that the GATT was the proper forum for dealing with trade issues and disputes, the UN General Assembly finally responded to these demands by convening the UN Conference on Trade and Development (UNCTAD).

The first UNCTAD was held in Geneva in 1964, and the Group of 77 used the opportunity to present a number of proposals for the reform of international trade. Among the proposals was one for the creation of a generalized system of preferences in the markets of the developed countries for the manufactures and semi-manufactures exported from Third World economies. The Group of 77 recommended that exports of primary products be stimulated and prices stabilized through a series of commodity agreements and an international financing scheme to compensate Third World governments experiencing fluctuations in foreign exchange receipts. There were also demands that UNCTAD be established as a formal institution of the General Assembly with a permanent secretariat. Only on this last demand did the Group receive enough support to proceed. Since 1964, UNCTAD has met at four-year intervals. Subsequent meetings involved detailed negotiations on the demands presented at the initial conference. Despite the lack of progress in implementing these recommendations, UNCTAD succeeded in keeping rather constant pressure on the Western states to respond to the concerns of developing countries.

Although the Group of 77 failed to win much support at UNCTAD, there were some signs of movement within the GATT in the late 1950s and early 1960s. In 1958, the GATT Contracting Parties established a panel of experts that examined, among other items, the place of developing countries in the world trading system. The Haberler Report, named after the panel's chair, Gottfried Haberler, released in 1958, 'did not find any general tendency towards discrimination, per se, but it did identify many factors, including trade barriers' that impeded the export earnings of the developing countries.[16] Among other matters, the report emphasized the need for co-operative action between the developed and developing economies:

> The underdeveloped primary-producing countries have an interest in obtaining from the highly industrialized countries aid and easier access to markets for their exports. The highly industrialized countries have an interest in the effects upon trade of these economic development policies of the underdeveloped primary-producing countries. The only chance of a successful outcome is a negotiated settlement involving a gradual shift away from the undesirable policies on both sides.[17]

The Haberler Report was a catalyst within the GATT in that it led, in Gilbert Winham's words, to the 'creation of a committee charged with the responsibility for trade policy

affecting developing countries'.[18] As a follow-up, and in response to the greater participation of the lesser developed economies in the GATT and to the threat of a rival organization in the UNCTAD, the Contracting Parties agreed in 1965 to a series of amend-
ments to the original agreement that dealt with trade and development. Part IV of the
GATT was added; it allows for (but does not require) three exceptions to the general
principles of the agreement: first, it calls on the Contracting Parties to refrain from
raising trade barriers against Third World exporters; second, it allows for the use of
preferential tariff schemes to be granted exclusively to Third World countries; and
third, it allows for the establishment of commodity arrangements. These changes did
not involve any firm commitments on the part of GATT members, many of which,
including Canada, were very slow in responding to the invitation offered by Part IV.
For example, Canada did not implement a system of preferences for Third World
exports until the 1970s and then did so only in a limited fashion. Furthermore, there
were few signs during the 1960s that there would be other changes in the GATT to meet
the aspirations of the developing economies. Despite substantial reductions in tariff
barriers to trade among OECD members as part of the Kennedy Round negotiations
(discussed later in this chapter), there was no significant reduction in the barriers to
trade affecting Third World producers. For some, the results of the round confirmed
Prebisch's view that the GATT continued to operate primarily to the benefit of the
developed market economies.[19]

Despite their growing political strength and persistent pressure, the Group of 77
had received few tangible benefits by the end of the 1960s. The developed countries
remained firm in their commitment to the Bretton Woods institutions and were
unwilling to consider alternatives. Nonetheless, the newly independent countries were
successful in presenting a formidable ideological challenge to the orthodox views
embedded in Bretton Woods. They were also successful in forcing some governments,
including Canada, to make some overtures, however limited, to the pressing needs of
the world's poor.

THE CANADIAN RESPONSE

The Canadian government's first sustained exposure to the problems of global
poverty came at a meeting of Commonwealth ministers in Colombo, Ceylon (now Sri
Lanka), in January 1950. Canadian policy was at this time concentrated on the
Western effort to reconstruct Europe and to shore up the economies of fellow NATO
members, but the Colombo meeting brought about a significant reorientation in
Canadian foreign policy. The Colombo Plan for Co-operative Economic
Development in Asia and the Pacific was initiated by and for the Commonwealth
countries of Australia, New Zealand, Great Britain, Canada, India, Pakistan, and
Ceylon. The Plan was a development assistance program with specific projects
arranged bilaterally. It was later joined by other countries, including the United States.
Canada's initial contribution was CAN$25 million. The decision to support the
Colombo Plan was the government's first major undertaking in the area of economic
development in the Third World. More important, it encouraged policy makers to

shift their attention to the problems of economic development in the Third World. For a number of years, the shift was not matched by a corresponding shift in funds. Through much of the 1950s, NATO members continued to receive the largest percentage of Canadian foreign assistance. This can be explained by the government's overriding interest in supporting collective defence in Europe and in responding to demands for increased defence spending from allies. When a significant competition between aid to NATO and aid to the Third World emerged during much of the 1950s and 1960s, NATO prevailed. The debate illustrated the competing demands that Canada's multiple multilateral connections were making on policy makers.

Launched with the Colombo Plan in 1950, Ottawa's foreign assistance program expanded slowly during the 1950s. In this respect, Canada was largely in line with other Western states. This slow expansion also closely reflected Canada's multilateral connections in the Commonwealth and NATO. Western attitudes to development assistance, including those of Canadian political leaders, began to change as concerns increased over the possible spread of communism to Third World countries. These fears increased significantly after Mao Zedong's successful revolution in China in 1949 and were very much in mind when Commonwealth leaders gathered in Colombo. In Lester Pearson's view, the fear of communism inspired the Colombo Plan:

> It seemed to all of us at the conference that if the tide of totalitarian expansion should flow over this general area, not only will the new nations lose the national independence which they have secured so recently, but the forces of the free world will have been driven off all but a relatively small bit of the great Eurasian land mass. . . . If southeast Asia and south Asia are not to be conquered by communism, we of the free democratic world . . . must demonstrate that it is we and not the Russians who stand for national liberation and economic and social progress.[20]

During this period, defence spending and foreign assistance disbursements were frequently compared as if they were different aspects of the country's overall security policy. In a candid commentary on the origins of Canadian aid to the South, Pearson once remarked that

> in order to test our real motives we should ask ourselves from time to time whether we would be doing what we are if the political and military menace of Soviet and Chinese communism did not exist. . . . It is a sorry commentary on the postwar period that without them and the threat which they represent we might not so readily have done what we should have been doing anyway.[21]

If the motives and the means were similar to those applied to Western Europe, the financial contributions were meagre in comparison. Canada's NATO connections may have necessitated some involvement in foreign assistance programs for the Third World (there was, for example, some pressure from the Americans to increase burden-sharing among the allies in this area), but it was clear that the government did not give such programs a high priority. In a critique of the Canadian government's policies, Hugh Keenleyside, then a UN official, lamented that 'as far as Canada is concerned, the present division of approximately $100 for direct defence and $1 for technical and economic aid to the fermenting and revolutionary areas of the world is about right'.[22]

There were, in addition to NATO, other multilateral connections of significance, most notably the Commonwealth. Commonwealth obligations were an important consideration in the St Laurent government's decision to agree to the Colombo Plan in 1950. Keith Spicer has noted that between 1950 and 1965, 'some 90 per cent of Canadian bilateral aid ha[d] gone to Commonwealth countries' and further that 'all Canadian parties have supported this emphasis, which is constantly defined in ministerial statements as deliberate and radical'.[23] When Commonwealth states acquired independence in Africa and the Caribbean and special programs were established for the countries in these regions (the Commonwealth Africa Aid Program and the Commonwealth Caribbean Assistance Program), Canada made commitments to participate in these programs. The effect was to spread the actual dollar disbursements more widely and more thinly than considerations of economic efficiency or political influence might warrant. The problems that resulted from dispersing aid so widely were further exacerbated in the 1960s when the government, in an acknowledgement of the country's bicultural heritage, began distributing aid to the former colonies of France.

The influence of Canada's multilateral connections on its development assistance programs are most evident in the timing and distribution of aid. Increasingly, however, the OECD, discussed later in this chapter, became a source of multilateral pressure for the level of foreign assistance. The Development Assistance Committee (DAC) of the OECD has been an important source of information on and accountability in assessing the size and character of members' foreign aid programs. Spicer, in his history of Canadian aid policy, writes that the 'DAC's confidential efforts to raise national levels of aid are noted for their persistence and frankness, both of which qualities have been used amply to coax improvements in Canada's volume of aid'.[24] The DAC was established to encourage a greater degree of 'burden sharing' among the member countries. At this time, it should be recalled, aid was seen as an important part of the Western struggle against communism. Whatever the initial motives behind the decision to establish the DAC, it obviously became an important forum for discussing and, most important, assessing the aid performance of member governments. Indeed, Spicer referred to it as 'undoubtedly the central and decisive organ of Western aid co-ordination' and to its annual report as 'usually one of the most instructive and realistic documents available on current aid'.[25] It is apparent that a good deal of Canada's foreign assistance programs has been influenced by an interest in maintaining good multilateral connections. It is also evident, however, that more narrowly defined national interests determined the precise character of the aid given.

The importance of multilateral considerations in convincing the government to undertake an aid program did not extend to Canadian support for giving the UN a greater role in the area of economic development. Canadian support for UN activities was instead tempered by a number of considerations, including an interest in keeping the UN from becoming over-bureaucratized and in protecting the primacy of the Bretton Woods institutions. In contrast with their general willingness to expand the scope and strengthen the capacity of the UN in other areas during this period, Canadian officials were hesitant in their support of proposals to expand the UN's development role. The response to the various proposals for reforms that would expand the role of the UN in international economic affairs, like that of many other developed market economies, ranged from indifference to fierce opposition. In this, the Canadians were in agreement with their closest allies. Soward and McInnis, in their review of activities in the UN in this area, noted that 'the Canadian attitude has mirrored that of the United States and other advanced industrial countries'.[26] This collusion was itself a reflection of the prevailing influence of Canada's other multilateral commitments, was apparent in a number of policy areas, and persisted over time.

Confronting the Third World

The 1970s and 1980s witnessed the rise and collapse of the North–South dialogue in international politics. Canada was an active participant throughout, but its record is clearly a mixed one. Jack Granatstein and Robert Bothwell, in their review of Trudeau's foreign policy, conclude that 'the balance is . . . ever so slightly favourable'; they argue that more aid went South during this period and that the government 'had maintained an attitude of engagement with the UN majority, and it had employed as best it could the techniques of diplomacy, with occasionally beneficial results'.[27] There were, however, clear limits to how far Canada was willing to go in reforming its own policies and in supporting reform in global institutions. There were also limits to how much influence the government and its prime minister could exert in the cause of a new international economic order. Despite these limitations, Canadian policy continued to reflect an overwhelming concern with the process of multilateral consultation and with maintaining an active role for international institutions, and especially the UN, in this ongoing dialogue.

During the 1970s, the developing countries of the South launched a major campaign to reform the international economic order. Inspired in part by the apparent success of the oil cartel OPEC and fed by a common feeling that the Bretton Woods system had little to offer them, members of the Group of 77 pressed through UNCTAD and the UN for a New International Economic Order (NIEO). Negotiations over the NIEO dominated interactions between the Northern industrialized countries and the developing economies of the Southern hemisphere until they ended in failure seven frustrating years later. Canadian officials took an active role in these negotiations and attempted to facilitate the negotiating process both inside and outside the UN. Such efforts were influenced by the personal, if sporadic, interest of Prime Minister Trudeau. Yet despite the prime minister's interest and attempted leadership, Canadian policy reflected a primary concern with process over substance. There was always an eagerness for negotiations, but there was little enthusiasm for policies that would push the NIEO beyond the talking stage and little willingness to challenge the position of leading members of the OECD—let alone that of domestic constituents at home.

The negotiations on the NIEO focused on three sets of issues. First, the developing countries demanded greater national control over economic development, including the right to nationalization of and control over resources. Second, they pressed for increased flows of resources from the North to the South through higher levels of aid, through trade provisions that would extend preferences without reciprocity, and through commodity programs that would both stabilize and index commodity prices. Finally, the Group of 77 advocated institutional reform that would give their members a greater voice in the deliberations of bodies such as the IMF and the World Bank. These concerns received full expression at a Special Session of the UN General Assembly in 1974, where they were included in a final document that was approved by a Third World majority despite the opposition of the leading members of the OECD, including Canada. The acrimonious nature of much of the debate was a foretaste of the opposition that was to develop within the OECD to the demands of the Group of 77. Nonetheless, the experience of the oil embargo of 1973 had convinced many Western political leaders that it was better to engage in negotiations on commodities than to run the risk of additional embargoes and future threats to their access to the resources of the South.

Negotiations on commodities were long, arduous, and eventually unsuccessful. They ended with agreement on a Common Fund that had been so emasculated as to prove ineffectual in supporting stable commodity prices. The negotiations are interesting, however, as an indication of Canada's commitment to the negotiating process and of its limited interest in policies of reform. These negotiations also served as one of the early tests of the implications of Canada's new-found status as one of the members of the annual economic summits.

Canada's economic policies toward the Third World have never been exemplary. The country has had an active aid program, and for a short time during the late 1960s and early 1970s, development assistance received the strong support of the Trudeau government. Aid began to increase as a percentage of the GNP, and Canada began to move to a level of support that was comparable with that of the OECD's leading aid givers, the middle powers of Northern and Western Europe. These contributions were partially offset by a high percentage of this aid being tied to the purchase of Canadian goods and services. During the 1970s, the percentage of Canadian aid directed through multilateral channels did increase, and between 'the period 1964/65–1973/74, two-thirds of Canada's multilateral-assistance funds went to the International Development Association and the United Nations Development Program'.[28] Some, however, have questioned the effectiveness of these aid programs.[29]

The development potential of the aid program was undermined by a trade policy that discriminated against Third World producers. Canada had not established an extensive trading relationship with Third World economies. Of all the members of the

OECD, Canada has the smallest trading relationship with developing countries: 'The relative share of developing countries in Canada's trade is considerably lower (about 9 per cent of exports and 12 per cent of imports between 1973–83) than their corresponding share in the trade of other major industrial countries—less than half the average for OECD countries as a whole'.[30] There also tended to be a concentration of trade with OPEC, Latin America, and the newly industrialized countries of Asia. Part of the explanation for this limited trading relationship was the entrenched bilateral trade between Canada and the United States that resulted from foreign investment, cultural similarities, history, and geographical access. Part may also be explained by Canada's lack of an imperial history. Finally, part of this trading picture can be understood as the result of discrimination.

Although it sought to maintain a good profile on aid, the government had been among the most discriminatory members of the OECD in the trade area. This was especially pronounced in areas such as textiles, shoes, and clothing, where potent domestic lobbies, many within the politically sensitive province of Quebec, had been successful in pressuring the government to retain protectionist barriers against Third World producers. This had at best a limited effect on employment in these sectors, and Jaleel Ahmad argues that 'the general lack of any strong pressures against the use of discriminatory protection against developing countries seems to have been more important than any disproportionate strength of lobbying for it' in accounting for Canadian practices.[31] As a result, while aid levels and the rhetorical support of Prime Minister Trudeau indicated a strong commitment to the position of Third World reformers, specific policies suggested more conformity with some of the more hardline members of the OECD. Ahmad observes that Canadian practices in many areas during the late 1970s were evidence of 'a hardening of Canada's trade policies toward the developing countries, which were not very generous to begin with. They are incongruent not only with Canada's long standing commitment to multilateralism in trade and tariffs but also with its general rhetorical support for North–South initiatives'.[32] This was evident in Canada's use of voluntary export restraints, which targeted particular countries, as opposed to global quotas under the Multifibre Agreement (MFA). It was also apparent in the government's approach to the commodities negotiations and to the attempt on the part of Norway and the Netherlands to establish a middle power coalition in support of the NIEO.

As a follow-up to UNCTAD IV in 1976, officials from the Netherlands and Norway instigated a series of meetings among middle power members of the OECD. The objective was to secure a strong base of support within the OECD for economic reforms that would go some way in responding to the demands of the Group of 77. In turn, this group of states might be able to exercise some influence over the more reform-resistant members of the OECD, such as the United States, Germany, and Britain. In establishing the Like-Minded Group, an effort was made to identify those members of the OECD who might be supportive of such reforms. Based in part on its high aid levels of the mid-1970s, Canada was included in the group and became a regular, if less than eager, participant. As an observer of this forum has remarked, 'In the main, the Like-Minded Group served as an informal caucus for a cluster of middle and small industrial powers which were anxious that some progress be achieved in the global North–South negotiations then in train'.[33] Canada was clearly supportive of ongoing dialogue, but there is little indication that it was prepared to accept substantial policy reforms that would challenge the accepted wisdom of the leading members of the OECD. As a result, the Like-Minded Group was unable to move beyond informal discussions of proposals that, while acknowledged, never received the full support of the members of the Group. The failure of the Like-Minded group cannot be explained only by the resistance of the hard-liners within the OECD; it must also be explained by the failure of the Group members, including Canada, to support the reformist proposals being offered by the main instigators within the Group—Norway, the Netherlands, and Sweden. Canada's support for the Group was clearly limited; A. Lovbraek observes that 'in several cases, and especially in the important case of Canada, member-states in the Like-Minded Group totally ignored what had been advocated in the group's discussions when forming their policies in the Common Fund'.[34] Indeed, the government seemed to be more protectionist than other members of the OECD; Vinod Aggarwal points out that 'Canada, while first dropping many of its old quantitative restraints and replacing them with bilateral agreements, invoked Article 19 on a number of goods to restrain imports into its market. This created a major uproar since such actions were not to be used until all MFA remedies had been exhausted'.[35] Aid contributions also began falling behind the level of other leading donors. As one British official pointed out, Canada fit more easily into the hardline mode than it did into the reformist mode.

What then accounts for Canada's continued participation in the Like-Minded Group? What, in turn, would explain its position as co-chair of the Conference on International Economic Cooperation (CIEC) and Trudeau's efforts to revive global negotiations of North–South issues in pressing for the Cancun Summit in 1981? An examination of Canadian policy reveals little support for economic reform in the interests of Third World countries. The contradictions can perhaps be explained by the inchoate policy direction coming from the prime minister, direction that had not touched the relevant bureaucratic actors. It may also have been a reflection of the government's primary interest in acquiring status rather than in economic reform. As Lovbraek argues, members of the Like-Minded Group 'welcomed the reputation thereby acquired that they were amongst the more internationalist of the industrialized countries'.[36] Such an image might enhance Canada's influence within other institutions such as the Commonwealth or at negotiations such as those on the law of the sea.

Perhaps a third contributing factor was the government's concern for its position within the Summit Seven. Having recently arrived in this elite plurilateral group, Canadian policy makers were reluctant to undermine their membership qualifications. Too close an association with the position of core members of the Like-Minded Group might have tarnished Canada's image with the leading lights of the global economy. Clearly, Lovbraek claims, Canada's 'other alliances and associations . . . [and its] special bilateral relationships with other states were far more important to them than those nebulous and loose links with the other like-minded countries'.[37] Cranford Pratt shares this view; Canada, he says, 'manoeuvred hard to be admitted to that inner circle [the economic summits]. Having secured this place, effectiveness in that group is regarded as incomparably more important to Canada than anything that might be accomplished through co-operation with like-minded Western middle powers'.[38] Elsewhere, Pratt discusses the influence of the prime minister:

> The brief excursion by Trudeau into a major mediating role is to be explained very largely in terms of his own values. Canadian policies on NIEO issues were not affected by this initiative. They continued to be primarily motivated by narrowly defined Canadian economic interests, tempered by a continuing concern to play an international role within the limits permitted by the world-view that predominated within the government.[39]

Not for the last time, Canada's overlapping memberships in middle power and great power clubs would place conflicting demands on policy makers.

It is, however, possible to identify another rationale for the government's apparently contradictory approach to North–South relations during the 1970s and early 1980s. Canada's high profile in North–South negotiations during the 1970s suggests a continuing concern with multilateral co-operation and with the process of negotiation in multilateral associations—with bringing a degree of procedural order to an increasingly contested realm of international relations, characterized by Hedley Bull as 'the revolt against the West'.[40] Canadian support for negotiations and for a right to be heard would have to suffice in the absence of a commitment to a more substantive form of justice. Such a posture may have taken on special importance in light of the government's unwillingness or inability to adopt more progressive aid and trade policies. Retaining credibility with Third World governments—necessary to secure their support in other forums—may have led the government to pursue high-profile positions in North–South negotiations, positions that enabled policy makers to escape taking firm positions that might have exposed the government's limited commitment to economic reform. There are some indications that Canada's active presence in these multilateral negotiating forums may have had some moderating influence on Canadian policy; the Cabinet overruled recommendations from the bureaucracy against debt relief and increased aid levels. These were, however, interim measures that did not address the fundamental concerns of Third World reformers.

The failure to revive global negotiations in the early 1980s brought an end to the period of intensive North–South negotiations. Developments on a number of fronts limited opportunities not only for improved North–South dialogue, but for any further multilateral leadership on the part of Canada. The severe economic recession of the early 1980s tended to reinforce the already extensive concern with narrowly defined national economic interests. In this harsh economic climate, whatever support there was for policies of global economic reform was effectively drowned out by those demanding protectionist responses to the changing global division of labour. The integration of trade and commerce into the Department of External Affairs also increased the likelihood that the foreign policy agenda would be dominated by commercial considerations and that activity abroad would be used to support these domestic economic objectives. Pratt argues that 'there has now emerged a new bureaucratic consensus on North–South issues, one that shows a marked shift of basic attitudes away from liberal internationalism and towards a realism that is narrowly national, preoccupied with economic objectives, and little interested in the Third World'.[41] The return to a harsher Cold War climate in the early 1980s also pushed North–South economic issues off the agenda, as governments in Canada and elsewhere turned their attention to reviving a system of détente. Finally, the debt crisis and the fragmentation of the Group of 77 when important manufactures emerged in the South upset the balance of global economic forces and shifted attention away from UNCTAD and toward the established institutions of the Bretton Woods system.

LIMITED (OR LIMITING) TRADE OPTIONS

Throughout this period, the GATT was viewed as crucially important for Canadian trade policy. As Stone and others have argued, the GATT provided considerable opportunities for middle powers such as Canada. First, it gave the country an opportunity to have some influence over the world trade-policy agenda. Second, the GATT could serve as a useful constraint on the policies and practices of larger economies such as the United States. Third, making trade policy in a multilateral framework was an effective means for resisting and overcoming protectionist pressures from inside the country. Fourth, the multilateral approach made it easier for relatively small economies, such as Canada, to gain better access for their exports to larger markets than would be possible under bilateral negotiations. Finally, the multilateral dispute settlement process, although inadequate in parts, could still be helpful in resolving trade disputes with other countries. For these and other reasons, it has been argued that 'Canada should regard the maintenance and progressive improvement of the multilateral trade system, in itself, as a major achievement'.[42]

Few substantial reductions in tariff levels emerged from early rounds of the GATT, and Canada retained relatively high tariff rates when compared with other industrialized states and was still disproportionately favoured in exporting to the American market. Progress in the GATT appeared stalled until changes in American trade legislation initiated the Kennedy Round of negotiations, which lasted from 1963 to 1967. For the first time since 1947, the Contracting Parties to the GATT participated in a comprehensive set of negotiations that would make substantial reductions in tariff levels.

The American move had been encouraged by a number of developments in the international economy, including the growth of the European Common Market (ECM), the need for a Western response to the Soviet Union's trade and aid offensive, the need to find expanding markets for the exports of Japan and the developing countries, and the need to revive the American economy, which had recently experienced balance of payments problems of its own.

In approaching the negotiations, the government confronted a range of opinions from both inside and outside official circles. Even the Cabinet was divided on the best approach to the GATT. Walter Gordon, then minister of finance, favoured a more protectionist stance and was concerned about the effects that changes in tariff rates would have on the country's balance of payments. The minister of trade and commerce, Mitchell Sharp, supported a reduction in tariffs and more liberalization of trade. To mediate the dispute and oversee the Canadian negotiating team, Prime Minister Pearson went to External Affairs and selected Norman Robertson. Robertson had been personally involved in numerous trade negotiations in the past, but now he had to confront many competing interests. His direct intervention with Pearson in the fall of 1964 enabled the Canadian delegation to overcome its internal rifts and meet the deadline of November 16 for the tabling of its negotiating position.

One of the principal issues for Canada was the proposal for 'linear tariff reductions' instead of the usual product-by-product bilateral negotiations that had been used in the past. Canadian negotiators were quick to demand that their country be excluded from the proposed linear tariff cuts. Their position was based on an argument that because of Canada's current trade structure, linear reductions would not yield a balance of advantages. This argument reflected the nature of Canadian trade in that Canada was heavily dependent on price-sensitive raw materials for most of the country's exports while its imports tended to be dominated by price-insensitive manufactured products. As John Evans writes, 'Canada expressed reservations about its ability to participate in negotiations on a linear basis, primarily on the ground that its common border with the United States would make Canadian industries particularly vulnerable to drastic tariff reductions'.[43] A Canadian official gave a more specific accounting to a group in Washington:

> Since we import about ten times more manufactured goods than we export, a linear cut in the Canadian tariffs to match a similar linear cut in the tariffs of our major trading partners would clearly be out of balance in terms of compensating benefits received and given by Canada, as well as being out of all proportion in terms of the degree of adjustment that would be required in Canadian industry as compared with the mass production industries of the US and Europe.[44]

Canadian objections were shared by other 'middle powers', such as Australia and New Zealand. The Americans were willing to support the Canadian request, but the Europeans, who for many years had been the subject of Canadian complaints, were reluctant to go along. After a rather intense session, writes Ernest Pregg, 'the Canadian view was finally accepted by the EEC [European Economic Community], but with deep resentment over the way it had been pressed upon by them [by the Americans]'.[45]

This provision eventually found its way into the declaration made at the start of negotiations.

Canada's success in gaining access to the centre of negotiations did not result in rapid progress, nor did it win substantial benefits from the Europeans. Once again, Canadian negotiators failed to achieve a significant diversification of trade, since the overwhelming majority of discussions were with the Americans. Pregg notes that throughout the negotiations, the Canadian delegation in Geneva 'was structured heavily toward negotiations with the United States' and 'up until the final weeks of the negotiation the Canadian talks were among the most difficult for the United States, mainly because of differing interpretations of reciprocity'.[46] Not only did Canada have a substantial trade deficit in excess of CAN$1 billion with the Americans, but Canadian tariff rates were also substantially higher. There were, however, other factors that complicated Canada's position during the Kennedy Round. The recovery and integration of Europe and the growth of Japan were changing the distribution of economic power in the system and resulted in the relative diminution of Canada. In addition, Robertson, for one, believed that Canada's 'niggling, cautious position' was out of synch with the more committed positions of governments such as the Americans.[47] The result was to suggest a government that was not only less influential than in the past, but also less interested in the longer-term objectives of liberalized international trade through the GATT and more concerned about protecting its immediate narrow interests. Once again, multilateral negotiations had tended to reinforce continental trade patterns, and although it brought these relations under multilateral surveillance, it brought little comfort to those concerned about the growing integration of Canadian–American economic relations.

Canadian participation in the Kennedy Round was a good indication of the changing position of Canada in the global economy. The country had long since lost its status as one of the core negotiating powers that it had held in the waning days of the war and the immediate post-war period. The Americans and the British had now been joined by a more united European Economic Community (the EEC, which negotiated as one in the GATT) and a recovering Japan. Yet Canada still held a strong position among other middle powers. It was the sixth leading trading member of the association and was an effective participant both in its effort to be exempted from the linear reductions and in its subsequent negotiations with the United States. While some disputed objectives, the government, having identified them, made effective use of the multilateral forum to achieve them.

THE TOKYO ROUND

In the midst of uncertainty about the American commitment to liberal trade, the Contracting Parties launched the seventh round of trade negotiations under the GATT. The Tokyo Round, as it became known, would have significant effects on the structure of Canadian trade policies and marked an important turning point in Canada's commitment to a liberal multilateral trading order. It did little, however, to stem the tide of ever-increasing bilateral trade contacts, and by the 1980s, policy makers in

Ottawa and key domestic interests moved to institutionalize these bilateral links in a free trade agreement with the United States. While the free trade agreement meant an important shift in Canadian trade policy, in certain respects this shift was set in motion by agreements reached during the Tokyo Round. For some observers, the Tokyo Round marked another significant advancement in support of the liberalizing objectives of the GATT trade regime.[48] Others have looked upon these codes in a more critical light.[49] From a Canadian perspective, however, the significance of the round is that unlike previous rounds of GATT negotiations, the Tokyo Round saw the government reject once and for all the national policy that had influenced Canadian trade policy for nearly a century.

The origins of the Tokyo Round are to be found in part in the successes and failures of the previous Kennedy Round of negotiations, which had been completed in 1967. The Kennedy Round had achieved substantial reductions in the tariff levels of many industrialized states. It had also encouraged a considerable expansion of global trade. Yet according to Stone, 'the reduction of tariffs achieved by the Kennedy Round had the effect of increasing the visibility of non-tariff trade barriers to trade'.[50] For this reason, many of the Contracting Parties, including Canada, favoured preparations for a new GATT round that would address these non-tariff barriers. Interest in Ottawa in a new GATT round also emerged from Canada's experience in bilateral talks with the Americans. The harsh treatment that Canadian officials received when they sought exemptions from the Americans following Nixon's address on 15 August 1971 raised concerns in Ottawa both about Canada's vulnerability to the American market and about the latter's support for liberal practices. The first concern led Ottawa to favour the Third Option policy announced by the external affairs minister, Paul Martin, Sr, in 1972. The second concern favoured a new round of GATT negotiations to get the Americans recommitted to the GATT regime and its liberal rules. Canada's ongoing commitment to the GATT process was evident in its participation in the Ginger Group, a collection of states with a strong interest in preserving the GATT system: 'In 1971, when the GATT system was seriously in jeopardy, a group of stalwarts drew together and began to make joint statements concerning the value of the multilateral trade system; they were Sweden, Switzerland, Canada, and Japan—the principal nonapplicants to the EEC'.[51]

Despite its commitment to a new round of negotiations, the government once again found it difficult to accept the basis for negotiations that the Contracting Parties agreed to in 1977. The so-called Swiss formula, described by Stone, proposed that 'average tariff levels in the industrial sector would be cut by 30–40 per cent, with a greater reduction in higher rates than in lower rates'.[52] The government argued that such a proposal would not result in a balance of advantages for Canada: 'It was noted that most of Canada's dutiable industrial exports faced relatively low tariffs in major world markets, while Canada's customs duties on industrial imports were relatively high; thus reductions in Canadian tariffs would be proportionately larger than the reduction of tariffs facing Canadian exports'.[53] This was similar to the argument that had been used to escape the linear tariff reductions of the Kennedy Round, and, according to Winham, 'the government was under pressure from domestic industry not to accept a formula approach at the Tokyo Round'.[54]

Once again, the Canadian proposals received little sympathy, but this time there was also no support for an exemption. Moreover, there appears to have been greater interest in Ottawa in accepting the linear approach. The national policy was out of step with the liberalization that was taking place under the GATT. Tariffs were becoming indefensible as a strategy for supporting domestic producers. In addition, commitment to these multilateral negotiating objectives was a way in which Ottawa could deflect those domestic pressures that favoured a continuation of high tariffs.

Equally important in shaping Canada's response was the growing influence of the EEC and Japan in international trade negotiations. The emergence of economic power in these centres gave them more influence over the agenda for and course of trade negotiations. As Stone writes, 'Within such new patterns in the world trade structure, the role of Canada and other middle-sized trading countries was inevitably modified and, to a degree, diminished'.[55] In response to these changing international and domestic conditions, the government decided to accept a formula approach in the Tokyo Round. This decision marked a significant political shift and one that was, as Gilbert Winham has argued, greatly assisted by the extensive consultation mechanism that the government had set in place in planning for the Tokyo Round.[56]

Canadian trade became increasingly diversified during the 1960s, such that by the end of the decade, the proportion of inedible end products had increased from about 8 per cent to over 30 per cent of total exports. The government's own reports indicate that 'the sharp increase in Canada's international trade in automotive goods associated with the Canada–United States autopact was a major factor in this transformation, but the increase in exports of end products other than automotive products has also been substantial'.[57] Not surprisingly given this expanding trade profile, the percentage of the country's GDP accounted for by trade had also grown during this period. This growing dependence on international trade made policy makers more sensitive to the GATT regime and reinforced the importance of continued progress in the GATT negotiations. This was especially the case at a time when the United States appeared to be turning its back on the regime. The American commitment to the GATT had always been seen as tentative, and one of the most important objectives of the GATT for Canada had been 'to restrain and discipline the trade policies and practices of the United States and other large countries'.[58] If the GATT regime was to continue to perform this function, Canada would need to make a stronger commitment to the regime in terms of its own policies. As a result of these factors, Canada's willingness to go along with a linear tariff cut, the so-called Swiss formula, was, in Winham's view, inevitable: 'Given Canada's interests in international trade, and given that Canada's interests are interdependent with the interests of other nations, there was little real choice about whether Canada would become committed to the formula procedures in the Tokyo Round. Instead the real issue was how to manage what was a necessary accommodation to a multilateral trading system'.[59]

The Tokyo Round pointed the direction for future trade negotiations, but it did not resolve the many problems that continued to plague international trading relations. According to Jock Finlayson and Stefano Bertasi,

> the round failed to achieve meaningful liberalization of agricultural trade; did not produce a new 'safeguards' code to stem the tide of managed trade arrangements and the proliferation of trade-restricting measures adopted outside the purview of the GATT; was unable to reach agreement on major new disciplines on the use of government subsidies; and did not result in significant overall decline in either the number or the trade-distorting impact of the wide array of non-tariff measures maintained by industrial countries.[60]

These issues would remain on the agenda. They would provide almost immediate interest on the part of some states, including Canada, for yet another round of negotiations. It would not be until 1986, however, that the necessary compromises could be reached and an eighth round of negotiations launched at Punta del Este, Uruguay.

CONTINENTAL TRADE: THE ONLY OPTION?

The Trudeau government's strategies of trade diversification and bilateralism failed to wean Canadian exporters from their dependence on the United States. Faced with an ever-increasing dependence on foreign trade, uncertainty over the future course of the GATT, and intractable problems in implementing an effective trade-diversification strategy, the Canadian government looked to the United States in the early 1980s as a way of compensating for the limitations of multilateralism. The GATT approach was proving increasingly cumbersome and time consuming and it tended to ignore much of what was most important in Canada–US trade. As a result of this and of a significant and increasing amount of political pressure, the Trudeau government began to look at selected free trade options with the Americans.

The 1980s witnessed a substantial increase in Canadian exports to the United States and a favourable trade surplus that grew to $20 billion in 1984. Despite this, there was growing concern within Canada about continued access to the American market. Most important, there was a desire to secure access against the protectionism that was intensifying as the American trade deficit increased and as political pressure mounted in the US Congress against foreign products in American markets. There were also a number of external considerations that fostered support for free trade, including the growth of regional trade blocs, the shift of dominant trade patterns to these blocs, the need for enhanced competitiveness, the ultimate reduction of Canadian tariffs as a result of GATT negotiations, and the GATT's inability to eliminate the increasingly restrictive non-tariff barriers to trade. In this environment, the Mulroney government decided to pursue a free trade agreement with the United States.

The Liberal government had taken the first steps toward a free trade arrangement with the Americans with the release of *Canadian Trade Policy for the 1980s*. As

Granatstein and Bothwell write, 'bilateralism, rather than multilateralism, became the watchword of the day. The third option was quietly and unobtrusively trundled off to the attic'.[61] In its approach to the Americans, the government attempted to negotiate a series of sectoral agreements comparable to the Auto Pact. By the early 1980s, a number of Canadians embraced the objective of a bilateral free trade agreement with the United States. Officials within External Affairs, prominent Liberal cabinet ministers such as Gerald Regan, and influential interest groups such as the Business Council on National Issues expressed support for a bilateral free trade arrangement. By the mid-1980s, following the election of a Progressive Conservative government led by Brian Mulroney, the sectoral approach had been abandoned. Not only would it be exceedingly difficult to negotiate a balanced package in different sectors, but such agreements might also violate the GATT. Political support was also growing around the free trade option.[62] Amidst an intense domestic debate, a free trade agreement (FTA) was concluded by the Conservative government in 1988, and it was implemented following an acrimonious federal election.

Throughout much of this period, however, Canadian policy makers were also actively involved in driving the GATT into the 1990s. As one of the early advocates of the Uruguay Round of negotiations, the Mulroney government seemed to undermine its support for the multilateral option by moving first into a bilateral pact. Nonetheless, support for the GATT remained strong and considerable efforts were made to insure that the FTA would be consistent with the GATT. It is clear that despite its failings, the GATT was still of considerable significance for Canadian traders. The dispute settlement procedures of the FTA had in many areas superseded those of the GATT, but the GATT continued to hold some promise of opening markets abroad and thereby encouraging a diversification of Canadian trade patterns. It would also act as a court of last resort in trade disputes. After more than 40 years of frustration, the dream of diversification was still apparent in the government's policy. In trade as in defence, the late 1980s suggested a noticeable shift toward a closer bilateral relationship at the expense of Canada's multilateral commitments. It was not that the government was abandoning the multilateral approach that had dominated for so long, but it clearly was now seen as of secondary significance. Despite this, the government remained active on the multilateral front.

CONCLUSION

Despite its efforts in the multilateral arena, Canadian officials could not escape the fact that Canadian trade increasingly tended to move along North–South lines. This was not completely unlike the experience of other countries, who also looked to the American market. None, however, were becoming as dependent on that market as Canada. The problem became even more pronounced during the 1950s and 1960s as two key industrial sectors became closely linked to the American market through formal agreements. The Defence Production Sharing Agreement in 1958 and the Auto Pact in 1965 significantly increased bilateral trade and reinforced Canada's dependence on the American market. These agreements did not, however, undermine the principle of Canadian support for the GATT, nor did they violate the rules of that agreement. They did, however, make it more difficult for the GATT to serve as a means by which trade could be redirected away from its continentalist concentration.

The newly independent states presented a different set of problems for officials in Ottawa. A desire to improve relations with the Third World came into conflict with other commitments—to rival multilateral organizations and, more important, to pressing domestic interests. While multilateral connections pressed the government to make some response to the demands arising from the South, domestic interests had other priorities.

Chapter Six

Bridging the East–West Divide: NATO in an Era of Détente

One of the compelling reasons for Canada to remain a member of NATO is the important political role that NATO is playing and that Canada is playing within NATO in reducing and removing the underlying causes of potential conflict by negotiation, reconciliation, and settlement. —Foreign Policy for Canadians, *1970*

INTRODUCTION

Canada's alliance commitments dominated many aspects of Canadian foreign policy during the 1960s and early 1970s. The pre-eminence of security considerations in the midst of the Cold War was largely responsible for the priority given to defence policy. Support for the alliance during the 1950s was strong despite the failure of the North Atlantic Treaty Organization (NATO) to evolve in a way that would best meet Canadian policy objectives. Instead of becoming more involved in political consultation and non-military affairs, NATO was devoted almost exclusively to military considerations, and by the late 1950s its strategy had become firmly based on nuclear weapons. In spite of reservations about the wisdom of these moves, in the spirit of alliance solidarity and out of deference to arguments presented by the military, the Canadian government acquiesced. In addition, the alliance did not put an end to American demands for Canadian territory and for Canadian contributions to continental defence. In making these demands, the Americans had the full support of many within the Canadian Armed Forces and the Department of National Defence (DND). But increasingly, differences emerged between Defence and External, and between both and political leaders, over the direction of Canadian defence policy. These problems led to a breakdown in the consensus on Canada's multilateral security policy. By the end of the 1960s, many Canadians, including members of the Cabinet, were calling for a complete withdrawal from NATO.

The shifting winds of East–West relations led to corresponding shifts in Canadian approaches to NATO. In the early part of the 1970s, when there were opportunities to pursue improved East–West relations and when there was an interest in developing improved economic and political linkages with European states, there was a much greater interest in displaying one's alliance credentials and in working with the alliance to develop common objectives. By the early 1980s, the 'second Cold War' had effectively obliterated most of the positive developments that had come out of the détente process.[1] The optimistic mood of the 1970s yielded to a profound pessimism nearly as grave as that which existed at the height of Cold War tensions in the early 1960s, and opposition to alliance policies and alliance membership grew in Canada and elsewhere.[2] When détente gave way to a new round of hostilities and pressures intensified for additional military commitments, the government adopted a more diffident attitude toward the alliance and its strategic orientation. Like that of its predecessor, the Mulroney government's 1987 white paper on defence tended to shift emphasis away from Europe and back to North America.[3] Throughout the 1970s and 1980s, however, and despite efforts to limit spending on European commitments, the governments of Pierre Elliott Trudeau, Joe Clark, John Turner, and Brian Mulroney all remained formally committed to continued Canadian participation, as did the majority of Canadians. The desirability of collective defence schemes and the opportunities the multilateral alliance presented for Canadian diplomacy seemed to outweigh the constraints NATO imposed on Canadian policy.

Throughout this period, Canadian officials continued to press the allies to engage in more extensive consultation between one another and between East and West. From the beginning, Canadians had called for more consultation and while such efforts were never entirely successful, the persistent demands kept the issue on the agenda and eventually led to the establishment of committees, such as the Nuclear Planning Group, which went some way in providing more opportunities for intra-alliance discussions on questions of strategy.

Ottawa officials also favoured keeping the lines of communication open across the 'Iron Curtain'. The Canadian government was one of the earliest advocates of NATO's 'two-track' approach to East–West relations, one that would emphasize diplomacy and arms control as much as force deployments and defence spending. In this way, Canada distinguished itself as one of the more progressive members of an arguably conservative group. In stressing the importance of such exchanges, Canada was identifying one of its own strengths in contributing to East–West relations. More important, it demonstrated an effective way for the alliance to make a contribution to the resolution of the East–West conflict. These efforts would ultimately reap some benefits. During the 1970s in particular, government policy statements and some of the practices of Prime Minister Trudeau in the security field often deviated from those of fellow alliance members and suggested disagreement with alliance strategy. The substantive decisions that were taken, however, were for the most part in accord with, and indeed supported, the alliance.

When asked why the Trudeau government had agreed to test American air-launched cruise missiles in the early 1980s, one member of the Prime Minister's Office (PMO) staff replied that the government 'did not have a choice. It was what we had to do as a member of the alliance'.[4] Trudeau had come to power in 1968 lamenting the extensive influence that Canada's membership in NATO exercised over foreign policy decisions. He had been especially critical of NATO's nuclear strategy, particularly of Lester Pearson's 1963 decision to accept nuclear weapons because of the country's obligations to the alliance. Trudeau seemed to favour a complete military withdrawal from Europe during the defence policy review of 1968–9, and one of his last major acts as prime minister in 1983–4 was a peace initiative that challenged many alliance orthodoxies and was openly critical of NATO's nuclear strategy. Yet despite this active criticism of the alliance and his less than wholehearted support for continuing Canadian involvement, Trudeau came to the defence of the alliance. In agreeing to test the cruise missile, one of the most advanced weapons systems then under development, the prime minister was not only casting doubt on his own 'strategy of suffocation'; he was also lending support to a nuclear strategy of which he was personally quite skeptical. The decision generated tremendous public opposition, but the prime minister held firm and justified his actions in terms of Canada's obligations to the alliance. It was a justification that his predecessor Pearson would have found convincing.

The very fact that Canadians were embroiled in a debate over defence policy and alliance commitments in the early 1980s was all the more remarkable because of the substantial progress that had been made in East–West relations during the 1970s. Following through on their decision to accept the Harmel Report in 1968, the member governments of NATO pursued both deterrence and détente, with the emphasis decidedly in favour of the latter. NATO and the Warsaw Pact met over many tables during the 1970s, negotiating on conventional arms reductions in the Mutual Balanced Force Reduction (MBFR) talks and discussing wide-ranging political, economic, and humanitarian issues as part of the Conference on Security and Cooperation in Europe (CSCE). The Americans and the Soviets were also active during this period, concluding agreements to limit additional deployments of strategic nuclear weapons and to accept limits on the further deployment and development of anti-ballistic missile systems. In Europe, led by West Germany's policy of normalization of its relations with East Germany, the Soviet Union, and other Eastern European governments (Ostpolitik), agreements were reached to recognize borders and to open these same borders to a freer flow of goods and people. Canada was an active supporter of détente, having been among the first members of the Western alliance to press for dialogue with the Soviet Union in the early 1960s.

In 1964, following the Cuban Missile Crisis and some early, albeit limited, successes in Soviet–American arms control measures, Paul Martin, Sr, then secretary of state for external affairs (SSEA), proposed that NATO should pay greater attention to its diplomatic role in the East–West dialogue: 'Canada, wishing to move NATO into fields of new endeavour, sought to contribute to a number of constructive changes affecting the conduct of East–West relations. From the outset, I favoured bilateral talks to reduce the forces of both NATO and the Warsaw Pact'.[5] Martin's initiative was designed in part to divert attention from the divisive debates over NATO's nuclear strategy and to attempt to find an area of common appeal, especially for France. The initiative was unsuccessful in preventing France's departure from NATO's military structure in 1966, but it did set in place a process that would lead to the Harmel Report in 1967.

The Harmel Report was important in calling member states' attention to the necessity of political dialogue with the Soviet Union and other members of the Warsaw Pact. It was an attempt on the part of certain members of the alliance to emphasize the diplomatic potential of the alliance and the need to work toward some sort of settlement of the issues that divided East and West. In a very significant way, the Harmel Report anticipated the policies of détente that would proliferate during the

1970s. The objective was to steer the alliance away from its overwhelming concentration on the military balance and its obsession with the distribution of military power in Europe and instead to pay more attention to the political context in which these forces were being deployed. In these respects, the Harmel Report was very much in accord with Canadian thinking. Indeed, it was the sort of reorientation that Canadian policy makers had been arguing in favour of for some time. It was certainly a policy that many in the government would support in the late 1960s. As Mitchell Sharp said, 'there is a coming together of events in Europe today that opens the way to profound change. Basic differences between East and West will not be resolved overnight, but there is reason to believe that a new era of genuine negotiation has begun.'[6]

The Road to Helsinki

In retrospect, it is evident that the Helsinki Accords signed on 1 August 1975 at the conclusion of the CSCE marked a turning point in East–West relations. The conference was a major foreign policy initiative of the Soviet Union, but in the end Western states, through effective multilateral diplomacy, were able to use it for their own objectives. The Soviets looked at the conference as an opportunity to acquire political and propaganda objectives. Some Western governments, especially the United States, tended to agree and looked upon the CSCE as little more than a way for the Soviet Union to gain a diplomatic advantage. Other Western governments, including Canada, saw in the CSCE an opportunity to open a substantial dialogue with the Soviet Union and its allies in the Warsaw Pact (Warsaw Treaty Organization), a dialogue that could be used to settle outstanding points of conflict and thus reduce the risks of war while encouraging a greater degree of liberalization within the member countries of the Warsaw Pact. The strong Canadian support for the CSCE was indicative of Canada's general approach to East–West relations, and indeed to many other areas of international politics.

Following the adoption of the Harmel Report in 1967, NATO member governments were provided with an opportunity to test their commitment to the second track of their avowed two-track approach toward the Soviet Union. The Soviet Union, through the Warsaw Pact, made various overtures during the late 1960s for a conference to discuss a political settlement of the issues that still divided Europe. The Soviets' prime motivation appears to have been to gain formal recognition for the then existing boundaries in Europe, especially those of East Germany and the Baltic republics. In addition, by initially proposing to limit the conference to European states, the Soviets appeared to be interested in severing the ties between the United States (and Canada) and the European members of the alliance. Only France on the Western side seemed anxious to support this aspect of the Soviet proposal, and it is one that they would continue to favour until the very start of the conference in 1973.

The possibility of a substantial dialogue between the Soviet and American blocs was severely tested by the Soviet repression in the Prague Spring of 1968, when Soviet tanks rolled into the capital of Czechoslovakia to crush political reforms in that country. In the aftermath of Prague, as the alliance debated how to respond, the Canadian delegation at NATO repeatedly linked the need for a restoration of NATO's military preparedness in the wake of such brute displays of Soviet force, which was the route favoured in some quarters, with a continuing effort to improve political contacts between the two blocs. Canada, along with a handful of other NATO members, refused to support the strong condemnation of the Soviet Union adopted in November 1968. The government was also the first NATO member to restore contact with the Soviets in the wake of the Prague Spring, when the Soviet foreign affairs minister Andrei Gromyko was invited to visit Canada in 1969.

Two years later, Trudeau made his own journey to Moscow. The trip was marked by the signing of a Canadian–Soviet Protocol on Consultations, which the Soviets viewed as a step on the road to détente and which Trudeau suggested 'had been prompted in part because the Canadian identity was endangered by the "overwhelming presence" of the United States from a cultural, economic and perhaps even military point of view'.[7] Trudeau, however, 'did not believe the protocol was in any way incompatible with Canadian membership in NATO or NORAD or with our traditional alliances'.[8] In spite of the suspicions of and criticisms from American officials, Trudeau was clearly interested in forging a new relationship with the Soviet Union, one not tainted by the Cold War and one that would be more independent of the alliance. In this respect, he was also pushing for the extension of détente between the Soviets and Western governments. Canada's ambassador to the Soviet Union at the time, Robert Ford, has commented on the significance of this visit:

> The visit marked an important watershed in the evolution of Canada's position in the world and in its international outlook and image. It impressed on Canadians and foreigners the idea of Canada looking beyond the traditional North Atlantic triangle and being capable of treating on a basis of equality with the other superpower without in any way diminishing our role in NATO. Indeed, it strengthened it as our importance on the international scene increased.[9]

The détente process was rescued not only by the alliance's recommitment to the principles outlined in the Harmel Report, but also by the important political support that it received in Bonn and Washington. The election of the Social Democrats in West Germany and incoming chancellor Willy Brandt's interest in reconciling inter-German and German–Soviet relations through his Ostpolitik were crucial ingredients in facilitating the CSCE process. In reflecting a strong European interest in détente, Brandt was also able to steer past one of the main impediments to an easing of tension in Europe, that being the divided German state and the divided city of Berlin. Brandt set about reconciling West Germany's relations with the Soviet Union and Poland, and the German legislature passed agreements with Moscow and Warsaw in May 1972. Restoring contacts with its next of kin was considerably more difficult, but with the Soviets pressuring East Germany (GDR), the Brandt government concluded an agreement with the GDR in December of the same year.

The challenge presented by the Soviet proposals was well received in Ottawa, where it was seen as a means of pursuing a more open dialogue between East and West. Alongside this objective, the Canadian government was also most anxious to ensure that any future discussions on European security would not exclude Canada's participation. Détente was now proceeding along three fronts: in Europe, bilaterally between the Americans and the Soviets, and multilaterally through the CSCE and the MBFR talks. Canada had direct access to only the last of these but was anxious to take advantage of the opportunity both to press its own agenda, for example, in the general area of human contacts, and to ensure that it would have a continuing role in the European security process. In the years preceding the commencement of the CSCE and throughout the conference itself, the Canadian delegations worked effectively to achieve these two objectives. The Trudeau government was especially sensitive to these considerations given its unwillingness to increase Canada's military contributions to the alliance. As Robert Spencer has noted in his excellent survey of the events leading up to the CSCE,

> Canada's early and sustained support for the proposed conference and its subsequent desire to work with its European allies in advancing it (with the United States being dragged along) was to a large extent a product of the wish to overcome the adverse effect of the new policy [the troop withdrawals] and a desire to assert the links with Western Europe for Canada's own political and economic reasons.[10]

A reassessment of Canada's participation in and military commitments to NATO was one of the first promises Trudeau made during the 1968 election campaign.[11] Opposition to Canadian participation in NATO had grown steadily during the 1960s. This opposition appeared in each of the three leading parties. Conservative Dalton Camp attacked Canada's defence policies of the 1960s and concluded that 'the major value of alliances today is to provide an umbrella of respectable sanction for the necessary actions of superpowers'.[12] While many New Democrats continued to express some favourable views toward NATO membership, by 1969 the majority of New Democrats had had enough and adopted a resolution calling for the country's withdrawal from the alliance. Even within ruling Liberal circles the sacred cow of alliance participation had been the subject of intense debate and considerable public criticism.

Incoming cabinet ministers Eric Kierans and Donald MacDonald argued publicly against continued Canadian membership in NATO. This was by no means the consensus view, for there were many who continued to see political value in Canadian involvement and threatened to resign if the new government withdrew, including Martin. The opponents, however, had an important ally in the new prime minister, who was suspicious of the value of alliance membership. Withdrawal from NATO and a declared policy of neutrality were options recommended by some within the Cabinet. Supporters of continued participation argued that such policies would have serious repercussions. Ford, for example, took the view that 'if we wished to adopt neutralism à la Suede, then we would have to be prepared to spend ten times what we did already on defence, unless of course we wished to give up all pretensions of being a truly independent country and rely totally on the United States for the defence of Canada'.[13]

Ultimately, the bureaucratic review endorsed the country's participation in the alliance, but Cabinet was not so easily persuaded. Instead, the prime minister turned to his own foreign policy advisor, Ivan Head, who was working out of the PMO, to draft a proposal that would reflect the new thinking that had come to power in 1968. Head accepted the continuing need for Canadian participation in NATO. In this sense, the recommendation was a reaffirmation of past practice. Head's proposals also, however, recommended a number of very substantial changes in the way in which Canada would contribute to the alliance. In addition to calling for an end to Canadian participation in the nuclear strike role and for a reduction in Canadian force contributions, the proposal argued that Canada should work toward changing the alliance from within. The proposals, although eventually accepted by the Cabinet, won little sympathy from the Canadian military, from many within External Affairs, or from other NATO members.

The government's decision was greeted with considerable opposition from the allies. Among the quietest were the Americans, who were perhaps thinking along similar lines themselves. The British took great exception to the proposed withdrawal of Canadian forces from the Central Front. Denis Healey, the Labour government's defence minister at the time, warned that 'if the Canadians go through with their planned reductions, and, even more, if this leads to a chain reaction from the other countries, conventional strength would fall, the nuclear threshold would fall, and the point at which nuclear weapons would be used would arise much earlier'.[14] Healey's concerns reflected the alliance's efforts to implement the flexible response strategy that had been advocated by American defence secretary Robert McNamara as a way of reducing the alliance's dependence on an early nuclear response in time of war, which would require an expansion of conventional forces. As D.W. Middlemiss and J.J. Sokolsky note, 'decisions to reduce the forces in Europe by half and cut back in defence spending were at odds with the NATO policy of the day since the alliance was looking for more of the types of conventional forces that Canada had been contributing'.[15] Despite the opposition, the government proceeded to implement the policy.

The Trudeau government, while keeping the ship, had clearly set sail on an alternative course. NATO would remain an important security commitment, but NATO force revisions were part of a larger package of defence policy reforms presented in a white paper in 1971. Unlike in the 1964 white paper, peacekeeping and NATO were demoted in terms of priorities and territorial defence and NORAD were highlighted. Although Canada retained its membership in two alliances that relied heavily on nuclear deterrence, the government attempted to enhance its nuclear-free image by formally disassociating the Canadian Armed Forces from roles that involved the use of nuclear weapons. The government also identified new objectives in the diplomatic realm that would support policies of détente between East and West. To identify this as a shift ignores the policies of earlier governments, which also worked within the alliance to push for greater accommodation with the Soviets. Unlike that of earlier governments, which were reluctant to move independently of collective support, however, Canadian policy under Trudeau was more unilateralist and visible even while displaying its alliance membership for all to see. At worst, this strategy suggested dissension within the ranks and alienated potential allies. At best, it reflected an alliance attempting to respond to changing international conditions. Either way, it suggested that if Canada was to pursue an influential role in East–West relations, it would need to retain its alliance membership. This became clear as the policies of détente and East–West negotiations continued in the 1970s.

The Trudeau government's decision to cut contributions to European defence had clearly antagonized many of Canada's European allies and thereby threatened Canada's ability to play an active diplomatic role in European security issues. Many European leaders resented the timing, substance, and method of Canada's unilateral reductions in the forces committed to the Central Front. The Dutch foreign minister Joseph Luns, for example, expressed the Western European Union's displeasure with Canada's decision and indicated that 'Canada need not be included in discussions on European security "because of her new attitude towards NATO".[16] This made it was more difficult for Canada to establish its credibility as a 'European' actor at a time when there was real opportunity for Canadian input.

For the Canadian government, there were more than practical considerations at stake in the CSCE: there was also a long-standing hope that the East–West conflict could be resolved through improved political contacts and that any opportunity for expanding such contacts could be supported. This hope motivated Canadian officials to work to keep the Soviets at the United Nations during the troubled early 1950s. Later it was most evident in NATO councils as Canada pressed its allies to pursue diplomatic contacts with the East.

In many respects, the CSCE was, from a Canadian vantage point, a highly significant event for both symbolic and substantial reasons. Not surprisingly given the importance of the CSCE to foreign policy objectives, Canada made a substantial and significant contribution to the conference. In addition to being among the most supportive members within the NATO bloc and encouraging alliance participation, the Canadian delegation played an active role in the negotiations. At preparatory meetings in the summer of 1973, the 35 participating delegations agreed on a four-point agenda. In addition to considerations of a follow-up process to the conference, the agenda consisted of three substantial areas, or 'baskets' as they were described. The first basket dealt with principles relating to the security of European states and relations among them. The second (and least controversial) basket pertained to co-operation in economics, science and technology, and environmental areas. The third (and arguably most controversial) basket involved co-operation in humanitarian and other fields. On these substantive issues, Canada was primarily interested in the broad range of matters that fell in Basket Three, including family reunification. On the procedural side, Canadian negotiators were regularly encouraged by Ottawa to maintain close consultation among the NATO allies in order to enhance Western interests in the negotiations: 'Unless [the] Alliance coordinates tactics and produces a united front . . . [the Warsaw Pact] will have disproportionate strength in CSCE. We believe that consultations both at NATO and Geneva should deal with detail as well as with general principles'.[17]

During the second phase of the CSCE, which was held in Geneva from September 1973 until the summer of 1975, the Canadian delegation adopted a tough negotiating stance across a broad range of issues. According to Peyton Lyon and Geoffrey Nimmo, Canadian negotiators 'emerged as among the toughest advocates, and quite probably the most effective, of squeezing every possible concession out of the Kremlin and its allies. They vigorously and consistently urged their associates to make and maintain maximum demands—"to press detente to its outer limit"—and to avoid any hint of allied disunity or impatience'.[18] The Canadian approach was strongly influenced by domestic considerations, especially in the area of free movement of people and family reunification. These had been prominent issues among some ethnic Canadians throughout the Cold War and had frequently followed Canadian officials in their trips to Moscow and other Eastern European capitals. In assuming responsibility for these issues as part of Basket Three at the CSCE, the Canadian delegation was able to demonstrate its commitment to opening a gap in the 'Iron Curtain'. The delegation was also motivated by a continuing interest in re-establishing its credentials as a committed ally. It wanted to be more European than the Europeans in order to convince those still uncertain over its intentions in the wake of the foreign and defence policy reviews of 1970. In both of these areas, the conference was a considerable diplomatic success for Canada.

For those officials who participated in the negotiations at Geneva, the Canadian contribution to the Final Act 'ranks among the major achievements of Canadian diplomacy'.[19] It is evident that the CSCE was the most significant achievement of the 1970s in East–West relations. It set the stage for continuing dialogue between East and West and provided a vital source of support for dissidents throughout Eastern Europe in their quest for improved standards of human rights. In this respect, although Canadian tactics at times reflected a hardline approach, the overriding objectives were fully consistent with previous efforts to improve East–West relations. Having secured an opportunity to participate in the first major comprehensive post-war conference on European security, the Canadian delegation also sought and acquired a guarantee to participate in follow-up conferences. Hoping that the CSCE would have an ongoing role in East–West relations, officials had, for the time being at least, secured a seat for Canada at the table.

Reassessing Canada's Defence Capabilities

One of the problems that confronted Canadian diplomats as they prepared for negotiations on the CSCE was their government's policy toward Western security in general and the North Atlantic alliance in particular. For many outside observers, the debate on Canada's policy toward NATO clearly revealed very substantial differences within the Cabinet on issues as fundamental as whether the country should continue as a member of the alliance. Although the government opted for continuing its membership, it unilaterally lowered the participation fee. What was perhaps most surprising in the government's decision was that it reduced the capabilities of the Canadian Armed Forces without in any way altering the commitments these forces had to European, continental, or national defence. Instead the government indicated that new commitments would be forthcoming without leaving much indication that additional capabilities would be provided to meet these commitments. The mix between capabilities and commitments, a long-standing problem in post-war Canadian defence policy, became a major issue during the 1970s and 1980s as first the Trudeau and later the Mulroney government attempted to restore Canada's credibility in the alliance and to purchase some much-needed political support in Europe.

The government's decision to withdraw Canadian forces from Europe was, for most observers, the highlight of the defence policy review undertaken by the Trudeau government in 1969. Troop withdrawals were, however, only a part of the government's efforts to restructure the country's defence policy. A white paper released in 1971 outlined the priorities that would govern the new policy and reflected an important shift from the Pearson government's statement released in 1964, which had emphasized Canada's international responsibilities. Not surprisingly, the 1971 white paper emphasized national and bilateral commitments over multilateral ones. The document identified the four primary roles for the Canadian Armed Forces as (1) the surveillance of Canadian territory, coastlines, and sovereignty; (2) the defence of North America; (3) the fulfilment of such NATO commitments as may be agreed upon by Canada; and (4) international peacekeeping roles. Middlemiss and Sokolsky point out that 'even though the White Paper did not specifically give priority to any of these roles and stressed Canada's continued adherence to its alliances, the emphasis was clearly on sovereignty protection'.[20] In affirming the prime significance of national and continental defence, the government was acting consistently with the foreign policy review, which also emphasized the central significance of domestic considerations over international ones. Yet despite the shift in emphasis, the government did not abandon any of its formal commitments.

The white paper was soon followed by an effective freeze on defence expenditures. Existing commitments were to be met with fewer personnel and no additional funds. As Middlemiss and Sokolsky write, 'Despite the Trudeau government's declarations about sovereignty protection and its public statements about the need to fashion a more distinct and independent defence posture reflecting national priorities, not a single major allied commitment had been abandoned. Indeed, with the creation of the CAST combat group, Canada had actually increased its commitments'.[21] The Canadian Air-Sea Transportable (CAST) group was to provide for the rapid deployment of Canadian forces to support NATO's Northern flank (e.g., Norway) in case of war. Maintaining commitments without any demonstrated willingness to supply the financial resources necessary to meet these commitments created what R.B. Byers referred to as a commitment–capability gap.[22]

Throughout the rest of the 1970s and into the 1980s, Canadian defence policy and the country's commitment to bilateral and multilateral alliances were influenced as much by economic considerations as by political or security objectives, if not more so. Increasingly, as defence spending was held in check, the government's ability to meet its widespread commitments faltered. Government spending on defence had increased from $1.7 billion in 1968 to $8.7 billion in 1984, but this apparent increase was at about one-half of the rate of growth in other federal expenditures. The relative decline in spending was even more pronounced when one considers the high rates of inflation experienced during this period and the relatively higher rates of inflation within the defence sector. Equally important for the Armed Forces was the real decline in the area of capital expenditures. Increasingly, the Armed Forces were attempting to carry out the same tasks with fewer personnel and with increasingly outdated and insufficient equipment.

The Trudeau government was able to escape these problems for a short time, but a number of factors forced a reappraisal in the mid-1970s. On the multilateral front, NATO military planners were attempting to implement a strategy of flexible response, which, although designed to delay the need for and use of nuclear weapons, required, in the view of NATO planners, substantial additions to the alliance's conventional forces. American military spending had been reduced in response to the ending of the war in Vietnam, and there were renewed pressures within the US Congress to bring American forces back from Europe. Finally, as mentioned earlier, the Trudeau government was looking for ways to improve its political and economic relations with Europe. In the midst of these developments, a defence structure review was established in late 1974, which undertook a detailed examination of the various tasks the Armed Forces were required to perform and their capability to perform them; but 'even before the full review was completed, there was a distinct change in the Trudeau approach to defence, one in which NATO re-emerged as the de facto top defence priority'.[23] The review confirmed this, and in November 1975, the government committed itself to re-equipping both the armoured brigade and the air squadrons in Europe. The end result was a series of capital acquisitions for the Armed Forces, including German-manufactured Leopard tanks and American-designed Aurora surveillance aircraft and CF-18 fighter aircraft, and a plan to produce a new generation of patrol frigates in Canada. Most of these acquisitions were made to meet alliance commitments and thereby reaffirm the country's commitment to NATO.

The decision to re-equip the forces reflected a mix of multilateral and domestic considerations. The decision to do so in a way that would facilitate meeting multilateral rather than exclusively national or bilateral commitments was in response to the Trudeau government's interest in using Europe as an economic and political counterweight to the further continentalization of Canadian foreign policy. Unlike in the 1950s, when such concerns were expressed primarily in terms of military security, in the 1970s the concerns were motivated more by economic and political considerations. The method of gaining access to Europe, however, remained the same. When the Liberal government made its first overtures to Europe for a contractual link, the

Europeans were not very responsive. At the time, it appeared that one obvious reason for this was the approach to NATO taken by the Trudeau government. In withdrawing troops from Europe and in doing so without prior consultation, Canada had suggested that it had little concern with European interests. Some European governments were further antagonized by the government's attempt to bring in strict controls on the export of uranium. They were therefore hardly sympathetic when the Canadians returned seeking special access to offset the signs of growing American protectionism. For Trudeau, who had apparently considered NATO to be nothing more than a military alliance and Canada at best a peripheral member, it might have come as a surprise to see how important Canada's contribution was viewed by the Europeans to be.

The foreign policy review of 1970 had explicitly indicated the continuing significance of Europe as a counterweight to the United States:

> The maintenance of an adequate measure of economic and political independence in the face of American power and influence is a problem Canada shares with the European nations, and in dealing with this problem there is at once an identity of interest and an opportunity for fruitful cooperation. Nevertheless, Canada seeks to strengthen its ties with Europe, not as an anti-American measure but to create a more healthy balance within North America and to reinforce Canadian independence.[24]

Such sentiments were strongly reinforced by the Nixon economic measures adopted in August 1971. Yet when the Trudeau government turned to Europe for support, little was forthcoming. The security link that had attempted to maintain the idea of a trans-Atlantic community had been broken by the government's earlier decision. Relations with the European Community had also been complicated by the freeze in Ottawa's relations with Paris that resulted from French intervention in Quebec in the 1960s. Restoring good relations would be a necessary first step on the way to a formal contractual link. The government's decision to retain its formal commitments to NATO may have been an attempt to do this. Middlemiss and Sokolsky suggest that 'by honouring all of its commitments . . . Canada avoided jeopardizing its valued seat in allied councils and continued to participate in important deliberations relating to East–West security issues'.[25] By the mid-1970s, however, the gap between commitments and capabilities was obvious and Trudeau was frankly told that he would have to improve the latter if Canada was to get a supportive voice in Brussels.

The government decided as part of its re-equipment program to purchase 138 Leopard tanks from West Germany. Not only were the Germans pleased with the purchase, but the acquisition also effectively confirmed the Canadian Forces' commitment to the Central Front in Europe, at least for the lifetime of the tank. In return, Canada acquired a supportive German voice in deliberations of the European Community (EC) in Brussels and was subsequently able to secure the contractual link with the Community. As Joseph Jockel and Sokolsky note, there has been a long-standing belief that Canadians could purchase access to European markets through contributions to European security.[26] While the inverse may indeed be true, there is little tangible evidence to support this prevailing belief. Increasingly, it has been evident that contributions to European security do not encourage Europeans to be more supportive of Canadian economic objectives. As the Canadian economy slipped ever closer into integration with its southern neighbour, efforts to counterbalance this by extending trade and investment contacts with the Europeans went nowhere. Canada did get a contractual link and this was in part because of Chancellor Helmut Schmidt's gratitude at Trudeau's willingness to buy German tanks for the Canadian army brigade operating in Germany. Gratitude had its limits, however, and certainly did not extend to the British or to other members of the EC. Thus although 'the notion . . . that Canada's military contributions to NATO should afford it special consideration in European economic policies' may have become 'dogma in the Canadian foreign policy establishment', as Jockel and Sokolsky claim,[27] it gave no signs of yielding tangible benefits. Europe remained a difficult market for Canadian traders to access, and the continentalization of economic policy continued apace.

THE BOMARC OF THE 1980S

Not since the early 1960s had Canadians displayed such tremendous concern with matters of defence policy, or such strong opposition to government plans in this sector, as they did in the early 1980s. Along with concerned citizens throughout Western Europe and in the United States, Canadians took up the banner against nuclear weapons. The underlying cause appears to have been growing fears that the Cold War rhetoric of the Reagan White House was leading the world ever closer to nuclear war between the superpowers. The immediate issue for Canadians was the proposed testing of American air-launched cruise missiles from the Arctic over the Northwest Territories and Alberta. Both the underlying cause and the specific issue were closely linked to a decision taken by the North Atlantic Council to deploy a new generation of intermediate-range nuclear weapons in Europe.

The NATO decision was taken in December 1979 amidst an intense debate within the alliance over Soviet and American intentions in Europe. On the Soviet side, Europeans were concerned about the deployment of a new generation of Soviet intermediate-range nuclear weapons that were not only mobile but could also be loaded with multiple nuclear warheads. These weapons, a worry under any circumstance, were more worrisome in the context of the deterioration of superpower détente. On the American side, and somewhat paradoxically, Europeans were concerned that the Americans had forsaken détente, which meant so much to the European governments, and that the United States was not doing enough to demonstrate its military commitment to defend the continent. A particular concern in this latter area was the apparent willingness of American negotiators to control levels of strategic weapons without reference to the shorter-range weapons that were targeted at European states. A further complication in this area was the political fiasco surrounding the proposed deployment of the neutron bomb to Europe, a deployment that was abandoned when the American government suspended production of the weapon.

The decision taken in Brussels at a special meeting of the foreign and defence ministers from member governments was not without controversy. Many within the alliance were reluctant to initiate yet another round of nuclear weapons modernization. Others wanted more weapons committed but wanted them at sea instead of on European soil. For many, however, the deployment of new nuclear weapons in Europe had taken on political overtones and was significant primarily as an explicit demonstration of American commitment to defend Europe. Oddly enough, less than four years later the deployment would be viewed as an explicit demonstration of the Europeans' willingness to be defended by the Americans. In an effort to meet these differing objectives, the representatives agreed on what became known as the 'two-track approach': NATO would deploy modernized nuclear weapons and would, at the same time, pursue an arms control agreement with the Soviet Union to control, reduce, and potentially eliminate these and other weapons. The two-track strategy left much to be desired. For one, the Americans and the Soviets were largely in control of the arms control agenda, whereas NATO was fully in control of the deployment of new weapons. This meant that although NATO had little direct control over the pace and substance of arms control negotiations, it had full control over deployment decisions.

The two-track decision created few immediate difficulties for Canada. It was largely a European issue, and Canadian representatives attempted to take into account European views. At the same time, the government had been more sympathetic to the desirability of pursuing arms control. In the end, it supported the decision in the hope that an arms control accord would be reached that would postpone indefinitely the need for modernization. Problems emerged when the government was presented with a request from the American government to test cruise missiles in 1979 following discussions of the Permanent Joint Board on Defence (PJBD). The primary reason for the American interest in Canada was the comparability of terrain between Canada and the Soviet Union. As with many previous aspects of continental defence relations, this agreement was initially negotiated between the USAF and the Defence Department in Ottawa.

The 10 February 1983 signing of the agreement to test American weapons in Canada launched a public outcry in Canada. Demonstrators hit the streets in numbers that although small by European standards, were nevertheless much greater than Canadian governments had experienced in the past. Not since the early 1960s had a military policy generated such an intensive debate among Canadians. The demonstrations reflected a deep-seated fear about the effects of the nuclear weapons modernization programs underway and about the Cold War rhetoric that was accompanying them in Washington. In short, as demonstrated clearly in public opinion polls, there was widespread and growing fear of nuclear war. Despite the sustained public protests, cruise missile testing proceeded, with the first test taking place in March 1984, shortly after Trudeau completed his peace initiative.

Trudeau did eventually respond to the many critics of the testing program through an open letter published in Canadian newspapers on 9 May 1983. The government's defence of cruise missiles was presented almost exclusively in terms of Canada's contribution to multilateral security:

> Canada has freely agreed to testing of the ALCM [air-launched cruise missile] in Canada because we realize that our security is inseparable from that of our NATO allies. By allowing these tests, Canada is accepting a responsibility born of collective security arrangements from which we benefit. Our NATO allies have chosen this weapon system to contribute to the deterrence of aggression and prevention of war.[28]

Once again, the view from within seemed to be that multilateral commitments would be more palatable than bilateral ones. This was perhaps as true for the politicians as it was for the public. Many of the critics contended, however, that contrary to what DND press releases stated, the cruise missiles being tested in Canada had nothing whatsoever to do with the intermediate-range nuclear forces being deployed in Europe. Critics also argued that cruise missiles, because of their small size, higher accuracy, and relatively low yield, were a destabilizing weapon, in that they might be more readily used in wartime and thus break the nuclear threshold. Testing was opposed on the grounds of Canadian sovereignty and arms control.

For policy makers in Ottawa, however, the issue was a political and not a technical one. Politically, Canada had to be seen to be doing something, especially given the political problems European governments were experiencing as they prepared to deploy a new generation of intermediate-range nuclear weapons. At the very least, the government did not wish to be seen as a weak link within the alliance as NATO entered the difficult year of 1983. As Allan MacEachen described it after meeting with Soviet arms control negotiators, 'if public opinion in Europe and North America weakens [NATO's determination to deploy] and if political will is reduced, then that will be an important factor in their deliberations, a very important factor'.[29] Perhaps in anticipation of the forthcoming peace initiative, or at the very least in an attempt to assert a Canadian view into ongoing arms control negotiations, the government was also interested in maintaining its diplomatic credit within the alliance. It would also appear that economic and commercial considerations were not incidental to the decision; an American subsidiary operating in the Toronto area, Litton Industries, had a lucrative piece of the cruise missile package. Finally, when viewed in light of these other interests in accepting the American request, the government could also help to improve the deteriorating state of bilateral relations with the Americans.

Despite the arguments, there was strong opposition to cruise testing even within the government. More than one cabinet minister was opposed, as were numerous backbenchers. For many of them, cruise testing ran counter to the government's previously displayed interest in a 'strategy of suffocation'. 'Basically we're a pro-disarmament Government of a middle power that is trying to deal its way through a difficult international situation', was how one PMO official described the government's predicament.[30]

The situation was even more difficult on the domestic front. The debate on cruise missile testing was as intense as on any foreign policy issue any government encountered in the post-war period. The New Democratic Party took up the anti-cruise banner in the House of Commons, and a broad coalition of groups rallied public opposition. The coalition included such groups as the Canadian Council of Churches, Project Ploughshares, and Physicians for Social Responsibility. The issue was also unpopular with the public at large; opinion polls suggested a slim majority in opposition to the tests. For many of these opponents, the issue raised the more fundamental question of Canadian participation in NATO. If cruise missile testing flowed from Canada's alliance obligations, as was argued by the government, then the only solution was to withdraw from the alliance. But while Trudeau and other members of his government had serious concerns with many aspects of NATO, and particularly with NATO's nuclear strategy, there was little interest in considering withdrawal.

The Trudeau government had come to accept the importance of Canada's multilateral security commitments. Part of the reason may have been a realization that the alliance did not, in practice, dictate the country's foreign policy options, as Gerald Wright says:

> NATO membership now appears less burdensome, no longer a policy straitjacket; it has not prevented Canada from increasing its ties with the Third World, concluding trade and cultural agreements with the Soviet Union, or sending Prime Minister Trudeau on a visit to Cuba. These were likely the major factors shaping the government's decision to modernize its contribution to European security.[31]

Having made the basic commitments to the alliance, the government seemed unwilling to do much more. Indeed, Trudeau's parting shots questioned some of the sacred cows of NATO strategy. Nonetheless, as suggested earlier, whatever success the peace initiative enjoyed was tied to Canada's membership in NATO.

CHANGING COURSE

The election of a Progressive Conservative government in Ottawa promised a considerable shift in Canada's defence policy, and particularly in Canada's military contribution to the North Atlantic Alliance. After receiving the largest majority in Canadian history, Prime Minister Mulroney confirmed his pledge to rebuild the Canadian Armed Forces in his first Throne Speech: 'Canada will once again play its full part in the defence systems of NATO. Only in this way do we earn the right to full consultation and participation in the policies of that alliance'.[32] As part of the pledge, Mulroney indicated that Canada would begin to replenish the strength of the Canadian Forces in Europe. At the same time, the government reached an agreement with the United States to modernize the continent's northern radar installations. The North Warning System would replace the more than 20-year-old DEW line of installations. Unlike its predecessors, the Mulroney government seemed inclined to give high priority to reinforcing the country's existing defence commitments by providing them with additional forces and equipment. Like its predecessor, the government ultimately let the Finance Department run the military, because budgetary considerations placed a close check on significant increases in defence spending. As two critics noted, 'except on the rhetorical level, there has been little real difference between the defence policy of the Progressive Conservative government and the one pursued by Pierre Trudeau as he left office in mid-1984'.[33]

The failure to meet the increasing demands that Canada's commitments were placing on limited financial resources led Byers to conclude that 'Canadian commitments to NATO and Western security are excessive and unrealistic given the current size and capabilities of the Canadian Forces'.[34] This view was echoed in parliamentary committees, by defence specialists, and by academics. For many the preferred solution was a major review of defence policy that would reduce and realign commitments at the same time as it would commit the country to refurbishing the Armed Forces with new equipment. A defence policy review and a refurbishing were among the main planks of the Conservative platform in the 1984 election campaign.

The new look at Canadian defence policy was in many respects a return to the themes that had been highlighted in the Trudeau government's 1971 white paper. The Mulroney government's defence policy review was not completed until 1987, after two defence ministers had been forced to resign from the Cabinet. When released, the document echoed the bellicose tones that had been emanating from the Reagan White House in the early 1980s. Even Ronald Reagan, however, had moderated his stand by 1987, and the document was widely criticized as being out of step with the changes in Soviet foreign policy and East–West relations. Less than six months after the release of the paper, the Americans and the Soviets had signed the Intermediate-Range Nuclear Forces (INF) Treaty, the first nuclear arms control agreement that would actually result in the reduction and destruction of the number of nuclear weapons in the superpowers' arsenals. The government's white paper, however, placed its emphasis on Soviet military power and the continued necessity for Canada to participate actively in supporting American nuclear deterrence. The paper included a proposal for a long list of equipment purchases designed to replenish a military that had been starved throughout much of the Trudeau era. Also implicit in the document was a substantial shift in emphasis in the future orientation of Canada's military commitments. Like its predecessor in 1971, the 1987 white paper placed its primary emphasis on defence of the North American continent; as Douglas Ross sums up, 'although the white paper justifies the traditional emphasis on Canada's role in NATO, there are indications of a drift towards a policy that emphasizes sovereignty and independence at the expense of a coherent purposeful alliance role'.[35]

Further evidence of the changing attitudes toward European security can be found in the Conservatives' interest in removing Canadian forces from Europe prior to the release of the white paper. As a way of increasing the cost-effectiveness of the country's various commitments to NATO, Minister of National Defence Erik Nielsen and Chief of Defence Staff General Gerard Theriault floated a proposal that would see the withdrawal of all Canadian forces—air and army—from the Central Front in Germany and shift the resources to support the Canadian commitment to Norway. As Howard Langille has described it, the proposal was a failure because of the political and economic significance of the Canadian forces in Germany. Their significance is not only in reminding Canadians of the formal links to European security, but in reassuring the Germans that North Americans (and others) will come to their aid in time of crisis. The net effect, however, in Langille's view, is that the alleged 'counterweight' has become a deadweight: 'In many respects the NATO "counterweight" had become an additional burden, tying Canadian forces to an antiquated role on the Central Front. It furnished the allies with a mechanism with which they could influence Canadian defence policy. With its range of policy alternatives further limited, Canada was, to all intents and purposes, trapped into the commitment'.[36] The response of the Germans and the British was a vehement no, and these two were able to convince the Americans to take the same view of the Canadian proposals. Two years later, there was no comparable reaction when the Canadians abandoned their commitment to Norway and shifted whatever resources there were for the CAST back to the Central Front; only the Norwegians complained. Like its Liberal predecessor, the Mulroney government was reluctant to antagonize the Germans and their powerful friends.

The government's efforts to shift Canada's military commitments closer to home met with little success. As much as ever, the Canadian forces in Europe were fulfilling diplomatic roles in support of political and economic interests. These interests were not affected by the state of East–West relations, or even by the pressing needs of the Canadian military. As long as Europe was seen as providing Canada with economic and political benefits, and as long as these countries wanted Canada to maintain its token military commitment on the Central Front, the government would accede. It was not until a more dramatic change in both of these factors had occurred that the government could, without apprehension, announce the withdrawal of forces from Europe.

A NEW AGE OF CONTINENTAL DEFENCE

Almost as soon as Canada was committed to active participation in continental air defence, the Americans lost interest. Throughout much of the late 1960s and the 1970s, the number of forces declined and the equipment at their disposal deteriorated. The simple reason was that intercontinental ballistic missiles had replaced bombers as the principal Soviet nuclear threat to the North American continent. There was no defence against missiles, and NORAD's role had shifted to surveillance and early warning. In recognition of these changes, its name was changed in 1981 from North American Air Defense Command to North American Aerospace Defense Command. In light of these developments, it was relatively easy for the government to ignore continental defence, and its drain on the defence budget continued to decline. The Americans took a similar approach, and the only point of concern arose in the late 1960s when the United States was exploring the possibility of deploying anti-ballistic missile (ABM) systems, designed to intercept and destroy incoming ballistic missiles. After a great deal of debate, the Americans concluded that such systems would be more destabilizing than their marginal contribution to improved security warranted. The Canadian government, however, had already decided that they wanted no part of any ABM system. Having already experienced the political fall-out that could occur as a result of American strategic and technological innovations, the government wrote a clause into the NORAD agreement that would prohibit the deployment of ABM systems on Canadian territory. This clause was subsequently removed when the likelihood of such systems ever being deployed seemed remote, largely in response to the conclusion of an ABM treaty between the United States and the Soviet Union in 1972 limiting the Americans and the Soviets to no more than two ABM sites. The Americans decided they were as well off without any.

All of this changed with a new round of technological developments and the election of Reagan to the White House. Within a very short time, continental defence was once again in vogue and Canada was confronted with a new set of demands for continental defence. The renewed interest in NORAD and continental air defence resulted from two developments. The first was a Joint Air Defence Study completed in 1980. The study, conducted by the American and Canadian air forces, recommended replacing the 33 distant early warning (DEW) stations with 50 installations (35 of them robot-operated) as part of a new North Warning System. The new system was approved by Reagan and Mulroney at their summit in March 1985, but not before a more substantial proposal generated considerably more debate.

In March 1983, President Reagan, with little prior consultation within his government and none with allies, informed the American public that his government was going to develop a ballistic missile defence system. Such systems had been prohibited by the ABM Treaty since 1972, and Reagan's announcement threatened to undermine the treaty. The Strategic Defence Initiative (SDI), or 'Star Wars' as it was popularly called, became a point of considerable conflict within the alliance and in Canadian defence policy. In an appearance on CTV at the time of the 1985 summit, American defence secretary Caspar Weinberger suggested that Star Wars components might be deployed in Canada. The reaction of Canadians was swift and highly critical of any sort of government involvement in the American plan. In a hastily organized parliamentary committee, hundreds of Canadians voiced their disapproval, and the government subsequently refused an American invitation to participate in Star Wars research. In rejecting the invitation, the government did not reject a continuation of NORAD or modernization of continental air defence. It appeared that the government was solidifying its continental arrangements as it searched for ways to loosen its trans-Atlantic commitments.

CONCLUSION

'Crisis' is a common word in discussions of NATO. A glance at the titles of books and articles suggests that the alliance has been in a permanent state of crisis since its formation in 1949. But for an association so racked by uncertainty, the alliance has

remained remarkably stable. The 1970s and 1980s were nonetheless somewhat different from earlier periods in that the member states were moving on two different
fronts at the same time.

For a number of years, the common perception of Canadian involvement in NATO
was that the country's military contribution brought it influence over collective decisions within the alliance and also translated into substantial economic and political
benefits in our relations with the Europeans such that NATO helped to maintain an
effective counterweight to the United States. By the end of the 1980s, the evidence on
both these accounts seemed clear. As Jockel and Sokolsky write, 'the size and compo-
sition of Canada's contribution to NATO translate into neither significant influence
nor measurable economic advantage'.[37] Perhaps to Canada's surprise, Canadian influence in the early 1970s in such areas as the preparation for the CSCE was largely undi-
minished by the Trudeau government's decision to reduce Canadian forces in Central
Europe. Influence could not be measured by the size of one's defence budget or by the
number of troops on standby. As Jockel and Sokolsky note, 'Canada owes whatever
influence it has within the NATO to the skill of its diplomats (and the political climate
for its proposals) rather than to its military contributions to collective defense'.[38] But
while there is little evidence to support the effectiveness of NATO as a counterweight
to the continentalization of Canadian commercial relations, the assessment on the
political and security sides is more difficult.

As in the 1950s, Canada in the 1980s could not easily escape American pressure for
a revival of continental air defence. Once again, the government attempted to present
this in light of the alliance, with questionable success. With the arrival of the Mulroney
government, the embrace of continental security was more explicit and enthusiastic.
Nonetheless, the alliance connections remained important in providing Canada with
a presence in multilateral negotiations on East–West relations and on the future of
European security. Keeping a seat at the table was important for Canada because
Canadians tend to be more effective in demonstrating diplomatic competence at the
table than they are at displaying military prowess. Canadian delegations took good
advantage of their opportunities to participate in East–West negotiations. The proliferation of such negotiations and their increasingly political character also played to
Canadian strengths. In these areas, Canada was able to demonstrate its independent
interests in East–West relations and its commitment to working toward a political
settlement. This also helped to distinguish Canada from its southern neighbour and,
in this respect, confirmed at least some of the objectives of those who first pressed for
Canadian involvement. Finally, through its continued participation in NATO, Canada
was able to establish a footing in the transformative structures that were being established to deal with a post-détente era. Acquiring membership in the CSCE and its
follow-up conferences insured that Canada would have a voice in discussions on
post–Cold War security in Europe.

Chapter 7

Multilateralism in Flux:
Looking for Order in the Post–Cold War World

We must not exaggerate the importance of the role Canada can play. But we must do our best to ensure that Canada plays an important a role as she is capable of playing. —Escott Reid, 1968

INTRODUCTION

The arrangement of multilateral institutions in which much of Canadian foreign policy was conducted since 1945 was shaken by the end of the Cold War, and with them so too has Canadian foreign policy been shaken. Spawned in part by the demise of the Soviet Union, in part by the rapid expansion of global capitalism, and in part by the activism of non-governmental organizations (NGOs), these institutions have entered a new era. Yet despite the profound changes in the global political economy, there remains a good deal of continuity both in the institutions and in Canada's approach to them. Multilateralism remains an important consideration in Canadian foreign policy, and both the Liberal and Conservative governments have remained strongly committed to the array of institutions that were established in the 1940s: the United Nations (UN), the North Atlantic Treaty Organization (NATO), the Commonwealth, and the institutions of Bretton Woods. In addition, however, new associations—the Group of Seven (or Eight) (G-7/8), the Organization of American States (OAS), and Asia-Pacific Economic Cooperation (APEC)—have taken on greater importance and the substantive content of Canadian policy has changed in significant ways. Perhaps most important, however, has been a relative decline in the government's financial and diplomatic support for foreign policy as both opportunities and demands for active participation in the post–Cold War period escalated. In this chapter, we examine the nature and effects of these changes on Canada's multilateralist practices and on the institutions in which these practices have been conducted.

The course of international politics has been radically transformed since the late 1980s. The Cold War that defined so much of Canadian foreign policy from the late 1940s on ended without any clear sense of future plans or direction. A proliferation of new issues and new actors crowded onto the international stage. In the absence of any clear overriding grammar by which to interpret and respond to these events, policy officials were left trying to refurbish old institutions to meet unforeseen demands and to conceptualize, articulate, and implement new norms to govern a changing world. Only in the arena of global capitalist practices did there appear to be a coherent approach and response on the part of states, institutions, and key actors in the private sector. In the arena of political security, the field has been more muddied and the vision more obscured. It was perhaps not too surprising that policy makers would look first to the institutions that had persisted through time.

The United Nations has been one of the principal cornerstones of post-war Canadian foreign policy. When the Cold War that had paralyzed many areas of activity for the organization ended, Canadians and other proponents of the institution anticipated a brighter future. Within the short span of a decade, the hopes for such a transformation were raised then dashed, and the UN retained the precarious position it has held for much of its history. While its existence seems secure enough, its relevance is still suspect as the rivals assert their respective capacities to act more effectively within their limited spheres. Nonetheless, the recent past has been a remarkable experience for the institution and for its Canadian supporters. For instance, for only the second time in its history, the UN Security Council sanctioned the use of force to repel aggression; it embarked on the most extensive and intrusive use of peacekeeping in its history when it worked alongside NATO in an attempt to settle the conflict in Bosnia, taking unprecedented steps in the direction of establishing and enforcing norms of international justice and human rights. The UN also convened a series of global conferences to address pressing political, social, and environmental issues. It has engaged with non-governmental organizations, including an unprecedented briefing that humanitarian NGOs provided to the Security Council. The Security Council in turn has seen its agenda expanded to include many new issues, including historic meeting on AIDS, the first time the Council ever discussed a disease. All of this has been done in the midst of ongoing financial crisis and uncertain American support. The Canadian government, however, has continued to promote the organization and this expanded agenda.

THE UN IN THE 1990S: EXPERIMENTING WITH NEW SECURITY ROLES

Joe Clark, then secretary of state for external affairs, outlined the factors that would guide Canadian foreign policy during the post–Cold War era in a speech delivered in September 1990. He identified nine areas that in his view exemplified Canadian foreign policy. A commitment to multilateralism and the need to work within multilateral institutions formed the core of these principles. Clark stressed the need for institutions to adapt to changing circumstances and the need for member countries to work within these institutions rather than abandon them, 'even when their failures are intensely frustrating'. He also stressed the need to maintain contacts with the different states and regions of the globe and to continue dialogue and negotiation rather than shouting and shooting. Multilateralism would remain a central element in Canadian foreign policy: 'While multilateral approaches to problems may be slower and the result less satisfying, the outcome can often be more significant and stable precisely because it was based on consensus'.[1]

The strategy for the new era sounds quite similar to the strategy that was used in the past. Many of the same themes were echoed in the Liberal government's white paper of 1994. For example, the Liberals made it clear that the UN would remain an important focus for Canadian foreign policy: 'The UN continues to be the key vehicle for pursuing Canada's global security priorities by working with other member states. The success of the UN is fundamental, therefore, to Canada's future security'.[2] It was also evident in the government's continuing financial support for the institution, as

Minister of Foreign Affairs Lloyd Axworthy made clear in his 1996 speech to the UN General Assembly (UNGA): 'Canada has in recent years undertaken some of the most severe expenditure cuts of any developed country. Yet we maintained our commitment to pay our UN dues in full and on time, because we believe that the UN responds to key international priorities'.[3]

The United Nations experienced a renaissance in the 1990s as a result of the dramatic changes in and subsequent demise of the Soviet Union. The end of the Cold War was first proclaimed at the UN. In 1986, Soviet leader Mikhail Gorbachev delivered a historic speech to the UN General Assembly that effectively reversed 50 years of Soviet foreign policy. As a result, there soon developed an unprecedented consensus in the Security Council that addressed conflicts between Iran and Iraq and in Afghanistan, that subsequently opposed Iraq's invasion of Kuwait, and that recommended forceful intervention in response. There has also been a resurgence of large-scale, multi-faceted peacekeeping operations. One of the most distinguishing features of the United Nations in the 1990s was an increase in both the opportunities and the demands for a more assertive and interventionist role in addressing threats not to only international peace and security but also from intra-state conflicts. Removed from the constraints of the Cold War, the organization was encouraged by some member governments to undertake more complex and dangerous operations in response to a range of local and regional conflicts.

Since 1988, the UN has established peacekeeping ventures at the rate of about two per year. There were 13 peacekeeping operations under UN auspices between 1948 and 1988, and none begun in the decade before 1988. Between 1988 and 1998, 36 new operations were established. Peacekeeping forces have been deployed to Afghanistan, Iran and Iraq, Namibia, Angola, Central America, the Western Sahara, Iraq and Kuwait, Cambodia, the former Yugoslavia, Somalia, Sierra Leone, East Timor, and elsewhere. Forces have been involved in everything from the standard monitoring of ceasefires to the repatriation of civilians and the monitoring of elections. In Cambodia, UN peacekeepers were in effect governing the country until a new government was formed. In 1992, the UN agreed to the supervision of humanitarian relief efforts in the war zones in Bosnia-Herzegovina and Somalia. They did so at considerable risk to the soldiers involved and without the support of the local warring factions. In Bosnia, UN forces seemed poised to engage in enforcement actions, only to yield in the end to NATO. In East Timor, they have been mandated to work alongside locals to construct a new country from the top down. Canadian forces have actively participated in the overwhelming majority of these operations, and by the early 1990s, more than 4,000 Canadian personnel, representing about 10 per cent of the total active UN forces, were deployed in 13 different operations under UN command. After a slight decline, Canadians were once again, at the end of the decade, contributing about 10 per cent of the personnel for UN operations.

The number of new operations was a result of a number of factors, including the dramatic improvement in co-operation among the permanent members of the Security Council. In the early 1990s, the permanent members of the Security Council delegated more and more tasks to the organization. The pressures for more assertive action most commonly came from the permanent five (P-5) members of the Security Council—the United States, Britain, France, China, and Russia—and initially suggested a political commitment to make the organization a more effective instrument for ensuring international peace and security. Yet the P-5 have been encouraged by countries such as Canada and by numerous NGOs that have persistently advocated a more interventionist role for the UN in response to civil conflicts and humanitarian emergencies.

In 1992, the first-ever summit-level gathering of Security Council members took place in New York, where the leaders asked the secretary-general to prepare a plan of action for the UN in the area of peace and security. The organization readily accepted the challenge. The result was *An Agenda for Peace*, prepared with significant Canadian input, released (later that year) with considerable fanfare, and received with generally favourable reviews.[4] *An Agenda for Peace* presented a plan for UN involvement in the resolution of international and civil conflict. It included proposals for the traditional sorts of UN activities in areas such as peacekeeping, but it also recommended a role for the UN in new areas such as peacemaking, peace building, and conflict prevention activities. The idea was to shift UN resources to focus on one or more of these approaches depending on the circumstances. To some extent, these proposals were a reflection of the expanded range of UN activities that had already begun to develop in the 1990s. As Kenneth Bush has noted, however, 'the cases acting as the major points of reference in contemporary international politics involve a combination of these activities'.[5] This meant in effect that operations would attempt to address all aspects of a conflict. These objectives were nothing short of grandiose. The secretary-general's program also forfeited three important characteristics that had in the past governed UN peacekeeping operations: (1) consent of the parties, (2) impartiality, and (3) the non-use of force except in self-defence. The organization was clearly moving to new ground, but as will be discussed later in this chapter, many of the same concerns remained.

The dramatic increase in UN activity during the early 1990s was also a result of member governments' adoption of a broader view of threats to peace in the international system and their apparent willingness to intervene in the domestic affairs of member states in order to seek to restrain and resolve violent conflict. The end of the Cold War may have solved some security problems, but it clearly created new ones, or at least made clear what had previously been obscured. As a result, there was a vocal demand for UN action and, alongside this, a Canadian government usually willing, if not always able, to make a commitment.

There was a certain unreality about the demands made on the organization, in that the resulting mandates for UN involvement have seldom been accompanied by a commitment of sufficient resources from member governments. Security Council resolutions to dispatch operations to Rwanda, East Timor, and Sierra Leone never received adequate support. Decisions to establish safe areas in Bosnia were not supported with sufficient forces to provide safety. Indeed, there have been clear limits established by member governments, among them the United States, on their willingness to be involved in or provide material support for these operations. As the record illustrates, pressures on the organization to move boldly into the area of peacemaking and conflict resolution have left it with a crisis of credibility. In 1993, then under-secretary-general for political affairs Marrack Goulding described the delicate balancing act these pressures presented for the organization:

> On the one hand, the Secretary-General has to try to ensure that peacekeepers are not deployed in conditions where failure is likely; on the other hand, he has to avoid appearing so cautious as to create doubts about the real usefulness of the United Nations or provide a pretext for member states to return to the bad old ways of unilateral military action.[6]

The far-reaching proposals of *An Agenda for Peace* also appeared to reflect a changed attitude on the part of the permanent members of the Security Council. This was especially true of the United States, where in the election campaign of 1992, soon-to-be-president Bill Clinton argued frequently and forcefully for the need to invest the UN with new responsibilities and additional resources. These views were more clearly articulated after the election when a series of policy statements proposed greater support for 'assertive multilateralism' conducted under the auspices of the UN. The much-needed financial resources were slower in coming, however, and effectively dried up once American forces experienced casualties in Somalia and the Republican Party gained control of Congress in 1994. American political support for an assertive UN role also vanished on the streets of Mogadishu when American soldiers fell victim to a poorly executed operation—an operation that was ordered by American commanders from military headquarters in Florida, not by the UN in New York. Blame, however, was placed on the UN's shoulders, and opposition to the organization flourished in policy debates in Washington. The Clinton administration reversed its earlier commitments, and the UN was left with significant responsibilities, inadequate resources, and its most influential member carping from the sidelines. The Americans were by no means alone in withholding support for these operations, but they and others had been active in promoting these undertakings from their seats on the Security Council. If nothing else, it was convenient to have the UN involved in areas such as the former Yugoslavia, where the United States lacked both a clear policy and the necessary political commitment to get directly involved. And while there have been many precedents for states using the UN for their own political objectives, one could not have devised a better scheme to demonstrate the limitations of the organization.

As well as for conflicts in which it had little real chance of success, the UN was also criticized for its selective involvement. As a result, many viewed UN intervention as arbitrary at best and biased at worst. Thus not only the credibility but also the legitimacy of the institution was threatened. The failures of the UN in Bosnia, Somalia, and Rwanda became fodder for critics of the organization. Many of the criticisms seemed designed more to undermine political support for the organization than to make it more effective. The reasons for the UN's failures have been frequently stated and included many institutional factors that needed to be addressed, among them inadequate resources, ambiguous mandates, misplaced impartiality, poor training and command of some troop contingents, and the lack of effective management from headquarters in New York. Left unstated and unexamined, however, was the fact that many of these operations were of unprecedented scope, in the midst of intense conflicts, and in areas of humanitarian intervention for which there were no established precedents and no clear consensus among member states. Moreover, some of these issues were so exceedingly complicated that even the most well-supported and expertly managed operations would likely have been unsuccessful. Finally, the attention given these failures also led many to overlook the positive and essential contribution that the UN made in facilitating peaceful change in places such as Mozambique, El Salvador, and Cambodia, as well as its work in other areas, such as eliminating weapons of mass destruction in Iraq and promoting the non-proliferation and comprehensive test ban regimes.

On balance, however, the experiences of the 1990s demonstrated that without a greater willingness on the part of member governments to make the commitment of material resources it is unlikely that the operations established by the P-5 will meet with much success. As events in Sierra Leone in 2000 indicated, there are as yet no firm indications that the necessary support for the organization's new security roles will be forthcoming. As Brian Urquhart has written, 'if they [the P-5] want the organization to intervene in some of the worst human tragedies, but, quite understandably, do not want to be physically involved themselves, they must provide the United Nations with at least the minimum capacity to act effectively'.[7] The limitations of the UN and the dilemmas confronting Canadian policy were made clear in Rwanda. In 1994 in Rwanda, the UN faced a certain massacre and a profound inability to marshal the necessary force to do anything about it. Canada, for its part, provided a C-130 to fly in and out of Kigali—the only government willing to do so during the worst of the fighting in Rwanda.

Much of the UN's initial enthusiasm for a more assertive multilateralism had been encouraged by the Mulroney government. Moreover, despite resisting an increase in defence spending and despite its later reluctance to approve NATO's use of force in Bosnia, the government was willing to match its rhetorical commitment with the deployment of forces abroad. By the end of 1994, more Canadians were serving abroad in theatres of action than at any time since the Korean War 40 years earlier. Canada was contributing a major share of UN peacekeeping forces. The supply of Canadian troops, along with Canada's commitment to this more assertive or interventionist form of peacekeeping, declined somewhat when the Liberals took over the government in 1994. The prime minister, Jean Chrétien, 'wasn't comfortable with this new sort of peacemaking'.[8] The Liberals' skepticism was also evident in their frequent consultations with Parliament as they sought to protect their position from public criticism. The public, for its part, appeared willing to maintain the degree of support it had exhibited in the past. Canadians also retained considerable credibility within UN peacekeeping quarters. In 1994, Major-General Baril became the senior military adviser on peacekeeping at UN headquarters and retained the position despite the French government's attempt to secure the position for one of their own.[9]

Events in the former Yugoslavia (discussed in greater detail in Chapter 9) provided the catalyst for Canadian policy, but the Mulroney government sought to apply the same interventionist principles elsewhere, such as in Haiti. In part, the government's response to these crises reflected the strong personal views of the prime minister as articulated in a series of statements in 1991, as well as domestic political considerations. A number of Canadian groups had been advocating for a more assertive policy in the promotion of human rights. It is also evident that considerable pressure from the general public influenced policy makers. Spurred on, it has been suggested, by the so-called CNN factor, or the media's presentation of conflicts, the public, moved by these humanitarian crises, pressed the government to do something. The DND and the Armed Forces also saw in UN operations an opportunity to stop the drain in, and perhaps restore, defence spending. Finally, pressure emanating from Canada's multilateral associations, and from governments' interests in strengthening these institutions, was also important. Canada's multilateral commitments in the UN, the OSCE, NATO, the Commonwealth, and the OAS encouraged policy makers to respond to crises that seemed to have no direct effect on Canadian interests. In his examination of the Somalian conflict, Bush writes that 'UN requests for Canadian participation in its missions provided the government with the opportunity to defuse pressure from both above and below while maintaining its traditional support for multilateralism, the UN system in particular'.[10]

In spite of diminishing resources, Canadian support for peacekeeping is as strong as it has ever been. It is also evident that the UN continues to rely on Canada and like-minded countries to contribute to these operations. Some have suggested that peacekeeping has been used by the government in the absence of policy and that Canadian officials should learn to say no. Yet the policy persists, in part because of the continuing influence of the factors cited here. Canadian support is reflected not only in the deployment of Canadian resources, but also in the government's contribution to the debate on reform at the UN. Through its work on the Special Committee on Peacekeeping Operations, Canada's UN delegation has persistently demanded that peacekeeping be put on a more secure financial and administrative footing. These efforts, which have been evident since the early 1960s, have been unsuccessful. They have become more imperative, however, as UN operations proliferate and because the UN appears to be the only organization capable of intervening in many conflicts around the globe.

Another, and equally difficult, problem arises in addressing the organization's inability to respond early and effectively to crises. In response to growing concerns about resourcing UN operations, Canada, Denmark, and the Netherlands each undertook a study on various aspects of a rapid-reaction capability for the UN. A UN Rapid Reaction Force was also discussed in the secretary-general's supplement to *Agenda for*

Peace. The Canadian portion of the study was presented to the United Nations in September 1994.[11] The study identified a capability gap at four levels. First, at the political level, there was a need for an effective and timely response from the UN Security Council. Second, at the strategic level, the reforms already undertaken in the Secretariat needed to be maintained and enhanced. Third, at the operational level, it was necessary to totally revamp the ad hoc manner of constructing UN operations. Finally, at the tactical level, there needed to be better co-ordination, especially between the UN and related agencies and NGOs. The Canadian study included a proposal to develop and implement a 'Vanguard Concept' that could be deployed quickly and early in conflict situations and thus move the UN closer to a prevention strategy. While many of the reforms recommended by the Canadians for the UN's Department of Peacekeeping Operations were undertaken, the UN has not yet advanced to the more significant and substantial areas involving deployable forces.

It became clear during the 1990s that the demands on the UN had exceeded its capacity to respond both in terms of the number and quality of personnel required and in terms of the operational mandates and practices that it had come to adopt. Traditional peacekeeping had given way to second-generation peacekeeping, and second-generation peacekeeping was yielding to peace-support operations. Operations increasingly had a substantial mix of military, civilian, police, and humanitarian contributions, each of which often operated under different authorities and with varying mandates. This was partly a reflection of the changing character of conflict in the world. During the 1990s, the more prevalent conflicts confronting the UN took the form of civil or intra-state conflicts, marked by insurrections, inter-ethnic confrontations, and failed states. The participants in these conflicts were more often than not irregulars—civilians, gangs, armed groups led by warlords. These were not the traditional armed forces of organized states, and their practices often looked more like banditry than like soldiery; the combatants did not adhere to the 'warrior's honour'.[12] New types of conflicts gave rise to new issues, such as breakdowns in civil authorities, refugee movements, and an increase in ethnic and religious fanaticism. Moreover, in these conflicts, combatants are often irregulars, commonly youth and children; they are diffused throughout the population and difficult to identify. The central government in question is at best weak and lacking in enforcement capabilities. As a result, politically and militarily enforceable ceasefires are often absent. The repercussions are usually felt by the local civilian population, who in addition to direct acts of violence, often directed against women, are also threatened by famine, disease, and displacement.

In response to these conditions of conflict, Canada began to shift its own focus, at least rhetorically, to place a greater emphasis on the non-military aspects of peace-support operations. In 1996, the Liberal foreign minister, Lloyd Axworthy, launched a peace-building initiative. Axworthy outlined the features of this approach in a speech to the UN General Assembly in September: 'In Canada, we are currently focussing our approach to these issues. We have started to rework our own tool kit to improve our ability to initiate and support peace-building operations in areas such as preventive mediation and dialogue; human rights monitoring and investigation; media and police training; judicial reform; and demobilization'.[13] The Canadian peace-building initiative was designed as 'a package of measures to strengthen and solidify peace by building a sustainable infrastructure of human security'.[14] The initiative suggested a concern for the multidimensional and integrated causes of civil war and thus acknowledged the need to address the economic, social, and political aspects of reconstruction and reconciliation. Rooted in a concern for human security, it also identified the need to address these issues at the level of individuals and groups within what is now commonly called 'civil society'. Axworthy's peace-building initiative focused on providing direct assistance to countries at various stages of civil conflict. It was also designed to support the capacity of the Canadian government and of individual Canadians to participate effectively in peace-building initiatives. The Canadian approach to peace building has been designed to co-ordinate the work of various government departments—the Department of Foreign Affairs and International Trade (DFAIT), the Canadian International Development Agency (CIDA), Justice Canada, Elections Canada, and the RCMP—that had become involved in conflict resolution activities at the international level as part of second-generation peacekeeping operations. The Canadian approach has also been designed to support work on a bilateral basis or in co-operation with international and regional inter-governmental organizations (IGOs) and Canadian and local NGOs. The overriding objective of Canada's peace-building policy is to 'support the emergence of participatory and pluralistic societies, with a well-functioning and responsible government administration acting under the rule of law and respect for human rights'.[15] In more specific terms, Canadian activities have included such things as humanitarian relief, demining and demobilization, repatriation and reintegration of refugees, police and justice training, support for an independent media, election and human rights monitoring, and reconstruction of schools and health centres. Thus although the government continues to support UN operations, both DFAIT and DND have accepted the need to redefine their approach to these conflicts and to shift to peace-support operations in which the military component would be significantly reduced and replaced with more civilian tasks and personnel. While continuing to operate under the auspices of multilateral institutions, the peace-building initiative reflected the Canadian government's interest in engaging more directly with NGOs both at home and abroad.

REFORMING THE UN

As the United Nations approached its 50th anniversary in 1995, much attention was focused on the matter of reform. Years later, the organization looks much the same and operates in much the same way as it did in the past. In spite of the many reports, conferences, commissioned studies, and debates, significant institutional and procedural reform remains beyond reach. The Canadian government and many interested Canadians were among the most vocal proponents of reform.[16] This reflected in part the government's and the public's ongoing commitment to the institution. It also reflected a very prevalent view that the institution was in need of major repair.

The problems fell in three main areas. First, and likely most pressing, were the never-ending financial problems encountered by the organization. Much of the pressure for reform in this area has come from the United States and as a result, the Americans have taken the lead here. Described in a 1995 *New York Times* article as 'a chief financial officer's nightmare', the UN has no liquidity, is unable to raise capital, has a highly unpredictable cash flow (few states pay their dues on time), cannot write off bad debts, and has too many delinquents, including its largest and most influential member.[17] Perhaps the worst problem, however, is that the 185 directors—many with their own interests at heart and with significant disagreements about what the organization should be doing—must agree to any significant reforms. Without an infusion of capital and a more stable and sufficient revenue base for the future, the UN may be forced to close its doors. The possibility is not as extreme as it might sound. In the words of *The Economist*, the world may very well 'get the UN it pays for'—or it may get no UN at all.[18] A number of administrative and budget reforms have been undertaken and others have been proposed, but significant problems remain.[19] One is the unwillingness of organizational interests and member governments to abandon unnecessary and redundant structures. A second is the outmoded scale of assessments that charges some governments too much and others too little. A third is the continued unwillingness of member governments to pay their dues in full and on time.

In September 1997, Secretary-General Kofi Annan brought forward a set of reform proposals intended to address some of the ongoing administrative and financial issues that have confronted the organization for decades. Much of the reform package was targeted at the US Congress, which had grown increasingly critical of the UN and had refused to provide financial contributions without significant administrative reform. Yet many of Congress's concerns were directed as much at the substantive policies being pursued by the organization as they were at its finances and administrative practices. They also reflected ongoing tensions and conflicts between the Congress and the US administration over the nature and scope of American involvement in the UN and in other arenas of global governance.

A second area of concern in the reform process has been the issue of representation and democratization within the UN. A good deal of the representation debate has focused on the Security Council. The Canadian delegation has supported expanding the membership of the Council and, while recognizing the desirability of increasing representation from the South on the Council, has reverted to its functionalist arguments of the 1940s in arguing that Council members should also be selected on the basis of their ongoing contribution to the organization.

A particular area of Canadian activism in the UN reform process has been in the support that the Canadian delegation has given to the representation of NGOs in the UN system. Non-governmental organizations have emerged as a significant element in both Canadian foreign policy and the activities of international institutions. The increased prominence of NGOs in the Canadian foreign policy process has been evident in many policy areas, including the negotiations of the land-mine treaty (discussed in Chapter 9), development projects, and human rights. Equally noteworthy has been the extent to which NGOs have assumed a higher profile in and around meetings of international associations. From a Canadian perspective, the activism of NGOs was most readily apparent at meetings of APEC in Vancouver, BC, in 1989; of the WTO in Seattle, Washington, in 1999; of the OAS General Assembly in Windsor, Ontario, in 2000; and at the 2001 Summit of the Americas in Quebec. These meetings attracted a number of NGOs and provided much fodder for the media. They also called attention to the prominence and salience of NGOs in Canada's approach to multilateralism. Although the Canadian government appeared to take up its position on the opposite side of the barricades at these meetings, it has, in fact, been one of the more active governments in promoting increased opportunities for NGO involvement in multilateral diplomacy.

Andy Knight has written that the active participation of NGOs in the politics of global governance represents a new multilateralism and a bottom-up approach to policy making within these institutional frameworks. The role of NGOs has entered a new era, Knight says:

> In some issue areas some NGOs are effectively positioned at the table with states. They have also been included as major partners in some multilateral conferences (e.g. the sustainable development conference in Rio de Janeiro, the Nairobi and Beijing conferences on women, the Vienna conference on human rights, and the population conference in Cairo). Also some governments have begun to include backbench members into their delegations at the UN General Assembly sessions, while others have even included NGO representatives in some of their delegations at major multilateral conferences. And NGOs have played a major role in helping the UN and other top-down multilateral bodies deal with humanitarian crises, such as in Somalia and Rwanda.[20]

In February 1997, representatives from selected NGOs (Oxfam, Médecins sans Frontières, and CARE) met with the UN Security Council to discuss the situation in the Great Lakes region of Africa. Although the meeting did not set any precedents (the UN Security Council carefully scheduled it outside of the Council's chamber), it reflected the extent to which NGOs have penetrated UN politics. The issue of NGO participation received additional attention when the UN General Assembly met to review the progress made in implementing Agenda 21, adopted at the Rio Conference. The Assembly heard from a number of NGOs but, once again, did so without precedent.

The Canadian government has been active in promoting NGO participation in a variety of venues. It has supported greater NGO involvement at a number of UN-sponsored conferences, worked closely with NGOs on the land-mines initiative, and developed mechanisms for consulting and working with NGOs in Canada in areas such as peace building, development, and trade. At the UN, the government has also been actively involved in the NGO cause. Canada's UN delegation sought to clarify the political issues surrounding NGO involvement by seeking to resolve a number of the more technical aspects of such participation. In 1998, Canadian representatives succeeded in commissioning a report that would summarize the current state of practice throughout the UN system with respect to NGO participation and would also address legal and financial implications of their greater involvement. The report settled nothing, as Peter Willetts describes:

> By the end of 1998, it appeared as if the long campaign for a permanent NGO presence in the General Assembly had lost all its momentum. Again, the Canadians, acting on their own, took the lead to prevent the question from disappearing from the agenda. They tabled a proposal to ask the UN's member governments and NGOs to give their views on the Secretary-General's report and to place the item on the agenda of the next session of the General Assembly.[21]

The issue remains unresolved, but its progress to date owes much to Canadian persistence. This action is reminiscent of Canada's approach to membership in the mid-1950s, when it sought a more inclusive organization. It is also a reflection of the current predilection of policy officials in Ottawa to foster greater NGO participation. Finally, Canadian support for NGO participation in the UNGA is consistent with its more flexible approach to matters of sovereignty and intervention.

While much of the attention—critical and otherwise—focused on the UN's involvement in conflict situations, the organization continued to address a vast range of social and development issues, primarily through its Specialized Agencies. Richard Falk argues that 'the UN has over the decades played an indispensable role in standard-setting in the human rights and environmental domains, creating a normative framework that can be invoked as authoritative by transnational social forces, especially by citizens' associations, as well as by conventional domestic oppositional politics'.[22] During the 1990s, this has been evident, for example, in the numerous UN conferences addressing such issues as the environment (Rio 1992), human rights (Vienna 1993), population (Cairo 1994), social development (Copenhagen 1995), women (Beijing 1995), and housing (Turkey 1996).

These conferences have dramatically increased opportunities for NGOs to gain a platform from which to proclaim their interests and demands to governments and to the world at large. This was especially evident at Rio and Beijing. In Cairo, Canadian representatives to the conference spent much of their time meeting with delegations from the NGO community. In a number of areas, the UN, generally with strong support from the Canadian government, has expanded the opportunities for NGOs to become more actively involved in the work of the organization.

These conferences have also attempted to address a number of pressing problems. Among the accomplishments of the Rio Conference were the adoption of Agenda 21, a global blueprint for sustainable development; new international treaties on climate change, biological diversity, desertification, and high-seas fishing; and the establishment of the UN Commission on Sustainable Development to monitor the implementation of the Rio agreements and serve as a continuing forum for negotiating global environment and development policy. Perhaps the most noteworthy feature of the conference was the extensive role played there by NGOs.

In June 1993 at the World Conference on Human Rights held in Vienna, the Canadian delegation worked closely with these NGOs to advocate for an international commitment to human rights and to strengthen the mechanisms for monitoring and promoting human rights. The conference resulted in the appointment of the first High Commissioner for Human Rights with the objective of reinforcing the UN's ability to act quickly and efficiently to prevent rights violations and promote fundamental freedoms. It also marked an attempt to increase the presence of human rights considerations in UN peacekeeping operations. The results also lent support to the Canadian government's good governance policy, as the conference also promoted the link between democracy, development, and human rights.

'A Principled Multilateralism'

The good governance policy of the Mulroney government was adopted in 1991 in an effort to promote democratic development and human rights abroad. Although the objectives and programs of the policy were not unique to Canada (other countries were experimenting with similar policies), Canada's promotion of good governance abroad and especially in selected multilateral institutions demonstrated a continuing commitment to use multilateral associations to advance foreign policy interests, an interest in making these institutions more effective in promoting substantive policy practices in member countries, and the ability of lesser powers such as Canada to help shape these institutions.[23] The Canadian initiative had ramifications for the mandate and operations of multilateral associations, including the Commonwealth and the Organization of American States. The proclamation of the good governance policy, while rooted in a substantial and growing domestic and transnational concern with the protection and promotion of human rights and democracy, moved Canadian policy beyond previous expressions of interest in such issues by focusing more directly both on how other states governed their societies and economies and on the right of external agents—governments, NGOs, and multilateral institutions—to intervene to protect or restore specific political and economic practices. It therefore represented a significant shift in the government's position on state sovereignty and on the role of multilateral institutions in protecting that sovereignty. Sovereignty was to be conditional, and multilateral associations were solicited to ensure adherence to these conditions.

Although the good governance initiative in its substance was more akin to American initiatives to inject political and economic values into other societies, the implementation of the strategy took on distinctively Canadian tones because the government pushed multilateral associations to adopt these values. Thus, the implementation of the policy involved not only adjustments to Canadian policies and programs (for example, in the area of aid policy), but also an attempt to reform and secure support from multilateral associations such as the Commonwealth, the Francophonie, and the OAS. Each of these institutions subsequently adopted declarations, mechanisms, or both in support of 'good governance'. The Commonwealth version is presented in the Harare Commonwealth Declaration, that of the Francophonie in a decision at the 1991 summit to establish a human rights and democracy unit, and that of the OAS in the Santiago Commitment to Democracy and the Renewal of the International System. These actions demonstrate an important dimension of the government's good governance initiative: to gain the support of other states for a more interventionist policy and to secure their commitment through revisions to the mandates of multilateral associations. These multilateral initiatives formed the core of the government's strategy to promote good governance abroad and an illustration of principled multilateralism. In each of these associations, Canadian political leaders attempted to make human rights and democratic forms of government the litmus test of a member's credibility. The objective behind Canada's initiatives appears to have been one of making respect for human rights and the adoption of democratic forms of government a requirement for continued participation in these regional associations. Along with an interest in promoting freer trade, good governance was one of the government's primary objectives as it turned to regional organizations in the 1990s.

MAKING THE HEMISPHERE SAFE FOR DEMOCRACY

The Mulroney government has most often been blamed for, or credited with, Canada's shift to regionalism.[24] While much of this was motivated by economic concerns (and will be discussed in the next chapter), the elaboration of a hemispheric policy contained both economic and political motivations and was advanced both by domestic interests and by the government's own desire to gain support for more globalist aspirations. Throughout the 1980s, domestic groups and parliamentarians had been pressuring the Canadian government to place a greater emphasis on peaceful change and human rights in Canada's foreign policy in Latin America.[25] The OAS provided a stable, if not exactly thriving, institutional base for Canadian policy in the region. For decades, successive Canadian governments had stood aside from the OAS, viewing it as an American protectorate and not wishing to be forced to confront American policy activities in the region. Latin America had traditionally been a peripheral area of concern for Canadian foreign policy despite the considerable economic, social, and political connections that exist between Canadians and Latin Americans.[26] Despite repeated American invitations, policy makers refused to take the Canadian seat. The embrace of regionalism in the early 1990s, especially in the Western hemisphere, was thus described by one observer as 'a major re-ordering of Canadian external relations.'[27] Officials in the Department of External Affairs pushed for a renewal of Canadian interest in the region and requested the Mulroney Cabinet to consider giving a higher priority to the region. In March 1989, the Mexican foreign minister urged Canada to join the OAS, and in October, the Cabinet gave its assent. In December, the Mulroney government took its seat in the OAS.

Coincidental with the Canadian decision to join was a move to revitalize what had become one of the world's more dormant institutions. Edgar Dosman notes that 'OAS institutional renewal provided Canada with a unique opening for starting out its claim in the inter-American agenda'.[28] Although some Latin American states may have looked upon Canada as a silent partner, one that would contribute dollars without taking too much interest in the institution itself, Canada's historical relationship with multilateral institutions indicates that such memberships are seldom taken lightly. Even knowledgeable Canadians, however, were likely surprised by the enthusiasm and activism that marked Canadian involvement in the OAS after it moved into the Canadian chair in January 1990.[29] As Dosman has written, 'Ottawa has pursued a stronger OAS and a more interventionist approach'.[30]

The government's initiatives in the region paralleled those being pursued in other forums. The government did not look to the region, in other words, as an alternative to the wider multilateral process, nor did it look upon its new relationship with the Americas as a replacement for trans-Atlantic or Commonwealth connections. Instead the relationship with the Americas enabled the government to secure support for the same initiatives being pursued elsewhere. These proposals included everything from fostering democratic development and promoting human rights to expanding trade and recommending harsh fiscal restraints for an organization that was often extravagant in its spending habits. Consider, for example, Joe Clark's comment in explaining the government's decision to join the OAS: 'Many of the problems which plague the globe have a direct relation to Latin America'.[31] The decision to enter the OAS was, in Stephen Randall's paraphrasing of Clark's words, 'a reflection of the larger trajectory of Canadian foreign policy—to pursue a distinctive Canadian role in international relations involving steady pressure and tangible support for peaceful change'.[32] It is perhaps for this reason as well that the Canadian government decided to adopt a very activist approach to the region once the decision was made to join the OAS. The FTA, in Andrew Hurrell's view, 'together with Canada's decision to join the OAS from 1990, marked a definite regionalist turn in Canadian foreign policy, which had previously been based on building-up extra-regional relations and active multilateralism as a means of balancing the power of the United States'.[33]

One of the government's first initiatives in the OAS was to gain approval for the Unit for the Promotion of Democracy (UPD). The Unit was approved unanimously at the OAS General Assembly in June 1990. As David MacKenzie describes it, 'the role of the UPD was envisioned broadly to promote and reinforce democratic institutions in the hemisphere, to help in the monitoring of elections, and to give practical training to men and women at both the grass-roots and official level'.[34] In addition to its diplomatic efforts, the Canadian government provided funding for the UPD, and former Canadian ambassador John Graham was appointed as the Unit's first director. The UPD's modest mandate of election monitoring and related work to strengthen democratic institutions was nonetheless the first major foray by the OAS into a more intrusive set of regimes.

An even more impressive set of measures emerged the following year when Canadian diplomacy helped secure the support of member governments for the Santiago Declaration. On the occasion of the 21st General Assembly of the OAS in

Santiago in June 1991, Canada was at the forefront of a proposal that became known as the 'Santiago Commitment to Democracy and the Renewal of the International System'. This ambitious-sounding declaration committed member governments 'to adopt efficacious, timely, and expeditious procedures to ensure the promotion and defense of representative democracy'.[35] The specific measures included an immediate response to the overthrow of democratically elected governments and assistance programs to preserve and strengthen democratic practices. The successful adoption of the Santiago Declaration reflected well on Canadian diplomatic skills as it created a more permissive environment for intervention in a region that had traditionally been opposed to such measures, with good reason. The region's troubled and turbulent historical experiences with American intervention, often under the guise of liberal democratic principles, raised a number of concerns among member governments when Canadian officials first made their proposal. Hurrell, for one, has noted that 'while democratic values are widely shared throughout the Americas, the dangers of abuse of hegemonic power have led, and will continue to lead, Latin American states to try to limit the scope for "democratic interventions"'.[36] Canadian officials were, however, able to secure the support of other governments in the region, especially those from the Southern cone, who were interested in securing the democratic reforms that had so recently been won; with this coalition Canadian officials won over the support of others. James Rochlin suggests that

> while it seems daunting enough these days simply to (re)establish some sense of community within Canada, let alone to engage in the historical project of construct- ing a global community which transcends spatial boundaries, reality dictates that we must try. Perhaps a starting point will be a regional endeavour aimed at forging a democratic and secure inter-American community. As a member of both the OAS and NAFTA, Canada is well placed to make a significant contribution to such a venture.[37]

The government's commitment to democratization in the region was tested imme- diately when Canada took the initiative to restore Jean-Bertrand Aristide to power in Haiti. Aristide had been elected to office in December 1990 only to be removed by a coup less than one year later. The Mulroney government reacted immediately to the overthrow of the democratically elected president and called upon other leaders and subsequently on the OAS to take action to restore democracy to the troubled island. Whether motivated more by democratic concerns at home in the face of Haitians in Montreal or by a commitment to principle, the government initiated action within the OAS, and for one of the rare moments in its history, the organization responded. Acting under the Santiago Commitment, an ad hoc Meeting of Consultation of Ministers of Foreign Affairs condemned the coup, demanded the reinstallation of President Aristide, and moved swiftly to isolate the new regime and impose sanctions on Haiti in what one observer described as 'undoubtedly the strongest resolution the OAS had adopted against any government'.[38] The meeting also recommended that 'member states take steps to isolate diplomatically the group that had seized control, to suspend all economic, financial and trade ties with Haiti, and to prohibit arms deliveries'.[39] The Canadian foreign minister, Barbara McDougall, joined a few of her OAS colleagues in a futile mission to Haiti to persuade the junta led by Lieutenant-General Raoul Cedras to restore the democratically elected government. A political standoff and economic sanctions ensued, bringing even more hardship to the people of Haiti.

As a regional institution, the OAS was limited in what it could do. For example, it could not extend its sanctions policy to other, non-member, states. It also had no history of peacekeeping or peace-enforcement measures. Moreover, there were strong political inhibitions against extending the institution's mandate in these areas, given the region's historical experiences with US-led interventions. In light of the lack of success and limited options, the OAS turned to the UN. The Ad Hoc Meeting of Ministers of Foreign Affairs met in December 1992 and decided

> to mandate the Secretary General of the Organization of American States to go to the extreme within the framework of the Charter to seek a peaceful resolution of the Haitian crisis, and, in conjunction with the secretary-general of the United Nations, to explore the possibility and advisability of bringing the Haitian situation to the attention of the United Nations Security Council.[40]

In response, Canada and others turned to the UN for support. As Joaquin Tascan has noted, the request for support from the UN came at a time when the organization 'realized that dialogue could not yield resignation by Cedras and that the type of measures prescribed in Chapter VII of the UN Charter were made necessary'. Moreover, he writes, 'by recognizing Aristide as the legitimate president and decreeing an economic, financial, commercial and arms embargo on Haiti, the OAS permitted the UN's involvement in what otherwise would be treated as a purely domestic matter'.[41]

The request for UN involvement overruled the objection of the organization's secretary general, João Baena Soares, who wanted to see the OAS retain responsibility for managing the conflict, but the request was otherwise widely supported. This support was particularly important in that it identified the strong consensus that existed in the region for something to be done and confirmed that this was not simply a case in which the United States was defining the interests of the region. This made it easier for the Canadian government to press the UN Security Council—a venue in which Canada was more comfortable—to take action. At the same time, by passing the issue to the UN, governments in Mexico and Brazil could ensure that the OAS did not undertake a military operation or establish any precedents that would encourage future interventions.

Unlike the UN's involvement in Bosnia (discussed in Chapter 9), there was a very concerted effort to co-ordinate the actions of these two institutions. Part of the problem with co-ordination was the very different tasks the institutions were capable of playing. Once the response to the crisis in Haiti involved a military presence, the OAS backed away from direct involvement. The most notable area of interaction was in the monitoring of human rights violations under the auspices of the OAS/UN International Civilian Mission in Haiti (MICIVIH), which in February 1993 replaced a comparable OAS mission. The inclusion of UN personnel with more extensive experience in human rights monitoring and the separation of the military peacekeeping and police-training activities (managed by the UN) from the monitoring and election-supervising activities (managed jointly or by the OAS) ensured that the OAS would not set precedents that its member governments wished to avoid while it retained some active presence in the conflict in order to enhance its role in the promotion of democracy and good governance. Co-operation was also facilitated by the Friends of Haiti group at the UN, which had been convened by the secretary-general and which included Canada among its members.

Canadian support for democratization has been sorely tested in Haiti. In 1993, in the middle of the federal election campaign, American and Canadian forces attempted to land in Haiti to implement a transfer of power that had been agreed to by the Haitian military. The troops never left the boat, and the embarrassing and politically significant retreat of the USS *Harlan County* from the harbour of Port-au-Prince in October 1993 sent a message to the Haitian military that neither the institutions nor their member governments were willing to use force to restore democracy. Both had been scarred by developments in Somalia and were unwilling to assume new risks. Under these conditions 'an angry mob of gunmen' was the only deterrent needed to prevent an intervention.[42] Within a matter of hours, the Canadian government withdrew a contingent of police monitors operating under a UN mandate and the MICIVIH evacuated its human rights observers. The Haitian military had effectively secured its position for another year. The Chrétien government subsequently refused to support the proposed American intervention on the island, but did promise to and subsequently did support the peacekeeping, or peace-building, operations in the country.

Four years after the coup, Aristide was returned to power. This occurred, however, only after the UN picked up the initiative and in the face of a threatened American military invasion in September 1994. As MacKenzie has written, the first venture by the OAS in the area of democratic reforms was marred by serious problems:

> The OAS was unsuccessful in diffusing the Haitian crisis: the missions and sanctions failed, the initial vigour with which the organization responded slowly faded. In the process, the OAS was edged from centre stage by the United Nations and the United States. Indeed, faint cracks began to emerge within the OAS and between the OAS and the United Nations over the issue of military invasion, and old concerns about American intervention in the hemisphere could be revived and potentially polarize the OAS once more.[43]

The Haitian experience was problematic for the OAS, but one should not discount the differences in the organization's response when compared with previous cases. The fact that the crisis was resolved without an American invasion and that Canada remained committed to sanctions may have protected the legitimacy of both OAS and Canadian efforts in this area. This may be especially true given that one of the major concerns is that such democratic initiatives will be used by the United States as a ruse for direct intervention in the region.

MOVING THE COMMONWEALTH BEYOND SOUTH AFRICA

The Commonwealth provided another forum in which the Canadian government of the day could articulate and seek support for its foreign policy initiatives of democracy promotion and peace building. The Commonwealth and human rights have a long, if somewhat checkered, history in Canadian foreign policy. The organization was for years nearly obsessed with the issue of apartheid in South Africa. Canada played a significant role in this issue, especially at the beginning and end of the Commonwealth's 30-year involvement. It was the Canadian government under John Diefenbaker that forced the vote on South Africa's apartheid policy at the 1961 Heads of Government meeting. Diefenbaker's comments at that time foreshadowed the approach of Brian Mulroney to good governance three decades later. 'No one wishes to interfere with the domestic affairs of any member', Diefenbaker said. 'But . . . any association that hopes to play an effective role in the world . . . must endeavour to bring about co-operation and understanding between races'.[44] Thirty years later, a Conservative government took a similar view.

An assertive Prime Minister Mulroney travelled to Harare in October 1991 to make the argument before the biennial Commonwealth Heads of Government Meeting that the Commonwealth needed to adopt stronger measures to protect human rights and promote democracy. The Commonwealth had assumed a very prominent place in the foreign policy of the government, and the prime minister relished his role as one of the senior leaders in the association. After all, as David Black notes, 'the Commonwealth offers a rare forum in which Canada is unambiguously important'.[45] Mulroney's stature within the group was also enhanced by his efforts to promote Commonwealth action against the apartheid regime in South Africa, especially his opposition to British prime minister Margaret Thatcher.[46] After the changes in South Africa, Canadian officials, and especially the prime minister, were concerned that the association find a new set of objectives around which members could rally in the years to come. New tasks needed to be identified and a new consensus developed in support of these tasks. The process would not be easy, however, because the anti-racist sentiments that had generated support against apartheid were not easily transferable to other human rights issues.[47]

The Canadian government's initiative to promote good governance provisions among the Commonwealth heads of government encountered varying degrees of support. Britain, now led by John Major, was a strong voice in support of such measures. Australia, however, reacted more critically to proposals by Mulroney to link aid and human rights. Prime Minister Bob Hawke, in adopting what would have been a more traditional Canadian view, said, 'I don't take the view that it is for us to hector and lecture. I am sensitive about telling others how to conduct their affairs'.[48]

The Canadian government had been working on different measures in preparation for the meeting and had identified three areas of concern: principles, instruments, and actions. They met with considerable opposition in all three areas. Among the dissenting voices were Ghana, which registered opposition to Western dictatorial tendencies; Zimbabwe, which resented the explicit linkage between aid and human rights (as was proposed by Mulroney); and India and Barbados, both of which were concerned about the emphasis given to political rights over economic ones. Indeed, this latter point of opposition led to the inclusion of a reference to 'development rights' in the Harare Declaration. The opposition clearly indicated that there was less consensus here than the Canadians had been able to identify in the OAS. As a result, the Declaration is more diluted; 'not a home run, but at least a standup double' was the prime minister's post-summit assessment.[49]

Nonetheless, in the end, the Harare Declaration was approved by Commonwealth political leaders. In the Declaration, member governments affirmed their commitment to the protection and promotion of democratic values and human rights. Along with this went a commitment to 'strengthen the capacity of the Commonwealth to respond to requests from members for assistance in entrenching the practices of democracy, accountable administration and the rule of law'.[50] The primary objective, in addition to setting standards that members were expected to meet, was to use the Declaration to hold governments accountable for any violations that might occur. Unlike the Santiago Commitment, however, the Harare Declaration did not provide for intrusive measures, nor did it provide for instruments to be employed when and if violations occurred. Subsequent efforts, in which Canadian officials played a major role, have been undertaken to rectify these 'shortcomings', but these have met with limited success. The problems experienced in responding to the persistent violations of democratic and human rights in Nigeria demonstrated the limitations of the Commonwealth's measures. The fact that the Commonwealth responded at all, however, reflects the increased significance of these values within the association.

At a meeting in Auckland in November 1995, Canada led the Commonwealth in suspending Nigerian participation in the association following the hanging of environmental activist Ken Saro-Wiwa and eight other activists in November 1995. The Nigerian government of General Sani Abacha also faced economic sanctions imposed by the Commonwealth. The Commonwealth actions were in part a reflection of the outrage that heads of government experienced as they met collectively. For the next two years, the Canadian government led the campaign to pressure the Abacha government into democratization and greater respect for human rights. A combination of the Commonwealth's importance for the conduct of Canadian foreign policy and the government's interest in pursuing a values-based foreign policy pushed the Chrétien government to the front of this campaign. Unlike the apartheid issue, however, there was little consensus within the Commonwealth and much opposition from African governments, who were either sensitive to the Nigerian government's position (and opposed to Western pressure for democratization) or unwilling to risk its umbrage. Subsequently, the Canadians, through the Commonwealth Ministerial

Action Group (CMAG), were able to secure a consensus on continued sanctions and suspension pending democratic reforms that, in Black's view, 'rescued the organization's strained credibility, at least temporarily'.[51] Events in Nigeria were subsequently overtaken by the death of General Abacha in June 1998. As the Nigerians moved, however tentatively, toward democracy in the wake of Abacha's death, the Commonwealth found the necessary opening to reverse its policy. Black has written that 'the most durable significance of this initiative for Canada and the Commonwealth will have less to do with Nigeria than with the longer-term educative process of deepening collective understanding of the meaning and salience of democracy and human rights'.[52]

Meeting Resistance: The Francophonie

The Mulroney government took an equally keen interest in the Francophonie, and in light of this, it is not surprising that Mulroney took the good governance message to its biennial summit in Paris in November 1991, where the prime minister proposed a similar initiative. Once again, the proposal called upon member governments to respect human rights and support democratic processes. The government also proposed 'to finance a unit within the Agency for Cultural and Technical Co-operation (ACCT) to support democratization and human rights' similar to the UPD in the OAS.[53] These initiatives met with even more resistance than Canada encountered in the Commonwealth, yet the government persisted in its efforts. Kirton offers a possible explanation for Mulroney's approach to the Francophonie:

> For Brian Mulroney the CHOGM [Commonwealth Heads of Government Meeting] and the francophone summit are not two unrelated ventures which can be tailored to the whim of the local customer. Rather they are cut from the same cloth, united by the doctrine that what is done by Canada for one must be done by Canada for the other. This involves rapidly building up the fragile French-dominated francophone summit to approximate in agenda, programme, and results the far more ample proportions of the much older Commonwealth.[54]

Thus, even as the agenda became more demanding, the same sets of concerns were taken to both meetings. This doubling can also be explained by the deliberate efforts to co-ordinate the government's good governance policy. However dim the prospects for success at the Francophonie, it would not be possible to abandon the effort without undermining the initiatives undertaken in other venues. So the government played its card, and with the exception of support for the beleaguered and, at the time, deposed leader of Haiti, returned home with little to show. There was still a lot of catching up to do.

On balance, what is most interesting about these initiatives is that they were undertaken in the first place. For the Canadian government, they represented a tangible demonstration of its efforts to promote good governance abroad. They also represented a fundamentally different view of these institutions from that to which previous governments had ascribed. In its attempt to get these associations to adopt substantial codes of conduct for member governments, the Canadian government was seeking a uniformity of values and practices in groups that had previously been appreciated as places of difference, as groupings of different states not only where other states might benefit from Canadian experiences, but also where Canada might learn and benefit from the different experiences of others.

THE INTERNATIONAL CRIMINAL COURT

The signing of the Rome Treaty establishing an International Criminal Court (ICC) stands as a considerable achievement in the drive to establish enforceable norms of global justice. It also represents a fairly significant achievement for Canadian officials, who were among those from a small group of states that led the effort for such a court. The Canadian action is noteworthy because it occurred in spite of fairly strong American opposition to the court. As Canadians had experienced on the issue of land mines and encountered in the debate over nuclear weapons (both discussed in Chapter 9), their multilateral polical objectives and those of the United States tended to diverge with greater regularity in the 1990s. The government's success in meeting its objections in spite of American objectives speaks not only to the strength of conviction and the diplomatic skill of Canadians, but also to the benefits of working through multilateral coalitions.

The International Criminal Court has a long pedigree, much of it unofficial. The momentum for the creation of a permanent ICC had been slowly building since the end of World War I. The Treaty of Versailles provided for the establishment of an international tribunal to prosecute the Kaiser, but trials were never held. The international tribunals at Nuremberg and Tokyo after the Second World War included the identification of the sorts of crimes that would fall under the jurisdiction of the ICC. The goal of establishing a permanent court has persisted. Instrumental in the process has been the International Law Commission (ILC), which has consistently advocated for such a court and which has also been actively involved in drafting charters for such a court over the years.

The Security Council's decision to establish the International Criminal Tribunal for the Prosecution of Persons Responsible for Serious Violations of International Humanitarian Law Committed in the Territory of the Former Yugoslavia Since 1991 (usually shortened as the International Criminal Tribunal for the Former Yugoslavia, or ICTY) and subsequently the International Criminal Tribunal for Rwanda (ICTR) reflected the more interventionist and human-rights-oriented mood of the Council and its supporters, including Canada. The Council's unprecedented step signalled the international community's commitment to supporting the principle of individual accountability for crimes under international law. The creation of these ad hoc tribunals also enhanced the prospects for establishing a permanent ICC.

The ILC submitted a draft statute for an International Criminal Court to the UN General Assembly in 1993. Upon receiving comments from governments, a revised draft statute was submitted by the ILC to the General Assembly in 1994, with the recommendation that it 'convene an international conference of plenipotentiaries to study the draft Statute and to conclude a convention on the establishment of an international criminal court'.[55] Because of political differences over the desirability of creating an effective criminal court and over the pace at which work should proceed, the UNGA set up an Ad Hoc Committee to review the ILC's revised draft statute. Member states and specialized agencies of the UN were invited to take part in the Ad Hoc Committee's debates and to submit comments on the draft Statute. A Diplomatic Conference to finalize and adopt a convention on the establishment of the ICC was held in Rome from 15 to 17 July 1998. Among the various reasons behind the creation of the Court, the foremost was a desire to end impunity. As Axworthy said,

> The reason why I think the international court has become so crucial is that the new body of humanitarian law . . . needs some way of holding not only presidents and prime ministers and ministers accountable, but to hold individuals accountable. Once you do that, it begins to provide its own deterrent to behaviour. All of the sudden you realize that sometime, somewhere, you're going to be held accountable.[56]

The Canadian delegation was led by Philippe Kirsch, who also assumed the position of chair of the Conference of Plenipotentiaries in Rome after the original chair fell ill. Schooled in the role of multilateral conferences and a former member of the Canadian mission at the UN, Kirsch 'played the role of Solomon during the talks' and was instrumental in moving the gathered representatives toward the objective of the ICC.[57] Canadian representatives were active throughout the months leading up to the conference, partly because, as Knight says, 'the discourse on the ICC served Canada's goal of drawing more attention to international humanitarian law and of supporting the creation and utilization of multilateral instruments to address problems that cannot be handled effectively or efficiently by national government instruments'.[58] The successful conclusion of the Rome Treaty and the establishment of the ICC (pending ratifications) demonstrate the government's ability to draw on its multilateral experiences and to work effectively in such settings to pursue foreign policy goals. Canadian interest and support for an ICC also demonstrated a growing interest in the more substantive and normative dimensions of multilateralism.

CONCLUSION

For the past 50 years, successive Canadian governments have turned to multilateral associations to support an international order that would facilitate Canadian interests, enhance Canadian influence in world politics, act as a counterweight to continentalist pressures in both security and commercial areas, and establish the basis for a stable and peaceful, if not often just, international order. In the changed environment of the post–Cold War world, the government, while relying extensively on existing associations, developed new coalitions with NGOs and turned to other institutions, such as the OAS, to achieve Canada's foreign policy objectives. In recent years,

Canadian foreign policy has shifted to take account of changes in the global order, as reflected in its approach to the UN, the Commonwealth, the Francophonie, and most recently the OAS. It has also been confronted with and willingly embraced an increased array of non-governmental actors, who have taken a prominent place in the world of multilateral associations. Indeed, much of the activity of NGOs has shifted from the national or local level to the multilateral level as they have actively pursued involvement with international institutions. Canada, although often at odds with the specific positions advocated by these groups, has been among the most active of governments in encouraging and, where possible, facilitating their involvement in the multilateral process.

Amidst the turmoil and turbulence of the far-reaching changes that have taken place in world politics in recent years, Canada's interest in searching for and working with multilateral associations to pursue foreign policy objectives continues unabated. Recent experiences, however, especially in the new forms of peacekeeping, indicate the difficulties that Canada faces in participating in the work of international institutions. The post-war network of international associations is undergoing a very significant transformation, particularly in their approaches to national sovereignty and their relationships with NGOs. In both of these areas, Canada has been actively (and at times aggressively) advocating and working toward significant change. Although it may lack the necessary power and has at times been reluctant to commit the necessary resources, it is in a position from which it can lend significant power or resources and in this way have a considerable influence on the emerging world order.

There has also been a significant growth in the number and capacity of regional organizations. It is apparent from recent experiences that the Canadian response to the trend toward regionalism has been to work from within these regional associations in pursuit of extra-regional policy objectives. It is also evident that the government's pursuit of such policies is much more likely to be successful if Canada can work from within an institutional framework. In the end, however, the ultimate success of these initiatives will depend on the extent to which these global objectives receive the support of—or, more specifically, serve the interests of—states and populations in different regions of the globe.

Chapter Eight

Globalization and Multilateralism:
Canada and the Reform of Global Economic Institutions

GATT rules are as important to us as the rules of our constitution. —Joe Clark, 1986

INTRODUCTION

The Trudeau government's white paper on foreign policy emphasized national interests over multilateral considerations and economic growth over social justice. In 1995, the Liberal government under Jean Chrétien issued its own white paper on foreign policy in which, once again, Canadian prosperity was given primacy of place. In the interim, the global economy had abandoned the embedded liberalism of the Bretton Woods system and had been overtaken by a process of globalization, shaped in large measure by neo-liberal ideas and practices. Governments and their citizens, with varying degrees of satisfaction, have claimed that globalization has reduced the capacity of the state to act in support of domestic economic objectives. The solution for many, including policy makers, is to yield to the market: to liberalize economic policy and to encourage and support liberal markets in trade and finance. Such ideas would have been alien to many of the economic nationalists of Trudeau's cabinet and Canadian society in the early 1970s. Indeed, they remain alien to many today. Among policy makers and Canada's economic elite, however, the heresy of the 1960s and 1970s has become the orthodoxy of the 1990s. This chapter reviews this transformation and examines the place of multilateralism in this process. It also discusses the evolution of Canadian policy and examines how successive governments have approached multilateralism in response to the process of globalization.

FROM BRETTON WOODS TO GLOBALIZATION

The Bretton Woods system was dealt a fatal blow on 15 August 1971. In a statement from Washington, American president Richard Nixon announced the implementation of drastic measures in an attempt to rescue the United States from its first trade deficit of the century. The New Economic Policy included provisions for domestic wage and price controls, a 10 per cent surcharge on a wide range of imports, an end to the convertibility of dollars into gold, and the elimination of a pegged value for gold.

These measures were a clear violation of the basic principles of the International Monetary Fund (IMF) and the General Agreement on Tariffs and Trade (GATT). They were also an explicit statement of American unwillingness to continue as the patron of the liberal multilateral economic order that it had led for the previous 25 years. For Canada, the 'Nixon shock' was a particularly devastating blow. It left the Canadian economy, which was so heavily dependent on the American market, particularly vulnerable. More important, the measures were directed at Canada; it was not an innocent bystander. There would be no special privileges for Canada this time. Despite the pleadings of the Canadian government—which sent a ministerial delegation, led by the prime minister, to Washington to argue for an exemption—the American secretary of the Treasury refused to consider any. The American action and the absence of any special privileges for Canada marked the end of an era in which Canada had been able to benefit both from American support of multilateralism and from American willingness to extend special benefits to Canada in order to keep the continental economy healthy. Three years later, Nixon would travel to Ottawa to remind Canadians that the United States looked upon Canada as an independent country. The meaning of the message was clear: Canada no longer carried a special position in Washington's foreign policy.

The Nixon shock was both a sign and a source of considerable disarray in the global economy, and 1971 marked the beginning of a period of turmoil. The decade began with a widespread rejection of the Bretton Woods commitment to fixed exchange rates in the international monetary system. It ended with a second upheaval in global energy supply and prices, the first having occurred in 1973–4. In between, the Canadian economy (along with those of other industrialized states) was ravaged by high inflation, slow growth, and increasing levels of unemployment. The Keynesian post-war boom had ended. By the early 1980s, the country experienced the worst recession since the Depression of the 1930s. While the effects of these developments in the industrialized North were bad, they were even more severe in the poorer regions of the world, where high energy costs, volatile commodity prices, reduced export earnings, and the increasingly protectionist practices of the North resulted in growing disparity between the North and the South. By the early 1980s, these countries were also saddled with insurmountable debt burdens brought on, in part, by the high interest rate policies of the leading capitalist economies.

The Nixon shock had its most significant impact in the realm of international monetary relations. In removing the American dollar from the gold standard, the US government had effectively and unilaterally removed the base of the fixed exchange rate system and the foundation of the IMF. Canada and other members of the IMF's Group of Ten acted quickly to minimize the damage. The leading members of the IMF met at the Smithsonian Institute in December 1971 and reached an agreement that was intended to re-establish a semblance of order and stability in the international monetary system. The agreement included provisions for the devaluation of the American dollar. It also included a proposal to return to fixed exchange rates, only this time with greater flexibility in allowing currencies to fluctuate within plus or minus 2.25 per cent of par value. This decision reflected the growing interest among members of the IMF for greater freedom and flexibility in determination of par values.

In addition to this multilateral activity, Canada took its case to the American government in an attempt to secure its support for Canada's exchange rate policy. After nearly a decade on a fixed rate, the Canadian government had decided in 1970 to return to a floating exchange rate. The government was anxious to protect this policy in whatever new arrangements were to be worked out multilaterally. From a Canadian vantage point, the agreement was a success; J.L. Granatstein and Robert Bothwell note that 'only Canada was not required to repeg its currency to the American dollar. That exemption had been arranged, carefully and discreetly; and, it was, quite definitely, an exemption'.[1] It was also an indication of things to come, because the IMF was finally moving in the direction that Canada had first advocated in the early 1950s. Within two years, the Smithsonian agreement had collapsed and the IMF abandoned the idea of fixing exchange rates.

The abandonment of Bretton Woods principles by the United States did not result in the collapse of the institutions that had been established in the 1940s. It did, however, alter their role in the global economy. American policy reflected the practical difficulties that these institutions were experiencing at that time. It also reflected a growing disenchantment with and discrediting of the Keynesian ideas and policies that had been so influential since the 1930s. In their place, economists and governments alike began to advocate for a return to more liberal policies, including the deregulation of financial markets, the privatization of state-owned enterprises, and the further liberalization of international trade. Over the next three decades, the embedded liberalism of the Bretton Woods era would be replaced by more market-oriented strategies advocated by these neo-liberals. John Ruggie summarized the situation:

> This shift in governments' policy postures runs deeper than swings in ideological moods and preferences, though such a swing is underway. It is also structural in character and, ironically, at least in part reflects the very success of the postwar trade and monetary regimes whose sustainability may hang in the balance. Point-of-entry barriers to international economic transactions have been virtually eliminated, financial markets are globally integrated, and entire sectors of production have become transnationalized. This transformation in the global economy has . . . undermined key conceptual and institutional premises of the postwar economic regimes as well as related aspects of national economic policymaking on the basis of which governments mediated the relationship between international and domestic stability: that the international economy consists of territorially distinct and disjoint national economies linked by external transactions; that these transactions are carried on at arms-length; that border measures are effective policy tools; that governments enjoy considerable policy autonomy within their domestic sphere; and that a relatively coherent and consensual policy framework exists for domestic governmental institutions.[2]

Canadian policy was deeply influenced by these developments, and policy makers and the country's economic elite rejected Keynesian policies in favour of freer markets. At the same time, however, they retained a strong commitment to the institutions of Bretton Woods, although this commitment was sorely tested by continental trade arrangements and by the country's participation in the elite club of the G-7.

Amidst the turmoil of the 1970s, Canadian policy makers sought initially to diversify Canada's economic relations. The Department of External Affairs' proposed 'third option' policy—'a comprehensive long-term strategy to develop and strengthen the Canadian economy and other aspects of its national life, and in the process to reduce the present Canadian vulnerability'[3]—became the centrepiece of the government's economic strategy. The third option suggested a new direction in Canadian commercial policy, but it had a long pedigree: similar objectives had motivated Canadian policy makers at the time of the GATT's formation in 1947. Since that time, successive governments had turned to Europe as the solution to Canada's economic dependence on the United States. This was a poor strategy because European countries had shown little interest in accepting a larger percentage of Canadian goods, and Canadian exporters, for their part, had also displayed little inclination to look beyond the North American continent.

This historical experience notwithstanding, the Trudeau government initiated yet another attempt at trade diversification. Trudeau signed framework agreements with the European Community (EC) and Japan in July and October 1976. These agreements were designed to facilitate the exchange of information and trade missions, but they provided little in the way of firm direction for changing trade policy. Each of the parties had little room to manoeuvre because they were prevented by the GATT from establishing preferential trading schemes even if there had been an inclination to do so.

Official interest in trade diversification waned as economic problems mounted, and the third option quickly passed from the government's priorities. Canadian trade continued to move in a north-south direction and its volume was increasing steadily. The third option, as past experience with the GATT had demonstrated, could not reduce Canada's trade dependency on the United States.

PURSUING REGIONAL AND MULTILATERAL OPTIONS

The negotiations on a bilateral free trade agreement (FTA) commenced in 1985. The Uruguay Round of GATT negotiations began in 1986. The FTA was completed in 1988, and the Uruguay Round in 1994. The slow progress of multilateral trade negotiations was one reason why the government opted first for the bilateral route. A second was the extremely complex nature of the Uruguay Round and the diverse nature of Canadian interests in the negotiations. There was, of course, the added difficulty of working within a multilateral system in which Canada had limited control over the pace of negotiations.

The Uruguay Round received strong support from middle powers such as Canada. Through its participation in various coalitions, such as the Cairns Group of Fair Traders concerned with agricultural issues and the de la Paix Group concerned with institutional reform, the Canadian delegation was among the more active proponents of a new round. According to Gilbert Winham, Canada also played a major role in the negotiations on subsidies in part 'because of its substantial trade with the United

States and the importance of this issue' in the bilateral FTA.[4] Such influence waned when the government was pressed by domestic interests to compromise its position on trade in agricultural products. The government was, however, able to secure sufficient support for its proposal to transform the GATT into a formal international trade organization, the World Trade Organization (WTO). This initiative reflected the continuing Canadian interest in supporting institutions at the multilateral level.

The Uruguay Round—the eighth round of GATT talks—was the most ambitious round to that time. Its agenda included items left over from the Tokyo Round as well as a number of new issues. One of the principal motivating factors behind the new round was the fact that more and more international trade was falling outside of GATT rules. This was in part a result of increasingly restrictive trade policy measures, the growth and emergence of regional trade blocs, and the increased significance of international trade in sectors such as services and foreign investment that had never been addressed by the GATT. Increasingly, international trade was also being influenced by domestic regulatory policies. If these were to be governed by international rules, it would require a more interventionist GATT regime than had been attempted or supported in the past. There was also a need to address the changing pattern of North–South trade. Reflecting both the failure of the UN Conference on Trade and Development (UNCTAD) and the increased diversity of economic development patterns in the South, more and more Third World governments accepted the necessity of working within GATT rules if they were to reform their domestic economies and reduce the ever-growing gap between rich and poor. Accommodating these new states would require an end to many of the discriminatory trade practices, such as the Multi-Fibre Agreement, that had governed North–South trade in the past. In addition, there was the perennial problem of agricultural products, which had been the source of long-standing disputes between the EC, the United States, and other major trading nations.

Canada was actively involved in promoting a new round in the early 1980s even as it considered the benefits of bilateral deals. Miles Kahler describes how Canada, Australia, New Zealand, and members of the European Free Trade Association (EFTA) proposed an agenda that received the support of a crucial bloc of developing countries and 'defined their [collective] interests as defending the multilateral trading system through support for a new round of trade negotiations'.[5] The government has viewed the two paths of bilateralism and multilateralism as complementary, but as Winham notes, there is a certain incompatibility between them: 'By definition, the establishment of preferential trading areas constitutes a threat to the universality of the GATT, although', he goes on to say, 'the effect of such developments on world trade liberalism may be less clear'.[6] Despite this threat, the government's trade negotiators attempted to ensure that the free trade deal met GATT rules:[7]

> When [the government] began to consider seriously a free trade arrangement with the United States, we believed that initiative was in full accord with Canada's commitment to multilateralism, in trade and other matters. The agreement would be consistent

with the [GATT], and, from a trade policy perspective, our view was that the region would lead the world. Indeed, we believed we would be more likely to create a climate for multilateralism by starting in the neighbourhood.[8]

Article 24 of the GATT, for example, does permit free trade agreements provided that they are comprehensive in nature and do not discriminate against other trading partners. In a strict sense, the FTA met these requirements. There were many people, however, both in Canada and outside, who viewed the agreement as a challenge both to Canada's commitment to the GATT and to the GATT process itself. Coming in the middle of the Uruguay Round, the FTA did suggest that Canada was less than whole-hearted in its support for the GATT. The subsequent negotiation of an expanded FTA to include Mexico in the form of the North American Free Trade Agreement (NAFTA), although not initiated by Canada, nonetheless suggested a further deviation from the multilateralist option.

The Uruguay Round negotiations were the most complicated round of the various GATT rounds, not only because of the wide range of issues involved, but also because of the increased number and interests of governments. Canada, as one of nearly 100 states involved in the negotiations, increasingly worked through coalitions along with other lesser powers to further its interests in the negotiations. The emergence of increased coalition behaviour within the GATT is, in part, also a reflection of the relative decline of the dominance of the United States in the negotiations. Decision making in the GATT became more diffuse, increasing opportunities for lesser powers to initiate demands. The increased importance of the GATT for these lesser powers also meant they had a greater stake in the negotiations, thus encouraging the use of techniques that will enhance their influence. Canadian support for these coalitions appeared at times more interested in furthering the process than in compromising to reach a common consensus.

The Cairns Group of agricultural traders illustrated the potential and problems of such coalitions.[9] On the difficult issue of agricultural subsidies, the Canadian government was unable to support the Cairns Group, which had been unequivocal in its opposition to subsidies. As a result of competing domestic pressures, the government attempted (with little success) to balance its opposition to subsidies with support for the continued protection of marketing boards through Article 11 of the GATT. In deciding to table a separate negotiating offer that protected Canada's supply management system from the common agricultural proposal of the Cairns Group, the government made it clear that as far as the Group was concerned, 'we're part of it, but we're not part of it'.[10] Speaking for the Cairns Group, a disappointed Australian official concluded, 'Clearly Canada found what the rest of the members were seeking was too hard politically'.[11]

The government was also active in soliciting the participation of and working with developing countries. While Australia, Colombia, and Switzerland championed the demands of the 'more pragmatic' developing countries, Canada served to represent their positions to the principal power brokers. Michael Hart describes Canada's position as follows: 'Canada, trading on its status as a member of the Summit and the Quads, proved an indispensable link between the smaller countries and the big three and learned to play the "honest broker" card with great skill, pursuing its traditional role of enthusiastic cheerleader for any agreement that advanced the cause of international rule making'.[12]

Reflecting Canada's ongoing interest in entrenching international rules within institutionalized settings, the government took up the cause of the World Trade Organization in 1990:

> At first hesitantly but with increasing confidence and the active support of the EC, Canada advanced proposals to establish a multilateral trade organization to implement and administer the many agreements under discussion. With the help of University of Michigan GATT scholar John Jackson, Debra Steger and other members of the Canadian team developed the contours of what would eventually become the Agreement establishing the World Trade Organization.[13]

The establishment of the WTO confirmed, for supporters and opponents alike, that the multilateral process worked.

While Canada's support for the liberalization of trade has generated a good deal of popular support, international economic policy has never been free from domestic conflict. No issue has generated as much domestic conflict as bilateral economic relations with the United States, and although the GATT has generally been guided by a stronger supportive consensus, it too has come under controversy. In 1999, the Standing Committee on Foreign Affairs and International Trade conducted hearings on Canada's participation in the WTO and its policy toward that institution in preparation for the Seattle ministerial meeting held in November 1999. The committee heard from over 400 Canadians in 30 public sessions. The public response reflected the growing concern on the part of many Canadians with international trade policy. It also reflected the growing importance of international trade to Canada. This marked a significant shift from earlier periods, when it would have been difficult to generate this much interest in international trade issues. It was thus with a keen sense of public interest and concern that the government approached the Seattle meetings, the second regularly scheduled ministerial meetings since the establishment of the WTO in 1995. Yet despite the significant demonstration of public concern and opposition, the government did not alter course: 'For at least the last fifty years, Canada has been helping to write the international rule book, to emphasize rules, not brute power, as the key to international peace and order. Our continued work at the WTO is a worthy chapter in that book'.[14]

The successful completion of the Uruguay Round of trade negotiations reasserted the viability of the GATT and of the multilateral trade regime that it helped established. In spite of the apparent change of heart in Canada's interests in multilateralism, as suggested by the amount of attention devoted to the bilateral and trilateral talks with

Mexico and the Americans, multilateralism retained a prominent place on the Canadian and global agendas. Hart writes,

> Pride of place has been restored to global approaches, with the WTO providing a cred-ible consolidation of many of the earlier experiments at the regional level. The region-alism of the 1980s, like that of the 1960s, challenged but did not overwhelm fundamental acceptance of the benefits of or, indeed, need for a multilateral frame-work of rules. A successful new round of multilateral negotiations was a useful coun-terpoint to the perceived benefits of regionalism. The Uruguay Round similarly ensured that a larger number of participants would pursue their regional interests in agreements that would complement rather than rival the multilateral trading system.[15]

Regionalism remained an important focus for Canadian trade policy in the 1990s, but it was most often directly linked to a wider vision of multilateral trade. This is evident in the Liberal government's pursuit of free trade arrangements in the Americas and in the Pacific. In the economic arena, NAFTA can be identified as the crit-ical move to regionalism for the Canadian government. Unlike the decision to join the Organization of American States (OAS), however, the decision to join NAFTA was a defensive action; it was not initiated by the government, and it did not initially reflect an interest in expanding the bilateral agreement. Indeed, the government was not predisposed to share its exclusive access to the American market. In the face of Mexican and American proposals, however, the Canadian government concluded that it would be best to join in. Yet even here, one finds the government's interest in a wider multilateral process. Among the issues that most concerned Canadian negotiators in NAFTA was the inclusion of an accession clause that would make it easier for new members to join the agreement. This would serve the twin objectives of limiting the possibility that the entire agreement would be renegotiated every time a new member joined and would also facilitate a more rapid expansion of the membership. It has been this more rapid expansion that has motivated Canadian policy makers since. Indeed, the subsequent trips by the prime minister to Central and South America can be seen as an attempt to do this. As Jean Daudelin writes, 'Canada, by calling for wider membership and in promoting the accession of Chile to the hemispheric free trade system, was acting in a manner consistent with this definition of the country's long-term interests. It was seeking to regain control over its involvement in a process it had not initially anticipated'.[16] One could go on to add that it was also trying to link regional initiatives with other policy goals in the form of an expanded system of global trade rules. This was particularly important with respect to the United States.

The so-called hub-and-spoke model of trade agreements, wherein the United States would conclude a series of bilateral pacts, was undesirable because the Americans would have full control over the timing and content of such agreements and as a result, a patchwork of trade rules might emerge. Daudelin writes, 'From Canada's standpoint, the hemisphere now appears above all as a trade area and, with

Asia, as one of the two ways to escape the overpowering influence of the United States'.[17] Former Liberal trade minister Roy MacLaren said that NAFTA 'can provide a nucleus for a more open, global trading endeavour'.[18]

A similar theme is evident in the government's approach to the Pacific. Even while policy makers continue to place much of their emphasis on global multilateral institutions, the response to regionalism has been to recognize its importance and to use it as a means of advancing these wider multilateral interests. Regionalism thus has become part of a larger multilateral project rather than a substitute for it. Prior to the 1993 Asia-Pacific Economic Cooperation (APEC) ministerial meeting, MacLaren said that

> the final building block will be to complement our multilateral efforts with regional efforts. Improved co-operation and dialogue with other Asia-Pacific governments are required to ensure that rules, rather than the unilateral projection of power or pressure policies, will rule in the Pacific trading relationship. While most of these rules will and should be multilateral, some may need to be regional, and indeed bilateral.

He went on to add, 'I am not saying, however, that this is only a regional process. We must recognize that the best way of achieving free trade in the Asia-Pacific is to get our global floor of multilateral trade rules up as high as we can'.[19] From such comments, it is possible to argue that Canada's concerns in getting involved in regional initiatives in the Pacific reflect an interest in keeping the region open to the global trading regime and in preventing a more exclusivist regional response. The policy did contain certain risks. To the extent that these regional arrangements suggested a preference for more limited trade blocs, they provided encouragement for others to follow a similar path. They also developed new interests within Canada that will be more motivated to protect and promote these regional arrangements at the expense of broader multilateral efforts.

The liberalization of trade has become a major—if not the major—foreign policy priority for the Canadian government. Partly as a reflection of the new security environment that substantially reduced direct threats to Canadian security and partly as a result of a powerful consensus within Canada that trade was the best means of ensuring continued economic growth, the Liberal government followed its Conservative predecessor in devoting an extensive effort and extensive resources to securing open markets for Canadian exporters. The foreign policy white paper of 1994 had identified the promotion of prosperity and employment as one of three key foreign policy priorities for the new government. As Claire Sjolander described it, 'foreign policy was trade policy',[20] and it certainly appeared to be the only sustained interest that Prime Minister Chrétien had in foreign relations. Chrétien's support for the trade policy agenda was evident in his participation in a series of Team Canada trade promotion missions abroad to the Far East in November 1994, Latin America in January 1995, South Asia in January 1996, and Southeast Asia in January 1997. On the multilateral front, the Liberal government oversaw the completion of the Uruguay Round and the establishment of the WTO. It has also continued to beat the free trade drum in the

Americas and the Pacific. By the end of the 1990s, the Canadian government had become one of the leading proponents of the Free Trade Agreement for the Americas (FTAA). Discussions on the FTAA dominated the preparations for the first Summit of the Americas to be held in Canada, in Quebec City in April 2001.

MAKING THE WORLD SAFE FOR INVESTORS

If Canadian trade policy demonstrated the emerging connections between the state and Canadian businesses actively pursuing export markets, negotiations on the Multilateral Agreement on Investment (MAI) brought policy makers into contact with those who were less favourably disposed to the process of globalization. Elizabeth Smythe has noted that much of the contact was of the virtual variety, as opposition groups relied extensively on the new medium of the Internet to press their opposition to the MAI.[21] Negotiations on a set of rules to govern international investment presented the Canadian government with a dilemma as it attempted to respond to the conflicting demands arising out of pressures for liberalization spurred on by globalization. Investment issues also demonstrated the underlying tensions in Canada's multilateralist policy and its attempt to balance bilateral and regional arrangements with a wider, more inclusive multilateral order.

Investment policy has been a significant issue in Canada's foreign policy for decades. Concerns about foreign investment in the late 1950s generated a wave of economic nationalism that still influences policy debates. A series of commissions and task forces during the 1960s and early 1970s examined the issue and kept it on the foreign policy agenda for successive Liberal governments. The main issue throughout this period was the extensive amount of foreign direct investment from the United States that had penetrated the Canadian economy. In response, the Foreign Investment Review Agency (FIRA) was established in 1974. Although the FIRA screening process is generally acknowledged to have had little substantial effect on the flow of foreign investment into Canada, it served as an important symbol of Canada's reservations about foreign investment and as a major irritant in bilateral relations with the Americans. When the Mulroney government sought to change Canada's investment policy, it renamed FIRA 'Investment Canada'. The signal went out that Canada would welcome foreign investment.

Defining a set of rules to guarantee the protection of Canadian investors in foreign markets has since become a priority for Canadian trade negotiators. This shift was not simply a reflection of an ideological preference for markets; it was also a reflection of a real change in Canada's position as not only a recipient but also a source of foreign investment. A clearer set of international rules was advocated to protect the expanding group of foreign investors operating from Canada. Many Canadian interests now argued that investment rules would protect their investments abroad and that opening Canadian markets was a necessary trade-off to ensure such protection. The issue then became one of how best to pursue that protection.

During the late 1980s and early 1990s, Canadian policy makers pursued these rules in two distinct, but in their view complementary, arenas: bilaterally (and later trilaterally) in negotiations with the Americans and the Mexicans and multilaterally as part of the Uruguay Round of GATT negotiations. The Canadian government under the Conservatives accepted the premise of the need to liberalize Canada's investment laws and also accepted the argument that it was necessary to strengthen international rules that protected the rights of investors against potential discrimination from governments. This was also one of the more important American objectives in trade talks, both with Canada and in the GATT. Given the sympathetic ear in Ottawa, the FTA, and later NAFTA, provided a set of rules protecting the rights of investors based on the GATT principle of 'national treatment'. With the exception of the important but deeply problematic sector of culture, NAFTA includes the strongest protection for investors yet to be included in an international agreement. Following the implementation of NAFTA, both Canada and the United States sought to multilateralize these provisions, although there was no consensus on how this should be done. Canadian officials leaned toward the GATT/WTO process because it would include a wider array of countries, most importantly developing countries, which often impeded foreign investment. The Americans and some European governments, not to mention individuals within the Organisation for Economic Co-operation and Development (OECD), favoured the OECD, and so in 1995, negotiations began under the auspices of the OECD on a multilateral agreement on investment.

As Smythe and others have ably documented, the MAI negotiations ended in failure. In part because of national differences and in part because of significant domestic protest in Canada and elsewhere, governments abandoned the negotiations in 1998. The issues, however, remain—as does the underlying public discontent with this and other aspects of globalization. The government's commitment to liberalization has failed to win the support of all Canadians. Many groups have taken issue with trade policy and other aspects of the neo-liberal economic agenda. Public protests in Vancouver at the APEC Summit of 1998, in Windsor at the General Assembly of the OAS, and in Quebec City at the Summit of the Americas demonstrated the extent of public concern. The demonstrations at the OAS General Assembly in Windsor also suggested that vocal sectors of the Canadian population were questioning the very fabric of Canada's multilateralist foreign policy. International economic institutions have become a significant target for groups and citizens concerned about the adverse effects of national and international economic practices, effects ranging from loss of employment to rapidly increasing inequalities to environmental degradation.

This has opened a new chapter in the evolution of international financial institutions, which once operated in virtual anonymity, and raised a dilemma for policy officials. Canadian officials at the UN and elsewhere have actively promoted increased involvement on the part of NGOs in the making and implementation of policy at the multilateral level. In the economic realm, they have adopted a quieter approach. In response to the increased attention that international economic issues have received, the government has encouraged greater NGO participation in this policy arena, but as Sjolander argues, it often takes a different form from the more inclusive participation of NGOs at the UN or in the human security arena discussed in the next chapter.[22]

REACHING THE SUMMIT

In an attempt to re-establish a mechanism for the collective management of the global political economy, five leading capitalist powers met at Rambouillet in France in 1975. As Sylvia Ostry writes, 'the innovation of the summit was an institutional response to the combined effect of two forces—the weakening of the established system of co-operation occasioned by the breakdown of the Bretton Woods arrangements and the advent of new problems requiring resolution at the highest level'.[23] Some also viewed it as a means by which the leading capitalist powers could manage the global economy free from the problems of the developing economies and from the Third World's demands for substantial economic reforms.[24] The annual economic summit was designed, in part, to re-establish the pattern of multilateral co-operation—albeit within a severely limited group of states—that had been unilaterally, if temporarily, suspended by the Americans in 1971.

The Canadian government's interest in participating in the economic summits was very much a reflection of its interest in gaining a voice in, or at least an ear at, deliberations that would have a profound effect on Canada's own economic policy options. For some observers, summit membership was an indication of Canada's arrival in (or return to) the core group of capitalist powers, a position that had been partially abandoned, partially superseded by others, in the 1950s and 1960s. The emergence of Canada as a principal power, as Dewitt and Kirton describe it, or as a state on 'the periphery of the core', as Resnick sees it, might also be viewed as an attempt to support a process of multilateral co-operation on which Canadian interests were quite dependent.[25] The government had already undertaken other actions in the GATT and had tried to forge extra-continental commercial links in response to the emergence of unilateralism and economic nationalism of the early 1970s.

The summits provided Canadian officials with yet another forum in which to respond to American trade and economic policies. Highly sensitive to exclusive bilateral dealings, especially when confronted with the American's rejection of Canada's requests for exemptions in 1971, the government obviously favoured a multilateral alternative, and the economic summits provided one. This is somewhat ironic given France's concern that Canada would be little more than an appendage of the Americans, controlled from Washington. Perhaps the Americans also saw it this way and favoured Canadian membership as a way of providing a 'North American' balance to a European-dominated grouping. Although Canadian participation in the summits was understandable in response to changed circumstances and status considerations, it was somewhat of a departure from previous policies that supported associations with wider memberships. In practice, Canadian contributions over the years have naturally (and inevitably) been constrained by Canada's relative position in the hierarchy of this economic elite group.

Canadian contributions to the summits are difficult to assess given the limited information available on the private discussions among the leaders and the rather general and vacuous tone of the declarations that pass for summit decisions. Understandably, contributions from Canadian prime ministers will vary depending on the personal dynamics of the individuals involved. Prime Minister Trudeau, for example, had greater difficulty in dealing with American president Ronald Reagan than with Reagan's predecessor, Jimmy Carter. Nonetheless, it is possible to identify instances in which Canadian leaders have attempted to shape the summit agenda. Stated Canadian priorities for the summits have frequently been actions designed to assist the developing countries. Such proposals have ranged from restarting global negotiations (at the 1981 Ottawa summit) to alleviating the debt burden of Third World countries (at the 1988 Toronto summit). There were also interventions on political issues, such as arms control in the early 1980s and South Africa in the late 1980s. In virtually all of these areas, Canadian efforts resulted in little, if any, success. The summits have very much reflected the interests and concerns of the capitalist world's leading powers: the United States, West Germany, and Japan. The other players, including Canada, have been limited to playing on the margins. According to former undersecretary and ambassador to the United States Allan Gotlieb, Canadian initiatives tended to place the country as 'the odd man out': 'Discussions at the Summits were often difficult. Canada found that the other Summit members saw it clearly as a developed industrialized nation. Accordingly they saw some of Canada's more interventionist and restrictive policies as a legacy of its self-perception as a weaker, or in the broadest sense, a developing nation'.[26]

With few exceptions, and these primarily in political areas, the summits have not been very successful in differentiating Canadian policy from that of the United States. In some cases, especially during the early 1980s, Trudeau often sided with the European leaders in opposing American economic policy. At times, on East–West issues, he would stand virtually alone. Under Brian Mulroney, however, Canada frequently supported the Americans on economic issues while differing with them on some aspects of North–South relations.

In the 1990s, the G-7 became one of the principal driving forces behind neo-liberal economic policies. Participation in the G-7 has clearly linked Canada with the policies being pursued by the other members of the club and, in turn, distanced the country from the policies and activities of other middle powers. As David Black and Claire Sjolander write, 'this concert-type form of multilateralism was very different in character from the notionally open, universal and non-discriminatory forms pioneered in the Bretton Woods era. While it did not preclude the continuation of the latter, the Summit process came to epitomize over time, a new and increasingly dominant form of more narrowly constructed multilateralism'.[27] This has imposed some constraints on the possibility of forging coalitions with these other states. In this respect, participation in this elite club, while no doubt an indication of Canada's senior status in the globe's capitalist economy, has created certain dilemmas for the government in terms of its foreign policy options.

Participation in the G-7 has also, however, given the government an opportunity both to support the rejuvenation of multilateral co-operation among the leading capitalist powers and to shape, albeit in an extremely modest way, its content. At the same time, it appears to have constrained assertive action on other fronts, most notably in the area of North–South economic reforms. As A. Lovbraek implies in his study of the Like-Minded Group of states during the late 1970s, Canada was unwilling to sacrifice its membership in the summit seven for more radical action in other forums.[28] Kim Nossal also suggests that this was a constraint on Canadian sanctions policy toward South Africa.[29] As will be discussed below, however, there were also other influential factors of a domestic variety that acted as a brake on a more progressive foreign policy in the ongoing North–South dialogue and there have been some opportunities to use G-7 participation to forge links with developing economies.

THE G-7 AND REFORM OF INTERNATIONAL INSTITUTIONS

It is not very surprising to find that Canada used its term as chair of the G-7 in 1995 to press its case for reforming international institutions, especially international financial institutions. The interest in institutional reform was partly a reflection of concerns about the ability of institutions to address a number of pressing global political, security, and economic problems: the peso crisis in Mexico in 1994, the extensive reform agenda at the UN as it approached its 50th anniversary, and concerns about co-ordinating the proliferation of institutions that had become active in the global community. Equally important, however, it demonstrated the importance of international institutions for the conduct of Canadian foreign policy. The emphasis that Canada placed on the governance issue also demonstrated that however important the G-7 might have become, it was very much rooted in a wider array of institutions that required support and care.

The Halifax summit set out an ambitious plan to reform international financial institutions, especially the IMF. It also included recommendations for other economic institutions, including support for closer collaboration between these institutions and other organizations, both regional and within the UN system, that had tended to be at the margins of the international financial institutions but that nonetheless dealt with the effects that these institutions had on states and societies. John Kirton has argued that these actions and subsequent Canadian diplomacy in the wake of the Asian financial crisis at the G-8 'recurrently displayed intellectual, policy, and structural leadership'. He goes on to argue that 'Canada's leadership was centered not on broad multilateralism, but on restricted membership plurilateralism, with an overwhelming emphasis on the concert that the G-7 represented'.[30] It is, however, difficult to separate Canadian diplomacy (and indeed that of other states) in one forum, such as the G-7, from the multiplicity of institutional connections in which Canada interacts. Moreover, as Andrew Baker has argued, 'more attention should be paid to linkages and relationships between different networks of officials from the G-7 countries, multilateral institutions, the private sector, and various emerging market economies. Ultimately it is these networks that facilitate the formulation and institutionalization of the consensual belief systems that are having an increasing impact on international politics and multilateral diplomacy'.[31]

Prior to the Halifax summit, Canada had engaged in a wide-ranging set of consultations both to inform and gather support for the government's reform agenda. After the summit, Canada undertook an unprecedented follow-up to its initiatives that has focused on reforms at the UN and in international financial institutions. Indeed, one of the primary objectives of the reform process was to seek greater co-operation between the UN and these global financial institutions. As part of their follow-up process, Canadian officials consulted with a wide range of members of the international community, including those within the Commonwealth, the Francophonie, APEC, the World Bank, UNCTAD, and the Association of South-East Asian Nations (ASEAN). The summit proposed an extensive plan to reform international financial institutions. These proposals were quickly picked up by NGOs, who, through the Sierra Club in Halifax, began to monitor and report on the reform process. The Halifax Initiative, as it was called, which represented a number of NGOs, was the face of the new multilateralism referred to elsewhere and reflects the growing salience and activism of NGOs on global and regional economic issues. In the fallout from the Halifax summit, not only did Canadian officials attempt to dilute the more elitist characteristics of the G-7, they also recognized the need to seek a wider base of consensual support from the international community if the G-7 was to have any influence. Moreover, the response of the Sierra Club, and the by now standard counter-summits of NGOs, demonstrated the inability of the G-7 to work free from these pressures, the same pressures that were challenging the authority and actions of many global and regional institutions. Canada, for its part, was well placed to 'facilitate the formulation and institutionalization' of the proposals launched at the Halifax and Cologne summits because of its many institutional connections that cut across the North–South divide.

At this and subsequent summits, one of the principal interests displayed by Canadian officials has been in addressing at least some of the concerns of the developing economies. And this raises the question of whether Canadian policy has been designed more to shape the process of liberalization to meet the needs of developing countries or to shape the developing countries to meet the requirements of liberalization.

LOOKING AFTER THE WORLD'S POOREST

In the 1970s, many Canadians took issue with the Trudeau government's proposal to place a higher priority on Canada's own economic well-being rather than on matters of social justice. So too the Chrétien government was criticized in the mid-1990s when its foreign policy white paper placed Canadian prosperity as its primary concern. For some Canadians, the idea that one of the wealthiest countries in the world should place a greater emphasis on increasing its own wealth than on addressing the gross inequalities that exist in the world was a heresy.

Development assistance is no longer the cornerstone of Canadian policy toward the developing economies of the South. 'Indeed', Tim Draimin and Brian Tomlinson write, 'government policy towards the developing countries since 1994 has focused almost exclusively on bilateral and multilateral trade and investment initiatives, meeting the primary foreign policy goal of *Canada in the World* of strengthening Canada's economic prosperity'.[32] This policy did not really distinguish Canada from other governments, as there has been a significant shift away from publicly funded capital flows to private capital flows between the North and the South. There has also been a notable, if troubling, shift in the direction of such flows. According to Draimin and Tomlinson,

> The North–South Institute recently calculated that in 1995 Canadian banks, public agencies, private firms, and individual investors had outstanding loans and investments of $60 billion in developing countries. The profits, interest, and other income flowing back to Canada from these investments was about $4.8 billion, more than one and a half times Canada's ODA [official development assistance] for that year.[33]

A good deal of Canadian foreign policy has been devoted to integrating countries from the South into the multilateral network of rules and institutions that govern the global economy. In addition to working in coalitions with developing economies during the Uruguay Round of the GATT negotiations, the government has supported financing schemes to encourage developing countries' compliance with international accords in areas such as environmental measures. The Canadian proposal to expand the membership of the Financial Stability Forum to include 'emerging markets' was accepted during the Cologne G-7 summit. These measures, when combined with the numerous free trade initiatives launched by Canadian officials in Asia and the Americas, suggest that the Canadian government has opted to encourage developing countries to look to the market rather than to public support to cure their economic ills.

At the same time, the government has placed even greater demands on the recipients of their shrinking development assistance disbursements. During the 1990s, the Canadian government identified four priorities in its development assistance program. These were governance, health, environment, and youth. In addition, the government increasingly attempted to link aid with such governance issues as human rights and reductions in arms expenditures.

These laudable objectives were circumscribed by successive years of budget reductions. The net result was a growing gap between the aspirations of foreign aid and the practical limitations of a shrinking budget, as the aid budget fell from over $3 billion at the beginning of the decade to less than $2 billion at its end. Fred Kunzle summarizes these cuts:

> At the end of the 1980s, Canada had been spending .5 per cent of its Gross National Product on foreign aid, well under the targeted amount of the .7 per cent pledged by the developed nations. Yet these cuts will reduce it to less than .3 per cent of our GNP. This will make Canada one of the least generous countries of the developed world.[34]

The OECD criticized Canada's declining aid budget: 'Canada's actual and planned decreases in aid volume could seriously weaken the highly regarded Canadian aid program and cause material and psychological setbacks for the global co-operative effort'.[35] Although the biggest drop occurred between 1992 and 1993, the Liberal government continued the pattern of raiding the foreign aid cupboard to address its ongoing deficit problems. As a result, Canada slipped from 5th to 11th place in the OECD's rankings. The OECD report recognized Canada's past achievement in this area, but this only served to exaggerate the adverse effects of the more recent declines: 'It is widely recognized that Canada has played an important role as a global partner in international development co-operation and has made distinctive contributions to the stability and economic progress of the developing world'.[36] Yet as the Canadian Council for International Cooperation (CCIC) stated, 'Canada, long seen as a leader in development aid, now has a tarnished image. . . . The aid program has borne a greater share of the burden of deficit reduction than have other federal programs'.[37]

Despite declining funds, the government hoped to use its depleted aid budget to reinforce its human rights campaign. Foreign Minister Ouellet proposed that foreign aid be used for three purposes: 'i) to persuade leaders to respect rights and govern democratically; ii) to develop the capacity of groups that protect and promote human rights in an effort to enhance individual security; and ii) to ensure that the public has more input in decision-making in society'.[38] How effective an emaciated aid budget would be was never questioned by the minister, but surely it speaks to the strength of the government's commitment to pursue these noble objectives. It was nonetheless evident that the principal effect was rhetorical rather than practical. The same could be said with regard to a subsequent proposal to use aid to influence the arms-purchasing practices of recipient governments. Invoking the mantra of doing more with less, the Liberal government increased its aid policy objectives even while it emptied the pot that was necessary to support these objectives in the field.[39]

CANADA AND THE JUBILEE 2000 INITIATIVE

In May 1998, a chain of people nearly seven miles long surrounded the meeting place of the G-7 in Birmingham, England, in a display of solidarity designed to demonstrate to the leaders of the world's most powerful economies the popular support for removing the burden of debt on the world's poor. The action represented the work of a major international campaign, Jubilee 2000, against the heavy debt burden facing many developing countries. The Jubilee 2000 campaign arose from widespread concern about the unbearable and unbreakable bonds of debt that shackle the world's poorest countries. Corruption, excessive military spending, declining export revenues, and questionable investments have left a legacy of debt throughout much of the developing world. Monetarist policies pursued through high interest rates in the early 1980s turned a serious problem into a major crisis, as the *Edmonton Journal* explained:

> Between 1980 and 1997, the total debt of the world's poorest nations grew from US$568 billion to over US$2 trillion, despite making US$2.9 trillion in principal and interest payments during that same period. The International Monetary Fund forced

them to implement Structural Adjustment Policies (SAPs) in order to receive new loans on which they have become dependent. As their debt continued to grow, the economies of these countries became geared toward export and revenue, rather than taking care of their own people. Health care, education, housing and other basic needs have been cut drastically in order to service the overwhelming debt facing these countries.[40]

The situation is particularly severe in certain regions. There has been a threefold increase in the level of public debt in sub-Saharan Africa, where it has risen from US$85 billion in the early 1980s to more than US$220 billion in the late 1990s. Enter the International Monetary Fund to rescue the banks while holding the profligate borrowers responsible for their practices. Borrowers in turn pass the burden on to their populations as currency flees the country for safer havens in other markets. Oscar Arias Sanchez has summarized the situation thus: 'From 1982 to 1990, debtor countries in the South paid their creditors in the North $6.5 billion in interest and $6 billion in principal payments per month—as much as the entire developing world spends on education and health. Yet their debts were 60 per cent greater in 1990 than in 1982'.[41]

The deteriorating situation in many African countries attests to the corrosive effects of debt on national economies. Wars, famines, and stagnant development are part of the legacy of debt facing many African countries. The politics of debt involves a complex web of national governments, private banks, investors, and international agencies working to serve each other's interests while individual citizens bear much of the costs. Throughout Africa, governments spend four times as much money servicing their debts as they do on health and education. And while figures suggest that Africa has among the world's highest growth rates, more than 50 per cent of the export revenue of countries such as Mozambique and Tanzania are devoted to servicing debt. Each day, more than US$700 million is transferred from the poorest countries to their creditor countries in the West. More than US$12 billion flows out of Africa annually to repay wealthy creditors. The IMF and its adjunct, the World Bank, impose structural adjustment programs to ensure that the debts are repaid and that sound credit status is retained. Meanwhile, other development needs must wait.

Since 1978, Canada has written off more than CAN$1.3 billion of debt to some of the poorest countries in the world. While this places Canada among the more generous of those governments that have forgiven debt, it does not address the full scope of the problem, nor even of Canadians' involvement in the issue. It is for this reason that many groups and individuals, led by representatives of various church communities, pressed the government to take action. More than 500,000 signatures from Canadians, representing but a small percentage of the international campaign to relieve the debt burden facing poor countries, were presented to the government prior to the G-7 meeting in Cologne in June 1999. Unlike the land-mines campaign (discussed in the next chapter), the government was reluctant to move too far in front on this issue: 'Whatever political pressure the petitions create, Canada would not act unilaterally to make further debt concessions. All Canadian debt reduction will be made in tandem with other industrialized countries as part of a sweeping worldwide Year 2000 plan to help the very poorest countries like Haiti, Sudan, and Equatorial Guinea'.[42] Canada and Britain led the charge for greater debt relief at the Cologne summit. Indeed, Kirton writes, 'it was on debt relief of the poorest that Canada's intellectual, policy, and structural leadership was most fully expressed'.[43] Canada's proposals included provisions of conditionality for those that would receive debt relief. The *National Post* reported at the time:

> A Finance official says that Canada is not likely to cancel all the debt owed by each poor country. Any policy is likely to be forgiveness of about 80–90% of the debt, so that Canada can maintain some influence over the governments concerned. The [remaining] debt they have to pay us gives us some leverage to educate them to the world of financial responsibility.[44]

In addition to 'financial responsibility', the government was also concerned about such practices as military spending. Former Costa Rican president Sanchez referred to Chrétien's proposal to link debt relief with military spending as 'truly encouraging for all who seek to create a more just and humane world—and it must be vigorously pursued and supported by concrete policy proposals'.[45]

The success of Canadian efforts at the Cologne summit suggests, perhaps, a renewed concern with the barriers to sustainable development in the South. It certainly reflects a continuing concern with working in concert and, in matters of economic policy at least, staying close to the other dominant economic powers. It also suggests Canada's continuing interest in using multilateral diplomacy and institutions to shape the political, economic, and social conditions of other countries in ways that are more direct and interventionist than those used in the past.

CONCLUSION

The G-7 has emerged as one of the government's main institutional connections for participating in global economic affairs. It epitomizes the tension between the more exclusive institutional connections that place Canada alongside a small but select group of leading powers and the more inclusive, if at times more chaotic, institutions such as the WTO or those based at the UN. Canada's important role in the Halifax summit and its active involvement in subsequent summits, including its role in addressing the Asian financial crisis, may indeed demonstrate Canada's position as a 'global financial power'. It would also seem, however, that Canada's priorities in this position say as much about its long-standing interest in building bridges rather than moats. This may reflect, as critical writers have argued, its role in legitimating the existing hegemonic order. Alternatively, it may suggest a desire to ensure that however this order might be maintained or transformed, that it be done through a process that respects ideas and diplomacy as well as, if not as much as, power.

Chapter 9

Redefining Security in the Post–Cold War Era

One of the most significant geopolitical ironies of the post–Cold War era has been endur-
ing centrality of NATO *to transatlantic security. Defying expectations, the old soldier has*
not faded away. —David Haglund, 2000

INTRODUCTION

The end of the Cold War was one of the most dramatic changes in the history of inter-state politics. The peaceful collapse of a major power and its empire was unprecedented. Not surprisingly, few knew how to react. The effects on Canadian security policy have been confusing at best. On one level, very little changed. Canada remained a member of the North Atlantic Treaty Organization (NATO) and continued to participate in the North American Air Defense Command (NORAD). Officials also continued to take an active role in international arms control initiatives. Even many of the issues were the same—alliance commitments, determining the proper level of military spending, the depleted state of equipment, nuclear weapons policy, and strategic defences. In each of these areas, one could easily be forgiven for assuming that there was little that was different in the practice of Canadian security policy from the Cold War years.

Yet the 1990s have been very different in many ways. Canada went to war twice during the decade, the first time against Iraq in 1991, the second time against the former Republic of Yugoslavia (Serbia) in 1999. On both occasions, the government went to war not to protect national security, but in defence of principles. On the first occasion, force was used to defend the principles of state sovereignty and territorial integrity. On the second occasion, these same principles of sovereignty and territorial integrity were violated to defend the principle of human rights, or 'human security' in Ottawa's vocabulary. On both occasions, Canada was a member of the UN Security Council in the months leading to war. On both occasions, the Canadian government sought to have the war conducted under the auspices of the UN, and on both occasions this failed. On both occasions, Canada's participation was limited to sorties flown by CF-18 crews. On both occasions, Canadian forces returned home without a loss of life. Between the wars, the Canadian Armed Forces were actively involved in numerous skirmishes as members of UN peacekeeping operations. At one point in 1993, the *Globe and Mail* reported that Canada had 'a greater percentage of its army on active service than any other country and more soldiers serving in combat conditions than at any time since the Korean War'.[1]

In the midst of these demands on the Canadian Forces and the expanded security agenda, there was an ongoing struggle between the UN, regional organizations, and the United States over which one would take the lead in addressing the evolving security environment. From the vantage point of Canadian foreign policy, and as evident in Canadian participation in these operations, there were competing interests in this struggle. Canadians seemed more than willing to maintain their commitments to a variety of associations, and even advocated taking on new ones[2]—provided, of course, that this could be done at little cost.

Defence spending continued to fall through the 1990s, and although not far enough for some, it was clearly far enough to put in question the government's ability to sustain the many commitments it was undertaking. Partly in response, the Liberal government began to promote the advantages of soft power and the country's ability to contribute to peace and security operations through non-military means. In addition, the government also resumed a more active arms-control policy, led by its work on the land-mines treaty and continuing through to its efforts in areas such as small arms, child soldiers, and NATO's nuclear strategy. This chapter reviews these many developments and attempts to describe some of the underlying features of Canadian security policy in this post–Cold War environment.

WAR IN THE GULF

On 2 August 1990, Iraqi forces invaded the independent state of Kuwait. In relatively short order, Kuwait was conquered, occupied, and annexed. This was a classic example of external aggression against a sovereign state. Yevgeny Primakov, one of Mikhail Gorbachev's close advisors and his personal emissary to Iraq, stated, 'However dangerous the gulf crisis may be in itself and however important it is to settle it, I think we should proceed from the fact that it offers a kind of laboratory, testing our efforts to create a new world order after the cold war'.[3] Joe Clark expressed a similar view, with a Canadian spin, in stating that the conflict in the Gulf provided 'a litmus test for what the United Nations can become. If we succeed here, the United Nations will send a clear and unambiguous signal to others that the world is now different; that it will not tolerate aggression and that international law is to be obeyed and not ignored'.[4] Bernard Lewis, in a commentary on the crisis, was even more categorical when he argued that the crisis presented 'a major challenge to world order and international law, confronting the United Nations with an awesome choice: either to discipline Saddam Hussein and restore the status quo, or to abandon the world to the violent and the ruthless and follow the path of the defunct League of Nations to ignominy and extinction'.[5] For some, the UN's response to and subsequent action against Iraq was a sign that the institution had been revived and restored to its original designs. For others, the organization had become a victim of American imperialism, little more than an instrument of American foreign policy. The record is more mixed than either position suggests.

The Iraqi invasion and annexation of Kuwait was a blatant violation of the sovereignty and territorial integrity of an independent state. As journalist Gwynne Dyer informed a House of Commons committee, 'the great majority of international conflicts have incredibly tangled pasts and there is always some wrong on both sides. This case, almost uniquely, is a nice open and shut case'.[6] Acting well within its mandate, the UN Security Council took swift action in response. The Council adopted a series of resolutions that condemned Iraqi actions 'as a breach of international security' (which brought into effect Chapter 7 of the Charter), nullified the annexation of Kuwait, called for an immediate Iraqi withdrawal, demanded the freeing of foreign nationals, imposed full economic sanctions against Iraq (Res. 661), and finally, on 29 November 1990, authorized 'member states cooperating with the Government of Kuwait . . . to use all necessary means to uphold and implement the Security Council Resolution 660 and all subsequent relevant Resolutions and to restore international peace and security in the area' if Iraq did not withdraw from Kuwait by 15 January 1991 (Res. 678). Significantly, the Council did not initiate action under Articles 42 and 43 of the Charter. This would have turned the coalition of forces into a UN operation.

The American military response to the crisis, unlike its diplomatic response, was largely independent of the UN, as were the responses of other governments, including Canada. Instead of working through UN channels to secure a resolution under Article 43 that would have created a multilateral force under UN command, the Bush administration rushed American forces to Saudi Arabia. They did this with some justification under Article 51 of the UN Charter, but in acting unilaterally, the Americans showed little interest in establishing a true UN presence in the region. American military deployments undermined the potential influence that a UN military presence might have provided and reinforced the image of the war as an American adventure that had little relevance for other members of the international community. As George Ball wrote at the time, a UN flag in the region 'would have provided some credible insulation from critics of the US while also making possible an authorized central command' for the armed forces of the more than 25 countries that participated in the coalition.[7] As in the case of Korea 40 years earlier, the United States had initiated a military response and then gone to the UN to gain legitimacy and political and military support. Unlike in Korea, the war in the Gulf was not conducted by the UN despite the unprecedented consensus.

The Mulroney government also responded to the crisis militarily.[8] The government's first action was to send two destroyers and a supply ship to the Gulf to monitor sanctions. The decision was announced on 10 August after the UN Security Council had approved comprehensive sanctions and on the day of an emergency meeting of NATO foreign ministers in Brussels. The NATO meeting confirmed the involvement of Italy and Germany in addition to that of fellow NATO members the United States, Great Britain, France, and Belgium. Meanwhile, the Canadian vessels needed to be re-equipped before they could move to the Gulf, and they did not arrive in the region until mid-September. The Canadian commitment of forces was subsequently increased by a decision in mid-September to send a squadron of CF-18 fighter aircraft from their NATO base in Germany to Qatar to provide air support to the Canadian vessels operating in the area. These CF-18s and their crews would eventually enter into combat missions. In deciding to participate actively, Canada was one of only a handful of coalition members actually to engage their forces in combat.

The speed and accord with which the UN Security Council went about its work was unprecedented, and Canadian support for a UN mandate was apparent at various stages during the crisis. As a member of the Security Council at the time, the Canadian

delegation and its ambassador, Yves Fortier, were actively involved in sponsoring resolutions and in encouraging the Americans to work within the organization. At times,
the Americans needed to be convinced to wait for UN approval. As Minister of
External Affairs Clark reported, 'the Americans were, as normal and usual, reluctant
to go into the UN. We were pressing very hard. We encouraged them to be patient and
to take the time to draft the resolution broadly enough that they would have support.
There's no question that we influenced them to the use of the UN'.[9] In mid-August
1990, when the United States said that it would impose an interdiction of Iraq to
enforce the sanctions, there was a quick and critical response from American allies
who saw this as a declaration of war. The *Globe and Mail* reported that 'Canadian
diplomats at the UN [were] among those quietly raising questions about whether the
United States . . . [had] any right under the UN charter to intercept shipping in the
Persian Gulf'.[10] Later, Canada's Fortier argued that 'the Security Council should
instead take a step-by-step approach under the Charter's Article 42, which provides
for blockades and other military actions but only with explicit Security Council
approval'.[11]

The record demonstrates that such efforts had mixed results. Articles 42 and 43
were never invoked, and the explicit UN command that many Canadians favoured
never materialized. At the same time, by securing UN approval for military action, the
Canadian delegation was able to demonstrate the extent of the international consensus in support of the Security Council's earlier resolutions. Differences over tactics
and motives were set aside in pursuit of common objectives. Nonetheless, Clark felt
justified in stating that 'when the history of this crisis is written, I think one of the very
interesting chapters will have to do with the effectiveness of Canadian diplomacy, not
least in the United Nations, where we have been able to play a quite significant role in
maintaining the consensus'.[12] Far from undermining the UN or Canadian contributions to it, the Gulf War, in Prime Minister Mulroney's view, had confirmed that 'the
United Nations has emerged from this crisis with new life'.[13] Some disagreed, and
many asked who was running the UN.

The actions of the United States, Canada, and the UN in the Gulf War raised many
criticisms in Canada and elsewhere. While the majority of Canadians supported
collective action through the UN, including the opposition Liberals in the House of
Commons, many others, including some Liberals and the New Democrats, were critical of the government's handling of the crisis. Critics focused on three aspects of the
government's policy: the government's support for American actions in advance of
UN resolutions, the apparent unwillingness to allow more time for sanctions to take
effect, and the apparent lack of diplomatic efforts to resolve the crisis short of war. In
addition, there were repeated concerns about the possibility that the government's
policies would tarnish Canada's peacekeeping reputation and undermine the future
effectiveness of the UN. In debate, opponents and supporters alike invoked the name
of Lester Pearson and the multilateralist tradition in Canadian foreign policy to
defend their positions. In response to a question in the House, Clark maintained that
Canada was working to bring 'this remarkable show of opposition' under the control

of the UN'.[14] Opposition members did not see Canadian support for the UN in such glowing terms. Liberal MP Paul Martin, Jr, for example, complained, 'I really do find it difficult that the Russians and the French have argued the United Nations case, all the while supporting the American initiative, stronger than we have'.[15] It is evident that although the government favoured a more formal UN presence in the conflict, it was quite willing to act in the absence of any UN role. In November 1990, the *Globe and Mail* reported that 'Canada would prefer to settle the gulf crisis by diplomacy. However, following the lead of the United States and Britain, it will not forswear the use of force without UN endorsement'.[16] The government was also quite willing to operate its forces in the field without UN command and control in place. The influence of American concerns on Canadian policy was seen by some as a change from past Canadian practice during such conflicts as the one in Korea in 1950, where Canadian diplomacy had been directed not only at restraining American policy, but also at reconciling the warring factions.[17] Such past actions indicated support for both the process and the substance of an institutionalized international order that some believed was missing during the Gulf crisis. The Mulroney government's response to the crisis was seen by some as little more than a poor reflection of that being pursued by the Bush administration in Washington.

After the war, the UN Security Council established an unprecedented instrument to prevent Iraq from acquiring the capability to produce weapons of mass destruction. Resolution 687, adopted on 3 April 1991, instigated by the United States, and enforceable by military action, included the requirement that Iraq accept unconditionally the destruction of all of its weapons of mass destruction and missiles with a range of more than 150 kilometres. This requirement was an explicit intervention into the affairs of a sovereign state. The United Nations Special Commission (UNSCOM) was mandated to search for and destroy production sites in Iraq in order to prevent the Iraqi government from developing and deploying weapons of mass destruction. The resolution also included a provision that sanctions on Iraq would remain in effect until the resolution had been implemented to the satisfaction of the UN Security Council. Canada actively supported UNSCOM and its wider objectives and has also maintained consistent support for the economic sanctions.

In 1993, and again in 1998, the United States launched military attacks against Iraq to force the Iraqi government to provide unfettered access to UNSCOM inspectors. In 1998, the Canadian government was asked to support these military attacks. In a statement in the House of Commons, Prime Minister Chrétien said that 'a military strike against Iraq would be justified to secure compliance with Security Council Resolution 687 and that Canada cannot stand on the sidelines at such a moment', especially because our 'allies led by the United States have asked for military support'.[18] In supporting military attacks against Iraq, the government demonstrated its continued willingness to use force against that country. The Canadian response also demonstrated the government's desire to be counted as a member of the coalition, despite many concerns that had been raised about the American-initiated bombing campaign. The ongoing sanctions against Iraq have also been subjected to much criticism for the tremendous hardships they have created for the Iraqi people and for their ongoing ineffectiveness against the Iraqi government:

> The failure of the UN to enforce a coercive process of disarmament of Iraq following the Kuwait war of 1991 has not only caused immeasurable suffering for the Iraqi people, but also led to a long period of tension and conflict between Iraq and the UN, or more specifically, between two of its powerful members, the United States and Britain. It has also generated a major split between the five permanent members of the UN Security Council (UNSC).[19]

And although the government has actively promoted studies on sanctions and how to make them both effective and humane, Canada has consistently supported these sanctions and has dispatched a frigate to the Gulf to help with the blockade against Iraq.

In the case of Iraq, the more specific interest of Canada's coalition solidarity has taken precedence over competing and conflicting concerns about the legitimacy and effectiveness of such actions. Part of the reason for this may have been tied to the government's reduced commitment of resources to NATO. A similar concern appears to have been at work in Canada's second war of the 1990s.

NATO AFTER THE COLD WAR: THE ROAD TO KOSOVO

Eight years after the Gulf War, Canada was at war again, but under very different circumstances. The issues and the process were even more problematic and the results, for some, little better than those experienced in the Gulf. In March 1999, NATO launched its first war by initiating an offensive aerial bombardment against Serbian forces and against military and non-military installations in Serbia and Montenegro in an effort to halt the Milosevic government's oppression of ethnic Albanians living in Kosovo. The decision on the part of the alliance to strike out on its own fell outside of its mandate as set out in the Washington Treaty of 1949 and demonstrated the extensive changes that had taken place in the alliance as it adjusted to a post–Cold War role. It also reflected the alliance's reaction to the war in Bosnia between 1991 and 1995. For Canada, NATO's war against Serbia once again called attention to the underlying differences between the UN and NATO. It also raised questions about the direction and implications of the Liberal government's human-security policy. Finally, it reinforced Canada's alliance credentials after more than a decade of uncertainty.

The 1992 budget brought an end to the deployment of Canadian troops in Europe and with it to a 40-year commitment of Canadian forces to the defence of NATO's Central Front. The closing of Canadian bases at Lahr and Baden-Soellingen brought complaints from Europe, but this time they carried no compelling weight strategically or politically. The end of the Soviet Union had brought an end to the one enemy that all NATO members could identify and with it an end to the perceived need to have forces in Europe. As European states become more integrated economically and politically and more isolationist in their approach to the rest of the world, the attractiveness of the continent as a counterweight also diminished. This was especially true for the Mulroney government, which was less concerned than many of its predecessors had been with economic and political counterweights to the United States.

Ironically, the withdrawal occurred while Canadian forces were becoming more actively engaged in the ongoing war in Bosnia. The incongruence between the government's activism in international peace and security issues and its willingness to provide the political and military resources to sustain this activism has persisted.[20] The commitment-capability of the Cold War years had been sustained, and even those who traditionally advocated lower levels of defence spending began to argue for military resources to support new security objectives.[21] The Liberal government, despite a white paper on defence that supported an all-purpose, combat-capable Armed Forces, showed no inclination to reverse the troop withdrawal and budget cutting at the Department of National Defence (DND) once they assumed power in 1994. In the absence of convincing arguments against withdrawal, immediate financial concerns over budget deficits at home provided a more compelling argument.

The repatriation of Canadian forces, argued the government, did not mean a withdrawal from NATO, nor did it mean a turning away from Europe. The government maintained that Canada could make a more effective contribution to European security through other means. Indeed, there was a certain validity to this; the Canadian forces in Europe did not return to Canada but were deployed to the former Yugoslavia as part of the UN operation there. There was also a rather strong view within NATO that the alliance itself must adjust its approach to European security and redefine its role. In its London Declaration of 1990, NATO political leaders had acknowledged that 'the Alliance's integrated force structure and its strategy will change fundamentally'. Among the proposed changes, the Alliance 'will field smaller and restructured active forces', 'will scale back the readiness of its active units', and 'will rely more heavily on the ability to build up larger forces if and when they might be needed'.[22] For an alliance that relied extensively on its military organization and capabilities, the idea of finding new tasks was not an easy one. Canada was among those NATO members that supported NATO reform, including the establishment of the North Atlantic Co-operation Council (NACC), which brings together NATO and the former members of the now defunct Warsaw Pact. The government also supported the Partnership for Peace program and the establishment of the Joint Task Force. In addition, the Liberal government took a strong stand in favour of NATO expansion. In the midst of all of these reforms, Canadians were actively involved as 'participant observers' when NATO and competing security institutions—the UN, the Organization for Security and Cooperation in Europe (OSCE), and the European Union (EU)—responded to a major challenge: containing and resolving the war in the former Yugoslavia.

For four years, a variety of European institutions and the UN attempted to work out an effective response to the breakup of the Federal Republic of Yugoslavia, and specifically to the war in Bosnia. For four years, they failed, until an American-brokered peace agreement among a group of war-weary combatants brought a measure of peace to the people of Bosnia. For four years, Canadian officials moved between the UN, the OSCE, and NATO, trying to make an effective contribution to this process. For some, the results appeared to confirm the greater legitimacy and credibility of NATO and paved the way for the alliance's actions in Kosovo. Others saw it as yet another example of the limited support available from member governments to make the UN an effective security institution. The international response to the conflict in the former Yugoslavia has repeatedly been cited as a prime example of the inability of international institutions to respond effectively to crises. The failings of institutions in response has not been for lack of attention. A parade of institutions responded to the conflict. Indeed, the number and variety of institutional options at times appeared to be part of the problem, for it was never clear which one would take the lead. Equally important was the fact that each institution (and its member governments) was responding to other interests beyond that of a resolution of an exceedingly complicated conflict.

The collapse of Yugoslavia presented the European Community (EC) with an opportunity to conduct a common, independent, and effective foreign policy. Differing national interests, even in the middle of preparations for the Maastricht summit, prevented the EC from becoming a more effective player in the conflict. Stanley Hoffman has said that

> Franco-German (and Franco-British) divergences about the policies the EC ought to follow made the Community look even more impotent than the situation on the ground obliged it to be. France was reluctant but Germany eager to acknowledge the breakup of Yugoslavia; France proposed to send a European force, but Britain opposed the idea so long as no cease-fire lasted more than a few hours.[23]

Under these conditions, it became clear that the EC would not be able to broker and implement a settlement on its own. The Americans had already willingly yielded the conflict to the EC and were not interested in getting directly involved. Instead, the EC turned to other institutions. In November 1991, it established a formal diplomatic relationship with the UN, with the appointment of Lord Peter Carrington and Cyrus Vance to launch an initiative designed to bring the conflicting parties to the bargaining table. The EC also looked to the Conference on Security and Cooperation in Europe (CSCE) to provide back-up support.

The CSCE and some of its member governments also had an interest in securing a place in the emerging European security architecture. Russia, which was excluded from the EC and NATO, saw the CSCE as a viable option. Canada looked at the CSCE as an alternative to NATO that would continue to provide it access to Europe, which the EC would not. Despite its meagre institutional framework, the CSCE attempted a response to the Yugoslav crisis. On 3 July 1991, it called for an immediate ceasefire in the fighting and dispatched a mission to Yugoslavia to undertake outside monitoring of the situation there. The CSCE, however, was no more predisposed to act than other institutions. It too was hampered by limited institutional capacity and by a membership reluctant to pursue a more active involvement in Yugoslavia. More specifically, the institution's procedural requirement for unanimity made it possible for the Belgrade government to block intervention in the early stages of the conflict. At the Helsinki meeting of the CSCE in July 1992, the institution and its members were criticized by the Canadian foreign minister for their failure to respond effectively. Barbara McDougall criticized the institution's lack of political responsibility, advocated that it work with NATO to establish the means to 'interposition forces, before or during a conflict', and noted that international and domestic opinion were demanding 'more action, more decisiveness, more leadership' from multilateral institutions. She concluded by warning that the failure of the CSCE to achieve significant progress beyond issuing pre-drafted and out-of-date declarations condemning the violence in Yugoslav would result in the CSCE's descent into disrepute and irrelevance.[24]

As mentioned in Chapter 7, the Canadian government favoured a prominent role for the UN in this conflict, both to reinforce the UN's security role and, perhaps, to legitimate the government's new interventionist strategy. One of the issues that emerged for the UN was how it would manage its relations with other institutions. At the political level, the formation of the diplomatic team of Carrington (later David Owen, later Thorvald Stoltenberg) and Vance established a solid working approach between the EU and the UN in the pursuit of a diplomatic solution. The problems that emerged in this area were primarily with respect to the diplomatic team's relations with the Americans and with NATO and the opposition of the parties on the ground.[25]

On the operational side, the principal relationship was between NATO and the UN. NATO's emergence as a major player in the conflict resulted from the alliance's desire to establish an effective and relevant role in the post–Cold War European environment. Peacekeeping missions in support of the UN and the CSCE appeared as an opportunity for the alliance, and the mission was pursued by NATO's secretary general Manfred Worner. By early 1992, the UN and NATO began working on a co-operative arrangement to address the worsening conflict. By July 1992, NATO was operating at sea alongside the Western European Union (WEU), enforcing economic sanctions as part of the multilateral response to the Yugoslav crisis. In mid-December, UN secretary-general Boutros-Ghali sent a letter to Worner asking for NATO support in implementing UN resolutions. The North Atlantic Council responded by confirming

> the preparedness of our Alliance to support, on a case-by-case basis and in accordance with our procedures, peacekeeping operations under the authority of the UN Security Council, which has the primary responsibility for international peace and security. We are ready to respond positively to initiatives that the UN Secretary-General might take to seek Alliance assistance in the implementation of the UN Security Council resolutions.[26]

In March 1993, with China abstaining, the UN Security Council authorized NATO to shoot down planes violating the no-fly zone. By May of that year, the Alliance was active in five areas: (1) the maritime embargo;[27] (2) no-fly zone enforcement;[28] (3) assistance in the command and control centre for United Nations Protection Force (UNPROFOR) headquarters; (4) contingency planning for a variety of specific tasks, including safe areas; and (5) contingency planning for implementing a UN peace plan.

The Yugoslav crisis had revealed, Worner candidly admitted in April 1992, that 'no institution has the full set of political, economic and security management tools to exercise decisive influence alone'.[29] The alliance displayed an institutional interest in playing a relevant role that superseded whatever reservations might have existed about getting involved under the authority of the UN. These assessments would change over the next three years. UN Security Council Resolution 816 of 31 March 1993, authorizing NATO's air forces to down aircraft violating the no-fly zone, marked a further departure from NATO's conventional role. The Russians were concerned that NATO was being given a free hand in responding to the conflict and that the UN would lose its authority. The Americans, on the other hand, favoured a larger role for NATO, both because of the Alliance's predisposition to using force and, arguably, because of their greater influence within the Alliance.

Canada for its part wanted the best of both worlds. It favoured the NATO option—under UN control. United Nations control was seen as an advantage not only because it was a way of retaining the institution's authority for conducting such operations, but also because of its support for more traditional peacekeeping operations. Alternatively, Canada's interest in encouraging a NATO role was related to its interests in maintaining a European connection in response to fears about Canada's future role in continental affairs after Maastricht.

Although Canada's military contribution to NATO in terms of men and *matériel* was modest and under constant erosion by budgetary cutbacks, Canada used its diplomatic resources to bridge the gap between NATO and the United Nations. At times the differences within governments were as great as those between governments, as military and diplomatic bureaucracies displayed preferences for different institutions. Such differences begin to account for the variation in national positions as one moved from New York to Brussels. The co-ordination of UN and NATO operations was complicated because the institutions operated in very different cultures, as General Lewis MacKenzie described:

> When people wonder why the military are frustrated, it is because our culture, training and background are completely different. That is why we both have to learn from each other. We on the military side have to learn that, of course, that is how agencies like the UN work and that is a fact of life. We are not going to change that by complaining about it or retiring or resigning or shooting ourselves. I have been immensely frustrated by the UN on this exercise because they played it very realistically.[30]

NATO was well experienced in operating under a centralized command and control structure with excellent intelligence and communications support. The UN not only lacked the sophisticated intelligence and communications support available to

NATO, but also suffered from inadequate command and control. Despite these differences, the UN and NATO worked out a standard set of procedures:

> The UN Security Council would pass a resolution dealing with a particular aspect of the Yugoslav crisis, the UN would then request NATO's assistance, the North Atlantic Council (NAC) would debate the political implications of the request and if consensus was reached, the mission would be accepted. The NATO military authorities would then review the resolutions and the NAC direction and propose a military capability to meet the stated political objective.[31]

For Operation Deny Flight, the situation was a little different in that NATO did not have sole operational control but was required to share operational control with UNPROFOR; this led to the exchange of liaison officers (NATO officials were sent to UNPROFOR headquarters). The problems of co-ordination proved exceedingly difficult and generated concerns at the highest levels in both organizations. NATO secretary general Worner referred to these problems early on, but maintained that NATO should, in his view, 'play its part in overcoming the obstacles that have hampered the smooth interaction of these institutions'. NATO would 'have to establish closer links to the UN. . . . The habit of cooperation and looking to each other for guidance has yet to be established at the working level'. He went on to say that 'a system of interlocking institutions, even if it can be perfected, will not be a panacea that moves automatically to manage crises. It will only work if there is determination, political will and leadership from the leading members of the international community'.[32]

At a NATO summit convened in January 1994 on the initiative of the French (who appeared inclined to support NATO air strikes to curtail Serb pressure on Sarajevo), Canada reiterated its opposition to NATO air strikes. Canada was willing to support only a UN resolution that 'provides Boutros-Ghali with the right to use air cover to protect the humanitarian aid convoys'.[33] Its position was complicated, however, by reports that Britain and other NATO members had recommended using NATO air strikes to relieve Canadians at Srebenica whose relief by Dutch forces was being prevented by Serbs who had encircled the city. The summit was designed to mend trans-Atlantic rifts, but the result was ineffective. As *The Economist* subsequently reported, 'the gap between the European allies and America over Bosnia looked briefly as wide as any since Suez in 1956'.[34] This gap was mended when France and the United States decided on a more assertive role for NATO in the conflict and dragged the others along for the ride.

Concerns over alliance solidarity began to overshadow strategic planning. As the operations in Bosnia became bogged down and time wore on, frustrations within both organizations grew and co-operation became ever more difficult. One area of particular difficulty was the arrangement whereby NATO was to provide 'close air support' to and 'air strikes' in support of UNPROFOR troops. This arrangement created unprecedented issues of command and control in that it involved a 'dual key' approach and in that:

in the absence of a precise agreement as to the circumstances justifying the use of force, each organization responded to its own priorities, which were different from or in some respects even mutually exclusive of the intentions of the other. . . . Under this arrangement, the UN and NATO, until the fall of Srebenica, operated with little success; it was only after a fundamental review of the arrangement, that the cooperation between the two institutions, under 'Operation Deliberate Force', became successful— illustrating that both organizations indeed can cooperate effectively, depending on the agreed conditions.[35]

A somewhat clearer separation of tasks emerged after the American-brokered settlement was concluded at Dayton, Ohio, in November 1995. The Dayton Agreement confirmed an effective federation of Bosnia, which had first been proposed by Owen and Vance in 1992. It also involved a separation of tasks between the UN and NATO, with the establishment of the military arm, IFOR, under NATO command and control and of the humanitarian tasks under the authority of the UN. Rather than a situation of NATO support for a UN operation, the post-Dayton arrangement is one of 'contracting out', whereby the UN provides a legitimate cover but is removed from the operation itself. By the end of 1995, NATO, with its more forceful approach and with the United States as its principal supporter, had emerged as the principal agent responsible for maintaining the peace in Bosnia. NATO's later decision to strike out on its own in Kosovo was very much influenced by an interest in establishing its credibility.

NATO's experience in Bosnia was one of the primary reasons why the alliance decided to act independently of the UN in the spring of 1999 when the Milosevic government failed to curtail its attacks on ethnic Albanians in the province of Kosovo. The war in Kosovo and the response of the UN and NATO raised concerns in Canada about the relationship between NATO and the UN, about the legitimacy of regional organizations in their claims to speak for the international community, and about the humanitarianism of military intervention.

The conflict in Kosovo was not a new issue. Officials at the UN and in Western governments had been monitoring the situation since the late 1980s, when the Yugoslav government of Slobadan Milosevic began to crack down on ethnic Albanians in the region. As early as 1992, US president George Bush issued a warning to Milosevic that the United States was prepared to use military force unilaterally if a conflict erupted in Kosovo. In spite of dire predictions of future conflict, no concerted diplomatic initiatives were launched until the conflict in the region took a more violent turn in 1998. Deteriorating civil relations in Kosovo were exacerbated by the increasingly violent struggles waged by the KLA and the Serbian military beginning in February 1998. In response, the UN Security Council adopted a series of resolutions that called upon the government in Belgrade to reduce its military presence in Kosovo and refrain from using excessive force in the region. The resolutions had little effect on the ongoing conflict in the region, and NATO issued its first warning of air attacks against Serbia in October 1998. The pressure on the alliance to do something in

Kosovo came from many sources, but one of the most frequently cited factors was the previous failure of the international community to stop the war in Bosnia. It was also evident, however, that the United States wanted the alliance to adopt a more aggressive posture to civil conflicts lying beyond NATO's member governments.

On 23 March 1999, NATO launched its air assault on Yugoslavia. The action was taken without the explicit approval of the UN. The Canadian government, after repeated attempts to secure UN support, concluded that acting with NATO was preferable to standing aside from or in opposition to the bombing. Paul Heinbecker has provided an explanation of Canada's approach:

> As President of the Security Council in February, and subsequently, Canada tried several times in several ways to see whether the Council could be brought to act responsibly. It became clear . . . in discussions Minister Axworthy had in New York, in Ambassador Fowler's repeated sounding of Council members, and in my own discussions with the Russians and others that a resolution to authorize intervention would have been vetoed. Our consultations also showed our allies preferred a 'connect-the-dots' legal basis for acting around an apprehended veto, to having to act in defiance of an actual veto. Had Canada pushed ahead regardless in New York, we might well have ended up destroying NATO unity of purpose and precluding NATO intervention.[36]

This view was more or less consistent with that of UN secretary-general Kofi Annan, who argued that the Security Council 'should be involved in any decision to resort to the use of force'. Yet in the same statement, he also acknowledged that force was likely justified: 'It is indeed tragic that diplomacy has failed, but there are times when the use of force may be legitimate in the pursuit of peace'.[37] Though the Council did not approve the action, it was also not willing to condemn it. Two days after the bombing started, Russia, joined by China, introduced a resolution into the Security Council condemning the bombing. The resolution was rejected by a vote of 12 to 3.

The decision by NATO to use force outside of its member states in response to an internal conflict and to act without the approval of the UN marked a significant departure from the alliance's original mandate as defined in the Washington Treaty of 1949. The Washington Treaty obligates the allies to 'refrain in their international relations from the threat or use of force in any manner inconsistent with the purposes of the United Nations'.[38] These principles were reiterated in NATO's 1991 Strategic Concept, which states that NATO's purpose is to 'safeguard the freedom and security of all its members . . . in accordance with the principles of the United Nations Charter'.[39] In rejecting these constraints, NATO embarked on a new and uncertain path: 'Kosovo has brought NATO into the never-never land. It has brought us into a situation where a regime that slaughters its own people is no longer sovereign and where the United Nations Security Council is no longer a requirement'.[40] NATO also for the first time established a presence in the area of humanitarian relief. Working in part through its Euro-Atlantic Disaster Response Coordination Centre (EADRCC), NATO was actively involved in establishing refugee camps and in transporting humanitarian aid into

Macedonia and Albania. As a result, the organization was involved with a variety of political, economic, and humanitarian institutions in already crowded post–Cold War Europe, and it took on a somewhat broader view of security.

Some observers saw Kosovo as a test of NATO's credibility. Simply put, said Joseph Biden, Jr, before the US Senate Foreign Relations Committee, 'if we do not achieve our goals in Kosovo, NATO is finished as an alliance'.[41] Peter Rodman wrote that

> NATO was demonstrating its relevance and effectiveness in the new era by combating ethnic violence in Europe. A success in Kosovo would guarantee the primacy of NATO in Europe's future. There would be no doubt that NATO was the preeminent and indispensable security institution on the continent. The controversy over whether a UN Security Council mandate was needed for such nondefensive NATO interventions seemed virtually settled. The Kosovo precedent validated an exception for 'humanitarian catastrophes', perhaps hinting of future unconstrained NATO action in other, more geopolitical emergencies.[42]

Although the air assault by NATO may have lent credibility to NATO's status as the world's principal agent for military intervention, it undermined the legitimacy and credibility of the UN. This was a concern for some NATO members, such as Canada and France. These concerns were one reason why the UN was brought back into the conflict in June and was given some responsibility for overseeing the peace-building process. The Security Council, through Resolution 1244, ratified the G-8 agreement. In the view of France's representative to the UN, Ambassador Alain Dejammet, the resolution re-established the role of the UN Security Council in the conflict: 'The resolution clearly said that it is the Security Council that authorizes the member states and relevant international organizations to establish the international security presence'.[43] Nonetheless, coming as it did at the end of the intervention, and effectively ratifying conditions that had been set elsewhere, one could question the extent to which the resolution reaffirmed the legitimate authority of the UN.

In supporting NATO's air war against Serbia, Axworthy maintained that 'NATO is engaged in Kosovo to restore human security to the Kosovars'.[44] For Canada, Kosovo provided an opportunity to promote many of its human-security initiatives, and despite the often-stated preference for UN action, Canada was an active participant in the air campaign, flying approximately 10 per cent of NATO's sorties. Clearly, in addition to the specific concerns with the security of Kosovo Albanians, the government was also interested in demonstrating its alliance credentials. As David Haglund has argued, 'one of the most important "interests" . . . is the maintenance of solidarity within a coalition whose core is the cooperative-security alliance'.[45] Maintaining coalition solidarity has been a long-standing feature of Canada's multilateralist tradition. It is a feature that remains important in a post–Cold War environment in which Canada has sought to limit its financial and resource commitments while retaining a right to participate in shaping the direction in which the coalition advances. Following the withdrawal of Canadian forces from Europe, alliance solidarity has become even more important as a tangible display of Canada's continued commitment to European security. Axworthy also took the position, however, that contributions should not be measured solely in military terms. In response to criticisms that the government might not be spending enough to support NATO's military forces, Axworthy countered that the government was making contributions in other areas, areas defined as 'soft power'. In addressing post–Cold War security issues, such views were not unique to the Canadian minister. Edward Luck has written that 'military strikes alone do not curb terrorism, civil strife, or aggression. Norm building, diplomacy, peacekeeping, arms monitoring, information sharing, nation building, and economic sanctions—areas where the United Nations has much to contribute— should remain part of the world's policy arsenal'.[46]

The events in Kosovo and the response of the United Nations, NATO, other institutions, and their member governments raised a number of concerns over who represents the international community and how that community should respond to civil conflicts. If the international community is to assume more responsibility for human security, as opposed to national or international security, it needs to clarify how that security is to be defined, who is going to define it, and how it is to be secured. Without some constraint, the failure to do so will result in others— organizations, states, NGOs—assuming responsibility on their own. For the alliance, Kosovo demonstrates a potentially very different role in international security affairs. It is a role that is not entirely inconsistent with changes in direction that have been occurring in Canada. Allen Sens argued in the debate over NATO expansion that these changes 'could also provide Canada with an opportunity to engage in such "soft" security roles as human rights monitoring, advising, and peacekeeping training, which rely more on expertise . . . and less on military capabilities'.[47] Haglund has speculated that NATO has been redefined as 'a political community sustained more upon the basis of common values and interests than upon the felt need to respond to a common threat, and, more importantly perhaps, an alliance that holds out the prospect of imposing low costs, and few risks, upon Canada'.[48] Seen in this light, NATO's evolution serves the Canadian government's interest in human security and has become 'the alliance of their dreams'.[49] For others, however, the attempt to present Canada's new security policy as consistent with that of the alliance are not convincing.[50]

ARMS CONTROL AND THE NEW SECURITY AGENDA

'We had no idea where the thing was headed', was how one official described the government's approach to the land-mines treaty in 1996.[51] After the fact, the ubiquitous references to the 1997 Ottawa Treaty to ban anti-personnel land mines in the speeches of Canadian officials suggest that this was the pre-eminent achievement of Canadian foreign policy during the 1990s. Canada's involvement in the land-mines treaty process and its work in bringing the process to a successful conclusion in December 1997 demonstrated a considerable amount of skill and tenacity. The diplomatic process surrounding the treaty also demonstrated the potential benefits of

Canada's multilateral connections. Perhaps most important, the treaty represents what Dolan and Hunt called the 'new multilateralism':[52] the growing activism and influence of non-governmental organizations in international politics and their active involvement in the diplomatic process.

The politics and diplomacy that led to the Ottawa Treaty have been extensively reviewed and analyzed, but it is worth recalling a few of the details here.[53] The origins of the treaty are generally traced to the work of the International Committee of the Red Cross (ICRC) and a small coalition of NGOs who first gathered in New York in 1992 and formed the International Campaign to Ban Landmines (ICBL). The following year, the group took their cause to France and gained the interest of French president François Mitterrand, who called for a review conference at the UN specifically to strengthen the 1980 UN Convention on Certain Conventional Weapons (CCW). The ICBL also appointed Jody Williams, who had been working with the Vietnam Veterans of America Foundation, as their coordinator. Action continued around the UN process, pressed by NGOs but led by the United States and France, both of which advocated the eventual elimination of anti-personnel mines. American president Bill Clinton called for the elimination of these mines in his address at the UNGA in 1994. The US government was also providing financial and political support to the NGO community. At this time, as a result of differences between the departments of Foreign Affairs and National Defence (DND), the Canadian government did not support the American proposal at the UN, and Canadian NGOs were not as vocal or influential as their American counterparts. As John English has pointed out, the change in Canada's position occurred as a result of an error at the UN that included Canada among those countries that adhered to an export ban. Instead of embarrassing the government by informing the UN that Canada had not adopted a moratorium on exports, DND agreed to a change in Canadian policy.[54]

The late arrival of the Canadian government to the land-mines ban process was quickly overcome when officials in the Department of Foreign Affairs and International Trade (DFAIT) decided to bypass the slow and cumbersome UN process and pursue a fast track to a treaty. The officials also decided, despite objections from other governments, including the United States, to invite NGOs to participate in a land-mines conference in Ottawa in October 1998. The conference 'would include pro-ban states and NGOs from around the world, and its purpose would be to develop a strategic action plan detailing concrete global and regional initiatives for the elimination of anti-personnel mines'.[55] Although the meeting generated considerable momentum to move toward a ban on mines, proposals by the United States, France, and Italy to send the issue to the UN's Committee on Disarmament were seen in Ottawa as a dead end. In response, and drawing on his experience in Canada's Open Skies initiative under the Mulroney government in 1989, Ralph Lysyshyn, director general of DFAIT's International Security Bureau, proposed that Canada host a follow-up meeting to conclude a treaty before the end of the following year. Axworthy agreed and the Ottawa Process was launched.

The process itself relied on the many connections that Canada had established in different regions around the world. Working with sympathetic states in these regions and building on the coalition of pro-ban states that had formed in Geneva as part of the CCW review process, Canada led what was already a fairly well-orchestrated campaign to what was now a clearly identifiable objective. The successful conclusion of the Convention on the Stockpiling, Use, Transfer and Production of Land Mines held in Ottawa was heralded by some as one of the major achievements in the history of Canadian arms control. Others took a dimmer view. As this review suggests, and without underplaying the importance of the government's initiative, Ottawa's success was based on the contributions of others. Yet it was the government's ability to assume a leadership role and to use its experience in working within multilateral coalitions to obtain support for the treaty that led to this success. It was also very much a reflection of the government's willingness and ability to work with NGOs in a variation of what has been described as the 'new multilateralism'. Indeed, the most revolutionary contribution of the process may very well prove to be the closer integration of NGOs into the treaty-making process.

The influence of NGOs is also readily apparent on another prominent arms-control issue: nuclear weapons and NATO's first-use policy. Canadian activism on nuclear weapons was not an isolated venture into an unploughed field. Opposition to nuclear weapons and to the alliance's nuclear strategy has a long history, including some significant Canadian chapters.[56] In the 1990s, the Liberal government was pressed to add Canada's voice to a vocal movement advocating the abolition of nuclear weapons. More immediately, these same NGOs advocated that Canada use its position in NATO to promote a change in the alliance's nuclear policy, most specifically the adoption of a no-first-use policy.

That nuclear weapons were still a salient political issue was itself somewhat of a surprise given the reductions that had been made in the nuclear arsenals of the super-powers at the end of the 1980s. The beginning of the post–Cold War era suggested a continuation of the Strategic Arms Reduction Treaty (START) process and additional and substantial reductions in the arsenals of the superpowers. There had indeed been rather substantial reductions, but both the Americans and the Russians retained significant and deadly nuclear arsenals. There was also increased concern over the potential for nuclear accidents, sabotage, and terrorism. Moreover, there remained the continual threat that other states would also deploy nuclear weapons. South Africa's decision in the early 1990s to eliminate its nuclear weapons program was a major move to a nuclear-weapons-free world, but the continued threat of acquisition in Iraq, Iran, and North Korea tipped the balance. The nuclear weapons tests conducted by India and Pakistan generated renewed concerns about increased insecurity and the continued threat of nuclear weapons, and even of nuclear war. Added to these events were the significant slowdown in Russian-American negotiations and the persistent interest that the United States has shown in ballistic missile defences. As a result, nuclear weapons rather quickly re-emerged near the top of Canada's arms-control agenda. On the other side, anti-nuclear advocates increased their profile and voice, spurred on by a number of developments, including the Non-Proliferation Treaty (NPT) renewal of 1995, in which the Canadian delegation played a significant role; the statements and actions of former officials, such as Lee Butler from the United States and Rob Green from the United Kingdom, both former nuclear commanders who now advocated abolition; and the World Court's decision questioning the legality of nuclear weapons and of a nuclear strategy based on their potential use.

In response to pressure from domestic groups, the government gave the House of Commons Standing Committee on Foreign Affairs the task of undertaking a review of Canadian policy on the issue. Following both public and in camera meetings and the high-profile visits of such anti-nuclear activists as Robert McNamara, Lee Butler, Rob Green, and Michael Douglas, the Committee submitted a report that included the following recommendations: (1) substantive moves toward eventual disarmament; (2) the 'de-alerting' of all nuclear forces; (3) ensuring an open debate on NATO nuclear policy; (4) aid to bolster Russia's missile early warning system; and (5) increased transparency of nuclear weapons stockpiles, fissile material, and doctrine. The Committee also took the view that Canada had a viable role to play in the nuclear-disarmament and arms-control process:

> Since Canada is not itself a nuclear-weapon state, some would discount its ability to encourage and influence further progress in this area. The Committee strongly disagrees. Canada, we believe, is uniquely qualified to lead, as the first State capable of developing nuclear weapons to decide not to do so, later as the first State to divest itself of nuclear weapons, and finally as a leader in the 1995 extension of the nuclear Non-Proliferation Treaty and a key player in the Ottawa Process which highlighted the need for creative diplomacy with respect to security and arms control. Despite its technical aspects, the challenge of moving toward the prohibition of nuclear weapons remains fundamentally political and moral. The Committee is convinced that Canada has the vision, talent and credibility to play a leading role in finally ending the nuclear threat overhanging humanity.[57]

The politics surrounding this campaign also reflected the new dynamics that were shaping Canadian foreign policy. Led by a coalition of NGOs, domestic interests were able first to press the Liberal government into holding the parliamentary hearings on nuclear weapons and then to convince the minister (who was also sympathetic to the cause) to advance the issue in NATO councils. Of particular concern was the alliance's unwillingness to consider abandoning its no-first-use policy. Instead, the policy was confirmed at the alliance's 50th-anniversary summit in April 1999. Moreover, certain allies, especially the United States, made it quite clear that they were displeased with both the style and the substance of Canada's challenge. Dean Oliver quotes one official as saying that Canada was 'outvoted eighteen to one'[58] on its proposal. Nonetheless, in response to Canadian concerns and those of other member governments, including Germany, the anniversary summit did put in motion a review of the alliance's policies with respect to nuclear weapons. Although the response from NATO members was certainly less than enthusiastic, the Canadian government's willingness to pursue the issue in the face of such vocal displeasure by the United States was reminiscent of concerns that Canada had raised in the past about the alliance's nuclear strategy. The government's response is also another indication of the increased salience of NGOs in Canada's multilateral diplomacy.

The nuclear weapons issue remains unresolved, but new issues are already appearing on the horizon. The American preoccupation with technological solutions to military insecurities, especially with ballistic missile defences, continues to pose a dilemma for Canadian officials. It raises not only important strategic issues, but also important political issues about the nature and future direction of NATO and the alliance's trans-Atlantic connections. Ballistic missile defences also raise important issues in Canada's bilateral relationship with the United States. Having been forced to confront and successfully dodge the SDI hot potato in the 1980s, continuing American interest in ballistic missile defences has presented a direct challenge to both Canada and the alliance as the Americans embark on yet another technological initiative. As with the previous SDI under the Reagan administration, the proposals for ballistic missile defences in the late 1990s required Canadian and alliance support for both political and practical reasons.

The problem that these arms-control issues present to Canadian policy makers is that the United States emerged as one of the principal barriers to Canada's arms control agenda in the 1990s. In their efforts to promote arms-control initiatives on issues as distinct as land mines, nuclear testing, NATO's nuclear strategy, ballistic missile defences, and small arms, Canadian policy officials have run into US opposition. Something close to a chasm has been developing between the two countries on these issues. This presents a formidable challenge to Canadian policy makers. First, advancing an arms-control agenda in the face of opposition from the most powerful state in the system is no small task. Advancing an arms-control agenda that is fundamentally at odds with the most powerful interests of your closest ally and most significant economic partner is even more worrisome. Increasingly, in the arena of arms control, Canadians and Americans are not just not on the same page, they are not even reading the same book.

HUMAN SECURITY AND THE MULTILATERAL ORDER

Human security has emerged as a major theme in the foreign policy of Canada, Norway, and a number of other countries. It has been used by these governments to account for an increased emphasis on individual rights, countering the effects of more traditional state practices on individuals, and thus has encouraged a more interventionist foreign policy. As described by Canadian foreign minister Lloyd Axworthy in 1998, the priority given to human security reflects the changing perceptions of threat and conflict in the contemporary international environment: 'Our basic unit of analysis in security matters has shrunk from the state to the individual. This human security lens produces new priorities—everything from countering terrorist bombs to child labour and climate change. These issues have now become the daily concern of foreign ministers and governments. They are the human security agenda.'[59] The theme of human security has also been highlighted by a number of prominent world leaders, such as UN secretary-general Kofi Annan and Czech president Vaclav Havel. They and others have cited human security as a promising guiding principle for international politics.

In addition to calling attention to individual rights and the conditions experienced by individuals, human security also presents a fundamental challenge to traditional principles of international politics, especially those of state sovereignty and non-intervention. As such, human security and its promotion explicitly question the legitimacy of these deeply embedded principles. This also challenges those governments that are promoting human security to reconcile their concerns with individual rights with the more traditional practices of international politics as reflected in the foreign policies of national governments and the operations of international institutions.

Among the more specific elements of Canada's human-security agenda are anti-personnel mines, child soldiers, small-arms trade, and international humanitarian and human rights law. As a priority in Canadian foreign policy, human security has been advanced in a number of multilateral settings, but especially at the UN. Human-security concerns dominated Canada's presidency of the Security Council in February 2000. They have also formed an important part of the government's OAS agenda. In pursuing this agenda, the government has worked closely with other middle powers, including Austria, Chile, Ireland, Jordan, Slovenia, the Netherlands, Switzerland, and Thailand. Norway has been a particularly important ally in this campaign, and the two governments have signed the Lysoen Declaration, in which they established 'a partnership commit[ting] Canada and Norway to a framework for consultation and concerted action in the areas of enhancing human security, promoting human rights, strengthening humanitarian law, preventing conflict, and fostering democracy and good governance'.[60] A variety of NGOs have also been extensively involved, as during the land-mines campaign.

CONCLUSION

Canada's approach to security since the late 1980s reflects a shift in emphasis away from state-centric security concerns to the individual as the primary subject of Canadian security policy. It also suggests a shift away from a concern with the process of multilateral co-operation through international institutions toward a greater concern with the establishment of substantive international norms and agreements. Indeed, one of the more interesting features of the human-security agenda as it has been pursued under the Liberal government has been the government's willingness to pursue this agenda outside of Canada's traditional multilateral associations. For example, the frequently cited treaty to ban anti-personnel land mines was moved outside of the UN and undertaken independently of any formal institution. On this and other issues, the government has demonstrated a greater concern with the substantive aspects of security than with the more procedural approach adopted by previous Canadian governments.

A number of events during the 1990s left a rather cloudy picture of the place of multilateralism in the future of Canadian security policy. The decade started with much hope for a revived UN and for a program of co-operative security exercised through the CSCE. It ended with the blunt force of NATO bombers exercising military power in the absence of a UN resolution and with Canadian-supported bombing missions against Iraq. Throughout this time, Canada pressed for a more aggressive arms-control campaign and constantly asserted the need to advance international security relations into new arenas using non-military measures. The incongruity is striking. The contradictions, of course, are not all of Canada's making. Nor is Canada the only country going through such dilemmas. In the balance hang the future security role of NATO and other institutions, including the UN, and the future direction of Canada's own security commitments.

Conclusion

It is obviously foolish to argue stubbornly that multilateralism is always best. —John Holmes, 1987

Multilateralism is very much under siege these days. To be sure, we have our moments of efflorescence—it may be that Kosovo and East Timor will be two of those moments—but multilateralism still has more trendy detractors than earnest proponents. —Stephen Lewis, 2000

John Holmes had the unique ability and insight to put Canadian foreign policy into perspective lest we turn good ideas into rigid dogma. Multilateralism is a good idea. To argue, however, as this book has attempted to do, that multilateralism has been persistently prominent in the conduct of post-war Canadian foreign policy is not to argue that it has been the only strategy pursued in Ottawa, that it has solved all of Canada's foreign policy problems, or that it has been an invaluable contribution to global peace and justice. The evidence does suggest, however, that in different historical circumstances and for different policy concerns, a multilateralist strategy involving the use of multilateral diplomacy under the auspices of international institutions has been effective in securing a number of important foreign policy objectives. It is also apparent that over time and across issues, Canada's multilateralist foreign policy has made a constructive contribution to world order. As Robert Cox and Harold Jacobson wrote in their review of decision making in international institutions, 'Canada . . . has been shown to have greater influence in several international organizations than in their specific environments or the general environment. The reason is that for a number of years Canada chose to make international organizations a principal vehicle for the expression of its foreign policies'.[1]

In the contemporary international system, a number of developments have led some to conclude that 'it is inevitable that Canada should encounter serious difficulties in applying a global policy built on multilateralism'.[2] Charles-Philippe David and Stephane Roussel identify three factors that have eroded Canada's ability to pursue an effective multilateralist strategy. First has been the end of the Cold War, which has allowed the great powers to settle their differences without the intervention of intermediaries such as Canada. Second has been the greater use of collaborative multilateral co-operative measures by the great powers themselves: 'This change in norms of conduct within the international community reflects a new emphasis on cooperative conflict resolution, humanitarian aid, democratization, and preventive diplomacy'.[3] This more interventionist approach to humanitarian issues also requires the capabilities of great powers if it is to be effective. Third has been the greater diffusion of power in the system, including the emergence of 'new' great powers and of growing pressures for regionalization; at the same time, there is often indifference or even opposition on the part of the major players for co-operative enterprises.

Despite these changes—indeed, arguably because of them—Canada, whose inter-national institutional reach is unmatched, might assume, in the words of Holmes, 'a greater responsibility for making the system work'.[4] Over the past five decades, Canadian foreign policy has often been dedicated to doing just that. Starting from a recognition that the country's interests required a stable international system in which Canadians had both opportunities and the necessary capabilities to inject their own views, policy makers favoured institutions that would guarantee Canada a voice. The support of successive Canadian governments for an institutionalized world order based on principles such as state sovereignty, liberal trading practices, and regional security arrangements reflects what Hedley Bull once described as a Grotian view of the world[5]—a view that privileged order above other values, in part because order served Canadian interests, but also because order allowed for the pursuit of more substantive goals. Canadian efforts in pursuit of these goals have not always been successful, and at times governments have deviated from this strategy in pursuit of either domestic or continental advantages. Yet one of the most important areas of activity for Canadian foreign policy makers has been in preserving the habit of inter-national consultation and co-operation.

Since the early 1940s, Canadian officials have devoted a considerable amount of skill and effort to keeping the multilateral machinery working. For more than 50 years, successive generations of Canadian foreign policy makers have pursued Canadian foreign policy interests primarily (though not exclusively) through interna-tional organizations. The role that these organizations played for the promotion of Canadian interests and what Canadian policy makers defined as global order interests was so significant that Canadian policy makers often devoted considerable resources to the maintenance of these organizations. At times it appeared as if the process of multilateralism was more important than the outcome. These efforts might also be seen as a sacrifice of principles and end results in favour of processes and institutions. What has been generally true of Canadian foreign policy is perhaps indicative of the place of middle powers in an anarchic system dominated by great powers. As Holmes wrote, 'foreign policies of middle powers are inevitably directed not only at the substance of an issue but also at the means by which they can affect the resolution of that issue. The machinery of world politics is their special concern'.[6] This approach, in my view, was based on a belief that the process was not independent of the outcome in two critically important ways: first, that the process of global governance was instrumental in shaping the outcome and that certain processes would tend to favour outcomes more likely to meet Canadian objectives than were others; second, that the process itself was a critically important part of global politics and that to encourage particular processes encouraged a particular form of global politics. It was not so much a matter of form replacing substance as it was a view that form *was* substance.

Since the end of the Cold War, Canadian governments have persisted along this multilateral course, albeit with some potentially important changes. In the 1940s, Canada's multilateralist strategy began with an interest in constructing the United

Nations as a universal, inclusive organization that would recognize the special capa-bilities of middle powers. The UN was to be the foundation of Canadian foreign policy and to serve as the forum in which Canada would contribute to international order. John Ruggie argues that much of what passed for international governmental organi-zations (IGOs) during the early years of the post–World War II period was shaped by the principle of 'embedded liberalism'.[7] One important aspect of this principle was that it recognized, legitimized, and to a considerable degree empowered state or national governments as significant actors in the management of both the domestic and the international political economies and in the process of global governance. IGOs were primarily statist institutions. Although the UN Charter began with the words 'We the peoples', the preamble ended by empowering states to carry out the provisions of the Charter. In subsequent documents, the organization reasserted the central place of sovereign states in the process of global governance. Similar patterns can be found in the actions and documents of regional organizations, such as the Organization of American States (OAS) and the Organization of African Unity, which reasserted such core principles as state sovereignty, non-intervention, political equality, and territorial integrity. Indeed, international organizations played a criti-cally important role in reinforcing the sovereignty and legitimacy of newly indepen-dent states in the post-1945 international system.

When the Cold War ended, the United Nations re-emerged as a vitally important organization for maintaining international order and for aiding the pursuit of Cana-dian foreign policy objectives. Yet it was not to be the only, or even the primary, forum. Canadian officials undertook initiatives in a variety of other associations. Across a wide range of issues from the environment to the promotion of free trade to the reconstruction of Eastern Europe and the protection of a democratically elected government in Haiti, Canadian officials have been actively promoting initiatives in a variety of multilateral settings. Working through institutions both old, such as the Commonwealth, and new, such as the Francophonie, and in joining others, such as the OAS, the government has emphasized the need to reinforce and enhance the insti-tutional basis of multilateralism to deal with the international agenda of the twenty-first century. Multilateralism, as both an objective and as a strategy of Canadian foreign policy, has not only survived the revolutionary changes that have taken place in recent years, it has prospered. The future of multilateralism holds considerable promise, but it is by no means secure. For just as Canadian officials seem to work well within multilateral associations, the nature of their involvement has changed; as Denis Stairs writes, 'Canada's initial contributions to postwar global governance . . . were rooted in real interests and were aimed at facilitating the pragmatic resolution of real problems as they happened to come along'.[8] And although today's problems are indeed very real, Canadian interests are more indirect and the motivation for policy makers, in turn, less pressing. Moreover, while Canadian official have supported the establishment of a rules-based international order, the nature and scope of these rules are changing. The rules governing many aspects of international relations, and espe-cially those managing global economic relations, have become more firmly entrenched. These rules have also evolved from procedural ones into more substantive ones fostering international norms and practices that would, in turn, extend this rules-based system to encompass not only relations between governments, but also relations within states and between governments and their citizens.

The post–Cold War international order has been dominated by international institutions. But the multiplicity of governmental institutions has been greatly exceeded by an ever-increasing variety of civil society, or non-governmental, organizations. Relations within this expanding network of institutions have increased attention to the structures and processes of global politics, or 'global governance' as it is frequently described. Interactions among institutions have been marked by consultation, collaboration, and concentrations of power. They have also been marked by confusion, competition, and conflict.

For Canadian policy makers, the proliferation and increased significance of these institutions stands as both an indicator of accomplishments and a source of consternation. Back at the end of the Second World War, Canadian officials argued and advocated incessantly for international institutions that would secure and sustain an international order rooted in the principle of state sovereignty. The new post–Cold War world order, however, must also include non-governmental organizations, both the more public-spirited civil society organizations and the more profit-motivated multinational business enterprises. No longer are states able to dominate these multilateral arrangements.

The increased participation of the non-governmental sector has been encouraged by the shift toward neo-liberal economic practices, or what a century ago was called 'laissez-faire'. This shift can be noted both within different national economies and in international institutions such as the International Monetary Fund (IMF) and the World Bank. The influence of these neo-liberal ideas is also evident in their promulgation by intellectuals such as Milton Friedman and politicians such as Margaret Thatcher and in the strengthened position of private interests, again within both national and international circles and in areas as diverse as health care, education, development assistance, and security. Neo-liberal economic practices have also had a dramatic influence on the role of the state and on the perception of the state's role both in its own national setting and on the world stage. In the view of observers such as the late Susan Strange, the contemporary period is defined by the 'retreat of the state' as private interests ranging from corporations to drug dealers move in to fill the void.[9] As Sylvia Ostry writes, 'it is the interaction between governments and global corporations that will determine the future of multilateralism'.[10] Although it may be too early to conclude that the era of embedded liberalism has ended, the writing, as the saying goes, may be on the wall. Ruggie, among others, has noted the longer-term significance of these changes: 'Because social purposes reflect configurations of state-society relations, it suggests that the foremost force for discontinuity at present is not "the new protectionism" in money and trade, which is most feared by observers today. Rather, it is the threat posed to embeddedness by the resurgent ethos of neo-laissez-faire'.[11] These neo-liberal ideas and practices have also influenced the process, and especially the content, of multilateralism at the regional and international levels. While this is most prevalent within international financial institutions, it has also influenced other institutions. At the UN, for example, officials are more frequently looking to the private sector to deliver assistance and security to war-torn countries.

At the same time that the state retreats from more direct involvement in managing the domestic and international economies, its legitimacy has been challenged by a second phenomenon: the growing influence of liberal ideas of human rights and human security. International concern and activity in the area of human rights is not a recent phenomenon. Although we have seen a great deal of attention directed to matters of human rights and human security in the past decade, human rights have animated governments, IGOs, and NGOs for more than a century. The late twentieth century, however, witnessed a return to these liberal themes and a renewed emphasis on individual, or human, security. The international status of human rights, for example, has been recognized in such documents as the UN's Universal Declaration and the final act of the Conference on Security and Cooperation in Europe (CSCE), the Helsinki Accords in 1975. The status of individual rights and human security has also been asserted by some Western governments, including Canada's, since the end of the Cold War. This in turn has led to demands for a more interventionist program of action by international and regional organizations.

A cursory review of the various instruments that have been used to support neo-liberalism and human security reveals a wide and diverse range, including aerial bombardment, economic sanctions, the creation of norms, and the provision of technical, financial, and military assistance. There has also been a variety of actors involved in the process, including national governments, international and regional organizations, NGOs, and even individuals, such as Ted Turner and Bill Gates. The mix of different instruments and actors has created what Emma Rothschild has described as 'problems of psychosocial and political incoherence'.[12] Advocates of neo-liberalism and human security have sought to empower both NGOs and international institutions as the principal agents for implementing these reforms. States are simply not suited to serve the menu of neo-liberalism and human security. This continues a persistent view within many quarters that challenges the legitimacy and capacity of states, as noted by Ngaire Woods:

> Indeed, in the 1980s and in the early 1990s, scholars began a full-fledged assault on state-centered international politics based on sovereignty. Since that time, new rationales for intervention and expanded conditionalities have been opened up, the increased participation of nongovernmental organizations (NGOs) has been encouraged, and concepts of 'global civil society' have been developed. There has been a tendency, in other words, to move away from state-centered views of international relations and toward a more global approach.[13]

Yet in Woods's view, 'as regards international organizations, . . . the tendency to dismiss sovereignty as anachronistic and illegitimate needs a further rethinking'.[14] At the very least, there are severe limitations to the legitimacy, credibility, accountability, and capacity of both NGOs and international institutions to implement the necessary provisions.

These emerging patterns of multilateralism have profound implications for the processes, institutions, and objectives of global governance. One result of these practices has been the transformation of international and regional institutions into agents of a selective and dominant world view. While this was perhaps less of a leap of faith for the IMF and its Bretton Woods sisters, it marked a more significant shift for the UN and its affiliated agencies and for regional organizations such as the OAS. It has also led to a very different form of multilateralism from that which existed in the immediate post-1945 period. David Kennedy has argued that one of the more significant effects of these changes has been to remove much of the politics from debates about multilateralism and international order:

> Internationalists are used to thinking that we have a robust international political order with only the thinnest layer of law. But the reverse is more accurate—we have a robust process of global law and 'governance' without a global politics. Real government is about the political contestation of distribution and justice. Governing an international order means making choices among groups. . . . Development policy means preferring these investors to those, these public officials to those, not the technocratic extension of a neutral 'best practice'. To make these choices we need a world which is open to a politics of identity, to struggles over affiliation and distribution among the conflicting and intersecting patterns of group identity in the newly opened international regime.[15]

These developments, although they may reflect the influence of liberal ideas and their successful application at the international level, pose a serious problems for the nature and role of international institutions in supporting multilateralism. As Woods says,

> In dealing with new issues, international organizations are being challenged in terms both of their legitimacy and their effectiveness. This challenge takes two forms. At the global level, institutions are being challenged by nonstate actors and domestic lobbies—raising broad issues of global democracy. The good governance agenda translates into questions about the very foundations of world order and the place of sovereignty within it. At a more modest level, the legitimacy of international institutions is being contested by states who feel inadequately consulted or represented within organizations. The old hierarchy of states within multilateral forums is being challenged and their effectiveness and legitimacy questioned by smaller or weaker states. Here, the good governance agenda can be applied to prescribe greater participation, accountability, and fairness among states within organizations.[16]

Recent practices in Canadian foreign policy suggest a considerable amount of support for these emerging practices of global governance. In areas as diverse as the rules of international trade and investment and protection against human rights abuses of various sorts, the Canadian government has advocated the establishment of international norms and the institutionalization of these norms by international organizations. It has also supported the increased participation of NGOs in many policy sectors and has favoured granting these NGOs and the private sector greater responsibility for implementing policy. The Canadian government has been prominent in advocating that international institutions adopt substantive criteria in assessing the credentials of member states, which would move global governance onto a more substantive and interventionist terrain. This differs from the view that Canadian officials took of the UN and the Commonwealth in the formative years of these institutions. During the 1940s and 1950s, Canada resisted efforts to turn the UN into an institution that would promote Western values and preferred to keep it as a place where competing values could collide peacefully and constructively. It was for these reasons that the government favoured the Commonwealth and not the OAS. Today the tendency among many inside and outside of government is to look at all three as platforms for articulating specific principles and enforcing a more selective set of solutions for global problems.

In addition, the Canadian government has supported international and regional institutions in assuming increased responsibility for the security and welfare of individuals in various parts of the world. This shift in responsibility alters the context in which states must operate. It limits their legitimacy, or at least questions it, at the same time as states have been encouraged to adopt more democratic forms of domestic government. The practices of global governance are also expanding the responsibility of the institutions through which global governance is being conducted. It often appears, however, that the aspirations for these institutions to act are not in line with the political will and the concomitant resource contributions of member governments. To date, both IGOs and NGOs have repeatedly demonstrated that they lack the capacity to provide welfare and security to people in need. Not only do they lack the necessary resources to make a difference, but they often lack the necessary interest, political will, legitimacy, and long-term commitment.

Thus, what is problematic in much of the advocacy and activity surrounding new approaches to multilateralism is the tendency to assume that institutions do indeed possess the capacity and will to act effectively in very difficult conditions. The capacity of institutions is at best a limited one, influenced by competing interests and by the commitment of supporters. Even the best IGOs and NGOs encounter donor fatigue and flagging volunteer spirit. To raise expectations beyond what one is prepared or able to deliver might create a false sense of security and thereby undermine the longer-term legitimacy and credibility of not only specific institutions, but the very process of multilateralism. As one embarks on a campaign for global governance, one must be sensitive to the limits of both ends and means. For a country such as Canada that has relied extensively on multilateralism and international institutions, and has made such a significant contribution to a multilateralist world order, these developments carry special significance.

Notes

Introduction

1. Joe Clark, 'Canada's New Internationalism', in John Holmes and John Kirton, eds, *Canada and the New Internationalism* (Toronto: Canadian Institute of International Affairs, 1988), 4.

2. For a discussion of foreign policy goals, see Arnold Wolfers, *Discord and Collaboration* (Baltimore: John Hopkins University Press, 1962), especially chapters 5 and 6.

3. Robert Keohane, 'Multilateralism: An Agenda for Research', *International Journal* 45 (1990): 731.

4. For a discussion of multilateral diplomacy and some of its applications, see Margaret Doxey, 'Strategies in Multilateral Diplomacy: The Commonwealth, Southern Africa, and the NIEO', *International Journal* 35 (Spring 1980): 329–56.

5. John Gerard Ruggie, 'Multilateralism: The Anatomy of an Institution', *International Organization* 46 (1992): 567.

6. Ibid., 571.

7. Michael Dolan and Chris Hunt, 'Negotiating in the Ottawa Process', *Canadian Foreign Policy* 5, 3 (1998): 27.

8. Ibid., 27.

9. Cited in ibid., 28.

10. Robert Cox, 'Multilateralism and World Order', *Review of International Studies* 18 (1992): 161.

11. Dolan and Hunt, 'Negotiating in the Ottawa Process', 28.

12. Denis Stairs, 'Global Governance as a Policy Tool: The Canadian Experience', in Raimo V. Väyrynen, ed., *Globalization and Global Governance* (Lanham, MD: Rowan and Littlefield, 1999), 70.

13. Mark Neufeld, 'Hegemony and Foreign Policy Analysis: The Case of Canada as Middle Power', *Studies in Political Economy* 48 (Autumn 1995): 7–29.

14. David Black and Claire Turenne Sjolander, 'Multilateralism Re-constituted and the Discourse of Canadian Foreign Policy', *Studies in Political Economy* 49 (1996): 8.

15. John Ruggie, *Constructing the World Polity: Essays on International Institutionalization* (New York: Routledge, 1998); Craig Murphy, *International Organization and Industrial Change: Global Governance Since 1850* (Cambridge, UK: Polity Press, 1994).

16. For a discussion of this episode, see Robert Bothwell and John English, 'Dirty Work at the Crossroads: New Perspectives on the Riddell Incident', *Canadian Historical Association Report* (1972): 263–85.

17. Cited in R.A. MacKay and E.B. Rogers, *Canada Looks Abroad* (Toronto: Oxford University Press, 1938), 269.

18. Ibid., 94.

19. F.P. Walters, *A History of the League of Nations* (London: Oxford University Press, 1960), 811.

20. R.A. Preston, *Canada in World Affairs*, vol. 9 (Toronto: Oxford University Press, 1965), 237–8.

21. Ibid.

22. Donald Page, 'The Institute's "Popular Arm": The League of Nations Society in Canada', *International Journal* 33 (1977–78): 49.

23. Escott Reid, *Radical Mandarin: The Memoirs of Escott Reid* (Toronto: University of Toronto Press, 1989), 124.

24. Lester B. Pearson, *Mike: The Memoirs of the Right Honourable Lester B. Pearson*, vol. 1 (Toronto: University of Toronto Press, 1972), 87.

25. Reid, *Radical Mandarin*, 125.

26. For commentaries on Canada's middle power status, see J. King Gordon, ed., *Canada's Role as a Middle Power: Papers Given at the Third Annual Banff Conference on World Development, August 1965* (Toronto: Canadian Institute of International Affairs, 1966) and the essays of John Holmes in *The Better Part of Valour: Essays on Canadian Diplomacy* (Toronto: McClelland & Stewart, 1970) and *Canada: A Middle-Aged Power* (Toronto: McClelland & Stewart, 1976).

27. See Carsten Holbraad, *Middle Powers in International Politics* (London: Macmillan, 1984).

28. Martin Wight, *Power Politics*, 2nd ed. (Harmondsworth, UK: Penguin, 1986), 66. Wight adds that middle powers 'can afford to champion international ideals because they do not have the responsibility for enforcing them'.

29. Robert Cox, 'Middlepowermanship, Japan, and Future World Order', *International Journal* 44 (1989): 824.

30. A. Leroy Bennett, *International Organizations: Principles and Issues*, 2nd ed. (Englewood Cliffs, NJ: Prentice Hall, 1980), 160.

31. John Holmes, 'The United Nations in Perspective', *Behind the Headlines* 44, 1 (1986): 13.

32. John Holmes, 'Canada's Role in International Organizations', *The Canadian Banker* 74 (1967): 116.

33. Cox, 'Middlepowermanship', 823.

34. Holmes, *The Better Part of Valour*, 2.

35. Michael Tucker, *Canadian Foreign Policy: Contemporary Issues and Themes* (Toronto: McGraw-Hill Ryerson, 1980), 5.

36. See, for example, James Eayrs, 'Canada's Emergence as a Foremost Power', *International Perspectives* 4 (May/June 1975): 15–24; David Dewitt and John Kirton, *Canada as a Principal Power: A Study in Foreign Policy and International Relations* (Toronto: Wiley, 1983); and Philip Resnick, 'From Semi-Periphery to Perimeter of the Core: Canada in the Capitalist World Economy', in his *The Masks of Proteus: Canadian Reflections on the State* (Kingston, ON: McGill-Queen's University Press, 1989), 176–204.

37. Dewitt and Kirton, *Canada as a Principal Power*, 43–4.

38. Pearson, *Mike*, vol. 2, 32.

39. Reid, *Radical Mandarin*, 252.

40. Dana Wilgress in a letter from London, 3 September 1952, Department of External Affairs, File 5296-A1-40-Part 1.

41. Reg Whitaker, 'The Cold War and the Myth of Liberal-Internationalism', paper presented to the Annual Meeting of the Canadian Political Science Association, Winnipeg, MB, 8 June 1986.

42. Neufeld, 'Hegemony and Foreign Policy Analysis'.

43. Stairs, 'Global Governance as a Policy Tool', 76.

44. Keohane, 'Multilateralism', 748.

45. John Ravenhill, 'Cycles of Middle Power Activism: Constraint and Choice in Australian and Canadian Foreign Policies', *Australian Journal of International Affairs* 52 (1998): 322.

46. National Archives of Canada, External Affairs Records, RG 25, Acc 89-90/029, vol. 9, file 7V(s), Part 1, Lester Pearson in a letter to Norman Robertson (1 February 1944).

47. Kim Nossal, *The Politics of Canadian Foreign Policy* (Scarborough, ON: Prentice Hall, 1985), 53.

CHAPTER 1

1. James Eayrs, *In Defence of Canada: Peacemaking and Deterrence* (Toronto: University of Toronto Press, 1972), 158.

2. Cited in Cordell Hull, *The Memoirs of Cordell Hull*, vol. 2 (New York: Macmillan, 1948), 1643.

3. Eayrs, *In Defence of Canada: Peacemaking and Deterrence*, 137.

4. The text of the Dumbarton Oaks proposals can be found in *Postwar Foreign Policy Preparation, 1939–1945*, US Department of State Publication 3580 (Washington, DC: Government Printing Office, 1949).

5. Cited in J.L. Granatstein, *The Ottawa Men: The Civil Service Mandarins, 1935–1957* (Toronto: Oxford University Press, 1982), 117.

6. Cited in Eayrs, *In Defence of Canada: Peacemaking and Deterrence*, 144.

7. For Reid's views, see his *Radical Mandarin: The Memoirs of Escott Reid* (Toronto: University of Toronto Press, 1989) and his *On Duty: A Canadian at the Making of the United Nations, 1945–1946* (Toronto: McClelland & Stewart, 1983).

8. National Archives of Canada (NAC), Escott Reid Papers, vol. 6, file 11, 'The United States and Canada' (12 January 1942).

9. Eayrs, *In Defence of Canada: Peacemaking and Deterrence*, 139–42.

10. For a discussion of Canadian policy at the ICAO conference, see Robert Bothwell and J.L. Granatstein, 'Canada and Wartime Negotiations over Civil Aviation', *International History Review* 11 (October 1980): 585–601.

11. W.L. Mackenzie King's statement to the meeting of Commonwealth prime ministers (11 May 1944); J.W. Pickersgill, *The Mackenzie King Record, I 1939–1944* (Toronto: University of Toronto Press, 1960), 678–9.

12. John English, *Shadow of Heaven: The Life of Lester Pearson, Volume One: 1897–1948* (Toronto: Lester & Orpen Dennys, 1990), 285.

13. Lester Pearson, cited in Eayrs, *In Defence of Canada: Peacemaking and Deterrence*, 154.

14. *Functionalism* has two distinct meanings. One definition found in the literature on international politics refers to a process of organizing international activity according to 'functional' or technical interests. This would, in the view of functionalism's principal proponent, David Mitrany, circumvent state sovereignty and depoliticize certain areas of international activity. In Mitrany's view, the proliferation of functional organizations would eventually lead to a more stable and peaceful international order. For details, see David Mitrany, *A Working Peace System: An Argument for the Functional Development of International Organization* (London: Royal Institute of International Affairs, 1943).

These ideas had some support in the Canadian government, but most of the attention was directed toward a second definition of *functionalism*, that being representation in decision making on the basis of one's contributions or ability to contribute to the matter at hand. For an analysis of the importance of functionalism in Canadian foreign policy, see A.J. Miller, 'The Functional Principle in Canada's External Relations', *International Journal* 35 (1980): 309–28.

15. J.L. Granatstein, *A Man of Influence: Norman A. Robertson and Canadian Statecraft, 1929–68* (Toronto: Deneau, 1981), 136.

16. *Documents on Canadian External Relations* (DCER), 9 (1942–43) (Ottawa: Supply and Services, 1980), 107.

17. NAC, External Affairs Records, RG25 Acc 89-90/029, vol. 9, file 7V(s), pt. 1, Lester Pearson to Norman Robertson (1 February 1944).

18. Granatstein, *A Man of Influence*, 139.

19. Ibid., 142.

20. Ibid.

21. John Holmes, *The Shaping of Peace: Canada and the Search for World Order, 1943–1957*, vol. 1 (Toronto: University of Toronto Press, 1979), 40.

22. Cited in Granatstein, *A Man of Influence*, 143.

23. Cited in ibid., 138–9.

24. English, *Shadow of Heaven*, 284.

25. Nicholas Mansergh, *Survey of British Commonwealth Affairs, 1939–52* (London: Frank Cass, 1968), 312.

26. Holmes, *The Shaping of Peace*, vol. 1, 28.

27. NAC , Pearson to Robertson (1 February 1944).

28. NAC, Escott Reid papers, Memorandum (14 March 1945).

29. Cited in Holmes, *The Shaping of Peace*, vol. 1, 235.

30. Reid, *On Duty*, 130.

31. Holmes, *The Shaping of Peace*, vol. 1, 236.

32. NAC, Escott Reid papers, vol. 6, file 10, Letter of instructions to the Canadian representative on the Security Council of the United Nations (28 November 1947).

33. Holmes, *The Shaping of Peace*, vol. 2 (Toronto, University of Toronto Press, 1982), 377.

34. Holmes, *The Shaping of Peace*, vol. 1, 269.

35. Cited in ibid., 18.

36. Cited in ibid, 147.

37. Cited in ibid., 150.

38. Lord Garner, cited in Nicholas Mansergh, *The Commonwealth Experience*, rev. ed., vol. 2 (Toronto: University of Toronto Press, 1983), 103.

39. Holmes, *The Shaping of Peace*, vol. 1, 152.

40. Margaret Doxey writes that 'the major structural innovation in the commonwealth (at this time) was the adoption of the formula that allowed republics to be members' and that Pearson 'made a significant contribution' to it (Margaret Doxey, 'Canada and the Commonwealth', in John English and Norman Hilmer, eds, *Making a Difference? Canada's Foreign Policy in a Changing World Order* [Toronto: Lester, 1992], 35).

41. Pearson's address to the UN General Assembly, 26 September 1949, in Deparment of External Affairs, *Canada and the United Nations* (Ottawa: King's Printer, 1949), 208.

42. F.H. Soward and Edgar McInnis, *Canada and the United Nations* (Westport, CT: Greenwood, 1956), 102.

43. Leon Gordenker, cited in Denis Stairs, *The Diplomacy of Constraint: Canada, the Korean War, and the United States* (Toronto: University of Toronto Press, 1974).

44. See the account in ibid., 9–12.

45. Ibid., 17.

46. Cited in ibid., 60.

47. Lester Pearson, 'Canadian Foreign Policy in a Two-Power World', Toronto, 10 April 1951, in Department of External Affairs, *Statements and Speeches* 51/14.

48. Stairs, *The Diplomacy of Constraint*, 50–1.

49. Ibid., 53.

50. United Nations Security Council, Document S/1508/Rev. 1, 27 June 1950.

51. Stairs, *The Diplomacy of Constraint*, 84.

52. Cited in ibid., 164.

53. Acheson, cited in ibid., 165.

54. Kenneth McNaught, 'Ottawa and Washington Look at the UN', *Foreign Affairs* 33 (1955). 667.

55. Stairs, *The Diplomacy of Constraint*, 52.

56. Holmes, *The Shaping of Peace*, vol. 2, 161.

57. Reid, *On Duty*, 77.

58. Cited in Arthur Menzies, 'The Roots of Complicity' (review of James Eayrs, *In Defence of Canada: Indochina: Roots of Complicity*), *Ottawa Citizen* (3 September 1983), 39.

59. Henry Wiseman, 'Peacekeeping and the Management of International Conflict', Canadian Institute for International Peace and Security, Background Paper 15 (1987), 1.

60. David Cox, 'Peacekeeping: The Canadian Experience', in Alastair Taylor, David Cox, and J.L. Granatstein, *Peacekeeping: International Challenge and Canadian Response* (Toronto: Canadian Institute of International Affairs, 1968), 46–7.

61. For a fuller discussion of Canadian policy at the time of the Suez crisis, see Terence Robertson, *Crisis: The Inside Story of the Suez Conspiracy* (Toronto: McClelland & Stewart, 1964); Holmes, *The Shaping of Peace*, vol. 2, 348–70; and Lester B. Pearson, *Mike: The Memoirs of the Right Honourable Lester B. Pearson*, vol. 2 (Toronto: University of Toronto Press, 1973), 239–316.

CHAPTER 2

1. Cited in Richard N. Gardner, *Sterling Dollar Diplomacy: Anglo-American Collaboration in the Reconstruction of the Multilateral Trade* (Oxford: Clarendon, 1956), 46, 47.

2. United States, Department of State, *Bulletin* 6 (1942): 192.

3. Cordell Hull, *The Memoirs of Cordell Hull*, vol. 1 (New York: Macmillan, 1948), 81.

4. Gardner, *Sterling Dollar Diplomacy*.

5. Cited in John Holmes, *The Shaping of Peace: Canada and the Search for World Order, 1943–1957*, vol. 1 (Toronto: University of Toronto Press, 1979), 53.

6. Ibid., 52.

7. Eric Helleiner, *States and the Reemergence of Global Finance: From Bretton Woods to the 1990s* (Ithaca, NY: Cornell University Press, 1994).

8. Louis Rasminsky, in A.L.K. Acheson, J.F. Chant, and M.F.J. Prachowny, eds, *Bretton Woods Revisited: Evaluations of the International Monetary Fund and the International Bank for Reconstruction and Development* (Toronto: University of Toronto Press, 1972), 34.

9. *Documents on Canadian External Relations* (DCER), vol. 9, 1942–1943 (Ottawa: Supply and Services, 1980), 612.

10. Ibid.

11. Ibid., 653.

12. J.L. Granatstein, *The Ottawa Men: The Civil Service Mandarins, 1935–1957* (Toronto: Oxford University Press, 1982), 146.

13. DCER, vol. 9, 651.

14. Cited in Granatstein, *The Ottawa Men*, 148.

15. DCER, vol. 9, 653–5 and 665–71.

16. Granatstein, *The Ottawa Men*, 148.

17. DCER, vol. 9, 654.

18. Richard Gardner, in Acheson et al., eds, *Bretton Woods Revisited*, 20.

19. Sir Roy Harrod, *The Life of John Maynard Keynes* (London: Macmillan, 1951), 579.

20. Granatstein, *The Ottawa Men*, 150.

21. See comments in ibid., 152.

22. DCER, vol. 9, 643.

23. Cited in Gardner, *Sterling Dollar Diplomacy*, 19.

24. Nicholas Mansergh, *The Commonwealth Experience*, 2nd ed., vol. 2 (London: Macmillan, 1982), 19.

25. Gilbert Winham, *International Trade and the Tokyo Round Negotiation* (Princeton, NJ: Princeton University Press, 1986), 38.

26. Gardner, *Sterling Dollar Diplomacy*, 148.

27. Ibid., 151.

28. Ibid.

29. Cited in ibid., 253.

30. DCER, vol. 11 (1944–1945), 67.

31. R.D. Cuff and J.L. Granatstein, 'The Rise and Fall of Canadian–American Free Trade, 1947–8', *Canadian Historical Review* 57 (1977): 481.

32. Jack A. Finlayson, 'Trade and Global Interdependence', in David Haglund and Michael Hawes, eds, *World Politics: Power, Interdependence and Dependence* (Toronto: Harcourt Brace Jovanovich, 1990), 292.

33. The text of the General Agreement on Tariffs and Trade can be found in Canada Treaty Series 1947, no. 27 (Ottawa: King's Printer, 1947).

34. DCER, vol. 12 (1946), 1054.

35. Cited in Frank Stone, *Canada, the GATT and the International Trade System* (Ottawa: Institute for Research on Public Policy, 1984), 22.

36. Gardner, *Sterling Dollar Diplomacy*, 361.

37. Ibid., 287.

38. Robert O. Keohane, 'Hegemonic Leadership and U.S. Foreign Policy in the Long Decade of the 1950s', in William P. Avery and David R. Rapkin, eds, *America in a Changing World Political Economy* (New York: Longman, 1982), 49–76.

39. Douglas LePan, *Bright Glass of Memory: A Set of Four Memoirs* (Toronto: McGraw-Hill Ryerson, 1979), 68.

40. Ibid., 63.

41. Glen Williams, *Not for Export: Toward a Political Economy of Canada's Arrested Industrialization*, updated ed. (Toronto: McClelland & Stewart, 1986), especially chapter 6.

42. Kenneth R. Wilson, 'The External Background of Canada's Economic Problems', in J. Douglas Gibson, ed., *Canada's Economy in a Changing World* (Toronto: Macmillan, 1948), 27.

43. Cuff and Granatstein, 'The Rise and Fall of Canadian–American Free Trade', 464.

44. For a discussion of this aborted agreement, see ibid.

45. Gardner, *Sterling Dollar Diplomacy*, 304.

46. Ibid., 346.

47. Ibid., 92.

48. NAC, Department of External Affairs, file 5296-A-3-40, 'The North Atlantic Community' (6 September 1951).

49. Stone, *Canada, the GATT and the International Trade System*, 101.

50. Ibid., 87–8.

51. Basil Robinson, *Diefenbaker's World: A Populist in Foreign Affairs* (Toronto: University of Toronto, 1989), 281.

52. Ibid.

53. A.F.W. Plumptre, *Three Decades of Decision: Canada and the World Monetary System, 1944–75* (Toronto: McClelland & Stewart, 1977), 96.

54. Cited in J. Keith Horsefield, *The International Monetary Fund, 1945–1965: Twenty Years of International Monetary Cooperation* (Washington, DC: International Monetary Fund, 1969), 161.

55. Plumptre, *Three Decades of Decision*, 147.

56. Ibid., 150.

57. Peyton Lyon, *Canada in World Affairs, 1961–63* (Toronto: Oxford University Press, 1968), 343.

58. Kenneth Dam, *The GATT: Law and International Economic Organization* (Chicago: University of Chicago Press, 1970), 32.

59. Lyon, *Canada in World Affairs*, 346.

60. Ibid., 156.

61. Gerard Curzon and Victoria Curzon, 'GATT: Traders Club', in Robert Cox and Harold Jacobson, eds, *The Anatomy of Influence: Decision Making in International Organization* (New Haven, CT: Yale University Press, 1973), 302.

62. Ibid., 171.

63. NAC, Department of External Affairs, file 5296-40, part 2, 'Canada's Economic and Financial Foreign Policy' (1951), 6.

64. Cited in Bruce Muirhead, 'Canadian Trade Policy, 1949–57: The Failure of the Anglo-European Option' (Ph.D. dissertation, York University, Toronto, 1986), 335.

65. NAC, Department of External Affairs, file 5296-40, part 2, 'Canadian Policy with Respect to the Commonwealth' (n.d.).

CHAPTER 3

1. Cited in Denis Smith, *Diplomacy of Fear: Canada and the Cold War, 1941–48* (Toronto: University of Toronto Press, 1988), 85.

2. Ibid.

3. Escott Reid, *Time of Fear and Hope: The Making of the North Atlantic Treaty, 1947–1949* (Toronto: McClelland & Stewart, 1977), 31.

4. Cited in ibid., 33.

5. Ibid., 36.

6. Canada, *House of Commons Debates* (1 February 1923), 33.

7. Cited in Reid, *Time of Fear and Hope*, 43.

8. James Eayrs, *In Defence of Canada: Growing Up Allied* (Toronto: University of Toronto Press, 1980), 52–8.

9. Cited in ibid., 67.

10. Cited in ibid., 66.

11. The initial members, in addition to Canada, were Belgium, Denmark, France, Iceland, Italy, Luxembourg, Netherlands, Norway, Portugal, the United Kingdom, and the United States. Greece and Turkey became members in 1952, West Germany in 1955, and Spain in 1982.

12. *Documents on Canadian External Relations* (DCER), vol. 12, 679–80.

13. National Archives of Canada (NAC), Escott Reid Papers, vol. 6, file 10, 'Letter of instructions to the Canadian representative on the Security Council of the United Nations' (28 November 1947).

14. Cited in Smith, *Diplomacy of Fear*, 189.

15. Reid, 'Letter of instructions'.

16. Lester Pearson, memorandum to King, 12 November 1946.

17. Smith, *Diplomacy of Fear*, 8.

18. Ibid., 73.

19. Leon Mayrand, cited in ibid., 78.

20. Ibid., 134.

21. Cited in Eayrs, *In Defence of Canada: Growing Up Allied*, 30.

22. Smith, *Diplomacy of Fear*, 10.

23. Joseph Jockel, 'The Canada–United States Military Co-operation Committee and Continental Air Defence, 1946', *Canadian Historical Review* 64, 3 (1983): 359.

24. Cited in Smith, *Diplomacy of Fear*, 157.

25. Hume Wrong, cited in ibid., 163.

26. See Reid, *Time of Fear and Hope*, 105.

27. Cited in ibid., 108–9.

28. Cited in Smith, *Diplomacy of Fear*, 117.

29. Cited in Reid, *Time of Fear and Hope*, 15–16.

30. Gregg Herken, *The Winning Weapon: The Atomic Bomb in the Cold War, 1945–1950* (New York: Vantage, 1982), 256–80.

31. Reid, *Time of Fear and Hope*, 28.

32. Cited in ibid., 264.

33. Cited in Eayrs, *In Defence of Canada: Growing Up Allied*, 126.

34. R.D. Cuff and J.L. Granatstein, *Ties That Bind: Canadian–American Relations in Wartime from the Great War to the Cold War* (Toronto: Hakkert, 1977), 127.

35. Cited in ibid., 126.

36. For some additional comments on this, see Eayrs, *In Defence of Canada: Growing Up Allied*, 56.

37. Cited in ibid., 182.

38. Cited in ibid., 186–7.

39. Cited in ibid., 187.

40. Cited in ibid., 188.

41. Reid, *Time of Fear and Hope*, 11.

42. Cited in ibid., 191.

43. Cited in ibid., 200.

44. Cited in ibid., 220.

45. NATO, *Text of Final Communiques, 1949–1974* (Brussels: NATO Information Service, 1975), 60.

46. Harald von Riekhoff, *NATO: Issues and Prospects* (Toronto: Canadian Institute of International Affairs, 1967), 104.

47. B.S. Kierstead, *Canada in World Affairs*, vol. 7 (Toronto: Oxford University Press, 1956), 138.

48. Cited in Eayrs, *In Defence of Canada: Growing Up Allied*, 223.

49. Kierstead, *Canada in World Affairs*, vol. 7, 144.

50. *Speeches and Statements* 52/24, 5.

51. Cited in Eayrs, *In Defence of Canada: Growing Up Allied*, 224.

52. Cited in ibid.

53. Cited in ibid., 359.

54. Kierstead, *Canada in World Affairs*, vol. 7, 89.

55. Editorial, *Montreal Star* (4 October 1954), cited in Donald C. Masters, *Canada in World Affairs*, vol. 8 (Toronto: Oxford University Press, 1958), 137.

56. Eayrs, *In Defence of Canada: Growing Up Allied*, 236–7.

57. *Globe and Mail* (26 March 1954).

58. Basil Robinson, *Diefenbaker's World: A Populist in Foreign Affairs* (Toronto: University of Toronto Press, 1989), 28.

59. Cited in ibid., 28.

60. Ibid., 30–1. This alignment within NATO was not uncommon.

61. Ibid., 28.

62. See, for example, James Minifie, *Peacemaker or Powder-Monkey: Canada's Role in a Revolutionary World* (Toronto: McClelland & Stewart, 1960) and Lewis Hertzman, John W. Warnock, and Thomas A. Hockin, *Alliances and Illusions: Canada and the NATO–NORAD Question* (Edmonton: Hurtig, 1969).

CHAPTER 4

1. Basil Robinson, *Diefenbaker's World: A Populist in Foreign Affairs* (Toronto: University of Toronto, 1989), 314.

2. Ibid., 148.

3. Ibid., 267–8.

4. Ibid., 148.

5. Paul Martin, *A Very Public Life*, vol. 2 (Ottawa: Deneau, 1985), 560.

6. Cited in Brian Urquhart, *A Life in Peace and War* (New York: Harper & Row, 1987), 216.

7. Martin, *A Very Public Life*, vol. 2, 563.

8. Urquhart, *A Life in Peace and War*, 213.

9. Ibid.

10. Martin, *A Very Public Life*, vol. 2, 569.

11. *Speeches and Statements* 64/12, 13.

12. For an analysis of Canadian policy, see Douglas Ross, *In the Interests of Peace: Canada and Vietnam 1954–1973* (Toronto: University of Toronto Press, 1984). For a critical view, see, for example, Victor Levant, *Quiet Complicity: Canadian Involvement in the Vietnam War* (Toronto: Between the Lines, 1986). Also see James Eayrs, *In Defence of Canada: Indochina: Roots of Complicity* (Toronto: University of Toronto Press, 1983).

13. Paul Bridle, 'Canada and the International Commissions in Indochina, 1954–72', *Behind the Headlines* 32, 4 (1973): 1–28.

14. See Ross, *In the Interests of Peace*, 300–1, for a discussion of Pearson's view on this.

15. John Holmes, *The Shaping of Peace: Canada and the Search for World Order, 1943–1957*, vol. 1 (Toronto: University of Toronto Press, 1979), 255.

16. Cited in F.H. Soward and Edgar McInnis, *Canada and the United Nations* (Westport, CT: Greenwood, 1956), 226.

17. Cited in Holmes, *The Shaping of Peace*, vol. 2, 347.

18. Cited in Frank Hays, 'South Africa's Departure from the Commonwealth, 1960–1961', *International History Review* 2 (1980): 458.

19. Ibid., 464.

20. Ibid., 470.

21. Cited in ibid., 473.

22. Cited in Arnold Smith, *Stitches in Time: The Commonwealth in World Politics* (London: Andre Deutsch, 1981), 8.

23. J.L. Granatstein and Robert Bothwell, *Pirouette: Pierre Trudeau and Canadian Foreign Policy* (Toronto: University of Toronto Press, 1990), 295.

24. Canada, Department of External Affairs, *Foreign Policy for Canadians* (Ottawa: Queen's Printer, 1970), 9.

25. Alan Gotlieb and Charles Dalfen, 'National Jurisdiction and International Responsibility: New Canadian Approaches to International Law', *American Journal of International Law* 73 (1972): 232–3.

26. Daniel Moynihan, *A Dangerous Place* (Boston: Little Brown, 1978).

27. United Nations, General Assembly, 22nd Session, 18 August 1967.

28. Clyde Sanger, *Ordering the Oceans: The Making of the Law of the Sea* (Toronto: University of Toronto Press, 1987), 31.

29. The Canadian delegation was also aided by a well-organized and effective management of domestic groups and government departments with an interest in the negotiations. See, for example, the discussion in Elizabeth Riddell-Dixon, *Canada and the International Seabed: Domestic Determinants and External Constraints* (Kingston, ON: McGill-Queen's University Press, 1989).

30. Canada, Department of External Affairs, 'The United Nations', *Foreign Policy for Canadians*, 16.

31. Patrick Martin, 'Canadians in Golan Heights Settling In for the Long Haul', *Globe and Mail* (25 February 1985), A2.

32. Cited in Akira Ichikawa, 'The "Helpful Fixer": Canada's Persistent International Image', *Behind the Headlines* 37, 3 (1979): 13.

33. Robert Mitchell, 'Peacekeeping and Peacemaking in Cyprus', Background Paper (Ottawa: Canadian Institute for International Peace and Security, October 1988), 6.

34. Chris Morris, 'Staying UN Course, US Urged', *Edmonton Journal* (2 February 1985), A3.

35. Cited in Preface to Harrod and N. Schrijver, eds, *The UN Under Attack* (Aldershot, UK: Gower, 1988).

36. Pierre Hassner, 'Europe and the Atlantic Relationship', *International Journal* 39 (1984): 417.

37. Robert Keohane and Joseph Nye, Jr, 'Two Cheers for Multilateralism', *Foreign Policy* 60 (1985): 148–67.

38. John Holmes, 'The United Nations in Perspective', *Behind the Headlines* 44, 1 (1986): 16–17.

39. Javier Perez de Cuellar, 'Secretary-General, Report on the Work of the Organization', in *Annual Review of United Nations Affairs 1982* (Dobbs Ferry, NY: Oceana Publications, 1983), 4.

40. Annual Report of the Secretary-General (New York: United Nations, 1985), 14.

41. Cited in Philip Geyelin, 'The Will for Peace Is Lacking', *Guardian Weekly* (11 May 1986), 18.

42. Cited in ibid.

43. Canada, Secretary of State for External Affairs, *Competitiveness and Security: Directions for Canada's International Relations* (Ottawa: Secretary of State for External Affairs, 1985), 2.

44. Canada, Parliament, Special Joint Committee on Canada's International Relations, *Independence and Internationalism: Report of the Special Joint Committee of the Senate and of the House of Commons on Canada's International Relations* (Ottawa: Supply and Services Canada, 1986).

45. Cited in Patrick Martin, 'Canada Blazes a Trail in Africa', *Globe and Mail* (29 July 1986), A7.

46. Granatstein and Bothwell, *Pirouette*, 284.

47. Canada, *House of Commons Debates* (9 September 1987), 8776–7.

48. Ian O. Cameron, 'Canada, the Commonwealth and South Africa: National Foreign Policy-Making in a Multilateral Environment', *Millennium* 18 (Summer 1989): 211.

49. Ibid., 212.

50. Ibid., 213.

51. Ibid., 217.

52. Brian Mulroney, 'Principles of UN Charter Signposts to Peace', *Statements and Speeches* 85/14 (Ottawa: Department of External Affairs, 23 October 1985).

CHAPTER 5

1. Walter Russell Meade, 'American Economic Policy in the Antemillenial Era', *World Policy Journal* 6 (Summer 1989): 385–468.

2. A.F.W. Plumptre, 'Perspective on Our Aid to Others', *International Journal* 22 (Summer 1967): 487.

3. For a discussion of Reid's work for the World Bank, see Escott Reid, *Radical Mandarin: The Memoirs of Escott Reid* (Toronto: University of Toronto Press, 1989). The Pearson Commission report was published as Commission on International Development, *Partners in Development: Report* (New York: Praeger, 1969).

4. Cited in A.L.K. Acheson, J.F. Chant, and M.F.J. Prachowny, eds, *Bretton Woods Revisited: Evaluations of the International Monetary Fund and the International Bank for Reconstruction and Development* (Toronto: University of Toronto Press, 1972), 47.

5. As described by Jock Finlayson and Ann Weston, the 'principal suppliers' rule worked as follows: 'Requests for tariff concession were usually made by the biggest supplier of a partic-ular product to an individual foreign market, not by secondary or smaller suppliers either individually or as a group'; Finlayson and Weston, *The GATT, Middle Powers and the Uruguay Round* (Ottawa: North-South Institute, 1990), 16.

6. Richard Gardner, 'The United Nations Conference on Trade and Development', in Richard N. Gardner and Max F. Millikan, eds, *The Global Partnership: International Agencies and Economic Development* (New York: Praeger, 1968), 121.

7. Edward S. Mason and Robert E. Asher, *The World Bank Since Bretton Woods: The Origins, Policies, Operations, and Impact of the International Bank for Reconstruction and Development and Other Members of the World Bank Group . . .* (Washington, DC: Brookings Institution, 1973), 383.

8. F.H. Soward and Edgar McInnis, *Canada and the United Nations* (Westport, CT: Greenwood, 1956), 172.

9. Ibid., 172.

10. Ibid., 175.

11. Mason and Asher, *The World Bank Since Bretton Woods*, 386.

12. Ibid., 380.

13. Mason and Asher, *The World Bank Since Bretton Wood*, 381.

14. Ibid., 397.

15. Ibid., 394.

16. John Evans, *The Kennedy Round in American Trade Policy: The Twilight of the GATT?* (Cambridge: Harvard University Press, 1971), 120.

17. GATT, *Trends in International Trade: Report by a Panel of Experts* (Geneva: GATT, 1958).

18. Gilbert Winham, *International Trade and the Tokyo Round Negotiation* (Princeton, NJ: Princeton University Press, 1986), 143.

19. Cited in Keith Spicer, 'Clubmanship Upstaged: Canada's Twenty Years in the Colombo Plan', *International Journal* 25 (Winter 1969–70): 25.

20. Cited in Raoul Prebisch, 'The Role of Commercial Policy in Underdeveloped Countries', *American Economic Review* 49, 2 (May 1959): 251–73.

21. Cited in Keith Spicer, *A Samaritan State? External Aid in Canada's Foreign Policy* (Toronto: University of Toronto Press, 1966), 22.

22. Cited in Douglas Anglin, 'Canadian Post-War International Assistance', *International Journal* 9 (Autumn 1954): 273.

23. Spicer, *A Samaritan State*, 54.

24. Ibid., 40.

25. Ibid., 73–4.

26. Soward and McInnis, *Canada and the United Nations*, 172.

27. J.L. Granatstein and Robert Bothwell, *Pirouette: Pierre Trudeau and Canadian Foreign Policy* (Toronto: University of Toronto Press, 1990), 307.

28. Peyton Lyon and Brian Tomlin, *Canada as an International Actor* (Toronto: Macmillan, 1979), 147.

29. See, for example, Robert Carty and Virginia Smith, *Perpetuating Poverty: The Political Economy of Canadian Foreign Aid* (Toronto: Between the Lines, 1981).

30. Jaleel Ahmad, 'Canada's Trade with Developing Countries', in Gerald K. Helleiner, ed., *The Other Side of International Development Policy: The Non-Aid Economic Relations with Developing Countries of Canada, Denmark, the Netherlands, Norway, and Sweden* (Toronto: University of Toronto Press, 1990), 31.

31. Ibid., 62

32. Ibid., 51.

33. A. Lovbraek, 'International Reform and the Like-Minded Countries in the North–South Dialogue 1975–1985', in Cranford Pratt, ed., *Middle Power Internationalism: The North–South Dimension* (Montreal: McGill-Queen's University Press, 1990), 26–68.

34. Ibid., 44.

35. Vinod K. Aggarwal, *Liberal Protectionism: The International Politics of Organized Textile Trade* (Berkeley: University of California Press, 1985), 139.

36. Lovbraek, 'International Reform and the Like-Minded Countries', 45.

37. Ibid.

38. Cranford Pratt, 'Middle Power Internationalism and Global Poverty', in Cranford Pratt, ed., *Middle Power Internationalism*, 15.

39. Cranford Pratt, 'Canada: An Eroding and Limited Internationalism', in Cranford Pratt, ed., *Internationalism Under Strain: The North–South Policies of Canada, the Netherlands, Norway, and Sweden* (Toronto: University of Toronto Press, 1989), 36.

40. Hedley Bull, *Justice in International Relations* (Waterloo, ON: University of Waterloo Press, 1984).

41. Pratt, 'Canada: An Eroding and Limited Internationalism', 59.

42. Frank Stone, *Canada, the GATT and the International Trade System* (Ottawa: Institute for Research on Public Policy, 1984), 26.

43. Evans, *The Kennedy Round in American Trade Policy*, 162.

44. Maurice Schwarzmann, cited in J.L. Granatstein, *A Man of Influence: Norman A. Robertson and Canadian Statecraft, 1929–68* (Toronto: Deneau, 1981), 365.

45. Ernest Pregg, *Traders and Diplomats: An Analysis of the Kennedy Round of Negotiations Under the General Agreement on Tariffs and Trade* (Washington, DC: Brookings Institution, 1970), 10.

46. Ibid., 91, 188.

47. Cited in Granatstein, *A Man of Influence*, 370.

48. Stone, *Canada, the GATT and the International Trade System*, 176.

49. G.E. Salembier, Andrew Moroz, and Frank Stone, *The Canadian Import File: Trade, Protection and Adjustment* (Ottawa: Institute for Research on Public Policy, 1987), 3.

50. Stone, *Canada, the GATT and the International Trade System*, 177.

51. Gerard Curzon and Victoria Curzon, 'GATT: Trader's Club', in Robert Cox and Harold Jacobson, eds, *The Anatomy of Influence: Decision Making in International Organization* (New Haven, CT: Yale University Press, 1973), 475.

52. Stone, *Canada, the GATT and the International Trade System*, 181.

53. Ibid.

54. Winham, *International Trade and the Tokyo Round Negotiation*, 334.

55. Stone, *Canada, the GATT and the International Trade System*, 178.

56. Winham, *International Trade and the Tokyo Round Negotiation*, 336.

57. Canada, Department of Industry, Trade and Commerce, *Canada's Trade Performance* (Ottawa: Department of Industry, Trade and Commerce, 1978), 13.

58. Stone, *Canada, the GATT and the International Trade System*, 209.

59. Winham, *International Trade and the Tokyo Round Negotiation*, 335.

60. Jock Finlayson and Stefano Bertasi, 'Evolution of Canadian Postwar International Trade Policy', in A. Claire Cutler and Mark W. Zacher, eds, *Canadian Foreign Policy and International Economic Regimes* (Vancouver: University of British Columbia Press, 1992), 31.

61. Granatstein and Bothwell, *Pirouette*, 332.

62. For a comprehensive account of the free trade negotiations, see Bruce Doern and Brian Tomlin, *Faith and Fear: The Free Trade Story* (Toronto: Stoddart, 1991).

CHAPTER 6

1. Fred Halliday, *The Making of the Second Cold War* (London: Verso, 1983).

2. Don Munton, 'Public Opinion and the Media in Canada from Cold War to Detente to New Cold War', *International Journal* 39 (1983–84): 171–213; Gregory Flynn and Hans Rattinger, eds, *The Public and Atlantic Defence* (Totowa, NJ: Rowman and Allanheld, 1985).

3. Canada, Department of National Defence, *Challenge and Commitment: A Defence Policy for Canada* (Ottawa: Department of National Defence, 1987).

4. James Rusk, 'The Cruise: A No-Choice Option?' *Globe and Mail* (21 February 1983), A10.

5. Paul Martin, *A Very Public Life*, vol. 2 (Ottawa: Deneau, 1985), 459.

6. Cited in Bruce Thordarson, *Trudeau and Foreign Policy: A Study in Decision-Making* (Toronto: Oxford University Press, 1972), 11.

7. Robert Ford, *Our Man in Moscow: A Diplomat's Reflections on the Soviet Union* (Toronto: University of Toronto Press, 1989), 119.

8. Ibid., 118–19.

9. Ibid., 123.

10. Robert Spencer, 'Canada and the Origins of the CSCE, 1965–1973', in Robert Spencer, ed., *Canada and the Conference on Security and Co-operation in Europe* (Toronto: University of Toronto Centre for International Studies, 1984), 35.

11. 'We wish to take a fresh look at the fundamentals of Canadian foreign policy to see whether there are ways in which we can serve more effectively Canada's current interests, objectives and priorities' (Thordarson, *Trudeau and Foreign Policy*, 1–2).

12. Dalton Camp, 'Introduction', in Lewis Hertzman, John W. Warrock, and Thomas A. Hockin, *Alliances and Illusions: Canada and the NATO–NORAD Question* (Edmonton: Hurtig, 1969), xix.

13. Ford, *Our Man in Moscow*, 115.

14. *Manchester Guardian* (31 May 1969).

15. D.W. Middlemiss and J.J. Sokolsky, *Canadian Defence: Decisions and Determinants* (Toronto: Harcourt Brace Jovanovich, 1989), 37.

16. Cited in ibid., 43.

17. Robert Spencer, 'The Curtain Rises: Canada in Stage One, Helsinki, July 1975', in Spencer, *Canada and the Conference on Security and Co-operation in Europe*, 103.

18. Peyton Lyon and Geoffrey Nimmo, 'Canada at Geneva, 1973–5', in Spencer, *Canada and the Conference on Security and Co-operation in Europe*, 111.

19. Ibid., 110.

20. Middlemiss and Sokolsky, *Canadian Defence*, 33.

21. Ibid., 36–7.

22. R.B. Byers, 'Canadian Security and Defence: The Legacy and the Challenges', *Adelphi Papers* 214 (Winter 1986).

23. Middlemiss and Sokolsky, *Canadian Defence*, 40.

24. Canada, Department of External Affairs, *Foreign Policy for Canadians: Europe* (Ottawa: Queen's Printer, 1970), 19.

25. Middlemiss and Sokolsky, *Canadian Defence*, 36.

26. Joseph Jockel and Joel Sokolsky, *Canada and Collective Security: Odd Man Out* (New York: Praeger, 1986), 54.

27. Ibid.

28. Canada, Department of National Defence, 'Air Launch Cruise Missile Testing in Canada', Backgrounder (September 1986), 7.

29. Cited in James Rusk, 'The Cruise', A10.

30. Ibid.

31. Gerald Wright, 'NATO in the New International Order', *Behind the Headlines* 36, 4 (1978): 16.

32. Canada, *House of Commons Debates*, 1st Session, 33rd Parliament (5 November 1984), 7.

33. Jockel and Sokolsky, *Canada and Collective Security*, 19.

34. R.B. Byers, 'Canadian Defence and Defence Procurement: Implications for Economic Policy', in Denis Stairs and Gilbert Winham, eds, *Selected Problems in Formulating Foreign Economic Policy* (Toronto: University of Toronto Press, 1985), 138.

35. Douglas Ross, 'A Maritime Strategy in the North Pacific', *International Journal* 42 (Autumn 1987): 880.

36. Howard Peter Langille, *Changing the Guard: Canada's Defence in a World of Transition* (Toronto: University of Toronto Press, 1990), 76.

37. Jockel and Sokolsky, *Canada and Collective Security*, 76.

38. Ibid., 52.

CHAPTER 7

1. Joe Clark, 'Canada in the World: Foreign Policy in the New Era', *Speeches and Statements* 90/11 (13 September 1990).

2. Government of Canada, *Canada in the World* (Ottawa: Government of Canada, 1995).

3. Lloyd Axworthy, 'Notes for an Address to the 51st General Assembly of the United Nations', Department of Foreign Affairs and International Trade, *Speeches and Statements* 96/37 (24 September 1996).

4. Boutros Boutros-Ghali, *An Agenda for Peace: Preventive Diplomacy, Peacemaking, and Peace-keeping* (New York: United Nations, 1992).

5. Kenneth Bush, 'Somalia: When Two Anarchies Meet', in Gregory Wirick and Robert Miller, eds, *Canada and Missions for Peace: Lessons from Nicaragua, Cambodia and Somalia* (Ottawa: International Development Research Centre, 1998), 83.

6. Marrack Goulding, 'The Evolution of United Nations Peacekeeping', *International Affairs* 69 (1993): 464.

7. Brian Urquhart, 'Some Thoughts on Sierra Leone', *New York Review of Books* (15 June 2000), 20.

8. Jeff Sallot, 'Redrawing the Lines of Battle', *Globe and Mail* (8 October 1994), D1.

9. See the account in Jocelyn Coulon, *Soldiers of Diplomacy: The United Nations, Peacekeeping, and the New World Order* (Toronto: University of Toronto Press, 1994).

10. Bush, 'Somalia', 92.

11. Government of Canada, *Towards a Rapid Reaction Capability for the United Nations* (Ottawa: Department of Foreign Affairs and International Trade, 1995).

12. See, for example, Michael Ignatieff, *The Warrior's Honor: Ethnic War and the Modern Conscience* (Toronto: Viking, 1998).

13. Lloyd Axworthy, 'Building Peace to Last: Establishing a Canadian Peacebuilding Initiative', Department of Foreign Affairs and International Trade, *Statement* 96/46 (30 October 1996).

14. Ibid.

15. Canadian International Development Agency, 'Canadian Peacemaking Experience', http://www.acdi-cida.gc.ca/cida.ind.nsf (6 November 1998).

16. A good collection of these proposals can be found in Eric Fawcett and Hana Newcombe, eds, *United Nations Reform: Looking Ahead After Fifty Years* (Toronto: Dundurn, 1995).

17. Christopher Wren, 'The U.N.'s Master Juggler', *New York Times* (8 December 1995), D6.

18. 'To Bury or to Praise', *The Economist* (21 October 1995), 24.

19. Erskine Childers and Brian Urquhart, 'Renewing the United Nations System', in *Development Dialogue* (Uppsala, Sweden: Dag Hammarskjöld Foundation, 1994).

20. Cited in Michael Dolan and Chris Hunt, 'Negotiating the Ottawa Process: The New Multilateralism', *Canadian Foreign Policy* 5, 3 (1998): 28.

21. Peter Willetts, 'From "Consultative Arrangements" to "Partnership"', *Global Governance* 6 (2000): 203.

22. Richard Falk, *On Humane Governance: Toward a New Global Politics* (University Park: Pennsylvania State University Press, 1996), 26.

23. For a discussion of middle power influence, see A.F. Cooper, R.A. Higgott, and K.R. Nossal, *Relocating Middle Powers: Australia and Canada in a Changing World Order* (Vancouver: University of British Columbia Press), especially 12–32.

24. Arthur Andrew, *The Rise and Fall of a Middle Power: Canadian Diplomacy from King to Mulroney* (Toronto: Lorimer, 1993).

25. See, for example, the final report of the 1982 Parliamentary Committee on Canada's relations in the region (Canada, House of Commons, Sub-committee of the Standing Committee on External Affairs and National Defense on Canada's Relations with Latin America and the Caribbean, *Canada's Relations with Latin America and the Caribbean: Final Report to the House of Commons* [Ottawa: The Sub-committee, 1982].)

26. For a review of these contacts, see James Rochlin, *Discovering the Americas: The Evolution of Canadian Foreign Policy Towards Latin America* (Vancouver: University of British Columbia Press, 1994), and J.C.M. Ogelsby, *Gringos from the Far North: Essays in the History of Canadian–Latin American Relations, 1866–1968* (Toronto: Macmillan, 1976).

27. Edgar Dosman and Jerry Haar, 'Conclusion: The Future Challenge', in Jerry Haar and Edgar Dosman, eds, *A Dynamic Partnership: Canada's Changing Role in the Americas* (New Brunswick, NJ: Transaction, 1993), 177.

28. Edgar J. Dosman, 'Canada and Latin America: The New Look', *International Journal* 47 (1992): 543.

29. For a discussion of Canadian policy in the OAS, see, among others, Jean Daudelin, 'The Politics of Oligarchy: "Democracy" and Canada's Recent Conversion to Latin America', in Maxwell Cameron and Maureen Appel Molot, eds, *Democracy and Foreign Policy: Canada Among Nations, 1995* (Ottawa: Carleton University Press, 1995), 145–62; Tom Farer, *Collectively Defending Democracy in a World of Sovereign States: The Western Hemisphere's Prospect* (Montreal: International Centre for Human Rights and Democratic Development, 1993); and Peter McKenna, *Canada and the OAS: From Dillettante to Full Partner* (Ottawa: Carleton University Press, 1995).

30. Dosman, 'Canada and Latin America', 545.

31. Cited in Stephen Randall, 'Canada and Latin America: The Evolution of Institutional Ties', in Haar and Dosman, eds, *A Dynamic Partnership*, 35.

32. Stephen Randall, 'Canada and Latin America: The Evolution of Instititional Ties', cited in Haar and Dosman, *A Dynamic Partnership*, 35.

33. Andrew Hurrell, 'Latin America in the New World Order: A Regional Bloc of the Americas?', *International Affairs* 68 (1992): 123.

34. David MacKenzie, 'Canada in the Organization of American States: The First Five Years', *Behind the Headlines* 52 (1994): 5.

35. OAS, 'Resolution on Representative Democracy', AC/RES, 1080 (XXI-0/91) (5 June 1991); for a more detailed discussion of these measures and their implications, see Farer, *Collectively Defending Democracy*.

36. Hurrell, 'Latin America in the New World Order', 135.

37. James Rochlin, 'Markets, Democracy and Security in Latin America', in Cameron and Molot, eds, *Democracy and Foreign Policy*, 272.

38. Domingo E. Acevedo, 'The Haitian Crisis and the OAS Response', in Lori Fisler Damrosch, ed., *Enforcing Restraint: Collective Intervention in Internal Conflicts* (New York: Council on Foreign Relations, 1995), 132.

39. Farer, *Collectively Defending Democracy*, 21

40. OAS Resolution 4/92, cited in Joaquin Tascan, 'OAS in Central America and Haiti: In Search of OAS/UN Task-Sharing Opportunities?', paper presented at ACUNS Workshop, Watson Institute, Brown University, Providence, RI (December 1996).

41. Ibid.

42. MacKenzie, 'Canada in the Organization of American States', 7.

43. Ibid., 9

44. Cited in Linda Freeman, *The Ambiguous Champion: Canada and South Africa in the Trudeau and Mulroney Years* (Toronto: University of Toronto Press, 1997), 25.

45. David Black, 'Canada, the Commonwealth and Nigeria', in Andrew F. Cooper and Geoffrey Hayes, eds, *Worthwhile Initiatives? Canadian Mission-Oriented Diplomacy* (Toronto: Irwin, 2000), 51.

46. For a fuller discussion of the Mulroney government's approach to the Commonwealth, see John Kirton, 'Shaping the Global Order: Canada and the Francophone and Commonwealth Summits of 1987', *Behind the Headlines* 44 (June 1987): 1–17.

47. David Black, 'Echoes of Apartheid? Canada, Nigeria, and the Politics of Norms', paper prepared for the annual meeting of the International Studies Association, Toronto (March 1997).

48. Cited in Ross Howard, 'PM Retreats on Aid, Rights', *Globe and Mail* (16 October 1991), A1.

49. Cited in Ross Howard, 'PM Fails to Forge Human Rights Link', *Globe and Mail* (17 October 1991), A18.

50. The Harare Declaration can be found in M. MacLeish and K. Szaniawski, eds, *The Commonwealth Ministers Reference Book, 1992/93* (London: Commonwealth Secretariat, 1993).

51. For the details see Black, 'Canada, the Commonwealth and Nigeria', 58–60.

52. Ibid., 61.

53. Monique Landry, in Canada, *House of Commons Debates*, 3rd Session, 34th Parliament, vol. 7 (20 March 1992), 8573.

54. Kirton, 'Shaping the Global Order', 15.

55. United Nations General Assembly, Resolution 49/73 (9 December 1994).

56. Cited in W. Andy Knight, 'Soft Power and Moral Suasion in Establishing the International Criminal Court: Canadian Contributions', in Rosalind Irwin, ed., *Ethics and Security in Canadian Foreign Policy* (Vancouver: University of British Columbia Press, 2001).

57. Christina Spencer, 'Can We Tell the US We'll See It in Court', *Ottawa Citizen* (12 August 1998), A13.

58. Knight, 'Soft Power and Moral Suasion'.

CHAPTER 8

1. J.L. Granatstein and Robert Bothwell, *Pirouette: Pierre Trudeau and Canadian Foreign Policy* (Toronto: University of Toronto Press, 1990), 70.

2. John Ruggie, *Winning the Peace: America and World Order in the New Era* (New York: Columbia University Press, 1996), 136.

3. Mitchell Sharp, 'Canada–U.S. Relations: Options for the Future', *International Perspectives*, special issue (Autumn 1972).

4. Gilbert Winham, 'GATT and the International Trade Regime', *International Journal* 15 (1990): 802.

5. Miles Kahler, 'Multilateralism with Small and Large Numbers', *International Organization* 46 (1992): 698.

6. Winham, 'GATT and the International Trade Regime', 798.

7. See, for example, the discussion in Christopher Thomas, 'Reflections on the Canada–U.S. Free Trade Agreement in the Context of the Multilateral Trading System', in A. Claire Cutler and Mark W. Zacher, eds, *Canadian Foreign Policy and International Economic Regimes* (Vancouver: University of British Columbia Press, 1992), 47–61.

8. Joe Clark, 'Preface', in Donald Barry and Ronald C. Keith, eds, *Regionalism, Multilateralism, and the Politics of Global Trade* (Vancouver: University of British Columbia Press, 1999), x.

9. Richard A. Higgott and Andrew Fenton Cooper, 'Middle Power Leadership and Coalition Building: Australia, the Cairns Group, and the Uruguay Round of Trade Negotiations', *International Organization* 44 (Autumn 1990): 589–632.

10. Madeleine Drohan, 'Canada at Odds with Trade Group', *Globe and Mail* (24 October 1990), B3.

11. Ibid.

12. Michael Hart, *Fifty Years of Canadian Tradecraft, Canada at the GATT 1947–1997* (Ottawa: Centre for Trade Policy and Law, 1998), 183.

13. Ibid., 190–1.

14. Pierre Pettigrew, Department of Foreign Affairs and International Trade, News Release (15 November 1999), No. 245.

15. Hart, *Fifty Years of Canadian Tradecraft*, 216.

16. Jean Daudelin, 'The Politics of Oligarchy: "Democracy" and Canada's Recent Conversion to Latin America', in Maxwell Cameron and Maureen Appel Molot, eds, *Democracy and Foreign Policy: Canada Among Nations, 1995* (Ottawa: Carleton University Press, 1995), 150.

17. Ibid., 151.

18. Department of Foreign Affairs and International Trade, 'Notes for an Address by the Honourable Roy MacLaren, Minister of International Trade, to the Canadian-American Business Council', *Speeches and Statements* 94/23 (Washington, DC, 24 May 1994).

19. Department of Foreign Affairs and International Trade, *Statement* 93/62 (16 November 1993).

20. Claire Turenne Sjolander, 'International Trade as Foreign Policy: Anything for a Buck', in Gene Swimmer, ed., *How Ottawa Spends 1997–98* (Ottawa: Carleton University Press, 1998), 111–34.

21. On the MAI and Canada's involvement, see, among others, Elizabeth Smythe, 'The Multilateral Agreement on Investment: A Charter of Rights for Global Investors or Just Another Agreement?', in Fen Osler Hampson and Maureen Appel Molot, eds, *Canada*

Among Nations 1998: Leadership and Dialogue (Toronto: Oxford University Press, 1998), 239–66; and William Dymond, 'The MAI: A Sad and Melancholy Tale', in Fen Osler Hampson, Michael Hart, and Martin Rudner, eds, *Canada Among Nations 1999: A Big League Player?* (Toronto: Oxford University Press, 1999), 25–54.

22. Claire Turenne Sjolander and Miguel de Larinaga, 'Mission Impossible: Canadian Diplomatic Initiatives from Mines to Markets', in Andrew F. Cooper and Geoffrey Hayes, eds, *Worthwhile Initiatives? Canadian Mission-Oriented Diplomacy* (Toronto: Irwin, 2000), 37–48.

23. Sylvia Ostry, 'Canada, the Summits, and the GATT', in John Holmes and John Kirton, eds, *Canada and the New Internationalism* (Toronto: Canadian Institute of International Affairs, 1988), 72.

24. See, for example, the comments in Robert Cox, 'Multilateralism and World Order', *Review of International Studies* 18 (1992): 61–80.

25. David Dewitt and John Kirton, *Canada as a Principal Power: A Study in Foreign Policy and International Relations* (Toronto: Wiley, 1983); Philip Resnick, 'From Semi-periphery to Perimeter of the Core: Canada in the Capitalist World Economy', in Philip Resnick, *The Masks of Proteus: Canadian Reflections on the State* (Montreal: McGill-Queen's University Press, 1990), 179–204.

26. Cited in Granatstein and Bothwell, *Pirouette*, 448.

27. David Black and Claire Turenne Sjolander, 'Multilateralism Re-constituted and the Discourse of Canadian Foreign Policy', *Studies in Political Economy* 49 (Spring 1996): 17.

28. A. Lovbraek, 'International Reform and the Like-Minded Countries in the North–South Dialogue 1975–1985', in Cranford Pratt, ed., *Middle Power Internationalism: The North–South Dimension* (Montreal: McGill-Queen's University Press, 1990), 26–68.

29. Kim Nossal, 'Out of Steam? Mulroney and Sanctions', *International Perspectives* 17, 6 (1988): 13–15.

30. John J. Kirton, 'Canada as a Principal Financial Power', *International Journal* 54 (1999): 622, 623.

31. Andrew Baker, 'The G-7 as a Global "Ginger Group"', *Global Governance* 6, 2 (2000): 183.

32. Tim Draimin and Brian Tomlinson, 'Is There a Future for Canadian Aid?', in Hampson and Molot, eds, *Canada Among Nations, 1998*, 157.

33. Ibid., 159.

34. Fred Kunzle, 'Canada's Cut in Foreign Aid Will Hurt the Poorest', *Edmonton Journal* (14 May 1995), A10.

35. Report cited in Eric Beauchesne, 'Canadian Cuts in Spending "Weaken" Global Aid', *Ottawa Citizen* (3 November 1994), A4.

36. Cited in ibid.

37. Cited in 'Canada "Far Below Average" Among World's Top Aid Donors', *Toronto Star* (17 October 1997), A6.

38. Allan Thompson, 'Foreign Aid to Be Used as Weapon for Rights', *Toronto Star* (10 November 1995), A12.

39. On the arms proposal, see Stephen Handelman, 'Canada Planning Arms-Cut "Reward": Third World Aid May Be Linked to Military Restraint, Ouellet Says', *Toronto Star* (18 April 1995), A3.

40. Chris Peters, 'Taking More than We Give; Foreign Debt Owed by Poorest Countries Is Unpayable and Unjust', *Edmonton Journal* (21 March 1999), A15.

41. Oscar Arias Sanchez, 'Cologne Summit: Canada Must Take Lead in Debt Relief', *Toronto Star* (16 June 1999), A24.

42. Finance Department official, cited in Philip Mathias, 'Canada Leads in Foreign Debt Forgiveness: Official: Jubilee 2000 Initiative: G8 Countries Under Pressure to Cancel Debts to Poor Nations', *National Post* (16 February 1999), A11.

43. Kirton, 'Canada as a Financial Power', 619.

44. Mathias, 'Canada Leads in Foreign Debt Forgiveness', A11.

45. Sanchez, 'Cologne Summit', A24.

CHAPTER 9

1. Paul Koring, 'Army Pushed to the Breaking Point', *Globe and Mail* (27 May 1993), A1.

2. A COMPAS public opinion poll in 1998 demonstrated strong popular support for an active Canadian role in international peace and security operations, including support for continued participation in NATO; see Giles Gherson, 'Canadians Reluctant to Pay for Expanded Involvement', *Edmonton Journal* (24 April 1998), A7. For the persisting public support of Canadian participation in UN peacekeeping operations, see Pierre Martin and Michel Fortmann, 'Canadian Public Opinion and Peacekeeping in a Turbulent World', *International Journal* 50 (1995): 370–400.

3. Cited in Francis S. Clines, 'Gorbachev Sends a Chief Advisor to Iraq in New Diplomatic Effort', *New York Times* (4 October 1990), A8.

4. Cited in Hugh Winsor, 'Canada Urging No Unitateral Move', *Globe and Mail* (27 September 1990), A5.

5. Bernard Lewis, 'At Stake in the Gulf', *New York Review of Books* (20 December 1990), 44.

6. House of Commons Standing Committee on External Affairs and International Trade (8 November 1990), 22.

7. George Ball, 'The Gulf Crisis', *New York Review of Books* (6 December 1990), 8.

8. For commentaries on Canadian policy, see, among others, John Kirton, 'Liberating Kuwait: Canada and the Persian Gulf War', in Don Munton and John Kirton, eds, *Canadian Foreign Policy: Selected Cases* (Scarborough, ON: Prentice Hall, 1992), 382–93; Martin Rudner, 'Canada, the Gulf Crisis and Collective Security', in Fen Osler Hampson and Christopher Maule, eds, *Canada Among Nations, 1990–91: After the Cold War* (Ottawa: Carleton University Press, 1991), 241–80; Ernie Regehr, 'Sailing to Iraq', *Canadian Forum* 71 (October 1990): 6–10; and Reg Whitaker, 'Prisoners of the American Dream', *Studies in Political Economy* 35 (Summer 1991): 13–27.

9. Norm Ovenden, 'Canada Played Unsung Diplomatic Role—Clark', *Edmonton Journal* (27 January 1991), A3.

10. Linda Hossie, 'O Canada, Must Thee Be on Guard?' *Globe and Mail* (18 August 1990), D3.

11. Elaine Sciolino with Eric Pace, 'Putting Teeth in an Embargo: How US Convinced the UN', *New York Times* (30 August 1990), A15.

12. Paul Koring, 'Clark to Visit Jordan During Mideast Swing', *Globe and Mail* (15 November 1990), A18.

13. Canada, *House of Commons Debates* (24 September 1990), 13232–3.

14. Ross Howard, 'Clark Pressed on Nuclear Ban in Gulf', *Globe and Mail* (23 October 1990), A11.

15. Hugh Winsor, 'Joe Where? Has the One-Time Leader of the Pink Tories Turned into a Hawk?', *Globe and Mail* (17 November 1990), D2.

16. Ibid.

17. See Whitaker, 'Prisoners of the American Dream'.

18. Canada, *House of Commons Debates* (9 February 1998), http://www.parl.gc.ca/36/1/parlbus/chambus/house/debates/055_1998-02-09/HAN055-E.htm#LINK75 (accessed 2 June 2001).

19. Amin Saikal, 'Iraq, UNSCOM and the US: A UN Debacle?', *Australian Journal of International Affairs* 53 (1999): 283–95.

20. Many observers have noted this incongruence. For a sample, see Kim Richard Nossal, 'Pinchpenny Diplomacy: The Decline of "Good International Citizenship"', *International Journal* 54 (1998–99): 88–105.

21. Paul Knox, 'Seeking a Battle Plan for the Forces', *Globe and Mail* (11 October 1999), A8.

22. NATO, 'Declaration on a Transformed North Atlantic Alliance Issued by the Heads of State and Government Participating in the Meeting of the North Atlantic Council ("The London Declaration")' (6 July 1990), http://www.nato.int/docu/basictxt/b900706a.htm (accessed 2 June 2001).

23. Stanley Hoffmann, 'French Dilemmas and Strategies in the New Europe', in Robert Keohane, Joseph Nye, and Stanley Hoffmann, eds, *After the Cold War: International Institutions and State Strategies in Europe, 1989–1991* (Cambridge, MA: Harvard University Press, 1993), 137.

24. Statement, Address by the Hon. Barbara McDougall to the CSCE, Helsinki, Finland (9 July 1992).

25. For a thorough if somewhat subjective account, see David Owen, *Balkan Odyssey* (London: Victor Gollancz, 1995).

26. NATO Press Service, Final Communique (17 December 1992).

27. Operation Maritime Monitor was the first active duty operation for NATO forces. It was implemented under the authorization of UN Security Council Resolutions 713 and 757. After Dayton, it was changed to Operation Sharp Guard, which in turn was cancelled on 1 October 1996 after elections in Bosnia and the UN Security Council's lifting of sanctions on 1 July 1996.

28. Operation Deny Flight was authorized by UN Security Council Resolution 816 under Chapter VII in March 1993 and began on 12 April 1993. On 28 February 1994, NATO fighters downed four Serbian aircraft in violation of the no-fly zone. Operation Deny Flight ended on 20 December 1995 when IFOR took over.

29. NATO Press Service, Brussels (2 April 1992), 1.

30. Cited in 'NATO, Peacekeeping and the Former Yugoslavia', Report of the Sub-Committee on Defence and Security Co-operation Between Europe and North America (May 1994).

31. Dick A. Leurdijk, 'Before and After Dayton: NATO in Former Yugoslavia', paper delivered at ACUNS Workshop, Watson Institute, Brown University, Providence, RI (December 1996).

32. Speech delivered by Manfred Worner at the North Atlantic Treaty Association's 38th General Assembly, Copenhagen (30 October 1992).

33. Juliet O'Neill, 'Peacekeepers Free to Leave War in Bosnia', *Edmonton Journal* (10 January 1994), A3.

34. 'A Ghost at the Feast', *The Economist* (19 February 1994), 21.

35. Leurdijk, 'Before and After Dayton', 8–9.

36. Paul Heinbecker, 'Human Security', *Canadian Foreign Policy* 7, 1 (1999): 21.

37. Cited in Judith Miller, 'The Secretary General Offers Implicit Endorsement of Raids', *New York Times* (25 March 1999), A13.

38. NATO, 'The North Atlantic Treaty' (4 April 1949), http://www.nato.int/docu/basictxt/treaty.htm (accessed 2 July 2001).

39. NATO, 'The Alliance's New Strategic Concept' (November 1991), http://www.nato.int/docu/comm/49-95/c911107a.htm (accessed 2 July 2001).

40. David Gompert, cited in Jane Perlez, 'NATO Confronts a New Role: Regional Policeman', *Christian Science Monitor* (22 April 1999).

41. Joseph Biden, Jr, Statement before the United States Senate Foreign Relations Committee, 106th Congress, 1st Session (21 April 1999).

42. Peter W. Rodman, 'The Fallout from Kosovo', *Foreign Affairs* 78, 4 (1999): 46.

43. Minh T. Vo, 'Shouldered Aside in Kosovo, UN Rethinks Global Role', *Christian Science Monitor* 91, 142 (18 June 1999): 7.

44. Peter Ford, 'World Weighs In on NATO's War', *Christian Science Monitor* 91 (14 April 1999): 10.

45. David G. Haglund, 'Here Comes M. Jourdain: A Canadian Grand Strategy out of Molière', *Canadian Defence Quarterly* 27, 3 (1998): 21.

46. Edward C. Luck, 'A Road to Nowhere', *Foreign Affairs* 78, 4 (1999): 119.

47. Allen Sens, 'Saying Yes to Expansion: The Future of NATO and Canadian Interests in a Changing Alliance', *International Journal* 50 (1995): 698–9.

48. Haglund, 'Here Comes M. Jourdain', 21.

49. David Haglund, 'The NATO of Its Dreams: Canada and the North Atlantic Alliance', *International Journal* 52, 3 (1997): 464–83.

50. See, for example, Dean Oliver, 'Canadian International Security Policy and the North Atlantic Treaty Organization: A Contradiction in Terms', in Penny Bryden, Raymond Blake, and Michael Tuckers, eds, *Canada and the New World Order: Facing the New Millennium* (Toronto: Irwin, 2000), 71–84.

51. Cited in Brian Tomlin, 'On a Fast-Track to a Ban', *Canadian Foreign Policy* 5, 3 (1998): 14.

52. Michael Dolan and Chris Hunt, 'Negotiating in the Ottawa Process', *Canadian Foreign Policy* 5, 3 (1998): 27.

53. For an excellent review of various aspects of the land-mines treaty, see the collection of essays in *Canadian Foreign Policy* 5, 3 (1998).

54. See John English, 'The Land Mine Initiative: A Canadian Initiative?', in Andrew Cooper and Geoffrey Hayes, eds, *Worthwhile Initiatives? Canadian Mission-Oriented Diplomacy* (Toronto: Irwin, 2000), 23–36.

55. Tomlin, 'On a Fast-Track to a Ban', 12.

56. See Albert Legault and Michel Fortmann, *A Diplomacy of Hope: Canada and Disarmament, 1945–1988*, trans. Derek Ellington (Montreal: McGill-Queen's University Press, 1992) for an excellent historical review of Canada's arms-control policies.

57. Canada, House of Commons Standing Committee on Foreign Affairs and International Trade, 'Canada and Nuclear Challenge: Reducing the Political Value of Nuclear Weapons for the Twenty-First Century', Report 7 (Ottawa: The Committee, 1998).

58. Oliver, 'Canadian International Security Policy and the North Atlantic Treaty Organization', 73.

59. Lloyd Axworthy, 'Canada and Human Security: The Need for Leadership', *International Journal* 52, 2 (1997).

60. Canada, Department of Foreign Affairs and International Trade, 'Canada and Norway Form New Partnership on Human Security', Press Release 117 (11 May 1998).

CONCLUSION

1. Robert W. Cox and Harold K. Jacobson, eds, *The Anatomy of Influence: Decision Making in International Organization* (New Haven, CT: Yale University Press, 1973), 410.

2. Charles-Philippe David and Stephane Roussel, '"Middle Power Blues": Canadian Policy and International Security After the Cold War', *The American Review of Canadian Studies* 28 (1998).

3. Ibid.

4. John Holmes, *The Better Part of Valour: Essays on Canadian Diplomacy* (Toronto: McClelland & Stewart, 1970).

5. See Hedley Bull, *An Anarchical Society: A Study of Order in World Politics* (London: Macmillan, 1977).

6. Holmes, *The Better Part of Valour*, 15.

7. John Ruggie, *Constructing the World Polity: Essays on International Institutionalization* (New York: Routledge, 1998), 62–84.

8. Denis Stairs, 'Global Governance as a Policy Tool: The Canadian Experience', in Raimo Väyrynen, ed., *Globalization and Global Governance* (Lanham, MD: Rowman and Littlefield, 1999), 79.

9. Susan Strange, *The Retreat of the State: The Diffusion of Power in the World Economy* (Cambridge: Cambridge University Press, 1996).

10. Cited in Michael Hart, *Fifty Years of Canadian Tradecraft: Canada and the GATT 1947–1997* (Ottawa: Centre for Trade Policy and Law, 1998), 212.

11. Ruggie, *Constructing the World Polity*, 84.

12. Emma Rothschild, 'What Is Security?' *Daedalus* 124, 3 (1995): 70–1.

13. Ngaire Woods, 'Good Governance in International Organizations', *Global Governance* 5, 1 (1999): 39–62.

14. Ibid.

15. David Kennedy, 'Background Noise?', *Harvard International Review* 21, 3 (1999): 52–8.

16. Woods, 'Good Governance in International Organizations'.

Index